Atlantic Crescent

ALAINA M. MORGAN

Atlantic Crescent
Building Geographies of Black and Muslim
Liberation in the African Diaspora

The University of North Carolina Press *Chapel Hill*

© 2025 Alaina M. Morgan
All rights reserved
Set in Arno Pro by Westchester Publishing Services
Manufactured in the United States of America

Library of Congress Cataloging-in-Publication Data
Names: Morgan, Alaina M., author.
Title: Atlantic Crescent : building geographies of Black and Muslim liberation in the African diaspora / Alaina M. Morgan.
Other titles: Building geographies of Black and Muslim liberation in the African diaspora
Description: Chapel Hill : The University of North Carolina Press, [2025] | Includes bibliographical references and index.
Identifiers: LCCN 2025013285 | ISBN 9781469688701 (cloth ; alk. paper) | ISBN 9781469688718 (pbk. ; alk. paper) | ISBN 9781469683874 (epub) | ISBN 9781469688725 (pdf)
Subjects: LCSH: Black Muslims—Political activity—20th century. | Islam and politics. | African diaspora—Religious aspects. | African diaspora—Political aspects. | South Asians—United States—History—20th century. | Caribbeans—United States—History—20th century. | Muslims, Black—Political activity—United States—20th century.
Classification: LCC BP221 .M67 2025 | DDC 297.8/7—dc23/eng/20250403
LC record available at https://lccn.loc.gov/2025013285

Parts of chapter 6 were previously published as Alaina M. Morgan, "A Practice Round for the Inner City: Circum-Caribbean Occupation, Crack Cocaine, and Religious Duty in Louis Farrakhan's Nation of Islam," *Journal of African American History* 108, no. 2 (Spring 2023): 244–72.

For product safety concerns under the European Union's General Product Safety Regulation (EU GPSR), please contact gpsr@mare-nostrum.co.uk or write to the University of North Carolina Press and Mare Nostrum Group B.V., Mauritskade 21D, 1091 GC Amsterdam, The Netherlands.

For Mom and Gaga

Contents

List of Illustrations ix

INTRODUCTION
The Serpent That Deceived the World 1

Part I
Discourses

CHAPTER ONE
Black Islam in a History of Overlapping Diasporas 19

CHAPTER TWO
The Atlantic Crescent from Lahore to Iowa 45

CHAPTER THREE
Muslims Speak to the Ummah in Black and White 72

INTERLUDE
Transitions, Crises, and Choices 103

Part II
Translations

CHAPTER FOUR
Bermuda Crescent: Black Muslim Resistance
and Decolonization in Translation 111

CHAPTER FIVE
The Bold Muslims We Were: Gender, Education,
and Anticolonial Islam 138

CHAPTER SIX
Who You Gonna Call?: Islam, American Neo-Imperialism,
and Dopebusting in the Inner City 159

EPILOGUE
The Bow, the Arrow, and the Crescent: Blackness and Islam
in the Past, Present, and Future 191

Acknowledgments 203

Notes 207

Bibliography 249

Index 261

Illustrations

0.1 *The World Serpent*, by Eugene Majied, *Muhammad Speaks*, March 25, 1966 2

1.1 Mufti Muhammad Sadiq, *Moslem Sunrise*, January 1923 21

1.2 Cover of *Moslem Sunrise*, January 1924 34

1.3a Denzel Carr (Abdullah Omar), *Moslem Sunrise*, January 1923 37

1.3b A. Mirza Ahmad (F. L. Andersen), *Moslem Sunrise*, October 1921 37

1.4 *Four American Moslem Ladies*, *Moslem Sunrise*, January 1923 38

1.5 An Eid gathering at the Ahmadiyya's London Mosque in Southfields, *Moslem Sunrise*, October 1923 42

2.1 Abdul and Zuleikha Naeem with five of their children, c. 1950s 46

2.2 Abdul Basit Naeem with members of the Camera Club of Western Michigan College of Education, c. 1948 55

2.3 Imagining of Islam in Africa, *Moslem World & the U.S.A.*, August–September 1956 65

3.1a Dakota Staton at home, *Jet Magazine*, April 19, 1962 85

3.1b Dakota Staton and Talib Dawud, *Jet Magazine*, April 19, 1962 85

3.2a Malcolm X and Fidel Castro laughing at the Hotel Theresa, September 20, 1960 96

3.2b Malcolm X and Fidel Castro talking at the Hotel Theresa, September 20, 1960 96

3.3 Eugene Majied, Messenger Muhammad's Idea, *Muhammad Speaks*, December 18, 1970 102

4.1 Stack of *Muhammad Speaks* magazines mistakenly delivered to Norwood Salaam, 2015 121

4.2 Photograph of the Bassett Building (Hamilton, Bermuda), 2015 129

5.1 Masjid Muhammad, 26 Cedar Street (Hamilton, Bermuda), 2015 145

6.1 Robert Muhammad, Reagan Stepping into Grenada, *Final Call*, April 27, 1986 169

6.2 Cartoon of Reagan and Bush stepping into Nicaragua, by Robert Muhammad 182

Atlantic Crescent

INTRODUCTION

The Serpent That Deceived the World

The year was 1966, and across the United States, the Caribbean basin, Europe, and Africa, impeccably dressed Muslim men with neat bow ties and pillbox hats stood on street corners at bustling intersections of the urban centers they called home. They carried with them stacks of newspapers professing that an insidious evil, represented by the Christian West, was spreading far and wide across the globe. These men, members of a paramilitary organization called the Fruit of Islam, were tasked with vending copies of the Nation of Islam's (the Nation's) institutional newspaper, *Muhammad Speaks*. This week, in late March, as the European empire continued to recede and American neocolonialism extended its reach through Southeast Asia, the publication included a nearly poster-sized reimagining of geopolitical power and its impact.[1]

Political cartoonist Eugene Majied's reimagination of the Earth's geography spread over a two-page centerfold in the middle of the newspaper and featured an alternative world map (figure 0.1). Rejecting the standard Mercator projection taught in primary and secondary schools across the United States, this map eschewed a depiction of Europe as the largest and most important continent. Instead, Majied centered the United States, North America, and the islands of the Caribbean Sea as the focal point. Representing a white, Western, and Christian threat, a poisonous "World Serpent" lurked, poised to exploit every population of the Earth in its search for global domination. In the center of the map, over the heartland of America, Uncle Sam's demonic visage hissed atop a serpent's form. As the snake's body crossed every body of water, it coiled over the Indian subcontinent, Southeast Asia, western and southern Africa, Latin America, the Caribbean, and Australia, emphasizing the role of American empire in the oppression of Black, Brown, and Indigenous people across the world. The only areas of the map safe from the grasp of the World Serpent were Cuba; Saudi Arabia, the birthplace and heart of the global Islamic tradition—a land never colonized by European forces; and the European continent. In Europe, which faded into the page's edge, Majied depicted the serpent's tail retreating from the continent, demonstrating the reconfiguration of geopolitical power during the Cold War.[2]

2 Introduction

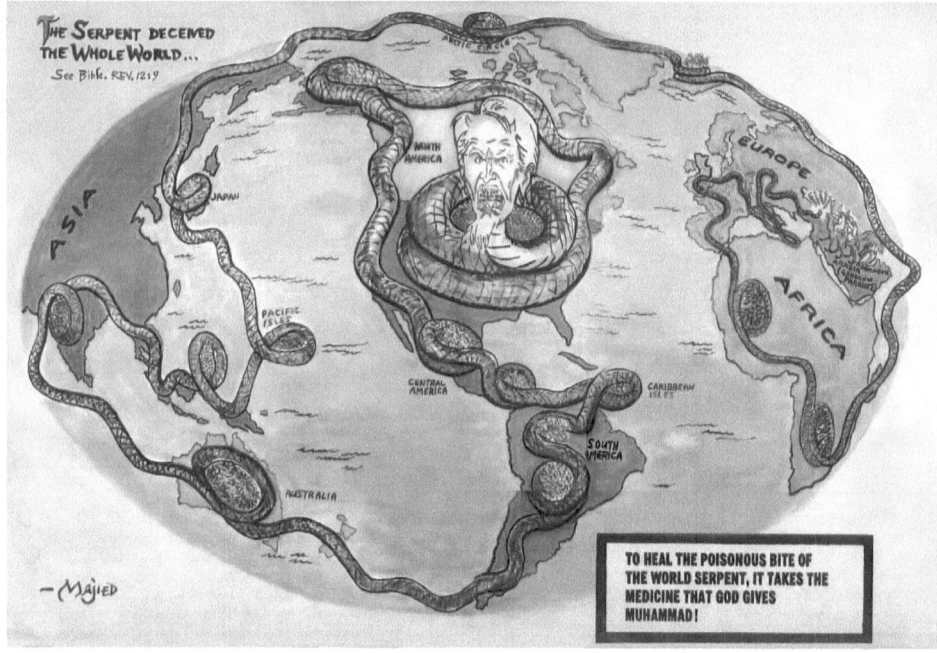

FIGURE 0.1 *The World Serpent*, in *Muhammad Speaks*, March 25, 1966, pp. 13–14. Cartoon by Eugene Majied.

At the top of Majied's cartoon, his caption paraphrased a verse from Revelations that speaks of a heavenly war between the angels and Lucifer's exile to the realm of evil and deception. It read, "The serpent deceived the whole world."[3] At the bottom of the map, the cartoon emphasized Islam's role in countering the sting of America's attempts at global domination. It declared, to "heal the poisonous bite of the world serpent," the antidote lay in the "medicine that God gives [Elijah] Muhammad!"[4]

This map appeared once in the Nation's *Muhammad Speaks* newspaper in 1966, but in the 1980s and 1990s, as the Nation's discussions turned to the shared impact of American neo-imperialism on the Black and Brown people of the Middle East, the Circum-Caribbean, and the American inner city, this exact cartoon regularly appeared. Through this repetition, the Nation visually and spatially asserted the critical importance of American empire in the existing global politics of the 1980s and 1990s. They also emphasized the central role of Islam in ameliorating secular evils like imperialism and colonial exploitation. This geography was asserted in public and private spaces throughout the African diaspora. On subway trains in New York, in the Panama Canal Zone, and in Trafalgar Square in London, readers casually consumed these sensational images and asserted the power of this transnational anticolonial Islam in forging critical diasporic connections and grounding grassroots action.

THIS BOOK IS AN INTELLECTUAL, political, and religious history. It traces the use of Islam, and the geographic space of the Muslim Atlantic, or "Atlantic Crescent," as an anticolonial and anti-imperial mechanism for people of African descent in the twentieth-century Atlantic world. I argue that from the First World War to the 1990s, these African-descended—or Black—people saw within Islam the potential to unify oppressed populations, remedy social ills, and achieve racial and political freedom.

The history of Islam practiced among Black people in the African diaspora—which we will call here Black Islam—has been extensively detailed by historians. Islam arrived in the Americas en masse in the bellies of slave ships, brought by enslaved Africans from heavily Muslim regions of the African continent.[5] Historians do not know the exact numbers of Muslim Africans who made—much less survived—the Middle Passage, but they estimate that their numbers were in the hundreds of thousands.[6] An exact accounting is complicated by the fact that colonial documents did not, for the most part, record the cultural lives—including religious beliefs and practices—of individual enslaved people or communities. Even paying attention to the percentages of enslaved Africans kidnapped and transported from heavily Muslim areas of West Africa, like Senegambia (present-day Senegal and Gambia), Sierra Leone, Gold Coast (present-day Ghana), and Bight of Benin (present-day Nigeria), does not give a full picture.[7] The numbers of Muslims forced to make the Middle Passage varied widely over time, as secular wars and jihads sweeping the African continent created a steady, but variable, stream of war captives.[8] In addition, these numbers were augmented over time and geography, as certain imperial powers sought out or avoided enslaving individuals from Muslim ethnic groups and regions.[9] Nevertheless, Muslims were never a majority of the enslaved population, and Islam was in constant competition with Christianity and other Indigenous African religious traditions.[10]

Even though enslaved Muslims struggled to retain their religious practices, by the turn of the twentieth century, these practices became increasingly disconnected from the Islam practiced on the African continent.[11] Although the open practice of Islam was always met with challenges—how would enslaved people, for example, avoid pork, pray five times a day, or fast during Ramadan when their nutritional allotments were already so meager?—the nineteenth century brought additional roadblocks. In the 1830s, African Americans were pushed toward Christianity by a Southern campaign to exert more complete control over enslaved people through religion. They were simultaneously pulled to Africanize Christianity and adapted the religion according to their experiences and worldview.[12]

By the 1930s, formerly enslaved people and their descendants in some isolated areas, like Sapelo Island in Georgia and the neighboring Sea Islands of Georgia and South Carolina, continued to recall certain Islamic referents and symbols in the religious practices of their parents and grandparents. These included the use of prayer beads and rugs, praying toward the East (the direction of Mecca), and giving sweet treats as gifts during the holiday season, called *saraka*.[13] There is suggestive evidence that still in the 1930s, the Christianity practiced by the residents of Sapelo Island was inflected with Islam.[14] Regardless, there is no evidence that the people of Sapelo Island, or any other community of formerly enslaved Black people, still considered themselves Muslim by the turn of the twentieth century.

Black Islam: A History of Overlapping Diasporas

My story begins here, in the years surrounding the First World War, at a moment in which the wispy memories of the connection of Islam to the Black past had been pulled incredibly thin. This link to the past was rebuilt and nourished at the intersection of three overlapping diasporas of Black and Brown people, instigated and facilitated by the violence and upheaval of World War I. First, the war precipitated the first half of the Great Migration (1915–30), a historic movement of African Americans from the Southern United States to the Northeast and Midwest in the years during and after World War I. During these years, over one million Black people traveled north with hopes, dreams, and aspirations of upward mobility, racial equity, and economic advancement.[15] But as these hopes and dreams were dashed by race riots, insalubrious housing, and subpar job opportunities, these migrants became disillusioned with the realities of continued racial violence, poverty, and constricted mobility.[16]

Religion and spirituality provided a fertile space for these migrants to reconfigure their racial identities, contextualizing them within the violent history of African America.[17] The religions that they created identified Christianity as complicit in upholding a white supremacist order and provided religious alternatives for Black people. Islam, in particular, lay at the beating heart of the religious movements that came to prominence during the Great Migration. Historians have argued that Black migrants were attracted to religious traditions that engaged Islam in part because they disrupted traditional understandings of religion and racial identity imposed on Black people from the outside. Adopting Islam served as a conscious rejection of the Christianity that was imposed on enslaved people by the slavocracy and that continued to oppress, demean, and subjugate them generations later.[18] Islam tapped into the existential frustrations felt by Black migrants as they experienced the déjà vu of racial violence, and it helped them take control of, and reframe, their racial identities and histories.[19]

I go further, however, and argue that Islam was able to take hold in Black communities in the United States—and to project, as we will see, both universalist and nationalist identities—during this period not only because of the migration of African Americans but because of the people and ideas that collided with this migration via two other diasporic phenomena. Here, I take up historian Earl Lewis's challenge to view the history of African Americans, and by extension, all Black people, as a history of "overlapping diasporas."[20] These individuals and discourses together were responsible for altering the intellectual foundation of Black migrant communities in the United States. This enhanced foundation was the building block upon which Black people built a distinctly Black and Muslim religious tradition. This religious tradition was designed to empower American Black people subjugated by centuries of American slavery, Jim Crow, and racist violence by helping them to reimagine themselves as part of a larger, powerful, African and Asian global community.

The first of these intersecting diasporic phenomena consisted of Afro-Caribbean intellectuals and skilled laborers migrating to the United States in the early twentieth century. From 1900 to 1937, concurrently with the first half of the Great Migration, over eighty thousand immigrants from the Caribbean (including the West Indies and Cuba) migrated to the United States. They came as a result of agricultural devastation, lack of educational opportunity, and rampant unemployment on their home islands.[21] The vast majority of these migrants arrived after 1914, during World War I, and most were from the Anglophone Caribbean. Many of these people chose the United States as a secondary site of migration after they completed service, support, or domestic labor jobs on the Panama Canal. They came in search of job opportunities opened by declining European migration during this period and an exodus of Americans shipped off to fight the war.[22]

Among these immigrants was Jamaican-born Marcus Garvey, whose Black nationalist philosophies would form the basis of his United Negro Improvement Association (UNIA) movement and would be incorporated as gospel in Black religious movements of the era. Garvey's Black nationalism helped to birth the Black and Muslim revival in the United States, and later formed the foundation of the religious texts of the Moorish Science Temple of America (MSTA), the first indigenous Black and Muslim religious movement in the United States. At the other end, Black nationalism would help to rationalize conversion to Islam for members of the UNIA.

Garveyism was critically important to the development and spread of Islam in Black communities at the turn of the twentieth century.[23] It is important to see Garveyism not as a hermetic philosophy, but rather as a discursive tradition responding to historical, global, and local realities in the African diaspora. Along with their trunks, hopes, and ambitions, Caribbean immigrants brought with them their experiences of colonial subjectivity. Gathered together in the same crowded tenements and ghettoes as their American counterparts, Caribbean intellectuals became further radicalized as they experienced life as racial minorities for the first time. In conversation and debate—and many times in disagreement—Black American and Caribbean intellectuals together refined ideas of Black nationalism, internationalism, and Pan-Africanism and brought them into public conversation. Garvey found himself at the intersection of debates and discussions on the plight and future of Black people in the world launched by his fellow Caribbean immigrants—radicals like his first wife and fellow Jamaican Amy Ashwood, St. Crucian Hubert Harrison, Trinidadian Claudia Jones, and Nevis-born Cyril Briggs—and prominent Black American intellectuals like W.E.B. Du-Bois and A. Philip Randolph.[24] The Caribbean—and the people, ideas, and philosophies it engendered through Black nationalism and radicalism—were at the core of early twentieth-century Black Islam. Garveyism, and its anticolonial sentiments, formed a critical basis for twentieth-century Black and Muslim religious texts and served as the impetus for the average Black person to convert to Islam.[25]

The second intersecting diaspora of interest is the migration of immigrants from the Indian subcontinent. From 1900 to 1930, the United States' population of documented residents from then-British India grew from 2,081 in 1900 to 5,850 in 1930, representing a net increase of approximately 3,800 immigrants.[26] In comparison to European (or even Caribbean) migration during the same period, migration from the Indian subcontinent seems miniscule. This was by design. From 1882 to 1924, Congress passed progressively more restrictive laws limiting immigration first from China, then Asia more broadly, and finally establishing a quota system that privileged Western European immigrants.[27] This legislative directive is reflected in the disproportionate immigration numbers during this period. For the same period, the population of documented European immigrants in the United States increased by nearly three million.[28]

It would be a grave disservice to the history of both Islam in America and the history of South Asian immigrants to the United States, however, to dismiss their influence based on these small numbers. Immigrants from the Indian subcontinent still entered the United States, either by evading detection by American immigration authorities or by fighting for admission under a number of loopholes created in these laws for professionals, entrepreneurs, educators, and religious missionaries.[29] In a nation fixated on a Black and white racial binary, darker-skinned immigrants from the Indian subcontinent occupied, at times, a fluid racial position.[30] They enjoyed greater access to mobility and to white audiences. But for darker-skinned South Asian migrants, their skin color prevented them from living in and blending into white communities. Taking up residence in Black neighborhoods—like Black Bottom in Detroit and Bronzeville in Chicago—these Muslim immigrants would have an outsized impact on the growth of Islam in Black communities in the years following the First World War.

Building Geographies of Imperial Resistance

Combined with burgeoning political and cultural movements based in anticolonialism and Black nationalism, different iterations of Islam forged at the intersection of these overlapping diasporas provided refuge for Black migrants to the northern and midwestern United States by reconfiguring prevailing ideas of race, space, and place.[31] Not only did these Muslim traditions redefine (or fully reject) racial distinctions—in particular, what it meant to be a Black person—but they also reimagined and reconfigured local and global geographies.[32] In these discourses, continents merged, populations thousands of miles apart were inscribed into the same histories, and global communities were united across distance by the bridge of religious belief and submission to the same God. As a result, I argue that these religious traditions, although they were in some ways conservative and regressive in their economics, gender politics, and politics of respectability, were radical in nature, as they imagined a racial reality dramatically different from the status quo. The overlapping of the three diasporas I discuss above—African American, Afro-Caribbean, and South Asian—fed these radical imaginaries, helping individual Black and Muslim leaders make sense of their historical subjugation by putting their local experiences into global context and allowing them to develop a powerful transnational tool to combat it.

I call the process by which Black and Muslim people reimagined their history, belonging, and solidarities, through reimagining space and their place in it, a Black Muslim "geography of imperial resistance," an imaginary where Black and Muslim identities became transposed onto global nonwhite populations engaged in antiracist and anti-imperial activity. This geography aligns with a similar theorization and pattern identified by the geographer and gender studies scholar Katherine McKittrick. McKittrick defines these formations as subaltern or "alternative patterns that work alongside and across traditional geographies" and identify "terrains of struggle" against domination.[33] Like McKittrick, and others, this study makes visible these alternative cartographic, geographic, and intellectual practices of place and space making by Black and Muslim people in the African diaspora over time, space, and national belonging.[34] These are alternative and supplementary ways of knowing, interacting, and understanding the world.

Leaders like Noble Drew Ali, Elijah Muhammad, Malcolm X, Warith Deen Muhammad, and Louis Farrakhan each created their own understanding of the ways that Islam connected Black and Brown people across the world. Some of this was done through mapping and utilizing images like the one with which I begin this introduction. Others, like that of Noble Drew Ali's Afro-Asian supercontinent, "Amexem," engaged with contemporary scientific models like continental drift to argue for a primordial connection between Black people and Islam. These imaginaries allowed Black and Muslim leaders to pull populations fighting against colonial domination in Asia, Africa, and the Middle East into their struggle. Some of this work had already been done for these thinkers through the processes of diaspora and migration that I emphasize in this introduction. But in dreaming, Black and Muslim people became able to discursively reconfigure their global status. Instead of powerless minorities, they became a powerful global majority with an unrecognized and untapped potential—a sleeper cell just waiting for the right moment to strike down the serpent of white supremacy. Through this geography of imperial resistance, Black and Muslim intellectuals included in their racial, intellectual, and religious communities far-flung populations who were not in the strictest sense Black or Muslim, but who they were able to identify as such.

In addition, Islam, a global religious tradition, imparts its own alternative and subaltern geography. Muslim people see themselves linked together by the concept of the *ummah*, or universal imagined Muslim community. In theory, this community transcends national boundaries, ethnic groups, languages, cultures, and styles of worship. Together, members of the ummah are united by one thing—their desire to submit themselves fully to Allah. In practice, however, this identity is often held in tandem with belonging in a local, or tribal, community called the *'asabiyah*.[35] As religious studies scholar Aminah McCloud has suggested, this tension between the ummah and the 'asabiyah—and the ways they each define the Black and Muslim experience—is the primary preoccupation for Black and Muslim people in the contemporary Atlantic world.[36] How do they demonstrate and profess belonging to a global community while dealing with the particularities of their histories?

In order to explain the processes by which Black and Muslim "freedom dreams" and discourses by elites, intellectuals, and leaders interacted with "freedom realities" by rank-and-file practitioners, I theorize a space I call the "Atlantic Crescent."[37] This space, a reimagining of the ubiquitous symbol of Islam's star and crescent moon, represents the fluid ways that Black and Muslim people intellectualized, understood, and acted on their religio-racial identities at the intersection of, and influenced by, these overlapping diasporas. These identities were, as the historian of religion Judith Weisenfeld argues, ways of understanding individual and collective identity as it was both formed and constituted at the intersection of religion and race.[38] The Black and Muslim people at the heart of this story shaped the Atlantic Crescent as they reflected their religio-racial identities upon it. Like the geometric shape, the "Atlantic Crescent" comprises both convex (outward curving) and concave (inward curving) sides. Its convex face stretches out transnationally, linking local Muslim communities to the ummah. By contrast, its concave face reflects inward, making sense of the unique local racial implications of colonialism and imperialism on various *'asabiyaat* throughout the African diaspora. Within this space, expansive global discourses identifying Islam as the key to the liberation of people of African descent were translated and applied at the local level, often in consultation with other Black and Muslim people passing through, and occupying, these shared spaces. As literary scholar Brent Hayes Edwards argues, these translations—between elite and rank-and-file, between global and tribal, and between overlapping diasporas—inevitably led to unevenness as the "trace or the residue, perhaps, of what resists translation" from one context to the other remained.[39] Edwards uses the French word *décalage* for this "residue," a word that can be loosely—but not directly—translated as a "gap, time lag, discrepancy, or interval." Essentially, décalage constitutes the differences, confusions, and jagged edges that occur when contexts are translated across time or space.[40] In this study, I explore these confusions, contradictions, innovations, reimaginings, and uneven encounters in all of their fullness.

Interventions

In exposing the contours of a globally conscious and locally relevant religio-political project, *Atlantic Crescent* makes interventions at the intersection of the literature on Black internationalism and the study of Islam in the African diaspora, two areas that have—for the most part—remained separate. Scholars of Black internationalism have sketched out a robust history of Black international engagement in politics, literature, and cultural production.[41] Yet, this scholarship has largely been a study of Black intellectualism and discursive production. When told from the perspective of Black and Muslim people, it has focused principally on the activities of visible, elite, male leaders—like Elijah Muhammad, Malcolm X, and Louis Farrakhan—and how they negotiated the tension between a particularist (*'asabiyic*) and universalist (*'ummic*) religio-political identity.[42] These tensions and explorations are equally important to the history I reconstruct in this book, and this study does not shy away from uncovering new perspectives and histories on these leaders. Part I of this book discusses these elite perspectives almost exclusively. But this story of Black and Muslim practice and politics is not just about visible intellectuals, elites, and prominent institutions. It is not simply about overarching ideas and discourses or imagined ideas of how the ummah incorporated and applied to Black people. Thus, I also focus on the people who molded these visions into practice according to their own geographical, historical, and personal circumstances. These rank-and-file Muslims, many of them women, created and adapted Black and Muslim politics, social activism, and intellectualism just as much as the elite, visible males who publicly broadcasted their views and left an obvious archive in their wakes. To understand the contours of this Black and Muslim geography of imperial resistance, we must examine—as some historians of Black Islam have begun to do—these interactions and exchanges between these visible elites and their rank-and-file practitioners.[43] For, despite painstaking efforts to mold a Black and Muslim geography of imperial resistance at the institutional level, individual expressions of Black and Muslim anti-imperial geography—whether articulated in New York, Lahore, or Kingston—were not only globally conscious but also locally rooted and specific. Thus, I position Black and Muslim people at the grassroots level as intellectuals and activists in their own right.

There is also an abundance of literature that brilliantly sketches out the contours of the experience of Muslims of African descent in the United States, the Caribbean, Europe, Asia, and Africa.[44] However, only a small number of these studies treats religion as a serious force in the forging of international community.⁴⁵ At the time of writing, only one considers the role of Islam as a catalyst of Black internationalist engagement and intellectual production.⁴⁶ In this monograph, I demonstrate that Islam was a critical driver of engagement with global Black and Brown subjugation that, in turn, produced, disseminated, and applied robust intellectual frameworks about the lives, experiences, and political fates of Black people in the Atlantic world. Here, I merge these two bodies of scholarship on Black internationalism and religious internationalism by focusing on the intellectual production of the Black and Muslim men and women who entered and negotiated the boundaries of the Atlantic Crescent in the United States, the British Caribbean, the Middle East, Asia, and Africa.

Finally, readers will note that many of the individuals and organizations that I write about in this book are not taken seriously by world Muslim leaders or scholars. Sects like the Moorish Science Temple of America, the Nation of Islam, the Ahmadiyya Movement in Islam, and the Muslim Brotherhood USA are seen as "quasi-Islamic," "heterodox," "heretical," and often simply "un-Islamic" in comparison to Sunni Muslims, who encompass the majority of the world's Islamic tradition.⁴⁷ I argue, however, that these opinions and statements reflect a false dichotomy between heterodoxy and orthodoxy. As such, I shy away from terms like "heterodox" and "orthodox," instead using the terms "particularist"—to describe certain locally and historically specific articulations of Islam practiced throughout this book— and "mainstream"—to describe the expectations and practices of a dominant Middle Eastern and South Asian Sunni Muslim tradition. This work aligns itself with scholarship that argues that Islam is by its very nature sectarian, and that even Sunni Muslim traditions—which are considered to be within the boundaries of "orthodoxy"—are articulations of particular geographical, cultural, and historical realities.⁴⁸ Islam—like many other religious traditions— adapts, transforms, and molds to the populations that adopt it, as much as they mold to the Sunnah, or the traditions and examples of the Prophet Muhammad.⁴⁹ In doing so, I attempt to respect the diversity of the Muslim tradition, and the self-identification of my historical subjects, by examining how Black and Muslim religious practice and political life are particular articulations of an Islamic tradition molded by the daily experience of racial violence, the realities of colonialism, and the global fight against white supremacy.

Sources and Chapter Outline

Inside the Atlantic Crescent, top-down and bottom-up processes were in constant tension and conversation with each other, and they were influenced—and sometimes challenged—by overlapping migrations of people and ideas. To demonstrate the ways in which these processes functioned, this monograph is divided into two parts, each consisting of three chapters. Part I explores the ways that Black and Muslim organizations and elites developed a geography of imperial resistance. Given their institutional and top-down focus, these chapters rely principally on institutional newspapers, Black and mainstream newspapers, official photographs, political cartoons, and government and institutional archives.

Chapter 1, "Black Islam in a History of Overlapping Diasporas," grounds this study of Black and Muslim people by placing the recovery of Islam among African Americans in the twentieth century in the context of the three overlapping diasporas and global migrations that I discuss earlier in this introduction. After establishing this landscape, the chapter concentrates on the way that two early Muslim movements, the MSTA and the Ahmadiyya Movement in Islam (AMI), and their leaders, used Black nationalism, Black internationalism, and Afro-Asian discourses to create a unique formulation of Islam appealing to Black people in the United States. I argue that these discourses were indebted to the internationalism and diasporic message of Garveyism and the internationalist vision of the AMI, which was born on the colonized Indian subcontinent. Together, these movements reclaimed connections to a Black and Muslim past and brought them into the present as liberation mechanisms. In this chapter, I draw on institutional newspapers, law enforcement surveillance, and photographs to reframe the early history of these two organizations in the context of the overlapping physical and discursive migrations of the early twentieth century.

In chapter 2, "The Atlantic Crescent from Lahore to Iowa," I use Black and Muslim newspapers, FBI and NYPD surveillance, and archival records to examine the role of immigrant Muslims and global decolonization movements in spreading Islam in Black and Muslim communities in New York and the Midwestern United States. To do this, I conduct a biographical study of an obscure Pakistani journalist and travel agent named Abdul Basit Naeem and his attempts to bring Black American Muslims into the fold of the global Muslim community. Naeem immigrated to the United States in 1948, a year after the independence and partition of his native Muslim Pakistan from India. Here, I examine Naeem's life genealogically and ask how his years in Pakistan, his relationship with Pakistani missionary organizations, his education in the United States, his marriage, and his hardships influenced his relationship to Black American Islam and his anticolonial outlook. I link Naeem's life and work to the growing popularity of the Nation in the 1950s and 1960s and examine his intimate relationship with Elijah Muhammad, the supreme leader of the organization from the 1930s until Muhammad's death in 1975. This chapter explores how this relationship, and Naeem's journalism, impacted the Nation's internationalist discourse and religious teachings. While scholars have briefly mentioned his relationships with the Nation and Elijah Muhammad, this chapter-length exposition demonstrates how Naeem's influence deeply affected those around him and contributed to the ways in which Black and Muslim people formulated, adapted, and projected their anti-imperial geographical imaginaries.[50]

Chapter 3, "Muslims Speak to the Ummah in Black and White," explores the outlines of the anti-imperial geography developed by Black and Muslim people in the United States through the lens of print media. In particular, this chapter examines the ways that Elijah Muhammad, Malcolm X, and the Muslim Brotherhood USA imam Talib Dawud—an Antiguan immigrant to the United States and a former jazz trombonist—used Black newspapers to connect Black and Muslim people in the United States to the rest of the Muslim diaspora. Throughout the 1950s, both Muhammad and Dawud regularly wrote columns in Black newspapers, including the *New York Amsterdam News* and the *Pittsburgh Courier*. In 1960, Muhammad launched the Nation's first newspaper, *Muhammad Speaks*. This chapter investigates how Dawud, Malcolm, and Muhammad used print media, most notably newspapers, to further their construction of a Black and Muslim anti-imperial geography and to apply this global vision to their national circumstances.

Part II incorporates the perspectives of grassroots and rank-and-file Muslims in the United States and in the Anglophone Caribbean. These practitioners and theorists were all, at some point in their lives, associated with the Nation and used its internationalist, anticolonial-inspired Islam to ground their own independence movements, remold their educational systems in ways that were nourishing and enriching for them as Black and Muslim people, and understand—and act on—an increasing subjugation of Black people in the United States and in the Circum-Caribbean. I decided to focus almost entirely on the Nation in part II because of the way that the practitioners themselves, in newspapers, oral memories, writings, and their personal collections, expressed their indebtedness to the Nation's anticolonial discourse and global worldview. It was an Initial belonging in the Nation of Islam, whether the subject stayed, converted to Sunni Islam, or left Islam altogether, that subjects attributed to the awakening of their political agenda, their anticolonial consciousness, and their understanding of third world solidarity and liberation. Thus, the sources themselves speak to the disproportionate impact of the

Nation's philosophies in undergirding and inspiring anticolonial political action. Part II of the book, therefore, reflects these realities.

In addition, readers will note that two of the three chapters in this section focus on the British Overseas Territory of Bermuda. During an era of rapid decolonization in the Caribbean, and the rise of the civil rights and Black Power movements in the United States, Bermudian people looked to the Caribbean and the United States to ground their own, ultimately unsuccessful, decolonization movement. Part of that gaze concentrated on the power of religion and, in particular, was directed through the Nation. In addition, because of Bermuda's geographic location in the middle of the Atlantic Ocean, the ideas that and people who circulated to its shores had freedom to transform in ways that were uniquely useful and relevant to Bermudian people. They looked different than they did in the United States, as Black Bermudian people seized their right to practice their religion as they wished and to apply it to their own political reality as it suited them. Thus, Bermuda presents an interesting case of the way that grassroots practitioners often ignored or circumvented institutional directives, took control of their own salvation and liberation, and implemented a living Islam relevant to their own needs and local circumstances.

Part II is likewise comprised of three chapters. Chapter 4, "Bermuda Crescent: Black Muslim Resistance and Decolonization in Translation," uses a case study to examine how Black and Muslim activists translated the anti-imperial geographies elucidated in part I into concrete action at the grassroots level. To do so, I investigate the conversations and political activities of Black Bermudians during the 1960s and early 1970s, a time when they were—as other nations in the Atlantic world—actively taking up the question of national sovereignty and independence. During the 1960s, the Nation had a growing and influential membership on the island of Bermuda. These Muslims were notably involved politically and spoke out regularly against British imperialism, supported Bermuda's decolonization, and engaged in protests and uprisings against state violence. As in recent work on the political lives of the followers of the Nation, this chapter demonstrates that Nation members were not apolitical, as argued by many scholars, but instead practiced a type of politics that was informed by their religio-political understanding of the world.[51]

Chapter 5, "The Bold Muslims We Were: Gender, Education, and Anticolonial Islam," continues to demonstrate the confluences and tensions between elite rhetoric and grassroots activism for Black and Muslim people in the African diaspora. In 1975, Elijah Muhammad died, and leadership of the organization passed to his son Wallace. Within nine months, Wallace transitioned the Nation's membership to Sunni Islam. This chapter explores the tensions and activism that took place during this transition by focusing on the Bermudian Muslim community and its allies from the United States Mid-Atlantic region. From the late 1970s through the 1990s, Bermuda's Masjid Muhammad was engaged in a public and internationally observed fight with the Bermudian government and Ministry of Education to open a Muslim parochial school on the island. Together with American Muslims, Bermudian Muslim men and women developed a curriculum rooted in Islam with the express intention of actively decolonizing their children's processes of education. In particular, this chapter exposes the critical contributions of the women who were publicly obscured during this battle. To bring this to light, this chapter uses privately held documents, school syllabi, and oral interviews to explore the ways that the activism that defined the membership of the Nation during the 1960s continued as the community embraced Sunni Islam.

Finally, chapter 6, "Who You Gonna Call? Islam, American Neo-Imperialism, and Dopebusting in the Inner City," explores how, at the beginning of the crack crisis in the 1980s, Nation members translated Louis Farrakhan's critique of American neo-imperialism in the Circum-Caribbean and Middle East into action. These followers created their own understanding of the combined crises of drugs and mass incarceration and attempted to implement Islamically motivated and inspired solutions to stem police brutality, remediate drug addiction, and put an end to gang violence in their communities. In the 1980s, as housing projects in American cities were assaulted by drug-related crime, HIV, and the incarceration of Black men and women, Black and Muslim leaders recognized the failure of local and federal law enforcement in protecting the Black community. The Nation's men, driven by a spiritual urge to wage jihad on haram activities and protect the women and children in their community, formed paramilitary organizations that intimidated drug dealers. In addition, these Muslims developed community-based solutions, like drug rehabilitation and detox centers, that spread Islamic *da'wah*—and eschewed temporary solutions like methadone—as a way to cleanse and redeem Black communities reeling from the drug crisis in America's inner cities. This chapter uses Black, mainstream, and institutional newspapers and government archives to examine the reception of these Muslim anti-drug programs throughout the 1980s and 1990s, the ways they explained their task in religious terms, and the experiences of the men who undertook this duty.

Conclusion

Over the course of nearly eighty years—from World War I to the 1990s—Black and Muslim people created, articulated, and implemented a vision of Black Muslim internationalism, solidarity, and anticolonialism. Operating at the intersection of three overlapping diasporas—of African Americans, Afro-Caribbeans, and South Asians—Black and Muslim people began to articulate a vision of liberation centering Islam and Blackness. These freedom dreams were part of a geography of imperial resistance pulling together Black and Muslim people from across the globe into one coalition against white supremacy, imperialism, and racist violence. Over time and space—from the American inner city to the island of Bermuda—real Black and Muslim practitioners transformed anticolonial discourses into practice as they sought to change their environments for the better. These rank-and-file members often adapted institutional discourses and directives, applying them to their own historical and geographical realities. This book celebrates and turns a critical eye on both the intellectuals at the helm of these organizations—the visible people who produced, disseminated, and performed an anticolonial and anti-imperial geography—and the people on the ground, the ordinary men and women who translated this discourse, molding the Atlantic Crescent with their praxis.

Part I

Discourses

CHAPTER ONE

Black Islam in a History of Overlapping Diasporas

From the moment the S.S. *Haverford* docked in the Port of Philadelphia on February 15, 1920, Dr. Muhammad Sadiq knew that he had an uphill battle ahead of him. Sadiq hailed from the Punjab region of British India. For the past three years, he had lived in London, where he worked as a missionary of Islam. On his disclosures to the United States immigration authorities, Sadiq was honest about his intentions in the United States. He openly declared himself a "preacher," indicating his intention to proselytize and convert Americans to Islam.[1] Sadiq hoped to make his way to New York City, where he would establish a branch of the Ahmadiyya Movement in Islam (AMI), a non-Sunni brand of the religion that emerged in the late nineteenth century in the Punjab region of North India. But it would be weeks before he set foot on American soil as a free man. Immigration officials, wary of Sadiq's religious mission and motivated by recent immigration restrictions on laborers from the Asian continent, demanded that Sadiq return on the vessel on which he came.[2] He refused. Instead, he began the lengthy process of fighting for his right to stay in the United States and launched an appeal to the Immigration and Naturalization Service in Washington, DC.

Unlike the thousands of Muslim immigrants from South Asia and the Middle East who came before him, Sadiq's case did not turn on his racial identity. He did not claim that he was white.[3] Instead, his case rested upon what he claimed was the United States' misunderstanding of Islam. He argued that he was not obligated to preach polygamy, as officials assumed, but rather would preach obedience to the laws of the United States, including monogamy.[4] Despite what seemed like an insurmountable bureaucratic battle ahead of him, his strategy worked. After seven weeks languishing in the Philadelphia Detention Center in Gloucester, New Jersey, Sadiq was released.[5] By that time, he had already converted twenty men of a diverse group of races and nationalities to Islam, taking advantage of his captive audience of the disadvantaged and downtrodden.[6]

As evidenced by his work on the *Haverford* and at the Philadelphia Detention Center, Sadiq's initial approach was multiracial and sought to take advantage of multiple diasporic communities coming together in a single space to augment his cadre of devotees. Sadiq arrived in the United States and settled in New York with an almost Pollyannaish view of race relations, but two years later in 1922, he moved to Chicago's South Side, where he began to focus on the Black migrant communities actively mushrooming around him. Living and working in the center of Bronzeville, in the heart of Black Chicago, he found himself baptized by fire into American racial politics.[7] In his writings for the Ahmadiyya's American publication, *Moslem Sunrise*, he began to directly recruit Black people and argued that Christianity was responsible for the continuation of racism and white supremacy.[8] By this time, 60 percent of the five-hundred-person congregation he ministered was identifiable as Black by outside observers.

Journalists began to race Sadiq as a Black man himself, using the context clues of his environment to identify and place him within the loose binary of the American Black–white racial hierarchy. A 1923 newspaper article pointed out his "Negro" features, describing him as an "aged man" with a "dark face . . . fringed with grey whiskers and horn-rimmed spectacles [that] surmount a thick nose"[9] (figure 1.1). These observations, many in mainstream newspapers and magazines, identified the Ahmadiyya as a religious project for nonwhite people. This was never Sadiq's intention, but the Ahmadiyya's demographic shift was due to his new surroundings and a newfound alliance with one of the most powerful Black nationalist organizations in the African diaspora: the Universal Negro Improvement Association (UNIA). Formed in 1914 by Jamaican-born Marcus Garvey, by the early 1920s, when Sadiq was gathering followers, the UNIA had become one of the biggest transnational Black nationalist organizations in the world, with chapters in the United States, West Africa, Central America, and throughout the Caribbean.[10] The previous year, Sadiq gave at least five speeches at a UNIA hall in Detroit, Michigan. He was awarded for his persistence and zeal with a windfall of forty new converts and a new Black imam, Sheikh Abdus Salaam, who would lead the Detroit congregation.[11]

Garveyism and Black nationalism provided the foundation for the rise of Black, radical Muslim traditions at the beginning of the twentieth century. The years Sadiq lived in the United States were part of a foundational period for the rise of these religions. This was the first half of the Great Migration (1915–30), a historic movement of over a million African Americans from the Southern United States to the Northeast and Midwest in the years during and after the First World War.[12] Simultaneously, from 1900 to 1930, refugees from the American South were joined by the historic migrations of 80,000 Caribbean migrants and almost 3,800 migrants from British India. This chapter explores the impact

FIGURE 1.1
A photograph of Mufti Muhammad Sadiq, *Moslem Sunrise*, January 1923, p. 155. Reprinted courtesy of the New York Public Library.

of these three diasporic and migratory phenomena together and the ways the ways they mutually influenced the social, political, and religious production of the time. As people and discourses moved within and across borders, ideas of space and place were reconfigured through the lens of Islam, allowing Black people to reframe their position of power and their relationship to other people of color throughout the world. In this chapter, I examine Mufti Muhammad Sadiq and the AMI as well as Noble Drew Ali, the leader of the Moorish Science Temple of America (MSTA). Both of these men would provide attractive theoretical and spiritual frameworks with which Black people could begin to reimagine themselves as a powerful majority connected to other Muslims and oppressed populations of color globally. Everywhere, these populations of color—whether fighting the British in the Punjab or repelling the Italians at Adwa—were fighting a protracted battle against colonialism, imperialism, and racial subjugation.[13] As historian Michael Gomez argues, these experiences were everywhere. They were "heard in the music ... felt in the dance ... expressed by stepladder advocates on the street corners and in the literature of the" moment.[14] And, as I argue, these experiences were expressed religiously and geographically through the embrace of Islam as well. In this initial adoption and engagement of Islam through and across diasporas, Black and Muslim people together began to sketch out the contours of an imagined geography of imperial resistance and began to define the Atlantic Crescent—and their understanding of their religio-racial identity as Black and Muslim within it.

Noble Drew Ali and the Afro-Asian Imaginary

Around 1913, a man by the name of Noble Drew Ali established a new religious order in Newark, New Jersey, called the Canaanite Temple.[15] In contravention of Sunni Muslim tradition, which holds that Muhammad ibn-Abdullah was the last prophet, Drew claimed that he was the second prophet of Islam and that he had come to establish the first "center of Moorish Science" among the "Asiatics of North America."[16] Noble Drew syncretized the theology of the Canaanite Temple by combining aspects of Islam, Christianity, Indigenous African American religious traditions, and Pan-Africanism. Drew taught that Black people were not "Negroes," but instead were an Asiatic people, descended from Moroccans, whose original religion was Islam. Drew defined his mission, thus, as an obligation to remind these lost Muslim Asiatic people of their true identity, history, and origins, linking them to other "Asiatic" nations, including Egypt, Japan, Turkey, and Latin America. Engaging with the teachings and symbols of the Islamic tradition, Drew taught his adherents to eschew pork, which they had been forced to eat during slavery; to sartorially identify themselves as a community by wearing the fez and turban; to rename themselves using "Bey" or "El" as their surname; to use signs and symbols of Islam, including the star and crescent moon; and to call their holy book a "Koran."[17]

What Noble Drew did, and where he went, prior to his appearance in 1913 Newark is unclear. His background is shadowy, purposely obscured equally by historical omission, lack of archival evidence, and a legendary cult of myth and personality surrounding him.[18] In the MSTA's official story, Noble Drew was born Timothy Drew in 1886. The legend surrounding him states that he was born in a fictional place called Simpsonbuck County, North Carolina, which does not exist in any current or historical map of the Carolinas or in any census records from this time period.[19] This claim, however, places Drew in the Carolinas at the end of the nineteenth century, close to the Georgia and South Carolina Sea Islands, including Sapelo Island. As discussed more fully in the introduction to this volume, these were communities in which historians found Islamic practices and referents as late as the 1930s.[20] Thus, as Michael Gomez argues, it is reasonable to assume that there was some "tangible, organic link between [this] nineteenth-century Muslim community and Noble Drew Ali."[21] If Islam was "vibrant and undeniable" in Sapelo Island as late as the 1930s, it would have been even more so at the time of Drew's birth and young adulthood, only twenty years after the abolition of slavery.[22] Although it is uncorroborated, some have even theorized that Drew might have been descended from Bilali Mohamet, the patriarch of Sapelo Island.[23]

The idea that Drew could have spent his early childhood a stone's throw from historic Black Muslim communities in the United States is only one theory, however. In addition, recent evidence has emerged that suggests that Noble Drew was actually a former child performer named Walter Brister who was born in Carlisle, Kentucky, in 1879.[24] As a young adult, Brister performed in circus shows as a fakir, or Sufi Muslim ascetic, under the pseudonym Armmah Sotanki.[25] This was a historical period in which the American and European publics were fixated on the aesthetics and trappings of the "Orient."[26] Brister, surrounded by authentically Arab and South Asian performers, adopted a fictive persona in which he performed "Hindoo magic," employing props, like turbans, snakes, beads, and scarves, that his audience would associate with the Middle East and South Asia. Here, Drew played with his racial presentation and identity, "passing" as a South Asian person by virtue of his appearance, dress, and associations.[27] In this role as a fakir, he would have been exposed to South Asian people who had migrated to the United States. Some of these people were undoubtedly practitioners of Hinduism, but it is also likely that among them were practitioners of a host of Indigenous South Asian religions, like Jainism, Sikhism, Christianity, Buddhism, and of course, Islam. However, the American public generally failed to distinguish between different types of South Asians and their unique religious and cultural traditions.[28] Although we cannot know the full extent, if either one of the above outlined theories is true, Noble Drew most likely had knowledge of Islam and South Asian religion, culture, and philosophy, and acquired this knowledge as a result of his movement across diasporic spaces. This would set up an ideal foundation for the MSTA, which would become an internationalist religious formation emphasizing the connections between people of African descent and the Asian continent.

When Noble Drew moved to Newark, one of the disembarkation points of the Great Migration, he found himself in a city that was increasingly populated by nonwhite people. From the beginning, Drew's theology and origin story were rooted in an Afro-Islamic imaginary, formed at the intersection of the migratory interactions that defined his life before and after he settled in Newark. Part of the legend of Noble Drew's rise to leadership includes the mention of a "Dr. Suleiman," a man who allegedly helped Noble Drew establish the Canaanite temple in Newark. Dr. Suleiman's identity, if he even existed, has been lost during the subsequent march of time. Perhaps the name was only engaged to give Drew legitimacy as he set up his fledgling movement, or maybe he was, indeed, a real person. But even if Dr. Suleiman was nothing but a figment of Drew's imagination, there were other Muslims in Noble Drew's orbit that could have served as mentors and advisors in constructing his particularist Islamic tradition. In the decades before and after Drew's establishment of the Canaanite Temple, New Jersey became home to a small number of South Asian Muslim traders. At the end of the nineteenth century, Muslim traders from Calcutta and Hooghly, West Bengal, made their way to the beach resort towns of New Jersey like Asbury Park and Point Pleasant with the determination to sell fine embroidered silks, rugs, and perfumes.[29] Some of these men would return to the Indian subcontinent each year, but increasingly as time went on, more of them stayed in the United States, where they established trading and kinship networks. They would regularly marry into African American, Afro-Caribbean, Creole, and Puerto Rican families. Outside of these communities, at work on the boardwalks, they would enjoy the slight racial advantages of being "exotic Orientals." At home, with their wives and children, or simply in Black-majority tenements, they were raced—like Sadiq would be decades later—as Black.[30]

Garveyism and the Roots of Islam in the North and Midwest

When Drew established his Canaanite Temple in Newark, he became part of a much larger regional social, political, and cultural movement sweeping New York City, one of the biggest destinations of the Great Migration.[31] Less than twenty-five miles southeast of Harlem, Newark was a part of the network of radical Black discourse, publishing, and art sweeping Harlem and the New York area via sound recordings, newspapers, and lecture circuits. During these years, Black intellectual production, art, literature, religion, and journalism flourished.[32] These patterns—of increased Black migration and intellectual vibrancy—were not confined to New York and its immediate environs but were replicated in American cities like Philadelphia, Chicago, and Detroit and internationally in places like Paris and London.[33] These changes were also not solely driven by African Americans but also by a historic migration of Afro-Caribbean people to the United States in the early years of the Great Migration.[34] This migration, while not Muslim in character, fundamentally altered the character of Islam in urban America. The Black nationalist principles and Pan-African foundation of Garveyism, which were brought during this migration, would become an integral part of the theology of the MSTA.

In 1916, Marcus Mosiah Garvey would become one of these Afro-Caribbean immigrants to the United States. Garvey had cut his teeth as a labor organizer in the Caribbean basin. As a young man, he followed the trail of Jamaican labor migration through Costa Rica, Panama, Ecuador, Nicaragua, Honduras, Colombia, and Venezuela. In 1910 and 1911, he founded newspapers in Costa Rica (*La Nación*) and Panama (*La Prensa*), attempting to expose the racist mistreatment and exploitation of Black workers by the United Fruit Company and in the construction of the Panama Canal.[35] In 1912, Garvey traveled to the heart of the British Empire—London—where he sought out the Sudanese-Egyptian Afro-Asian and Pan-Islamist thinker Dusé Mohamed Ali. During his time working at Dusé Mohamed's publication, *The African Times and Oriental Review*, Garvey published his first article, "The British West Indies in the Mirror of Civilisation," in which he discussed the history of slavery and its impact in Jamaica and identified British imperialism as the biggest ongoing threat to Black advancement in the West Indies. In his conclusion, Garvey predicted that one day, the people of the West Indies would be "the instruments of uniting a scattered race who, before the close of many centuries, will found an Empire on which the sun shall shine as ceaselessly as it shines on the Empire of the North to-day."[36] This dream of his own Black empire would drive Garvey's Black nationalist aspirations for decades to come.

In June of 1914, Garvey took what he learned working for Dusé Mohamed and returned to Kingston, looking to the future of his political and social organizing.[37] When Garvey returned to Jamaica, his mind "afire" with the possibility of Pan-African unity and sovereignty, he established the UNIA.[38] In doing so, he invoked the universalist language that Dusé Mohammed weaved throughout *The Review* on his new institutional letterhead, which was emblazoned with the motto, "One God! One Aim! One Destiny!"[39] Two years later, when Garvey arrived in Harlem, he attempted to carve out a place for himself amid these intersectional diasporic migrations and among competing manifestations of Black nationalism and internationalism. In addition to standing on soapboxes at the corners of major thoroughfares in Harlem, Garvey founded another newspaper in 1918, the *Negro World*, which would become the primary press organ of the UNIA.[40] The *Negro World* served as the chief means through which Garvey's ideas spread out of Harlem where they were dispersed into the winds of the diaspora. The *Negro World* quickly became one of the leading Black newspapers in New York, and by 1920, the newspaper was distributed globally to approximately 50,000 people.[41]

Garvey's influence was impossible to avoid in New York, and this would soon be true throughout the world.

Garvey's location in New York by 1916 put him a quick train, carriage, or car ride away from Noble Drew's Newark temple, where both men and their ideas would have been circulating, transforming, and coming into contact with each other, even if inadvertently. Although there is no evidence of a direct impact of Noble Drew's thought on Garvey, it is likely that the presence of conversations about Islam by the MSTA, which was operating in the UNIA's periphery and which many UNIA members would have been knowledgeable about, influenced Garvey's attitude toward Islam. Garvey's movement was not fundamentally religious in nature, but it often used religion to further its political goals. This environment was permissive toward Islam—among other religious traditions—using Islamic referents and symbolism to promote Garvey's ultimate goal of Black sovereignty and liberation. In 1922, after he was indicted by a federal grand jury on charges of mail fraud, Garvey gave a speech at Liberty Hall in New York in which he compared his suffering to the Prophet Muhammad, arguing that both he and the Prophet were both exemplars of radical persistence and leadership, men who had both "paid the price" for their activism on behalf of the people.[42]

Even when Garvey did not directly mention Islam, it was in the air and the culture of the organization. In May 1922, with Garvey's federal trial pending, Dusé Mohamed Ali reentered his life and began editing a column in the *Negro World* on Afro-Asian affairs. Dusé Mohamed's articles were in line with his goals in *The Review* and emphasized the necessity for Afro-Asian unity and the utility of Islam in the burgeoning anticolonial and nationalist movements of the Afro-Asian world.[43]

Even the music played at UNIA meetings directly referenced Islam, positioning it as a religion of Black people and the African diaspora. Composed by Arnold Josiah Ford, who had converted to Judaism by the time he became involved with the UNIA, the "Universal Ethiopian Hymnal," composed from 1920 to 1922 at the height of the Garvey movement, contained eighteen songs, which members of the UNIA were required to sing at hall meetings.[44] One of these songs was titled "Allah-Hu-Akbar," which took as its title the first line of the Muslim call to prayer.[45] At the top of the first staff, the word *quiblah* appeared, a reference to the wall niche featured in most mosques that helps to orient the congregation toward Mecca.[46] In two additional songs, Ford included lyrics suggesting that Garvey and his mission were sanctioned by Allah as leader of the UNIA and the global Black community. In "God Bless Our President," Ford asks the "Father of all creation, Allah omnipotent," as the supreme being of the universe, to bless Garvey as president of the UNIA and Africa.[47] In "Potentate's Hymn," Ford asks Garvey to proclaim that the UNIA's mission is being conducted in the name of Allah. He writes, "Long live our Potentate . . . May he our rights proclaim/ In that most sacred Name/ 'Allah'—One God, One Aim,/ One Destiny."[48] Finally, in "The Password," Ford encourages UNIA members to focus on their universal brotherhood and to not, as Cain, "spill or drink [their] brother's blood/ When LOVE is Allah's Word."[49] This music created a spiritual connection between Islam and the UNIA. This connection was so prominent that in 1922, a delegation of Muslims from an unidentified sect approached Garvey at a UNIA meeting and asked him to declare Islam the official religion of the UNIA, arguing that Islam was the religion of the majority of the Black world. These delegates were most likely Ahmadiyya Muslims, who—as we will see later in this chapter—like Mufti Sadiq, frequented UNIA meetings and recruited heavily from their membership.

Garvey ultimately declined to designate Islam—or any other faith—the official religion of the UNIA. He argued that Garveyism was a secular movement. But these questions of whether Islam was the natural choice of religious affiliation for Black people persisted, and these arguments unfolded among Garvey's followers in the *Negro World*. In August 1923, Jamaican-born Garveyite J. A. O'Meally published an article titled "Crescent or Cross?" in the *Negro World*.[50] In this article, O'Meally concluded that Islam, represented by the crescent, was preferable to Christianity and would be a "wonderful spiritual force in the life of the colored races, uniting us in a bond of common sympathy and interest."[51] This bond of common interest was, for O'Meally, forged very explicitly in a mutual desire to see the defeat of the European imperial powers. In a call for Garveyites to convert to Islam, O'Meally concluded, "With millions of Moslems in India, China, Arabia, Persia, Afghanistan, Turkey, Negroes would find valuable allies, who would bring pressure to bear upon the white world."[52] O'Meally's article reflected the Afro-Asian and Pan-Islamic solidarity that Dusé Mohamed Ali regularly emphasized in his column, and that Garvey himself highlighted in his speeches.

And even though Garveyism was not a religious movement, per se, it also found itself in competition with religious movements among, and led by, Black people in the urban North, like the MSTA. When Garvey was imprisoned in 1925, Noble Drew immediately took advantage of his absence to recruit Garveyites to the MSTA. In 1927, while Garvey languished in federal prison, he wrote to a Detroit member, Leonard Smith, who had written to him complaining about the UNIA's dwindling numbers on account of Noble

Drew's *da'wah*. Garvey responded, "I know nothing of the man referred to."[53] The claim that Garvey was unaware of Noble Drew Ali, however, is hard to believe. From 1916 to 1923, they lived less than twenty-five miles from each other in the New York Area. In 1923, Ali moved to Chicago, a central hub of the Garveyite movement. At this time, Garveyism was in its apogee, and in 1922 alleged that it had three million members worldwide.[54] Chicago alone had nine organized groups of UNIA members, with the largest, on Chicago's South Side, claiming twenty thousand.[55] Noble Drew did not command an international audience, but by 1930, his movement claimed thirty-two thousand enrolled members nationally with ten thousand in Chicago alone.[56]

Even if Drew and Garvey did not know each other prior to Leonard Smith's letter, they remedied this in November of 1926, when Noble Drew visited Garvey while he was imprisoned in Atlanta. The *Chicago Defender* reported that Garvey seemed "very much pleased with the splendid uplift work being done" by the MSTA.[57] Perhaps Garvey's resistance to acknowledge Drew initially had to do with the competition the men found themselves entangled in for the minds and souls of Black people in the urban North. By 1935, Garveyites in Philadelphia wrote to the attorney general begging for Garvey's return from exile to combat the exodus of members from the UNIA to the MSTA. Apparently, Drew had been invoking Garvey with greater frequency, alleging that he was Garvey's heir to the movement in the United States in his absence.[58]

Reimagining Asia and Africa in Noble Drew's Islamic Theology

Despite Noble Drew's reliance on Garvey's principles, or perhaps because of this, Garvey's absence was a boon for the MSTA. Beginning with Garvey's 1925 imprisonment, Noble Drew consolidated his movement and his power and moved his headquarters to Chicago.[59] In 1927, he codified his teachings, theology, and worldview in the *Holy Koran of the Moorish Science Temple of America*, or the *Circle Seven Koran*. Although not a true Qur'an, Noble Drew called his followers "the Moslems of North America," self-consciously used the name of Islam's holy book, called upon Allah as his deity, and used passages from the Qur'an along with Islamic referents and symbols.[60] Practitioners of the MSTA acknowledged themselves to be Muslims by the laws of the Holy Qur'an. Noble Drew distinguished this text from his own by calling it the "Holy Koran of Mecca" and the "Great Koran of Muhammad," acknowledging that his formulation was a distinct local manifestation of Islam.[61]

In the *Circle Seven Koran*, Drew used biblical references to establish an ancient and primordial connection between African and Asiatic people that rooted transnational Black and Muslim identity within a new history and geography of Black glory and anti-imperial resistance. Drew taught that Canaan (located in parts of present-day Palestine, Lebanon, and Jordan) was the heart of civilization. From the land of Canaan, Noah's son Ham and his family inhabited the African continent. They were soon joined by other Asian populations who founded great civilizations, including the Kingdom of Morocco. These people, according to Drew, were the forefathers of Black people in the United States—who were more properly referred to as the "Asiatics of America."[62]

To argue that the Black people of North America were Asiatic, Noble Drew engaged in a radical reframing of the Old Testament story of Noah's son Ham, his descendants, and their enduring legacies on the Earth's continents. This story was tied to a passage in Genesis that tells of the story of Noah and the repopulation of the earth by his sons. Ham, after emerging from the ark with his brothers and father, saw his father "drunken ... [and] uncovered within his tent."[63] His brothers, Japheth and Shem, covered their father, managing to avert their eyes from his naked body. When Noah woke from his wine-induced slumber and discovered what happened, he cursed Ham, declaring that Ham's son Canaan would thenceforth be a "servant of servants" to his uncles.[64] The exact details of this story are debated extensively by Old Testament scholars—did Ham simply look at his naked father, therefore exhibiting unforgivable disrespect? Or was it something much more sinister, something unspeakable, like incest or castration?[65] But no matter the context, on first glance, the story seems to have little consequence to someone like Noble Drew, a Black American trying to establish a Muslim religious movement and living in the urban United States centuries after Noah and Ham allegedly lived.

However, Noble Drew was fully aware of the significance of the story of Ham for the historical subjugation of people of African descent across the world. The story of Noah's ark is a tale not only of the repopulation but also the reorganization of a human race destroyed by their own wickedness, obsession with the profanity of the secular world, and disobedience to God. In deciding which of his sons would repopulate the continents, Noah demonstrated his preferences. Shem, his favorite, repopulated Europe. Japheth was the patriarch of Asia. And Ham, given his disgraceful behavior, would populate Africa and the Middle East with descendants who would be enslaved to his two brothers.[66]

From the fifteenth century, the curse of Ham (or the Hamitic curse)—and the racial hierarchies it was used to create—was mobilized to justify the enslavement of people of African descent. By the nineteenth century, as the United States marched to a civil war driven by the question of whether chattel slavery should be allowed to persist, defenders of the institution continued to point to the curse of Ham as justification for the condition of Black people in bondage.[67]

While white defenders of slavery used the Hamitic curse to justify the institution of bondage, Black Christian intellectuals like David Walker and Alexander Crummell began to reframe the story of Ham and Canaan, using it to argue that the Black past was a "utopia ... in which their ancestors, a race of supermen, had erected civilizations from the banks of the Indus to the British Isles."[68] These discourses identified the Assyrians, Babylonians, Egyptians, Cretans, and Druids, among others, as great Black, Afro-Asiatic civilizations that had fallen into decline.[69] These fascinations continued into the twentieth century, spearheaded by thinkers like W.E.B. DuBois, Dusé Mohamed Ali, and Garvey who promoted ideas of a historic connection between great African and Asian civilizations. Drew's focus on Ham as the progenitor of African people is consistent with this already existing discursive strain in nineteenth- and twentieth-century Pan-African and African diasporic thought.[70]

Drew also imagined a primordial geographical connection between Africa and Asia. Canaan's descendants traveled overland from Morocco to Canaan, traveling across a part of a supercontinent that Drew dubbed "Amexem." Drew created a geography that, through the idea of Amexem, created an expansive supercontinental mass that extended from "Northeast and Southwest Africa, across the great Atlantis [sic]" and continued to "North, South, and Central America and also Mexico" and the "islands of the Atlantic."[71] As historian Judith Weisenfeld argues, Drew's conception of an "Asiatic" world was not the same as contemporary understandings of "Asian." Instead, this was an "expansive religio-racial category which included a range of peoples," including "Moorish" or Black Americans.[72] Influenced by the zeitgeist of Black nationalism and Pan-Africanism, Drew created an imagined, but historically rooted, geographical and religio-racial space in which all people of African descent were not "Black," "negro," or "colored" but genealogically Muslim and Asiatic.

As much as Drew was influenced by Pan-Africanism and Black nationalism in his construction of Amexem, he was also likely influenced by the popular scientific theories of the day. Amexem was Drew's version of Pangaea, a supercontinent originally theorized by German scientist Alfred Wegener in 1912. In a theory that is now widely accepted by geologists, Wegener posited that Pangaea broke up over the course of millions of years, slowly becoming the configuration of continents and subcontinents that make up the Earth's present-day geography. In 1924, three years before Noble Drew codified the *Circle Seven Koran*, Wegener published the first English translation of his book *Origins of the Continents and Oceans*.[73] These ideas were circulating in mainstream publications like the *New York Times* as early as 1925, two years before the publication of the *Circle Seven Koran*.[74] Thus, although Drew never mentioned Pangaea, the similarities between Pangaea and Amexem suggest that he was building on and borrowing from cutting-edge theories of continental drift to give a scientific basis to his contention that there was a historical connection between African Americans, Africa, and Asia.

Amexem thus allowed Drew to geographically solidify and scientifically back his teachings that there was a brotherhood and a unity between people of the African diaspora and "Asiatics" of all shades, colors, and geographical locations across the world. The *Circle Seven Koran* beseeched Drew's followers to recognize that they were the "children of one father, provided for by his care; and the breast of one mother" who "hath given [them] suck."[75] The exact identities of this "mother" and "father" are up for interpretation, but given the arguments that Drew makes throughout the remainder of the *Circle Seven Koran*, the "father" that Drew is referring to is most likely Allah, and the "mother" that nourished these scattered children could be the bitter experience of slavery and racial subjugation uniting people of color across the world. All of these people, from Egypt to Japan, from China to the Indian subcontinent, and across the Americas were, for Drew Ali, Muslims.[76] Islam was their ancestral religion, created and introduced to them for their specific salvation and liberation. As punishment for forsaking their ancestral religion, and "stray[ing] after the Gods of Europe," Allah subjected them to racial subjugation and suffering.[77] But Drew offered a solution. By readopting Islam, Black and Brown people—the Moorish nation—would once again thrive.[78] However, Drew's solution was not the only one available to Black people in the urban North; it was not even the only Islamic solution. Simultaneously, Muhammad Sadiq's group of acolytes began to carve out its own own Atlantic Crescent by preaching their own solution to the problem of American racism and subjugation through Islamic faith.

A Punjabi in Chicago: The Rise of the Ahmadiyya Mission

On November 27, 1922, Mufti Muhammad Sadiq was a lone brown face in a sea of white at the Exchange Club of Grand Haven, Michigan. He waited patiently while local club president John Hoffman addressed the membership who had gathered to hear him speak about Islam. Excited about Sadiq's lecture on Islam, Hoffman unwittingly acknowledged the long history of religious colonialism on the Indian subcontinent when he noted the uniqueness of Sadiq's presence. He said, "We are used to hearing of our missionaries going to India, but here is something extraordinary, a missionary sent by the Indians to preach about their religion to the Americans."[79]

Sadiq's presence in Grand Haven probably did seem extraordinary to this group of white men, who in 1911 founded the Exchange Club as a civic organization dedicated to the ideals of Americanism, community service, and youth protection. In 1912, the Exchange Club made clear its interpretation of "American values," when they took the side of Detroit Tigers player Ty Cobb after he mercilessly beat a physically disabled patron who dared to suggest that Cobb had African ancestry. Cobb was suspended by the American League Baseball Association, and in response his teammates launched a strike, refusing to play until he was reinstated.[80] In a unanimously passed resolution, the Exchange Club declared its solidarity with Cobb and the Detroit Tigers, writing that Cobb's actions were the "only right one[s] for a man to take who has good, red American blood in his veins" and expressing the "highest respect for the members of the club who have by their acts shown that they are of the kind of mettle that is willing to suffer that wrongs may be made right."[81] Although these actions occurred in Detroit, and not in Grand Haven, it is reasonable to assume that these were values shared by Exchange Club members in the same region of Michigan, if not nationally. There is no evidence of statements issued by individual clubs condemning the Detroit club's resolution.

As Mr. Hoffman suggested in his introduction for Sadiq, the members of the Exchange Club would have been well versed in the history of white missionaries going to Africa and Asia with the intention of "civilizing" what they viewed as "backward savages."[82] Conversely, they were most likely much less versed in the history of resistance to colonial missionaries and education—a fact represented by the existence of the Ahmadiyya and Sadiq—and this must have seemed "extraordinary" to them.[83] In formulating their international missionary strategy, the AMI took a page out of the theoretical book of the American and European Christian denominations that had impacted the education system of the Indian subcontinent beginning in the nineteenth century.[84]

The AMI, founded by Hazrat Mirza Ghulam Ahmed in the late nineteenth century in Qadian, Punjab, India, was deeply rooted in the experience of

British colonialism and subjugation on the Indian subcontinent. Less than twenty-five years before Ghulam published his first book, *Al-Barahin-al-Ahmadiyya* (Arguments of the Ahmadiyya) in 1880, the British consolidated their imperial rule on the Indian subcontinent after the failure of an 1857 mutiny of Indian soldiers against British rule.[85] This event was only one in an era of contestations surrounding what seemed like endlessly expanding European colonial control over the Middle East, Asia, and Africa. And throughout the Muslim world, religious renewers like Ahmad stood poised to reinterpret Islam for the masses in light of their new modern experience as imperial subjects.[86] Ahmad's version of Islam, which he consolidated in 1890 and 1891, differed markedly from the mainstream Sunni Islam practiced around him. In contravention of the idea that Muhammad ibn-Abdullah was the seal of prophets, Ahmad—like Noble Drew later—preached that he himself was a prophet and that he continued to receive revelation. He also preached that he was the Mahdi, a figure in Islamic eschatology who would appear at the end of the world to redeem the faithful; the messiah; and an avatar of the Hindu god Krishna.[87] These claims angered mainstream Muslims, who persecuted the Ahmadiyya. Even at a time when many in the Islamic world were claiming to be prophesied renewers of the religion, most Muslims were united in their belief that Ahmad's claims were *bida'*, or impermissible innovation, and heresy.[88] But the Ahmadiyya's most enduring legacy was their commitment to religious proselytization, and they took their tactics from the Christian missionaries who increasingly populated Qadian and other cities throughout the Punjab. The Ahmadiyya began in 1913 by sending missionaries to Great Britain, flipping the tactics of the European Christians, who had so often come to the Punjab with dreams of mass conversion, on their heads.[89] And then, in 1920, the Ahmadiyya sent its first missionary to the United States in the form of Mufti Muhammad Sadiq.

Although the AMI began as a response to colonialism, it did not begin as a critique of British imperialism. Ahmad was vocally pro-British during his lifetime, but in 1908, he passed away, leaving the organization to the first of many *khalifat*, or successors.[90] These men reframed the AMI's missionary goals, which by 1922 they viewed as their own type of colonial project. In July 1921, Sadiq launched the *Moslem Sunrise* from Highland Park, Michigan, to serve as the North American press organ of the organization. The cover art of the newspaper, which remained the same from the second issue in October 1921 until late 1948, depicted a map of the North American continent from Canada to Panama with a resplendent sunrise, representing Islam, emerging behind it (figure 1.2).[91] This "Muslim Sunrise" on its surface represented Sadiq's vision

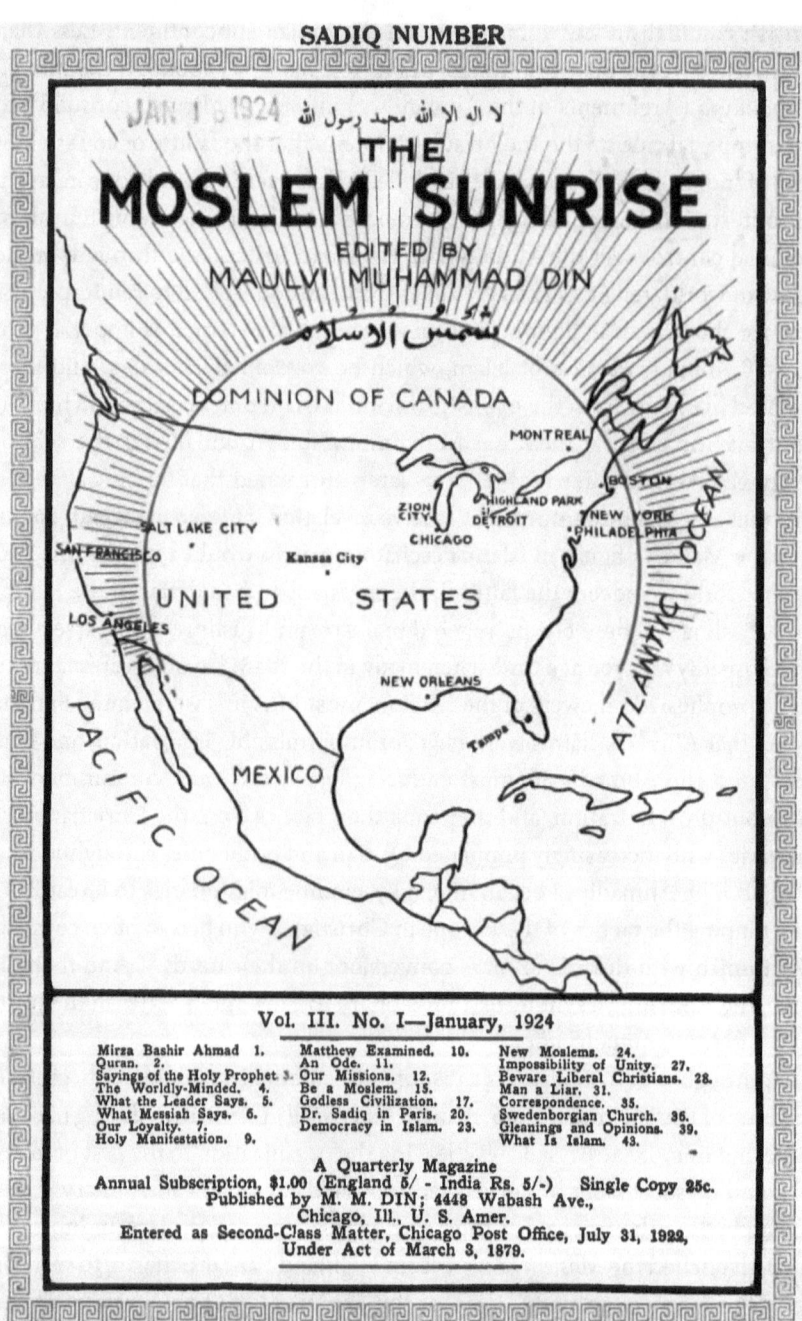

FIGURE 1.2 The cover of *Moslem Sunrise*, January 1924. Reprinted courtesy of Columbia University Libraries.

that one day Islam would enlighten the people of North America, but it also suggests that Sadiq was articulating a deeper anti-imperial motive through the publication's art. At this juncture, Sadiq did not critique the British monarchy or empire, even sending a letter of condolence to Queen Consort Mary after her son, Prince Edward, was involved in a railway accident.[92] But by depicting a sunrise over the North American continent, Sadiq appears to be rejecting the supremacy of the British Empire and, specifically, responding to the long-standing historical reality that Britain was the heart of a "vast empire, on which the sun" would never set.[93]

As a spiritual matter, the imperial ambitions of the AMI were reflected in the inaugural issue of *Moslem Sunrise*. In a greeting to the publication's readers, then-*khalifa* Hazrat Mirza Bashirud-Din Mahmud Ahmad wrote, "The pioneers in the Colonization of American land are always looked back upon with great honor and respect. Their work was temporal, but now, my dear Brothers and Sisters, Allah the Almighty has made you the Pioneers in the spiritual Colonization of the Western world."[94] It is unclear how literal Mahmud Ahmad was being when he claimed that the initial colonizers of America were honored and respected, but from his statement, it is clear that Ahmad saw the spiritual and transcendental work of the AMI to be a higher and more righteous form of imperialism. This work would happen not through a jihad, or struggle, of the sword—a method that had facilitated the growth of the Islamic empire historically—but rather, through a jihad of intellectual conquest and discourse.[95]

It is unclear exactly what Sadiq spoke about during his visit to the Exchange Club. Perhaps he reiterated the AMI's central teachings that Ghulam Ahmad was the Mahdi and a redeemer of the Islamic faith.[96] Or maybe Sadiq focused instead on the commonalities between his practice of Islam and that of other sects, of which there were many. At any rate, the lecture was undoubtedly consistent with the multiracial strategy he employed during his 1920 trip to the United States aboard the S. S. *Haverford* and his subsequent detention with which this chapter began.

Among the diverse group Sadiq converted upon his 1920 arrival were people of a host of nationalities, including Argentinian, Azorean, Belgian, British Guianese, Chinese, French, German, Honduran, Italian, Jamaican, Polish, Portuguese, Russian, South African, Spanish, Syrian, and Yugoslavian origin.[97] Sadiq's strategy was simple—the more converts, the better, no matter their racial or ethnic background. Consistent with this approach, Sadiq moved the headquarters of the AMI from New York to Chicago by October 1920, citing its "central position on the continent" and other reasons of convenience.[98] These reasons of "convenience" may have been linked to the protest of his neighbors against the simple sight of him in his turban prostrating to perform prayers five times daily. According to his own recollections in his Urdu language memoir, Sadiq was forced out of the vicinity by local residents who complained to his landlord that he was an Indian magician.[99] It is equally likely that Sadiq moved to Chicago in order to be closer to the sizable population of Muslim immigrants from the former Ottoman Empire, including the Levant, Turkey, Bosnia, and Albania.[100] This move would have simultaneously taken him away from the concentration of Muslims from the Indian subcontinent in the New York area who would be aware, and potential wary, of the Ahmadiyya's particularist interpretation of Islam.

After a brief stint in Chicago, Sadiq moved the AMI to Karroub House in the Highland Park suburb of Detroit in the summer of 1921, where he felt stable enough to launch the *Moslem Sunrise*. Karroub House was a mosque and Islamic center used by Muslims from various ethnic groups and located in the center of a Syrian enclave.[101] Karroub House embodied Sadiq's vision of a multiracial and multiethnic faith coalition, a vision similar to what the Ahmadiyya had sought in India. In July 1921, in the same issue of *Moslem Sunrise* that established its intention to spiritually colonize the world, Sadiq wrote that Americans, who were a "mixture of nationalities, languages, races, and colors ... are ready to accept the truth [of Islam]."[102] At this point, despite being chased out of New York and finding little support in Chicago, he probably still believed this was true. He boasted several white converts whose pictures were reprinted in *Moslem Sunrise* (figures 3.1a and 3.1b), and the world still seemed open to the possibility of the AMI's multiracial religious movement.[103] But by 1922, despite his own reports of success, Sadiq moved his headquarters back to Chicago, finding—as the mainstream press had reported—that Islam, at least as he preached it, had "found no root."[104]

By 1923, however, Sadiq had obviously changed tactics, moving away from the pan-racial approach that had characterized his *da'wah* previously. In January 1923, *Moslem Sunrise* featured four Black converts, Sisters Khairat, Zeineb, Ahmadia, and Ayesha, with a caption identifying them as "four American Moslem ladies" (figure 1.4).[105] In the caption, Sadiq notably does not identify these women as Black or African American. He makes no specific mention of their race, just as he made no mention of the race of the numbers of white converts whose pictures graced the pages of *Moslem Sunrise*. However, the photograph—which is displayed prominently on its own page of the *Moslem Sunrise*— is clear regarding the racial identity of these women. It could be that Sadiq wanted to allow the picture to speak for itself and the readers to come

MR. DENZEL CARR
Abdullah Omar

FIGURE 1.3A A photograph of convert Abdullah Omar, formerly known as Denzel Carr, in *Moslem Sunrise*, January 1923, p. 163. Reprinted courtesy of Columbia University Libraries.

MIRZA AHMAD F. L. ANDERSEN

FIGURE 1.3B A photograph of A. Mirza Ahmad, formerly known as F. L. Andersen, in *Moslem Sunrise*, October 1921, p. 25. Reprinted courtesy of Columbia University Libraries.

FOUR AMERICAN MOSLEM LADIES
Right to left: Mrs. Thomas (Sister Khairat), Mrs. Watts (Sister Zeineb), Mrs. Robinsin (Sister Ahmadia), Mrs. Clark (Sister Ayesha)

FIGURE 1.4 A photograph of four Black Muslim women, sisters Khairat, Zeineb, Ahmadia, and Ayesha, in *Moslem Sunrise*, January 1923, p. 165. Reprinted courtesy of the New York Public Library.

to their own conclusions. Or, given the Ahmadiyya's multiracial approach, it may have seemed counterproductive to boast about racial statistics at this juncture.

Nevertheless, any apprehensions about specifically targeting or mentioning Black Americans dissipated by mid-1923. In July, Sadiq published an open letter to "the American Negro," in which he called Islam the "real solution of the Negro question."[106] Sadiq had previously held that Islam was the solution to the problem of "color prejudice" in the United States. He argued that in Islam there was no racism or colorism, ignoring hundreds of years of evidence of the same, and he condemned Christianity for upholding these racial divisions.[107] Watching white Christians drive past Black churches to attend their own racially segregated churches, and vice versa, seemed to Sadiq a "comic opera of the highest order."[108] However, in this open letter, Sadiq was suddenly much more explicit about the reasons that Black people should embrace Islam. He wrote, "The Christian profiteers brought you out of your native lands of Africa and in Christianizing you made you forget the religion and language of your forefathers—which were Islam and Arabic.... Christianity cannot bring real brotherhood to the nations. So now, leave it alone. And join Islam the real faith of Universal Brotherhood."[109] Although this is overly simplistic, Sadiq made an argument for an ancient connection between African Americans and the Islamic world and argued for bringing African-descended people back into the ummah, where they claimed an ancestral inheritance.

Sadiq was not content to simply promote Islam. Instead, he became an increasingly loud voice condemning Christianity. He reported with schadenfreude on the disillusionment of a Congolese immigrant to the United States, named Brother Hakim, who converted to Ahmadiyya after serving as a Christian minister. After rejecting Christianity, Sadiq divulged that Hakim had become a "zealous worker" for Islam, converting "many."[110] This bold and radical approach was new for Sadiq and was evidence of his three years of directly experiencing racism and racial violence firsthand in the United States. But it was also practical. By the time Sadiq permanently relocated his headquarters to Chicago, he was in competition with several other manifestations and interpretations of Islam—not to mention the other Black religious formations that were cropping up throughout the urban North. In addition to AMI, those who were attracted to Islam could choose from MSTA, Sunni, and Shi'a variations.

Sadiq's ability to reach and convert Black people in Chicago and Detroit was due to his increasing understanding of Black social and political movements in the post–World War I period. By the time Sadiq moved to Chicago in 1922, it was a hotbed of Black religious and political activity. Surrounding himself with a Black congregation and focusing on issues that were important to Black Americans helped to racialize him as Black, lending credence to his ministry to Black people. When the *Chicago Herald & Examiner* reported that this "dark face[d]" and "thick nose[d]" man was leading a congregation of five hundred people, three hundred of whom were "Negro," it associated the rise of this movement with Black identity, community, and religious culture.[111] Indeed, it appeared that Sadiq's Black converts were gaining positions of power and authority, and were consistently promoted to local "sheikhs" in places like New Orleans, Saint Louis, New York, West Virginia, Florida, Indiana, and South Carolina.[112] Realizing the potential for a coup of new converts, Sadiq spoke at the UNIA hall in Detroit in November 1922. Within months, the fruits of Sadiq's revised strategy were clear—his congregation had transformed, surrounding him with a majority of people who identified themselves as Black or African American. These affinities were clearly reciprocated. A year later, J. A. O'Meally published his article "Crescent or Cross?" in Garvey's *Negro World*, arguing that Islam was the ideal language to drive the liberation of Black people.

Part of the ease of the alliance between the UNIA and the American AMI at this juncture came from a similar way of viewing colonialism and imperialism. Garvey envisioned a defeat to European imperialism through the colonization of the African continent by Afro-Caribbean, Afro-European, and African American people. Similarly, the AMI had, from the outset of its journalistic presence in North America, identified its project as imperial in nature.[113] Even if Sadiq wasn't of African descent, he was still one of the "darker races of the world" that Garvey followed, lauded, and cheered on in the *Negro World*.

In late 1923, Sadiq boarded a steamship and returned to Qadian.[114] In reuniting with his family, Sadiq left behind an American wife, Edith Hoffman, a Pennsylvania resident who converted to Islam in late 1922.[115] He was replaced by Maulvi Muhammad Din, who came from Qadian in March of 1923 and took over the AMI's American offices and the editorial responsibilities of the *Moslem Sunrise*.[116] Din continued Sadiq's jihad of words among American Black people and continued to solidify an alliance between the UNIA and the AMI. In his inaugural issue, in October 1923, Din reprinted O'Meally's article from the *Negro World* arguing that Islam could be a useful mechanism for the liberation of Black people and other people of color globally.[117]

Under Sadiq and then Din, the American AMI had, over the course of its three-year mission, slowly adapted its views on colonialism and imperialism.

Ghulam Ahmad had been a massive proponent of the British presence in the Indian subcontinent, and as the issue of Indian independence emerged at the beginning of the twentieth century, the Ahmadiyya were politically apathetic.[118] Having a positive view of the British Empire served them well in certain parts of the world. For example, whereas the American Ahmadiyya was 60 percent Black, in London, the membership skewed much whiter, and these native Britons would have not been as receptive to a message indicting them for their complicity in the subjugation and exploitation of the Indian subcontinent (figure 1.5).[119]

The AMI's official views on British imperialism did not change, even as the leaders of the American AMI were forging new alliances on a new continent and manifestations of Muslim nationalism cropped up all over the Indian subcontinent.[120] In the January 1924 issue of *Moslem Sunrise*, Din published an editorial that had the tone of a public relations statement mandated by AMI head officials in Qadian. Published after the October 1923 reprint of O'Meally's article, Din clarified claims made by a New Orleans newspaper that alleged that the Ahmadiyya were "anti-British." Din stated affirmatively that the Ahmadiyya were not pro- or anti- any government. He wrote, "We are neither loyal to this government or that, nor are we opposed to any. Our position is clear; we are loyal to ourselves and to our principles."[121] Din is diplomatically reserved here, but his views on British imperialism glint through his reframing of the Ahmadi position. Whereas Ghulam Ahmad had explicitly lauded the British presence in India, Din wrote, "It was our duty then to have fought against the [British] enemy tooth and nail and kept our house in order, safe as well as protected. But we did nothing of the kind. In spite of the numbers on our side, thanks to our own inefficiency, disunion and treason, we suffered a heavy defeat and then submitted to a handful of foreigners."[122] Although Din seems like he is toeing the party line, he reflects themes that were shared by O'Meally in his August 1923 *Negro World* article. Din highlights the role of unity and universality—through Islam—in overcoming racial and ethnic subjugation and exploitation. For him, that is the ultimate reason that Allah punished the people of the Indian subcontinent by taking away their sovereignty and self-governance.[123] Given the demographic realities surrounding the AMI, and perhaps their own experience of racial prejudice in the United States, Sadiq and Din began to adapt the AMI's views on colonialism and imperialism. Far away from their governing body in the Punjab region of India, they used the distance to their advantage to create a uniquely local manifestation of the AMI tradition.

After-noon 'Id gathering at the Mosque Ahmadia, 63 Melrose Road, Southfields, London, England

FIGURE 1.5 An Eid gathering at the Ahmadiyya's London Mosque in Southfields, in the *Moslem Sunrise*, October 1923, p. 256. Reprinted courtesy of Columbia University Libraries.

In part II, we will see examples of local chapters of national and international Muslim movements that implement their practice in a dramatically different way than prescribed by central leadership. Many of these local practitioners, adapting Islam to their own needs, histories, and experiences, continued to do so with no reprisal from central authority figures. The tale of Sadiq, Muhammad Din, and the AMI is not one of those cases. In 1924, the *Moslem Sunrise* abruptly terminated publication. It does not appear that Din anticipated this turn of events. In his quarterly reporting of the latest converts to the AMI, Din noted that the organization had obtained 113 new converts in the preceding three months but that he was only at liberty to list the details of thirty-four of these converts. He promised to print the names of the remaining seventy-nine in the next issue of *Moslem Sunrise*.[124] This statement suggests that he had no reason, even as late as April 1924, to predict that he would never edit the *Moslem Sunrise* again.

It is possible that part of the decision to pause *Moslem Sunrise* had to do with the fact that even as a quarterly magazine, the journal was running at a loss. Din reported that annual expenses to run the magazine were over $1,500, while the income did not exceed $600. In the last issue of 1924, Din made a plea for subscribers to donate money to keep the magazine afloat.[125] But it is likely that other factors were at play. As historian Richard Brent Turner observes, Din had "not been politically astute."[126] Din's support of Islam as a potential anticolonial mechanism was in direct contravention of the organization's long-standing policy and teachings. Despite his promise to update his followers in July 1924, the AMI leadership had other plans for Din.[127] In late August 1924, he boarded a steamship from New York for Southampton, United Kingdom. He listed on his travel documents that he would be going to 63 Melrose Road, Southfields, London, the location of the British AMI mosque.[128] This was a place where he would, given the demographic realities of the overwhelmingly white membership of the AMI's British mosque, not be tempted to make statements on race, Islam, or British colonialism.

When Maulvi Muhammad Din departed for London, he left the future of the AMI in the hands of a diffuse network of Black sheikhs from Detroit to New Orleans. These sheikhs, as well as the zealous congregation of new Muslims he had succeeded in converting, kept the AMI together for six years in the absence of stable central leadership. In July 1930, *Moslem Sunrise* suddenly returned, reporting that despite the "great handicaps and prejudices of the past twelve months [that the organization] had witnessed great changes and marvelous success."[129] One of these changes was the relocation of the Chicago headquarters from the Southside of Chicago to the Loop, the city's central business district. From this location, a new imam and editor, Sufi Mutuir Rahman Bengalee, would head the movement until 1947.[130] These were years of transition back to a less radical and more multiracial positionality, but the AMI's emphasis on racial justice remained at the core of its recruitment and missionary strategy.[131]

Conclusion

Although Bengalee's 1930 appearance in Chicago took the Ahmadiyya back to its roots as a multiracial movement, the groundwork for the return of Black communities in the United States had already been laid. This foundation was built by the physical and discursive migrations of South Asian, Caribbean, and American Black people, and allowed Islam and the Atlantic Crescent to—against what contemporary observers noted—take root. Bengalee's predecessors, Sadiq and Din, as well as Noble Drew Ali and his MSTA laid the foundation for the return and rise of Islam as a radical form of religious practice among Black people in the United States. Their early interventions—positioning Islam as an antidote to Christianity and a driver of Black and Brown freedom and salvation from colonialism and imperialism—were critically important to how Black people would continue to refine their use of Islam as a spiritual tool against empire into the 1930s and 1940s, as the world once again found itself embroiled in violent conflict in World War II. In these years, the Atlantic Crescent developed by these Black and Muslim people would directly reflect a resistance to European and American empire and would continue to exhibit the unique religio-racial identities and political engagements of these practitioners in their unique temporal and geographical realities.

Bengalee's arrival in the United States coincides with a period of uncertainty in the history of Islam in the United States, and with a transformation in the Black nationalist discourses circulating through the diaspora. In 1927, Garvey was deported from the United States after serving two years of a five-year prison sentence for mail fraud. In 1929, Noble Drew Ali died at his home in Chicago under suspicious circumstances. The disorganization of the AMI, the death of Drew Ali, and the deportation of Garvey left a spiritual and power vacuum, a space waiting to be filled by another charismatic Muslim leader.[132] In June of 1930, a month before the AMI restarted its publication of the *Moslem Sunrise*, this leader would appear in the Black neighborhoods of Detroit. He would have passed through the doors of the AMI, the UNIA, and the MSTA at some point, taking these philosophies with him as he created his own religious synthesis, passing them on to Black women as he entered their homes under the pretext of selling them beautiful silks and oriental goods, just like the traders of Hooghly. This man, W. D. Fard Muhammad, would start the Nation of Islam, a movement that built on the foundations of Garveyism, the UNIA, and the AMI.[133] This movement, also built and facilitated through an anticolonial, anti-imperial, and Afro-Asian world view, would come to be—over the course of the next three decades—one of the most powerful, most influential, and most feared Black nationalist movements—religious or otherwise—in the African diaspora. And just like its predecessors, it was influenced deeply by the overlapping diasporas of the early twentieth century. It would leave an indelible mark on the spiritual, political, and social fabric of Black and Muslim America.

CHAPTER TWO

The Atlantic Crescent from Lahore to Iowa

In 1956, twenty-nine-year-old Abdul Basit Naeem moved with his wife, Zuleikha, and his five young children to Bushwick, Brooklyn (figure 2.1).[1] With so many people relying on him, Naeem was hungry for power and influence. The year prior, from his apartment in Cedar Rapids, Iowa, Naeem launched the *Moslem World & the U.S.A.*, a magazine that aimed to unite Muslims across the world and to make Islam intelligible to non-Muslim Americans. At first, *Moslem World* relied on a strict Cold War dichotomy—siding squarely with the United States in its battle against the Soviet Union—but events thousands of miles away changed that. As anticolonial movements across what would soon be called the Third World bore fruit in the form of independence, the magazine became fixated on Islam's role in decolonization and anti-imperialism. In 1955, after twenty-nine African and Asian nations met in Bandung, Indonesia, to discuss their postcolonial futures, *Moslem World* became focused on the challenges that awaited Muslim-majority countries as they transitioned to independent nations.

Naeem was fascinated by these transnational solidarities, but he was also influenced by what was happening around him. In the one hundred square miles of Brooklyn and Manhattan, Naeem could pray with Sunni Muslims from Sheikh Daoud Faisal's Islamic Mission of America and exchange ideas with Ahmadiyya missionaries from his native Pakistan. But no movement inspired Naeem more than Elijah Muhammad's Nation of Islam (the Nation), which was then in the process of breaking out of its regional Midwestern confines to become an international organization. Muhammad employed Naeem as a consultant for the Nation, using his expertise and his identity as a Pakistani Muslim to bolster the organization's authenticity and make an argument that it was a legitimate, although decidedly Black and American, interpretation of Islam. Together, Naeem and Muhammad used glossy magazines and inky black-and-white newspapers to communicate a diasporic, anti-imperial identity reflecting the liberatory potential of Islam for all colonized people, especially those of African descent.

This chapter conducts a biography of Naeem, a Pakistani Muslim intellectual, traveler, and missionary, and places it in conversation with the early history of the Nation. Naeem came to the United States at a pivotal moment

FIGURE 2.1 Abdul and Zuleikha Naeem with five of their children. Photograph taken circa late 1950s. Courtesy of Shahid Naeem.

in the decolonization of the African and Asian worlds and settled in the midwestern and eastern United States. There, he sought intellectual and physical community with Muslims of African descent living in the United States. As a resident of Michigan and Iowa, Naeem launched *Moslem World & the U.S.A.* with the intention of facilitating Muslim understanding across the ummah and helping non-Muslims make sense of the complexity of Islamic history and Muslim life. In New York, Naeem took advantage of long-standing Black internationalist movements and networks, helping to enhance their connections with the decolonizing world.

Naeem's migration as a member of the Pakistani diaspora intersected with the ideas, theories, and cultural production of the Great Migration. This brought him into contact with the theories, ideas, and interpretations of Islam that would motivate his connections with Elijah Muhammad, Malcolm X, and the Nation. From this vantage point, he began to help Muhammad and the Nation build an internationalist, Third World–centered, Afro-Asian focused Atlantic Crescent and Islamic identity. Although Naeem's intimacies with Elijah Muhammad and the Nation are his longest—and most studied—relationships with Black Muslims in the United States, Naeem was much more than just a booster for the Nation's particularist interpretation of Islam. He was a theorist in his own right, making sense of the political upheaval taking place around him and finding a place for Black and Muslim solidarities in these spaces. Scholars have observed the way Naeem played with different solidarities on his way to the Nation's doors, noting the difficulty of pinning down his exact motivations.[2] I, however, argue that Naeem intentionally altered his racial and religious solidarities—as any intellectual, scholar, or theorist would—in view of the overlapping diasporas and momentous political changes happening around him globally, nationally, and locally.

A Glossy Haired Peddler: The Early Afro-Asian History of the Nation of Islam

It wasn't so strange that Naeem would eventually find his way to the Nation's doors, especially given that imagined connections to Asia provided a strong foundation for the organization's theology and mythos. In July 1930, a "glossy haired" Muslim immigrant who went by some variation of the name Fard Muhammad went from house to house in Detroit's Black migrant neighborhoods.[3] A skilled salesman, Fard Muhammad enchanted the Black housewives and working-class women of neighborhoods like Black Bottom and Hastings, who allowed him into their homes to examine the beautiful textiles and oriental goods that he sold.[4] They would have seen men like him before, traveling salesmen from Bengal and the Punjab, who sold imported goods by day and, at night, sometimes went home to Black, Creole, or mixed-race families.[5]

Once he had gained entry, Fard Muhammad switched from peddling silks to pushing membership in the ummah, the imagined transnational Muslim community. After he gained their trust, Fard Muhammad told these women, as Noble Drew Ali and the MSTA did before him, that they were not Negroes, as they had been led to believe, but instead lost members of an Asiatic tribe. For Fard, who adapted Drew's theory and made it his own, American Black people were part of the lost Asiatic Tribe of Shabazz.[6] In their "home country," which Fard explained was Saudi Arabia, they were never slaves or servants, but instead the descendants of a powerful ruling class and merchant tribes who practiced Islam, spoke Arabic, and invented math and science.[7] Instead, Fard Muhammad reversed the American racial hierarchy. It was Caucasians who were the real barbarians, wicked "blond blue-eyed devils," who were unnaturally created in a laboratory by a mad scientist named Yakub, and who used Christianity to rob Black people of their religion, language, culture, and accomplishments. One day, these "white devils" would be destroyed for their wickedness by a contraption called the Mother Plane, or Ezekiel's Wheel, a flattened disc of a spaceship approximately half a mile in diameter. To survive this destruction, and to revive their lost history, Black people needed to separate themselves from white people and live within the boundaries of Islam's holiest text—the Qur'an—and reclaim their identities as Muslims.[8] They needed to accept rigid gender roles, with men as heads of household and protectors of the Black woman, and women as the "master[s of] the domestic sphere"—a corrective to the destabilization of the Black family during slavery.[9] They needed to reject the use of drugs and alcohol, refuse to eat pork and bottom-feeding fish, and live "clean" and "respectable lifestyles." They also needed to accept Fard Muhammad as their messiah and as an incarnation of God himself. Then, on Earth and in the afterlife, they would construct a utopia free from sickness, disease, poverty, and racial violence.[10] By 1938, when anthropologist Erdmann Doane Beynon published the first academic study on the Nation, these teachings and many others had been codified in both textual and oral forms.[11] By the 1950s, when Naeem came into contact with the Nation, Fard's teaching had been reorganized and republished several times.[12]

Fard's inspirational message and reinterpretation of Black history filled a void left by the arrest and deportation of Marcus Garvey in 1927 and the death of Noble Drew Ali in 1929.[13] From the Nation's early days, observers noted an overlap between the teaching and membership of the UNIA, the Nation, and the MSTA. Writing less than a decade after the founding of the Nation in 1930, Beynon observed, "The story of the Nation of Islam cannot be considered as complete in itself. [These] movements among migrant Negroes in the cities of the North have formed a sort of tree."[14] There is evidence that Fard Muhammad, in a sense, may have been one of the acorns that fell from this Black nationalist tree. In the 1920s, using the alias of George Farr, Fard may have joined the UNIA in San Francisco. In 1929, as Wallace D. Fard, he moved to Chicago where he joined the MSTA and dabbled in Ahmadiyya Islam.[15]

Contemporaneous reports indicate that by 1934, Fard Muhammad had converted between five thousand and eight thousand men and women, began renting a meeting hall, and stoked the fears of the Detroit Metropolitan Police and the ire of competing Black organizations in the city.[16] In these temple hall meetings, early members reported hearing Fard say that he was from the Holy City of Mecca and directly related to the Prophet Muhammad.[17] Over the decades since he disappeared, rumors have circulated about where Fard went, but the matter of where he went is far less important here than another hotly debated question: Where did he come from in the first place?

Fard's self-proclaimed Saudi identity became indispensable to the Nation's origin story and lore. Although there is much conflicting information about Fard's origins, linguistic analysis conducted by the journalist Karl Evanzz provides compelling evidence that Fard was most likely an immigrant of Pakistani descent from New Zealand named Wallace Dodd Fard, born in 1891 to Zared and Beatrice Fard.[18] In developing the eschatology of the Nation, particularly the idea of the origins and genealogy of Black people, Fard pulled from these Pakistani roots, combining them with anti-white and pro-Black—but notably not pro-African—rhetoric that appealed to African Americans. When he told Black Midwesterners that they were a part of the lost "Tribe of Shabazz," he was not referring to a real geographical location. Instead, he was likely referring to the cult of the Sufi saint Lal Shahbaz Qalandar, who is widely revered in Pakistan.[19] Qalandar's cult of personality is small but is followed by a relatively large proportion of Sufi Muslim believers of African descent. These Muslims mostly hail from the Balochistan and Sindh regions of Southern Pakistan and are referred to variably as *Sheedi* (or *Sidi*), *Dada*, *Syah*, *Gulam* (meaning slave), and *Nokir* (or *Naukar*, meaning servant). Pakistan's African-descended Muslims are in large part, but not exclusively, the descendants of East Africans who were brought to modern-day Pakistan by slave traders in the eighth century CE.[20] Fard, thus, was a part of the diasporas that created the foundation of Islam in the early twentieth-century as much as he was influenced by them.

Muhammad and the Nation were vehement about protecting their institutional version of Fard's origins in Saudi Arabia, and rejected any idea that he could have hailed from elsewhere. In July 1963, for instance, after the *Los Angeles Evening Herald-Examiner* published an article alleging that Fard Muhammad was really a white New Zealander, fraud, and ex-convict named Wallace Dodd, Elijah Muhammad went on the offensive. Two weeks later, on the front page of *Muhammad Speaks*, Muhammad offered the Hearst company, which owned the *Herald-Examiner*, $100,000 to definitively prove their allegations.[21]

To the present day, the Nation maintains that Fard Muhammad was Saudi.[22] The self-serving nature of each side of the archive—on one side the government's desire to discredit and incarcerate Nation leadership and the Nation's project of projecting themselves as a strong, unified Black organization grounded in Islamic legitimacy—makes it difficult to know for certain what is true. However, Fard's potential identity as Pakistani, although speculative, is important. For one, it gives us additional insight into why the Nation's lore is focused on the Asian instead of the African continent and how it was able to incorporate the existing Black nationalist affinity for Asia—which we saw in the previous chapter—so easily. Second, it explains the pro-Asian sentiments that flourished within the organization during the lead up to World War II, and why they strengthened after 1955, the year of the Bandung Conference of Afro-Asian nations. And finally, it explains why Naeem pursued the Nation vigorously, why he accepted and excused their particularist teachings, and why he developed a close intimacy with Elijah Muhammad and vice versa.

A Transition Period

By June 30, 1934, thirty-seven-year-old Elijah Muhammad, a migrant of the Great Migration and former sharecropper from Georgia, had ascended to leadership of the Nation.[23] Muhammad was slight, soft-spoken, and had not finished the fifth grade, but what he lacked in stature and formal education he made up by being an "astute observer" of his environment and an expert delegator of responsibility.[24] He arrived in Detroit in 1923 with his young wife, Clara, and their two children, Emmanuel and Ethel, following the beaten trail of Great Migration migrants determined to find a better life free from poverty and the violence of the Jim Crow South. But the racial violence of white supremacy followed them northward, as did the poverty.[25] Elijah was unable to keep any of the unskilled jobs for which he qualified in Detroit's factories, and like many Black women, Clara took on low-paying and exploitative domestic work for white families.[26] Elijah became despondent, self-medicating to the point of oblivion with alcohol and putting his faith in gambling.[27]

One day, in 1931, overwhelmed and holding her family—which had swelled to five children—together single-handedly, a pregnant Clara stumbled upon Fard preaching, and she took his message of the transformative and salvific qualities of Islam and the righteousness of the Asiatic Black man home to Elijah.[28] Perhaps she had heard of the organization from Elijah's father, who had recently encountered a friend, Abdul Muhammad, who had started attending Fard's lectures. Or perhaps she heard news of Fard's teachings from any of the other women whom Fard had enticed throughout Black Detroit.[29] We don't know the nature of their private interactions on the nights Clara came home from Fard's meetings, but as many married women do, she may have shared her experiences and her transforming worldview with her husband. Fard's idea of a world where white people were naturally demonic and directly responsible for Elijah and Clara's suffering must have been incredibly appealing to them both. And yet, Elijah stayed home, letting Clara attend meetings alone. One day, however, Clara came home with a direct request from Fard himself: for Elijah to teach the message of Islam to his brothers and sisters in Detroit. Driven by Clara, and by his new purpose, Elijah rose to the helm of the Nation. From this vantage point, he was poised to assume complete control of the Detroit temple's eight thousand members upon his teacher's disappearance three years later in 1934.[30]

In Fard's message, Elijah and Clara saw not only an explanation for their suffering but also the means to emerge from it, and nothing would stop their march out of poverty and powerlessness. As early as 1932, the organization had attracted negative attention when one of its followers, who alleged he was compelled to plunge his knife into his victim's heart due to Fard's teachings, was charged with murder.[31] Although the organization vehemently denied any involvement, that incident resulted in a new era of surveillance and persecution by the Detroit police, by local Black Christian leaders, and by elite Black organizations like the Urban League.[32] In April 1934, Elijah, who had by then been elevated to minister of Islam, was arrested on charges of "contributing to the delinquency of minors" after refusing to close the Nation's University of Islam parochial schools at the demand of the Detroit Board of Education.[33] In September 1934, under a campaign of persecution, Muhammad left Detroit for Chicago, where he would make the Nation's fledgling Temple No. 2 the organization's new headquarters.[34] But even in their new home city, the Muhammads would continue to be harassed by police and by federal agents.[35]

Seven years later, in 1942, the FBI began to take broad notice of Black Muslim refusal to register for the selective service. In order to uncover the reasons behind this trend, the agency enlisted Black men and women to infiltrate the Nation and uncover its subversive teachings.[36] Agents found plenty of evidence of anti-American sentiment, including rejection of loyalty to the United States, derision of the American flag, promotion of the idea that Japan had superior weapons, including the Mother Plane, and the belief that a Japanese win would bring about an immediate end to white supremacy.[37] In September of that year, after months of investigation, the FBI raided Nation headquarters in Chicago and arrested Elijah Muhammad, seventy male members of the Chicago temple, and one solitary woman, the national secretary of the Nation, Sister Pauline Bahar.[38] When all was said and done, Muhammad and sixty-three of his male followers were each sentenced to three years in prison for sedition and violation of the Selective Service Act.[39] All charges against Bahar, who was initially charged with promoting draft evasion and sedition, were dropped in 1943 despite her high level of involvement in the organization.[40]

After the raid in Chicago, the FBI tried to piece together the primary reasons for the mass selective service violations committed by Nation members. For the FBI, the most obvious reason was that members were taught by Fard, and later Muhammad and Bahar, that registering for the draft was a violation of their religion. Almost all FBI interviewees reported that they believed themselves to be citizens of "Mecca," citizens of "Islam," or citizens of "heaven," and therefore unable to pledge allegiance to two "governments" at once.[41] Although FBI agents dismissed this as simple sedition, these interviewees were expressing their belief that they had a national identity, driven by their religion, which superseded their commitments and obligations to any geographical entity, in this case the United States.

The refusal of Nation members to register for the draft was not only religious, however; it was also grounded in their understanding of race and racial solidarity. Interviewees indicated that they refused to register for the draft because of Fard's teaching that Black Americans and all members of the "dark races" were Muslim and, as a diasporic transnational body, were citizens of a global nation of Islam. Interviewees did not use this terminology, nor did they likely know this language at the time, but this was a nascent idea of membership in the Muslim ummah. For these Nation members, the Islamic religion—not the United States—stood for "freedom, justice, equality and for the furtherance of people [of color] in the world."[42] Given this logic, instead of registering to support the European and American imperial drives for domination, they instead gathered behind the Japanese and the "dark races in their fight for supremacy."[43]

Yet, for all of these dramatic calls to Japanese support, Nation members were not physically joining the ranks of the Axis powers. At least, there is no evidence to support that this was ever the case. Nevertheless, both men and women were willing to be imprisoned for holding steadfast to the belief that their belonging in the ummah transcended and negated any obligation they had to the American government. In the words of historian Ula Taylor, "Persecution can sometimes have the opposite effect of its intent, inspiring a more profound commitment to one's original purpose."[44] For Muhammad, this was also true. When he was imprisoned in 1943, prison authorities recorded that he believed there existed "a marked persecutory trend both against himself and his race." Prison authorities chalked this up to unfounded paranoia. However, as Muhammad's biographer Claude Clegg observed, Muhammad often recognized that he was, in fact, being "pursued and slandered by enemies."[45] Muhammad's observational experience, therefore, was used by prison authorities to slander him, to discredit him, and to depict him as a man suffering from mental illness and schizophrenia.[46] However, this campaign of persecution by the FBI would only serve as proof of Muhammad's assertion of the white race's inherent "adverseness to truth and fairness" and would bolster his teachings of the redemptive nature of racial separation and of the Muslim faith.[47]

A Different World

The FBI's raid on the Nation was catastrophic for the organization. From 1943 to 1946, the Nation held on by a thread, buoyed by Clara and Sister Pauline Bahar.[48] Clara assumed a primary leadership role and kept Muhammad abreast of organizational matters through constant communication. By the time Muhammad exited the Federal Correctional Facility at Milan, Michigan, on August 24, 1946, the membership of the Nation had dropped to approximately one thousand.[49] But global changes were also afoot. At the end of World War II, nationalist movements that had been steadily simmering since the turn of the twentieth century came to a rolling boil. Kicked off by Sukarno's Proclamation of Indonesian Independence from the Netherlands on August 17, 1945, European powers began losing control of their colonial strongholds in Asia and Africa at a dizzying pace. New imperial tensions began to arise as the United States and the Soviet Union battled for global domination. By the end of the decade, Jordan, Vietnam, Korea, the Philippines, India, Pakistan, Myanmar, and Sri Lanka had joined Indonesia as sovereign states and raised questions of how to maintain their independence amid the powerful geopolitical currents of the Cold War between the United States and the Soviet Union.

Although Japan and the Axis Powers did not win the war, at least to Elijah Muhammad, his followers, and the rest of the "dark world," it seemed that the demise of white supremacy was nonetheless imminent as the demands for liberation that had preoccupied Asia and Africa began to yield fruit in the form of independence. For the Nation, these ideas of international solidarity and connection to the larger Asian and Islamic worlds had been integral to the organization's foundations and teachings, and World War II strengthened the intellectual connective tissue holding these ideas of diasporic solidarity together.[50] The war, the global shift in power it forced, and the circulation of these ideas in the Black press forced connections between African American suffering and third world decolonization to snap together like ideological puzzle pieces.

These conversations took place, not only among governments but also among citizens. Facilitated by wartime advances in communication technologies like syndication, newspapers and magazines served as the backbone of nationalist and independence movements throughout the world.⁵¹ In the United States, Black newspapers, like the *Pittsburgh Courier*, the *Chicago Defender*, and the *New York Amsterdam News*, were able to facilitate a sense of global solidarity and community by easing communication over geographical distance.⁵² These technologies lessened the burden of international political organizing by enabling more rapid communication between populations separated by oceans. Thus, whether readers were experiencing segregation in Harlem or decolonization firsthand in Accra, they had a shared language upon which to build an imagined diasporic community.⁵³ These technologies ensured that even when people couldn't travel across space to interact with each other, their ideas could.

It was in this global context that on January 27, 1948, a nineteen-year-old Abdul Basit Naeem left his birthplace in Lahore and boarded a steamship headed for the United States. Over six days, he traveled across the Indian Ocean, around the cape of Africa, and over the Atlantic Ocean until he was greeted by the sight of the Statue of Liberty thrusting her torch to the heavens.⁵⁴ From Ellis Island, Naeem made his way across the Appalachian Mountains to Kalamazoo, Michigan, where he would begin his studies at Western Michigan College of Education. At Western Michigan, Naeem was an active member of several student organizations, including the Camera Club, the International Relations Club, and the Foreign Students Club (figure 2.2).⁵⁵ Not yet in his twenties, Naeem was already interested in forging connections between Americans and Pakistanis and, on at least one occasion, was invited by the International Relations Club to share about his homeland.⁵⁶ Indeed, there was plenty of news to share. The year prior, in 1947, Britain's rule over the Indian subcontinent came to an end, and the Muslim nation of Pakistan was carved off from India. The exceptionalism of this historical event was not lost on the young Naeem.

After leaving Western Michigan in 1949, Naeem briefly enrolled as a journalism graduate student at Iowa State University in Cedar Rapids. By 1951, he was a graduate student at the University of Pennsylvania's School of Southwest Asian Studies. In the two years since he had left Western Michigan, Naeem's interest in American perceptions of Islam and the Islamic world— and vice versa—continued to blossom. And his determination to facilitate mutual understanding only increased. In 1951, during his graduate study at the University of Pennsylvania, he published his first-known essay, titled "Pakistan and the U.S.A." The essay lamented that most Americans were ignorant of both the new nation of Pakistan and the religion of Islam.⁵⁷ From that point forward, Naeem's activities would be focused on correcting this

FIGURE 2.2 Abdul Basit Naeem (*second from right*) at the age of nineteen with members of the Camera Club of Western Michigan College of Education. From the *Brown and Gold Yearbook*, 1948, p. 148. From the Western Michigan University Archives and Regional History Collections.

dearth of knowledge not only from the American side but also from the Muslim world at large.

By 1952, the twenty-four-year-old Naeem had experienced massive and momentous life changes. He was a new husband to his wife, Zuleikha, who also emigrated from Pakistan and enrolled at Western Michigan.[58] He had abandoned his studies at the University of Pennsylvania. He moved to an apartment on Baker Street in San Francisco, where he tried his hand working at the new Pakistani consulate.[59] And on October 16, 1952, the Naeem family doubled in size when Naeem and Zuleikha welcomed twins Shahid and Shereen.[60]

On June 13, 1953, the Naeem family reversed course.[61] Naeem and his family traveled overland to New York City, sailed across the Atlantic, around the horn of Africa, through the Indian Ocean, and arrived back home on the Indian subcontinent. On their disclosures, the Naeem family indicated that they intended to be gone for five years, but less than a year later they returned. Between June and December, Naeem solidified his membership in a Pakistani missionary group called *jam'iat-ul-falah*, translating to the Society of Salvation, an organization with a singular aim to "work for the exposition, propagation and implementation, in all its fulness [sic], of the scheme of life promulgated by Islam, and thereby, to promote the all-around well-being of humanity."[62] *Jam'iat-ul-falah* sought to do this through ambassadors like Naeem, through the public writings of these missionaries, and through its own journal, the *Voice of Islam*, which began publication in 1952.[63] Carrying a "mandate" to "deliver Islam's message of Peace and Goodwill to the people of America," Naeem returned on Trans World Airlines Flight 967/14 via London to New York City in December 1953 with new baby Selma in tow.[64] His intended destination was Sacramento, where he was supposed to make the city a "real centre of Islamic life and light" in California, but it is unclear if he ever made it there.[65] Six months later, the Naeems were back in Cedar Rapids, where they would soon become a family of six.[66]

The Muslim World, the United States, and the Afro-Asian World

In 1954, Zuleikha Naeem wasn't the only one who was pregnant. The Naeems arrived in Cedar Rapids at a time that was expectant with the possibility of real Afro-Asian cooperation, self-government, Muslim global leadership, and the end of white supremacy. Even the struggles of non-Muslim nations became a powerful basis for optimism and imagination among Muslims in the African diaspora. In 1954, Malcolm X—who joined the Nation in 1952 from prison and quickly rose to leadership in the organization—used the ongoing struggles of the Kukuyu *Mau Mau* fighters against the British colonial government of Kenya and the defeat of the French by Ho Chi Minh's communist forces at Dien Bien Phu as examples of imminent change.[67] As these nations achieved independence, or saw it more clearly on their horizon, they reached out across oceans to forge diplomatic ties—reaching past the United States and Europe to their peer nations. But the Cold War created an omnipresent danger. Any diplomatic, developmental, or military misstep, and these young nations could find themselves drawn back into the imperial orbit of their former colonizers, the United States, or the Soviet Union. The idea of nonalignment was not yet articulated, but within a year it would form the zeitgeist of the era.

Naeem had dabbled as a diplomat, but he was also a writer, an intellectual, a journalist, and a missionary. Based on these constant shifts, historians have been unkind to him and suspicious of his motivations.[68] But a more generous assessment is that Naeem was a young man whose worldview was shifting as quickly as national boundaries moved after the Second World War. He was also ambitious, willing to shift his alliances and allegiances in order to achieve his goals. At this point in his life, consistent with the *jam'iat*'s views, Naeem was strongly anti-communist and suspicious of Soviet attempts to influence or control Muslims in the Islamic world through publishing and propaganda.[69] Thus, he was motivated to create an American press organ that would combine the *jam'iat*'s missionary agenda with his own interests: *da'wah*, or religious proselytization; diplomacy; anti-communism; and promoting Muslim unity and understanding across the ummah. He would do this through a glossy monthly periodical he would call *The Moslem World & the U.S.A.* The title *Moslem World* was a reference to a journal published by in 1893 by Mohammed Alexander Webb, the first American Muslim convert to Islam, and thus connected Naeem to a longer history of Islam in the United States.[70]

Since his arrival in Cedar Rapids, Naeem had audited classes in magazine production at the University of Iowa and toiled sixty-five hours a week at a local restaurant to make ends meet. But in early 1955, he was exceptionally close to making his dream of publishing *Moslem World* a reality. He had fifty-six advance orders from local Muslims, libraries, and universities. One hundred fifty copies sat on his ink-smudged desk in his family apartment, waiting to be mailed. But Naeem didn't have money for stamps, or even rent for that matter. In December 1954, he left his job at the restaurant to take care of Zuleikha, who had contracted a viral infection, and their children. He did not have the credit for a bank loan, and he had depleted nearly all of their savings on the magazine. By January 1955, he was two months in arrears on his rent and on the verge of eviction. In order to save the project, Naeem needed several hundred dollars and a stroke of dumb luck. That windfall came in January after celebrity journalist Dorothy Thompson heard about Naeem's difficulties and offered the help of an organization called the American Friends of the Middle East (AFME).[71]

AFME claimed that its intentions were to help Americans and people from the Middle East engage in a process of mutual understanding and respect. Ultimately, this was thinly veiled language for the promotion of anti-communism and American oil interests in the Middle East.[72] The group was likely funded by the CIA's Office of Policy Coordination, a division chartered with the intention of carrying out "covert operations" in ways that "if uncovered, the U.S. government [could] plausibly disclaim any responsibility for them."[73] As a practical matter, these organizations looked like AFME and a host of other groups that, on the surface, seemed simply like groups of elite, rich, private citizens engaged in benevolent activities. If, as some historians have argued, the AFME was funded in part by money from the CIA's Office of Policy Coordination, when Thompson offered to help Naeem in January of 1955, she was likely aware of the CIA's investment. But this agenda was probably hidden from Naeem, as it was from the public more broadly.[74] Whether Naeem ever knew about AFME's ties to the government is unclear, but their anti-communist stance suited him just fine at that moment. The relationship gave him access to the capital he needed to finish the project, opened up a world of new subscribers, and supported his vision of promoting Muslim sovereignty.[75]

Just six months after its maiden issue, *Moslem World* was up to two hundred subscriptions, twenty-seven of which were by subscribers in Malaysia and the Middle East. The remaining subscriptions were held by American Muslims and institutions. For the benefit of non-Muslims, each issue of *Moslem World* featured primers on Islamic practice, shariah (Islamic law), and basic Muslim cultural traditions.[76] Geographically, Naeem included news from the entire Muslim world but focused heavily on his home country of Pakistan, using it as an example of the diversity of Islam in the world. Through the example of Pakistan, Naeem highlighted Ahmadiyya, Sufi, Shi'a, and Sunni Islam.[77] His embrace of Ahmadiyya Islam as a node on the spectrum of Muslim experience and practice is, itself, unusual. As discussed in greater detail in chapter 1, the majority of Muslims consider Ahmadiyya beliefs to be blasphemous and to violate the most basic tenets of Islam, including the idea of the oneness of God and the assertion that Muhammad ibn-Abdullah was the last prophet in the Abrahamic tradition.[78] Nevertheless, Naeem's propensity to think outside of the box of Sunnism would eventually pave his road to the Nation's doors. For Naeem, Islam had a clear role in the process of obtaining freedom from colonialism and racial oppression. This was true whether the subjugated were living in the ghettos of Chicago, the banlieues of Paris, or the occupied lands of North Africa. And for these purposes, Naeem believed that the religion could be—and in some cases needed to be—malleable.

By forging Muslim diasporic connections, Naeem hoped to realize his secondary goal, which concerned ensuring the ongoing sovereignty and decolonization of the Muslim world. The allies that he identified in this struggle, however, changed over the course of the publication in response to the conversations taking place in newly independent and decolonizing nations. These nations found themselves newly threatened in the Cold War scramble for power between the United States and the Soviet Union. In the first issues of *Moslem World*, Naeem adopted a clearly pro-West and pro-American slant, encouraging both Muslims and Americans to see themselves as friends and allies in the struggle for global democracy. One such article detailed how two

Turkmen hajjis uncovered a devious plot by Soviet propagandists to sow antireligious, anti-American, and pro-communist information in Jeddah, the key port of entry to Mecca. Naeem celebrated this victory of Islam over communism through a jihad of words, detailing how these men worked quickly to print a pamphlet expounding on the long history of religious persecution of Muslim people by Russia. By the time the Soviet delegation arrived, a group of Arabs and Muslims had gathered together to pelt the Soviets with tomatoes, and the word had spread to Saudi leader King Saud, who refused to receive the delegation.[79] Naeem cautioned that these types of efforts by the Soviets would become more frequent as the "pro-West" tendencies of Islam became apparent.[80] To emphasize this point—and perhaps to up the ante for potential subscribers—in the second issue of *Moslem World*, Naeem reprinted a US military briefing on the dangers of communism in Southeast Asia and North Africa.[81]

At this time, democracy and the United States were synonymous for Naeem. And yet, the fact that Muslim-majority nations were steadily obtaining independence was not lost on him. In a subscription advertisement on the last page of *Moslem World*, Naeem lauded the two hundred million Muslims of India, Pakistan, Indonesia, and Libya who had recently obtained independence, and he noted that the independence of others, including Morocco, Tunisia, and Sudan, was on the horizon. *Moslem World* promised to keep its readers informed on these current events monthly.[82] But at this stage of his life and publishing career, Naeem—like many others at the time—could not view the potential for Muslim democracy and liberation outside of the Cold War dichotomy of the United States and the Soviet Union. As global diplomatic alliances shifted, however, so did his worldview.

Bandung and the Muslim Imaginary

Naeem continued to be plagued by problems throughout the first year of the publication of *Moslem World*. The magazine took a hiatus from February 1955 until April 1956 when the Naeem family left Iowa and moved to the rapidly diversifying neighborhood of Bushwick, Brooklyn.[83] By then, there had emerged another, third, option in world diplomacy. In April 1955, India, Pakistan, Ceylon (present-day Sri Lanka), and Burma (present-day Myanmar) hosted twenty-five other nations in Bandung, Indonesia. Here, these nations discussed their commitment to sovereignty and Cold War nonalignment. They committed themselves to organizing a third diplomatic space apart from the United States and the Soviet Union. And in refusing to align themselves with either, these nations expressed their unwillingness to be used as strategic pawns in the Cold War race for global power.

There is no April 1955 issue of *Moslem World*, and thus, we cannot locate Naeem's "eureka moment" after the Bandung Conference—if this moment even occurred. From April 1955 to March 1956, *Moslem World* paused publication due to unspecified "problems of great magnitude."[84] However, in the issues of *Moslem World* published after Bandung, Naeem notably detached himself from a view of the United States as an ally of the Muslim people, and instead focused on enmeshing himself ideologically and diplomatically into the African-Asian Third World molded by the Bandung Conference itself. After Bandung, Naeem became committed to practicing and projecting the spirit of Bandung through *Moslem World* in two ways. First, after April 1956, Naeem gave plenty of attention to the ongoing processes of decolonization in Muslim countries of the newly defined "Third World." Naeem lauded the frequency with which Muslim-majority and plurality nations, including India, Indonesia, Libya, Pakistan, and Tunisia, had "thrown off the yoke of foreign colonialism" and predicted that this was a harbinger of a "great future" for the ummah.[85] These nations were obliged to come together to assist in the emancipation process for their brother nations like Algeria, Malaysia, and Nigeria, to ensure that they too would "shatter the shackles of slavery."[86] Islam, above all else, was the glue that held these nations together. It was an overarching identity that defied national boundaries.[87]

Second, by the third issue of *Moslem World*, the blind support that Naeem had previously expressed toward the United States had dissipated. When *Moslem World* returned in April 1956, it had shed its decidedly pro-American and pro-West perspective. In the year since *Moslem World* began publication, Naeem came to see Christianity, the dominant religion of the United States, as antidemocratic. This was in stark contrast to what he viewed as the inherently democratic nature of Islam.[88] In the case of Muslim countries, Naeem believed that this Islamic spirit of democracy and self-determination was driving the independence movements that were beginning to enjoy success across Africa and Asia.[89] In supporting Christian, European imperialists, the United States had proven itself to be a hypocrite. In the case of Algeria, for instance, *Moslem World* explicitly condemned the United States for supporting the imperial designs of a murderous and bloodthirsty France over Algerian self-rule.[90]

Naeem did remain anti-Marxist and anti-Soviet. He argued that Soviet ideology was anti-God and anti-religious, and he condemned the ongoing persecution of Muslims in the Soviet Union.[91] But he encouraged political, economic, military, and cultural diplomacy between Muslim nations of the decolonizing world and a mutual commitment to self-defense. Naeem wrote, even though these types of alliances might "displease the West or Russia," they were the only way to Muslim independence and sovereignty, even if it resulted in warfare.[92] These articles reflected a spirit of Afro-Asian brotherhood—and a refusal to engage in the Cold War binary—that was lacking in previous issues of *Moslem World*. But as much as large-scale, explosive events like Bandung delivered a shock to Naeem's point of view, so too did the new relationships he made in Brooklyn. There, he consulted with African Americans and Afro-Caribbeans and prayed with Black Muslims as they contemplated the question of the role of their faith against racialized violence in America.

Building Bandung in Bushwick and Harlem

In Bushwick, Naeem began to make the diasporic connections he had discussed in his magazine a physical reality. Between his years at Western Michigan and his editorship at *Moslem World*, Naeem's worldview had transformed as he realized the diversity of the American, and specifically Black, Muslim experience. When Naeem moved to Brooklyn in 1956, he immediately gravitated toward Sheikh Daoud Ahmed Faisal's Islamic Mission of America and his mosque on State Street in Brooklyn.

Like many early Black and Muslim leaders, including Fard Muhammad and Noble Drew, Sheikh Daoud's early life is obscured by legend. Evidence suggests that even though he alleged to be Moroccan born, he came from Trinidad. As anthropologist Robert Dannin has argued, Sheikh Daoud's claim of Moroccan ancestry suggests that at some point, he had an association with the MSTA, which promoted the idea that African Americans were originally Moors from Morocco. His adoption of the honorific title of sheikh suggests an affiliation at some point with the Ahmadiyya. Like these sects, he argued that Islam was an original and transformational religion for Black Americans, and Sheikh Daoud rejected Christianity as an oppressive religion.[93]

It is unclear how or when Naeem and Sheikh Daoud met, but in April 1956, Naeem reported that *Moslem World* had been offered permanent office space at the Islamic Mission of America's upstate New York facility, *Madinat-asslam*, meaning the City of Peace.[94] Naeem's attraction to Sheikh Daoud made ideological sense. Since Sheikh Daoud's founding of the Islamic Mission of America in 1924, he maintained an internationalist vision of Islam where religious legitimacy for African American Muslims would come through diplomatic and diasporic connections with Muslim and Arab nations. He envisioned the vehicle for this solidarity as the United Nations, and through his diplomatic efforts with Arab nations, he was granted United Nations observer status in 1960. Moreover, Sheikh Daoud viewed the anticolonial movements awakening across Africa and Asia in the post–World War II period as examples of a righteous jihad against both Cold War dualities of warring capitalism and communism.[95] In Sheikh Daoud, Naeem saw a man who shared his own vision uniting the liberatory capabilities of Islam and the anticolonial struggle. His diasporic identity, as a South Asian man from a newly independent nation, overlapped with and was enriched by that of Sheikh Daoud, an Afro-Trinidadian man with a large African American following. In this way, Naeem began to understand this dynamic of the Atlantic Crescent—the marriage of the local and national focus of Sheikh Daoud's teachings and his larger global Islamic vision.

However, it does not appear that Naeem ever took Sheikh Daoud up on his offer of office space in the City of Peace. Records from the time period indicate that the *Moslem World* publication continued to operate out of Naeem's apartment in Bushwick.[96] Instead of joining Sheikh Daoud's international Sunni brotherhood, however, he chose to create a partnership with Elijah Muhammad and his Nation, a seemingly much more unorthodox ally. Through this relationship, Naeem would not only be influenced by Black Islam but would also serve to shape its contours and focus as well.

The Nation had been on Naeem's radar since 1948 when he read an article on the organization in *True Confessions* magazine. However, Naeem lacked the connections and social capital to make contact with Muhammad until Sheikh Jamal Diab, a Palestinian Muslim who acted as a consultant and Arabic teacher for the Nation at the time, introduced him to Muhammad in 1955.[97] The next year, in 1956, Naeem visited the Nation's headquarters in Chicago.

After Naeem's visit to Chicago and his initial report on the Nation in *Moslem World*, every single issue of the magazine from April 1956 until it ceased publication a year later, featured at least one article on the Nation, its politics, and its impact on the Islamic world. Naeem claimed to be committed to communicating the diversity of the American Muslim community to Muslims abroad, but he regularly fell short of his stated mission. For the purposes of *Moslem World*, Islam practiced by American Black people was synonymous with the Nation. Naeem had been so close to Sheikh Daoud that the Sheikh had offered him a permanent office space in a private compound, so Naeem knew that the Nation was not the totality of the Black and Muslim experience. Regardless, from 1956 to 1957, *Moslem World* contained sixteen articles and editorials on the Nation in five issues, including editorials by Malcolm X and Elijah Muhammad.[98] Of these five issues, three covers featured the Nation and one issue was dedicated entirely to the Nation's annual Saviour's Day convention. Naeem's sudden focus on the Nation has led some scholars to proclaim that *Moslem World* transformed "overnight" into a promotion vehicle for Elijah Muhammad.[99] Contemporary critics of Naeem held the same view. Indeed, there is no doubt that the Nation intended to use *Moslem World* as a publicity tool. In a temple meeting at Muslim Mosque No. 12 in Philadelphia, Malcolm advertised Elijah Muhammad's editorial in the August–September 1956 issue of *Moslem World* and sold copies of Naeem's publication to the congregation.[100] The relationship between the Nation and the young Pakistani publisher was no doubt beneficial; it was so much so that after publishing articles concerning Elijah Muhammad and the Nation in three consecutive issues, Naeem felt it necessary to publicly disclaim his relationship with the organization and affirm the *Moslem World*'s status as a financially independent publication.[101] He would do this repeatedly over the course of the next year.[102]

In retrospect, it is easy to see why Naeem's critics were suspicious of the attention he gave the Nation. After April 1956, the Nation featured more prominently than any other Muslim movement, American or global. By featuring Elijah Muhammad, Malcolm X, and their followers, Naeem took on two roles; first as a translator of the Nation's beliefs for the rest of the ummah, and second as a cheerleader for Muslims in the Nation, assuring them that they were, indeed, legitimate even in the face of a chorus of arguments to the contrary.

In his role of translator, Naeem tried to help Arab and South Asian Muslims in the United States and abroad understand why the practices and teachings of the Nation were so different from those with which most Muslims were familiar. In 1957, Naeem was engaged by Muhammad to write the introduction to the *Supreme Wisdom*, a written compilation of the teachings, practices, and religious beliefs allegedly passed down from Fard Muhammad to Elijah Muhammad. Explaining the Nation's teachings to the rest of the ummah, Naeem pointed to slavery, brainwashing, and anti-Black racism as the primary reasons why the Nation's practice of Islam looked different from the Sunni tradition practiced by Muslims in the Middle East and South Asia. However, according to Naeem, these differences were "of relatively minor importance ... because these are not related to the *SPIRIT* of Islam."[103] Part of the problem, as Naeem saw it, was that the Nation's followers had not yet had the opportunity to be educated on the Qur'an and hadith. Naeem explained, "Not many of Mr. Elijah Muhammad's followers have had the opportunity to read and understand the Holy Qur'an or fully comprehend the concept of Moslem prayers, fasting, *zakat* (alms-giving) and the institution of *hadj* (pilgrimage to Mecca)."[104] Education on daily prayer and the other pillars of Islam would soon come to the Nation, however, as Naeem encouraged his fellow Muslims to simply have patience, to understand the movement on its own historical terms, and to accept them as Muslim brothers.

In February 1957, Naeem gave an address at the Nation's annual Saviour's Day convention where he discussed the role of women in Islam. Naeem's argument centered on the benefits of Islam for Muslim women. In this speech, Naeem seized on Islam's ability to provide protection, political and economic rights, and family security for women. These were common tropes in the Nation's organizational discourse, but Naeem's address placed the Nation's patriarchal restrictions on women in the context of the history and practice of Islam more generally. In this way, he assured the Nation's followers that they were righteous, moral, and authentically Muslim.

At the end of his speech, Naeem conferred upon Elijah Muhammad the Muslim title of Ameer Maulana, meaning chief religious leader. With this gesture, Naeem assured the Nation's followers that they were part of a longstanding Islamic tradition and culture.[105] In addition, Naeem affirmed, as the Nation had argued for decades, that Islam was the "natural religion" of Black people and that it had a unique role in uplifting the downtrodden and oppressed. Here, he used the example of Islam's role in elevating the Hindu Dalits of the Indian subcontinent.[106] Beyond the role of Islam in uplift, Naeem defined it as a naturally anticolonial and anti-imperial religion and argued that Islam suited the needs of African people in expelling European imperialists. *Moslem World* reminded readers of this with its articles and also reinforced it visually through the use of political cartoons and sketches. For example, next to an article titled "The Black Man and Islam," Naeem included a sketch of Africa with the majority-Muslim areas of the continent highlighted. Superimposed across the majority of the continent was a Black figure in a white tunic. Over only South Africa, a small white figure appeared. In the corner, a blurb explained the graphic by linking the religion to independence. Naeem wrote, "In Africa, where Blacks outnumber whites 41 to 1, Islam is the dominant religion, not Christianity. Besides, practically all the Moslem-majority areas are independent, and those not yet free are rapidly nearing their goal of gaining sovereignty"[107] (figure 2.3). In his introduction to the *Supreme Wisdom*, Naeem continued to make these types of connections between liberation and Islam, arguing that "Islam alone, undoubtedly, will elevate the status of those among the so-called 'Negroes' in America who

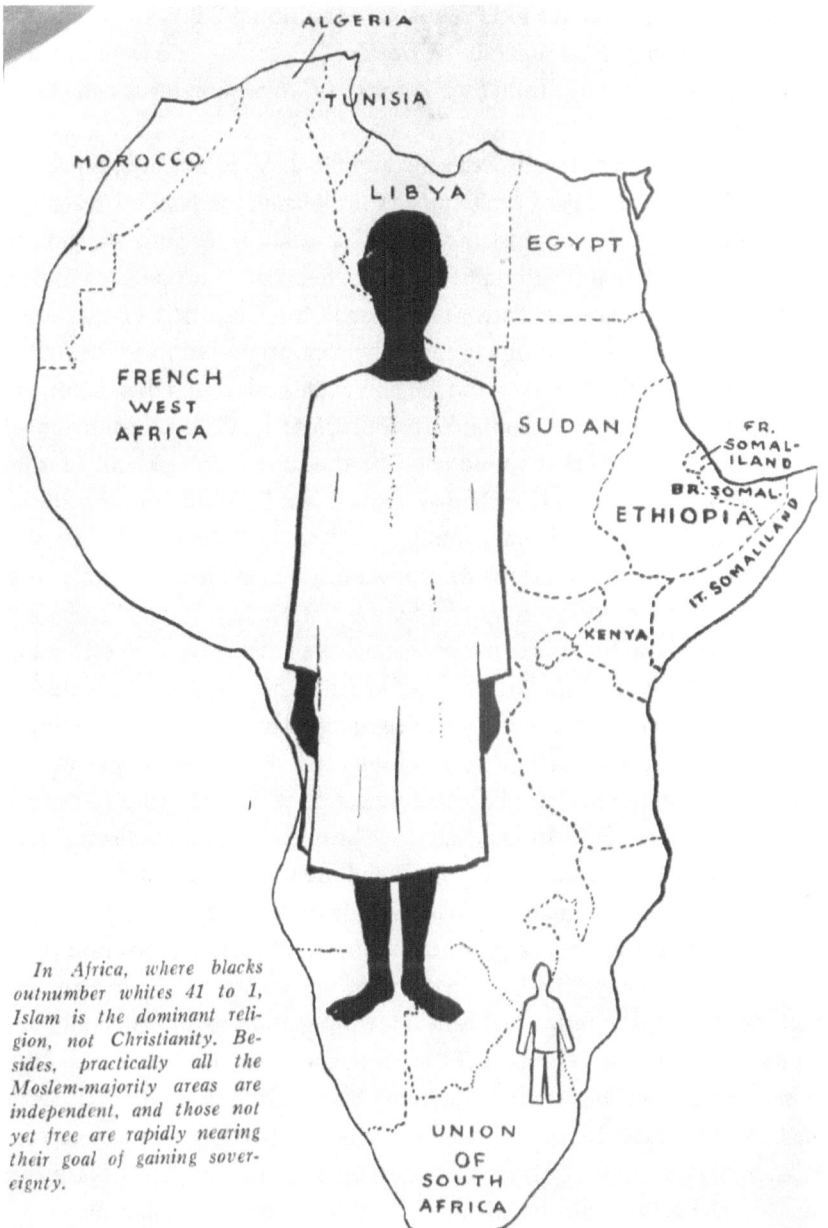

In Africa, where blacks outnumber whites 41 to 1, Islam is the dominant religion, not Christianity. Besides, practically all the Moslem-majority areas are independent, and those not yet free are rapidly nearing their goal of gaining sovereignty.

FIGURE 2.3 Drawing from *Moslem World & the U.S.A.* titled *Imagining of Islam in Africa*. Reprinted courtesy of University of Iowa Libraries.

are down-trodden and in a pitiable mental condition."[108] Like the new Muslim nations emerging throughout the world, Islam could—and would—allow these believers to emerge from their cocoons of white supremacy and Christian propaganda.

For the Nation's followers, Naeem's arguments were not new. Since the 1930s and the days of Fard Muhammad's leadership, the Nation's teachings had expressed the idea that Islam was the "natural" or "original" religion of Black people and that it had transformative effects on Black people's minds, bodies, and purse strings. Fard Muhammad's teachings that Black people were a part of a larger Muslim community that originated in Saudi Arabia rooted them into the history of the religion while connecting them to others throughout the Islamic diaspora. Fard Muhammad and Elijah Muhammad argued for decades that it would soon be the time for Black and Muslim people to rise up against Christianity—which had been the source of Black people's subjugation and brainwashing—and white supremacy. What was new, however, was the vocal media support of a Muslim from abroad, a man who was willing to act as a translator for the Nation. In this role, Naeem not only explained the Nation's brand of Islam to the ummah through the lens of slavery, Jim Crow, and the historical subjugation of American Black people but he also explained the global practice of Islam to the Nation, bringing it into the fold of the ummah. Before Naeem arrived, the Nation was already beginning to understand its plight in connection with the freedom struggles of Asian, and eventually African, nations. The organization's intellectual solidarities with Japan during World War II and their elation about the military gains of the Viet Minh and the Mau Mau made these nascent Afro-Asian connections clear. But Naeem helped the Nation to understand its position vis-à-vis the decolonizing Afro-Asian nations of the world, and to explain the Nation's teachings in terms that Muslims throughout the ummah could understand. Naeem found himself at the confluence of several diasporas, diasporas that sparked conversations between Black and Muslim intellectuals in the United States and abroad about the role of Islam in the process of decolonization. By extension, Naeem is a critical figure in the history of Black and Muslim intellectualism and anticolonial politics in the twentieth century.

Naeem's support gave the Nation new confidence and provided additional evidence of its embrace of the Afro-Asian world. In August 1956, as Malcolm vended copies of *Moslem World & the U.S.A.* from temple to temple, he reflected Naeem's view on the political and cultural importance of the newly formed Third World, and the critical role of African Americans in it.[109] In a speech in or around August 1956, Malcolm emphasized that the US government was quickly losing its authority abroad and at home as the postwar global balance of power shifted and the world became "filled with fast-awakening DARK nations, who are tossing off the yoke of white imperialism."[110] Moreover, at home, the rise of forums like Bandung demonstrated to Black people in the United States that they had political power. Malcolm preached, "We [Black people] affect both foreign and domestic policy. The majority of the earth's people are non-white (Africans and Asians)."[111] That realization flipped the hegemonic power script. The United States was not more important culturally or politically than Indonesia, Pakistan, or Sudan. Instead, Malcolm implored his followers to recognize that "America is of as equal importance to the entire Dark World.... Our people of the East must learn to see that our fight is theirs and their fight is ours."[112] These processes of building mutual insight are definitive of Naeem's relationship with Elijah Muhammad, Malcolm X, the Nation, and the American Black Muslim community. Their relationship, and the doors it opened into the world of Black Islam and internationalism, would not only help the Nation to transform its commitment to Afro-Asian solidarity but would also help Naeem to shape his own worldview as well.

The Magic of Harlem Internationalism: Naeem in the World of the Hotel Theresa

Naeem's Muslim internationalism was not just the product of his awareness of international affairs; it was also cultivated locally in Harlem and Brooklyn as he moved between the people and ideas brought by the historic migrations that transformed New York's demography. When the Naeem family moved to Bushwick in 1956, Naeem became deeply immersed in a world of African American intellectualism. This was a world to which he had not been previously privy in East Lansing, Cedar Rapids, or even San Francisco. Across the East River, Harlem had been at the center of two complementary migrations since the beginning of the twentieth century—one of Black people from the Southern United States and the other of mostly Caribbean immigrants from the African Diaspora. Both populations sought to take advantage of an increased demand for labor in the Northern United States during World War I. In these segregated neighborhoods, like Harlem, Caribbean intellectuals like Marcus Garvey, Hubert Harrison, and Claude McKay came into physical and intellectual contact with American-born Black people like W.E.B. DuBois, Alain Locke, and Zora Neale Hurston. The result was that Harlem's Black political and cultural movements were necessarily diasporic and international in nature. These Black people were forced to consider the intersections of issues like socialism, colonialism, class, labor, and race, and they did so through conversations in Harlem and with intellectuals of color in European metropoles and colonized spaces.[113] World War II only strengthened these connections, creating a sense of shared history and destiny between African Americans and other people of color throughout the colonized world. The rise of new communication and printing technologies during the war, including syndication, made international reporting easier and less expensive, allowing readers throughout the world to see their own struggles reflected across the Atlantic or Pacific oceans.[114]

In August 1950, New York City became home to the United Nations Secretariat.[115] As a result, the leaders of new and emerging nations regularly made their way through New York City and often came to Harlem to beseech American Black people to give their moral support. For Black nationalists and internationalists who had been working in Harlem for decades, the presence of the United Nations in New York added a new dimension to their movements and provided a new level of direct access.[116] Along with the Nation and Sheikh Daoud Faisal's Islamic Mission of America, one of these movements was the United African Nationalist Movement (UANM). Like the Nation, UANM had also emerged from the ashes of the UNIA. From the beginning, UANM engaged politically with foreign delegations to the UN. In April 1951, the organization began to hold weekly meetings at the Hotel Theresa, where invited speakers discussed the effects of African nationalism on the destabilization of European power on the African continent.[117]

The view UAMN had of Africa was expansive and included the entirety of the continent, both above and below the Sahel. As these nationalist movements met resistance from imperial powers, UANM regularly held conferences to build on the issues raised at Bandung, to establish moral support for African and Arab decolonization in the Black community, and to celebrate successful movements.[118] In 1952, one such press conference was held for Bahi Ladgham, the secretary-general of revolutionary Tunisia. As revolutionary leader Habib Bourguiba languished in prison, the UANM held a press conference for Ladgham at the Hotel Theresa, where he made a racial appeal for solidarity asking African Americans to sign a petition to convince African nations to condemn the French occupation of Tunisia.[119] As more nationalist and revolutionary leaders, like Bourguiba, and soldiers at the center of these movements were imprisoned, UANM gathered support to protest their imprisonment and to lean on the UN and United States to condemn their oppression.[120] When it became clear that the United States was not on the side of these nationalist movements, the UANM president, James R. Lawson, declared, "By her refusal to take sides in the U.N., America is aiding and abetting the colonial powers [by] ... continuing to give material aid [in order to help these powers] keep African colonies under their domination."[121]

Lawson's condemnation sounded a lot like the critiques of American support for French Algeria that Naeem presented in *Moslem World*. One of the reasons for this intellectual similarity was that, beginning in 1956, Lawson and Naeem cultivated their own intellectual relationship, which was facilitated by Naeem's existing relationship with Elijah Muhammad and the Nation. Throughout the 1950s, UANM and the Nation worked together to bring to light political issues having to do with African nationalism and to support Black pride and culture. Members of the Nation's temples regularly attended UANM's Friday meetings at the Hotel Theresa, and Nation leadership invited Lawson to attend its meetings and events. In October 1956, when UANM held a meeting on Nasser's plans to nationalize the Suez Canal Company, several members of the Nation were in attendance. Although he had no particular expertise on the subject besides his editorship at *Moslem World* and his short stint at the Pakistani consul general, Naeem was asked to speak on this topic.[122]

By the end of 1956, Lawson and Naeem had deepened their partnership and were together seeking charter subscriptions for a new magazine titled the *African-Asian World*, which they promised would speak on behalf of the "common interests of people *native* to Africa and Asia."[123] The effort was a failure. Although Naeem and Lawson managed to print the magazine in time to gift a copy to the Indian prime minister Jawaharlal Nehru during his December visit to the United States, Lawson and Naeem never published another issue. In June 1957, Naeem expressed optimism that *African-Asian World* could resume publication "soon," but this never came to pass.[124] That month, the publication abruptly terminated. No copies of this venture have survived; the sole mention of its existence is encapsulated in a brief mention in *Moslem World* and a photograph of Naeem and Zuleikha meeting Prime Minister Nehru.[125] In June, *Moslem World* abruptly terminated as well. It would not, however, be the end of Naeem's relationship with the Nation, with Black internationalists in the United States, or Pan-Africanists and Arabists abroad.

Conclusion

After *Moslem World* folded, Naeem struggled for career and financial stability. He appears very little in the historical record for approximately three years.

But in May 1959, Naeem reappeared in a new supporting role. He had dreamed for a decade of facilitating connections between the African and Asian worlds, and after Gamal Abdel Nasser extended an invitation to Muhammad and Malcolm to visit Egypt as official guests, Naeem stepped into his second act as travel agent. In 1962, Naeem launched his own travel agency, Shalimar International, named after the Lahore gardens built by the Mughals to reflect their vision of an earthly utopia. Naeem described Shalimar as the first "completely Muslim owned and Muslim staffed Worldwide Travel Service in the United States" and promised that Shalimar would specialize in forging connections through its travel bookings to Africa and the Muslim world.[126] Shalimar's offices hosted a rotating cast of international Afro-Asian and Muslim dignitaries, including at least on one occasion the Nigerian ambassador to the United Nations, Alhaji Muhammad Ngileruma, and United Arab Republic consulate general, Issa Serag, who attended the opening of the agency.[127]

Throughout the decade, Naeem would reprise his role as consultant and facilitator of Afro-Asian connections and understanding for the Nation. In April 1962, Elijah Muhammad contracted with Naeem to edit a pull-out "magazine-like" section of the Nation's new newspaper, *Muhammad Speaks*, dealing with international political and religious issues. Muhammad offered Naeem a salary of $600 per week part-time or $12,000 per year full-time to complete this work. If satisfactory, Muhammad promised to raise this salary to $20,000 annually. It is unclear which option Naeem chose; however, he was also hired as a foreign correspondent for the newspaper, making as much as $1,000 per month.[128] In the 1960s, Naeem would use his journalism studies to spearhead the Nation's transformation of its *Muhammad Speaks* newspaper to an internationally distributed, and internationalist, publication. He continued to write for the Nation until the end of the 1960s, writing columns on international foreign relations, on theology, condemning Malcolm X after his separation from the Nation in 1964, and beseeching his fellow Muslims to accept Elijah Muhammad's teachings. He continued to educate Black Americans in his home in Bushwick through the 1970s and 1980s.[129] His last known address locates him right around the corner from where he published *Moslem World & the U.S.A.*, still in Bushwick in the year 1993, where he unceremoniously exits the historical record.[130] According to his son Shahid, he returned to Pakistan at the end of his life and died sometime around 2004.[131]

Naeem spent decades of his life working to build Afro-Asian connections and promote international understanding throughout the ummah. Although he was not of African descent, Naeem inserted himself in—and was absorbed into—Black and Muslim anti-imperial geographies developed by the Nation and other Black and Muslim organizations in the mid-twentieth century. Although just one man, Naeem's life represents an impressive, and exceptional, microcosm of the ideas circulating in New York City and the Midwestern United States during this time. His influence would shape the Atlantic Crescent—and the Black and Muslim internationalism that defined it—in new and important ways, and most notably, would change the way that the Nation itself thought of its relationship to the Afro-Asian world.

CHAPTER THREE

Muslims Speak to the Ummah in Black and White

By mid-1959, Abdul Basit Naeem had dreamed of uniting the ummah for over a decade. His first attempts at doing so, through publishing *Moslem World & the U.S.A.*, had presented nothing but challenge after challenge. But as he prepared to usher in a new decade, Naeem took a brief sabbatical from his life as a publisher and journalist and assumed the position of Elijah Muhammad's travel agent. In May, Elijah Muhammad and Malcolm X received the invitation of a lifetime. After months of cordial correspondence from Egyptian president Gamal Abdel Nasser, Nasser extended an invitation to Malcolm and Muhammad to visit Egypt as guests of the state. Naeem had served as an intermediary between the Nation and the rest of the Muslim world before, and now he would reprise his role facilitating physical connections, this time as a travel agent. Working with the Black travel agency Hilton G. Hill, Naeem booked Muhammad and his sons, Akbar and Herbert, on SAS Flight 912 to Copenhagen, Denmark, where they would begin their travels to Istanbul, Jordan, Lebanon, Egypt, Saudi Arabia, Ethiopia, and Pakistan. In the sole photograph capturing their departure, taken by an unknown photographer, the Messenger posed unsmiling alongside the plane as it idled on the tarmac, standing beside Naeem, his sons, Herbert and Akbar, and his wife, Clara.[1] In the 1950s, government agents did not enforce checkpoints at every stage of a traveler's journey, but the FBI was still close at hand, anxiously watching the trio and their interactions and thinking about what the trip might mean for Muhammad's burgeoning relationships with the Afro-Asian world.

Naeem's editorial efforts throughout the 1950s had exposed the Nation to a dizzying world of Afro-Asian politics and possibility to which they had previously not been privy. As 1955 came and went, the white supremacy that Malcolm had promised would be vanquished was still intact. But the Afro-Asian world was transforming into a diplomatic force to be reckoned with. On the heels of the Bandung Conference of 1955, newly independent African and Asian nations of the United Nations coalesced under an Afro-Asian bloc, voting together on issues related to the sovereignty and right to self-rule of colonized and formerly colonized nations. These nations racialized their discussion, seeing themselves united as people of color against white, wealthy, and exploitative colonizers. Black nationalist and Muslim organizations in the United States keenly watched these interactions, seeing themselves not only in solidarity but also among the nations of the Afro-Asian bloc.

As we will see, the articulation of this Afro-Muslim religio-racial identity was complicated, conflicted, and constantly shifting. In the case of many of these Muslims, although they saw their religious and political projects as intertwined, the mandates and teachings of their versions of Islam were much more conservative than the internationalist political projects they supported. Some, like the Nation—which occupies a large part of this chapter—had a vision of a united Muslim Third World that was much more radical and progressive than its religious teachings. The Nation taught its adherents to support capitalism, to adopt a patriarchal worldview and community orientation, and to enforce a middle-class politics of respectability. These expectations are in line with the Black nationalist thought of Marcus Garvey, which the Nation, and other Black Muslim organizations, were influenced by.

This chapter is about how Black and Muslim leaders and organizations navigated the tensions between their religious and theological practices and their politics, and how they articulated them for the public through the press. Newspaper and magazine production was critically important to the spread, transfer, and transformation of ideas about religion, race, and colonialism. Through media production, Ahmadiyya Muslims like Afro-Caribbean jazz trumpeter Imam Talib Dawud of the Muslim Brotherhood USA, South Asian Sunni Muslims like Abdul Basit Naeem, and Nation leaders like African American Malcolm X and Elijah Muhammad together crafted a geography of imperial resistance that discursively connected the rise and success of African and Asian anticolonial movements with the brutal fight for racial justice at home. Through regular publication in Black newspapers and magazines, Black Muslims put forth a dual national and international identity. Here they pushed and pulled on the borders of the Atlantic Crescent. They expressed a locally rooted identity as Black American Muslims while simultaneously positioning themselves as part of a larger transnational community, an ummah connected to the Afro-Asian Muslim world.

Media, Islamic Internationalism, and Diplomacy

Elijah Muhammad got plenty of attention in Abdul Basit Naeem's *Moslem World*, but he was working on controlling his own image as well. For about a year before the final issue of *Moslem World* in 1957, the Nation slowly built its media presence through regular columns in major Black urban newspapers.

In June 1956, Muhammad became a columnist for the *Pittsburgh Courier* where he published a feature titled "Mr. Muhammad Speaks" each week.[2] Naeem would, on occasion, reprint these columns in *Moslem World*, arguing that by making the teachings of Muhammad and Malcolm X available across the Muslim diaspora, he was "rendering the Moslem world a real service."[3] In 1957, after the demise of the *Moslem World* publication, the Nation's media presence exploded in the form of new columns by Malcolm X and Elijah Muhammad in the *New York Amsterdam News*. Malcolm's column, "God's Angry Men," premiered in the *New York Amsterdam News* in April of 1957 and moved to the *Los Angeles Herald-Dispatch* beginning in August of that year. Muhammad's column, "Islam World," first appeared in July of 1957 in the *New York Amsterdam News*.[4] For the most part, these publications served as a means to fish for converts and to publicize and interpret the Nation's teachings for a wide audience. However, Malcolm regularly incorporated the Afro-Asian political situation into his sermons. In June of 1957, he stood in front of his followers at Harlem Temple No. 7 to praise the growth of the Afro-Asian bloc of the United Nations, which had recently grown to twenty-eight countries. Teaching that these nations were both Black and Muslim, Malcolm cited their growing strength in the United Nations as "just a bit more proof that the Black Men are beginning to see the light" and that they were "beginning to realize that there is strength in numbers."[5] In hindsight, Malcolm was prescient. Sovereignty had been elusive for much of the Third World, but as it played the game of Cold War diplomacy in the UN General Assembly, it grew to possess power that had previously eluded it. By 1962, the Afro-Asian bloc nearly doubled and constituted the strongest regional voting bloc in the General Assembly. Its members numbered fifty-one, almost half of the 104 nations in the United Nations.[6]

As Afro-Asian diplomats and world leaders communicated about their collective fates in the Cold War world, Malcolm and Muhammad viewed themselves as a part of these conversations. They certainly argued that they were partners in Afro-Asian diplomacy among their followers. In 1956, the New York Police Department (NYPD) received intelligence that a "bus load" of Nation members from Baltimore would soon be on their way to New York City in order to meet "Moslem[s] from the East . . . to show that there is great Muslim activity in the United States."[7] The NYPD's intelligence suggested that the Nation had great interest in diplomatic contact with Muslim leaders, but it does not appear that this meeting ever happened.[8] It was not until 1957 that Nation leaders made direct diplomatic overtures to leaders in Muslim countries in Africa and Asia. In June of that year, Malcolm and Adam Clayton

Powell came together at Harlem's Abyssinian Baptist Church to welcome two Indonesian leaders, echoing back to the Bandung Conference itself.[9] Malcolm praised Powell for what he called "great wisdom and foresight, inviting [two Indonesian statesmen] to Harlem to study the conditions here first hand," arguing that naturally their Muslim brothers in Indonesia would have a "great interest in [their] welfare."[10]

Later that year, on December 31, 1957, as forty-four countries gathered together in Cairo at the Afro-Asian People's Solidarity Conference, Elijah Muhammad sent a cable to President Nasser affirming his support for the conference principles, including nonalignment and the ongoing struggle for sovereignty for African and Asian peoples.[11] Muhammad's cable invoked Islam as a shared point of convergence between the American Muslims of the Nation and the participants of the Cairo Conference. Muhammad wrote, "Your long lost Muslim brothers here in America pray that Allah's divine present [sic] will be felt at this historic African-Asian Conference, and give unity to our efforts for peace and brotherhood."[12] In this communiqué, Muhammad repeated a motif that dated back to the pro-Japanese propaganda disseminated by the movement during the Second World War—he intertwined the fates of the "dark races" across the globe with those of African Americans. Discursively closing the oceanic divides between them, Muhammad wrote, "Freedom, justice and equality for all Africans and Asians is of far-reaching importance not only to you of the East, but also to over 17 million of your long lost brothers of African-Asian descent here in the West."[13] Muhammad's message reflected the direct articulation of a strong sense of shared destiny between African and Asian people. In addition, he used Islam as an entrée to advocate for the Nation's belonging as one of the decolonization movements sweeping the African and Asian world.

Muhammad and the members of the Nation were not invited to Cairo, but that didn't stop them from trying to engage diplomatically and internationally on their own home turf. Immediately after the Cairo Conference, in early January 1958, the Nation hosted its own conference at the Wayside Casino in Harlem where, over the course of four hours, Muhammad and Malcolm entertained diplomats from Egypt, Iraq, Sudan, Ghana, and Morocco. Hosting seven hundred people, the Wayside Casino conference exceeded the participation in Cairo by about two hundred attendees. In addition to the aforementioned diplomats, representatives of various Black nationalist organizations, including James Lawson's United African Nationalist Movement (UANM) and organizations like United African-Asian Friendship and the Africa House were present.[14] Just a few weeks later, at an African-Asian

Exposition held at the Park Palace Hotel, Malcolm triumphantly announced that Nasser answered Muhammad's cable thanking him for his sentiments.[15]

It is unclear whether it was Afro-Asian brotherhood or Islam that served as the true basis for Nasser's diplomatic courtesies to the Nation or for his invitation, but there is no doubt that there was some level of mutual interest between Nasser and Black American internationalist groups. NYPD intelligence revealed that Nasser saw Muslim groups like the Nation and the Muslim Brotherhood USA, and secular organizations like UANM as a way to gain support for the nationalization of the Suez Canal and to place pressure on the United Nations to force Israel and the British to withdraw troops from the Suez Canal Zone.[16] Their efforts had been effective. As early as 1956, Malcolm was openly repeating Nasser's talking points about the occupation of the Suez Canal, Palestine, and the open possibility of war in the Middle East.[17] As early as 1957, the Nation was met with accusations that they were receiving foreign funds from Arab leaders, and in particular from Gamal Abdel Nasser.[18] The Nation denied these accusations but flagged its relationship with Nasser and similar leaders as concrete evidence of the Nation's rightful place at the juncture of the Afro-Asian world and the ummah.

As the Afro-Asian bloc of the United Nations began to gain more influence and the Nation continued to build their Afro-Asian geography, Imam Talib Dawud of the Muslim Brotherhood USA took to the *Pittsburgh Courier* to proffer his own take on the connections between Blackness, imperialism, and Islam. Dawud, born Alfonso Nelson Rainey in the British colony of Antigua, came to New York at the age of eighteen. After studying brass instruments at Julliard, he played with Duke Ellington and Louis Armstrong before jazz legend Dizzy Gillespie took him under his wing. Historians have previously noted the number of Gillespie's bandmates who attained international renown as jazz musicians, and the unusual frequency with which they converted to Islam. Joining bebop musicians and former Gillespie understudies, Yusuf Lateef, Hajj Rasheed, Liaquat Ali Salaam, and Mustafa Dalil, Rainey converted to Ahmadiyya Islam in the early 1950s and changed his name to Talib Dawud.[19] Dawud, who was reported to have a knack for *da'wah*, was likely responsible for converting the other members of Gillespie's band, although Gillespie himself would remain ambivalent to the religion.[20] In 1950, Dawud founded the Muslim Brotherhood USA, an Ahmadiyya-affiliated sect. In the early 1950s, Dawud and his wife, jazz vocalist Dakota Staton, moved to Philadelphia where he opened the Islamic and African Institute with fellow Muslim and Caribbean immigrants, Egyptian Mahmoud Alwan and Jamaican J. A. Rogers.[21] Each man brought his own specialty to the institute, which served Philadelphia's

Black community. Alwan was a member of Egypt's militant *Ikwan al-Muslimun*, or Muslim Brotherhood, and advocated social revolution through Islamic education and practice. He taught Arabic at the institute. J. A. Rogers, a journalist and historical anthropologist who attacked racial segregation, taught African history. And Dawud, as imam of Muslim Brotherhood USA, taught Islam. Although Staton was not directly involved in teaching at either the institute or within the Muslim Brotherhood, she was front and center as the organization engaged in African pride events. During the late 1950s, as African leaders frequented Harlem, she often appeared on behalf of, and in concert with, her husband and the organization.[22] In addition, Staton's celebrity status opened doors to partner with elite allies. It was Dakota's "star power" that put into motion the couple's ability to host a luncheon for Guinean president Sekou Touré and his wife on their visit to Harlem in November of 1959.[23]

In his music, religion, and community outreach, Dawud was committed to interpreting tradition in an explicitly African diasporic way. In the same way he allowed his identity as an Afro-Antiguan to drive his music, Dawud allowed his intersectional experience as a British colonial subject and his life as a Black immigrant in America to shape his religious beliefs and teachings. Like Malcolm and Muhammad, Dawud agreed that Islam presented a critical challenge to white supremacy and imperialism, and he characterized the central tension among African-descended people as one between Christianity and Islam. For Dawud, Christianity's main drawback was its obsession with color prejudice and the racial superiority of the white race. Islam, by contrast, was a religion that eschewed racial hierarchy, where "the color of the skin of a person carries no value, no importance ... Religious pride is the strength of Islam in Africa, while racial pride is the peculiar weakness of Christianity."[24] In this way, Dawud differed markedly from Elijah Muhammad, who argued for the superiority of Black people over white, flipping instead of erasing the hegemonic racial script. For Dawud, the battle between racism and racial equality was reflected through the ongoing tension between Islam and Christianity. This tension was acutely palpable by the late 1950s because of the steady dismantling of colonialism on the African continent, and Dawud taught that Islam played a key role in this process because, in his interpretation, Islam unified populations, and as such made "all men ... free, all men ... equal, [and] all men ... brothers."[25] This unifying potential carried an incredible danger for white supremacy in Africa, and as it spread unchecked, Christianity, and by extension white supremacy, would find itself "up against a stonewall, the wall of Islam."[26] Although Dawud's tone was incredibly civilizationist—he argued that Islam could play a role in civilizing the remaining "pagan tribes" and "naked savages"—he was arguing for a role for Islam in building brotherhood, uniting political movements, and fighting inherently racist imperial and colonial subjugation.

Dawud left big band life to focus exclusively on the Muslim Brotherhood, but his interpretation of the role of Islam in global racial liberation struck a different type of chord across racial and ethnic lines. In December of 1957, a letter to the editor from a reader named Ahmad Jamal praised Dawud's publication, proclaiming that it was "the most accurate and authentic information on Islam, its doctrines and progress, than any previously read ... in your ... publication."[27] These previous articles cited by Jamal were undoubtedly Elijah Muhammad's "Mr. Muhammad Speaks" column and Malcolm X's "God's Angry Men." It is impossible to tell Jamal's racial identity from this letter to the editor. He does not cite it, but the fact that he does not use an "X" after his name would at least suggest that he did not belong to the Nation and was thus aligned with either the Ahmadiyya or one of the more mainstream movements in the United States at the time. Jamal would not be the first or the last Muslim to write to the *Pittsburgh Courier* siding with either Dawud or Muhammad, and opining on the validity of each of their teachings. In August 1956, a reader named Yusuf Ahmad wrote that Muhammad was nothing but a fake who was not accepted by Muslims as part of their brotherhood.[28]

Executing an Afro-Asian Agenda

Since Malcolm's 1954 lecture in Philadelphia where he engaged the *Mau Mau* and the Viet Minh as evidence that white supremacy was in its death throes, the Nation had thought about, and then executed, an agenda that actively built a sense of Afro-Asian solidarity and community.[29] In addition to reaching out to Nasser and hosting Indonesia statesmen, Malcolm developed relationships with Saudi, Pakistani, Iraqi, and Ghanaian officials. In early 1958, Malcolm accepted an invitation from Saudi Arabia's King Saud to meet at the Waldorf-Astoria Hotel in New York. Later in March, the Nation held a celebration in Los Angeles to commemorate the independence of Pakistan. In August, Malcolm and Muhammad attended a gathering to honor President Kwame Nkrumah of Ghana.[30] In April of 1959, at an African Day celebration in Harlem attended by secular leaders like Manhattan Borough President Hulan Jack and Staton and Rogers on behalf of the Muslim Brotherhood, Malcolm called for Black leaders to put their "petty differences of religion and politics aside, and hold a Bandung Conference in Harlem" in order to collective progress toward freedom.[31] To some extent,

Malcolm was being redundant. The Nation had already hosted and attended several Bandung-type conferences and meetings over the preceding three years, and internationalism was the zeitgeist of the era, but as the Nation's profile began to grow nationally and internationally, it was time for both the Nation and the Muslims it courted in the United States and abroad to take their relationship to the next level.[32]

The Nation's opportunity to strengthen its direct relationships with the Arab and Muslim world came in May of 1959 when Nasser extended an invitation to Muhammad and his family to visit Egypt as guests of the state.[33] The initial plan, in addition to visiting with Muslim heads of state, was for the family to make the pilgrimage to Mecca, or hajj, which took place that year during the month of June.[34] Naeem was hired to make travel arrangements for the Messenger and his family, which included acquiring travel documents for Muhammad, his wife Clara, and sons Herbert and Akbar.[35] The process, however, would not be easy. Once the American government became aware that Muhammad was planning this trip, it did everything in its power to thwart it.[36] By the time the Muhammads finally received their passports in late June 1959, it was too late to make hajj.[37] The State Department could not prevent them from leaving the country later that year, but it did make sure to forward an information sheet on Muhammad to the consulates of every country he intended to visit. The intelligence community would be watching even beyond the United States' borders.[38]

While Muhammad and his entourage were having trouble obtaining clearance to leave the country, on May 27, 1959, the Department of State issued a passport to Malcolm X under the name Malik el-Shabazz.[39] Malcolm headed for Cairo in early July without the Muhammad family. He spent the majority of his trip there where he passed most of his time with Anwar El-Sadat, then vice president of Egypt, as well as religious leaders at Al-Azhar University, one of the most prestigious institutions of Islamic education in the world.[40] He intended to travel to Eritrea, Ethiopia, Sudan, and Nigeria but was sidelined by an unexpected illness in Cairo. Instead, Malcolm recalibrated his itinerary and traveled straight to Saudi Arabia, and from there to Sudan. For Malcolm, this trip was transformational, and it reaffirmed his commitment to Pan-Arabism, Pan-Islamism, and Pan-Africanism. He had recognized the importance of an international perspective and transnational solidarity before, but now on his trip to Egypt, Saudi Arabia, and Sudan, he witnessed firsthand how freedom dreams could transform into liberatory realities for Black people. Of course, Malcolm ignored both the rainbow of skin colors he saw in Jeddah and the long-standing history of racial subjugation of Africans from below the Sahel. Instead, at least publicly, Malcolm clung to the idea of Black supremacy in Muslim countries, reporting that "Muslims in Egypt and Africa are blacker" than he himself.[41] Any suggestions to the contrary, or any mentions of racial hierarchy in these places, were framed by Malcolm as an insidious campaign in the United States to "make it appear that Saudi is the 'land of bondage' . . . that Mecca is the Slave capitol [sic], and that Islam is a slave-making religion."[42]

Until recently, most scholars have focused almost entirely on Malcolm's 1964 hajj as the turning point in his faith and internationalism, but I argue that it was that first trip abroad that kick-started the expansive ideas of Black Afro-Asian solidarity that defined his later years. All of this happened while he was still in the Nation. One of the reasons for this lack of attention is that Malcolm's trip received very little press. One solitary piece in the *New York Amsterdam News* announced that Malcolm was leaving the country with intentions to visit Mecca, Medina, Jerusalem, and "several African-Asian countries."[43] Upon his return in August 1959, only one article—in the *Pittsburgh Courier*—was published concerning his tour, consisting of two jubilant letters that he sent home from Jeddah and Khartoum about the close watch that African people were keeping on the ongoing civil rights struggle in the United States and his observation that "Africa is the land of the future."[44]

The lack of press attention about Malcolm's trip and growing Afro-Asian internationalism was likely due to the fact that from nearly the moment that Malcolm left the United States, the Nation was beset with a media crisis. A week after Malcolm's departure, on July 13, 1959, WNTA-TV's *News Beat* aired the first installment of an investigative piece on the Nation and its partner in Black internationalism, UANM, called the *Hate That Hate Produced*. The show, which aired nightly from July 13 to 17 and then again on July 22, whipped the mainstream media into a panic. When Malcolm returned from Khartoum on the night of the second broadcast, there was no time to revel in the international connections that he made in Africa. Instead, Malcolm immediately turned his attention into managing the simultaneous public relations boom and bust related to the broadcast.[45] Inside the Nation, however, Malcolm's travels were the focus of a speech he gave at St. Nicholas Arena in New York City immediately upon his return. He marshaled his special treatment by the government of Egypt, which he claimed had "squired [him] around due to the fact that he was Muslim," and he boasted that he was taken on a cruise by Egyptian officials in forbidden territory, presumably to the Sinai Peninsula, which Israel had seized during the Suez Canal crisis.[46]

Malcolm was not the only Black leader who traveled to the Middle East on a diplomatic tour, although he may have been the most famous and controversial at the time. Throughout 1959, Nasser had extended several invitations to Muslim and non-Muslim Black leaders to visit Egypt as guests of the government. On June 9, 1959, over a month prior to Malcolm's departure, Imam Talib Dawud also left the country on his own tour of the Middle East and North Africa.[47] Imam Dawud embarked on a seven-week trip to Mecca, Egypt, and Lebanon. His impressions of the region were colored by his position as a Black man living in America, and although he had preached race neutrality, his recollections were not starkly different from Malcolm's. Imam Dawud also emphasized the rainbow of brown skin tones that he found in the region, noting that he was struck by "the general color and faces of the peoples.... Were it not for language and dress, I could fancy myself among people of African ancestry in Harlem or Mississippi. You could see the African strain running almost the entire population. In fact, the people on the whole are darker than those in America."[48] On the subject of his hajj, Dawud did not mention seeing white people specifically but instead avoided the subject, noting that he had "never ... seen such a variety of peoples before."[49] The picture that Dawud painted was, like Malcolm, one of a nonwhite, African-dominated society untouched by white supremacy. Unlike Malcolm, however, Dawud was granted an audience with Nasser, with whom he discussed issues of diplomacy and Afro-Asian relations, including Nasser's commitment to the independence of all nations and his relationship with Ethiopian Emperor Haile Selassie.[50] In Egypt, Dawud spoke to exiled African nationalist leaders, including Jomo Kenyatta and Ahmed Ben Bella, about the status of independence in their countries. He reveled in the realization that the French were despised by many Egyptians because of their history of colonial domination. In Mecca, Dawud asserted himself and his followers as full members of the ummah, and he attended a meeting of the Pakistan-based World Islamic Congress, a Pan-Islamic Congress founded in 1931 by Palestinian-born political and religious leader Haj Amin al-Husseini and Bangladeshi Maulana Shawkat 'Ali, as a guest of Colonel Sadat.[51]

On November 21, 1959, five months later than planned, Muhammad, accompanied by his sons, Akbar and Herbert, finally left for the Middle East and Africa. Clara, although included in the original travel plans, did not go with them. On November 22, 1959, after about forty-eight hours of travel, the Muhammads finally arrived in Istanbul to begin their whirlwind tour of the region.[52] From Istanbul, the trio went to Lebanon and Jordan before arriving in Cairo for the main political event. For two weeks, Muhammad, Akbar, and Herbert met with Nasser and el-Sadat and were treated as dignitaries and esteemed guests of the Egyptian state. After a fortnight in Egypt, Muhammad visited Sudan, Ethiopia, and Pakistan—which the Nation emphasized was the first nation founded for Muslims.[53] While Cairo was the main political entrée, religiously, the most important destination in the Muhammad family's itinerary was Saudi Arabia, the home of Mecca, the holiest city in the Islamic tradition. There, the trio performed *umrah*, a lesser pilgrimage.[54]

On January 6, 1960, about a month ahead of schedule, Muhammad and his sons returned to the United States.[55] Originally, they had intended to visit other countries in North and West Africa, including Morocco and Ghana, but they never made it. This may have been due to the bureaucratic roadblocks the United States had thrown up to complicate their plans. The FBI, for example, had sent requests to consulates all over the world asking local authorities to deny the Muhammads entry.[56] But more likely, the trip may have been cut short because it was already costing the Nation thousands of dollars. Muhammad owed a balance of $8,8016.16 to various vendors and had spent $1,400 on film and photography equipment alone.[57] Perhaps not a cent more could be spared.

Although shorter than anticipated, Muhammad's trip abroad served several critical purposes, and Muhammad immediately took to Black newspapers in order to report back on his travels. First, the trip was used by Muhammad as evidence that the Nation was not marginal as it was being made to seem in the mainstream media, but instead was an important movement recognized as such by foreign leaders, like el-Sadat, who went out of their way to treat Muhammad and his sons as dignitaries. Even in recounting his trip to Mecca, Muhammad wrote that Saudi authorities greeted him at customs with "handshaking and praises to Allah, and many wishes for [his] blessing and success."[58] In addition to these well-wishes, Muhammad claimed that a personal guide was waiting for the trio to usher them through customs and bring them to Jeddah, Mecca, and Medina. This was likely true, but it was not special treatment for Muhammad and his sons. In June, Talib Dawud had also been assigned a guide who took him and several others around Mecca.[59]

Second, since the birth of the Nation in Detroit, it had been in a constant battle with Sunni Muslims and the American government to prove that the Nation was not a "cult" or simply an antiwhite Black supremacist organization. Rather, it aimed to show that it was an authentic Muslim sect with its own specific practice of the religion influenced by four hundred years of slavery and racial subjugation. This is one of the reasons that the Nation employed Muslim immigrants like Jamal Diab, at first, and later, Abdul Basit Naeem, to act as translators and intermediaries between the Nation to the rest of the Muslim world. But the publicity from the *Hate That Hate Produced* prompted even more criticism, and in some cases, disgust from Muslims who identified themselves as Sunni.

The fight over Muslim authenticity and for converts was at the heart of a growing conflict that would dominate the Black press and the American court system beginning in the summer of 1959. In August, Imam Dawud took to the *New Crusader* to lambast the Nation and Elijah Muhammad, arguing that they were not "bona fide Muslims" and that they would be prohibited from entering Mecca by the Saudi government and Muslim authorities. Dawud even claimed to know that Malcolm X had not "decided" to skip hajj, but instead that he had been barred from entry.[60] Both Dawud and Staton used the Black press to disclaim all connection between their faith and the Nation. In August 1959, Staton decried Mike Wallace's unbalanced focus on the Nation, calling this lens "very bigoted." A balanced picture would, according to Staton, have included a representation of Dawud's Muslim Brotherhood USA.[61]

In October, Imam Dawud contrasted his "bona fide" movement with the teachings of Elijah Muhammad, who he claimed was a "phony" whose followers do not pray properly, follow Muhammad's teachings of hate, and believe Allah to be a living man in the person of W. D. Fard Muhammad, who he claimed was "once a Nazi agent."[62] Dawud also accused Muhammad of working in concert with Ku Klux Klan grand wizard J. B. Stoner. In response, Muhammad and Malcolm launched a series of misogynist and gendered attacks against Staton, critiquing her songs as "filthy," her dress as "immodest," and claiming that she should be ashamed of her attempts to critique Muhammad and his followers because she was "publicly serving the devil in the theatrical world."[63] He then took a stab at Imam Dawud as a Black Muslim man, questioning his masculinity for allowing his "wife [and the believing women who follow him] to go before the public partly dressed." Expressing a control over the bodies and behavior of the Nation's women, Muhammad claimed that if women in the Nation acted and dressed like Staton, that he would cast them out, and "claim them to be [his no] more."[64] Muhammad challenged Dawud's credentials as leader of his movement, cast doubt upon his doctrinal teachings, and stated that he was erroneously calling himself an imam. Instead, subverting all of his teachings about the inherent unity of Black people in the diaspora, he wrote that Dawud was both a "devil" and a British subject, referring to Dawud's birth in Antigua.

Imam Dawud regularly wrote in the *New Crusader* and the *Pittsburgh Courier* calling Muhammad's movement "fake," but it was Dakota Staton who was the most public and, by virtue of her celebrity, effective voice condemning the Nation. To be sure, given Malcolm and Muhammad's misogynist attacks on Staton's moral standing as a Muslim woman in the music industry, she had all the more reason to lash out with vitriol. In April 1962, Staton was the focus of a *Jet* magazine article where she discussed her Muslim faith and how it was actually integral to merging the "double life" that she led in private as a dutiful Muslim wife, and in public as a jazz singer.[65] This was the same Muslim life that Muhammad and Malcolm had repeatedly condemned in their misogynist attacks on Staton in the *Pittsburgh Courier*, but Staton defended herself against these accusations, claiming that the lives she lived were not at all contradictory. Instead, she found a way to reconcile both her personal and professional lives and maintain a fully Muslim existence. After Staton's profile in *Jet*, which included photographs of her tending to her home, wearing a demure argyle sweater, and dutifully sitting with her husband, her stardom grew, and accordingly, her platform for critiquing the Nation expanded as well (figures 3.1a and 3.1b). In June 1962, Staton and Dawud filed an action in the United States District Court for the Eastern District of Pennsylvania seeking to enjoin Muhammad from using the term "Muslim" or "Islam" in connection with the Nation, or from claiming to be a Muslim.[66] Staton argued that the media's focus on the Nation had resulted in the sect becoming virtually "synonymous" with Black Islam, and as a result had caused her career irreparable harm. In order to launch this suit, Dawud and Staton allied themselves with white detractors of the Nation, including Arthur Gottschalk, a Republican state senator from Illinois who had previously attacked the Nation's University of Islam, the Nation's network of parochial schools, and sought to have it shut down.[67] In response, Malcolm continued to unleash a tirade of misogynist attacks, suggesting that because she sang "sexy songs, half-naked in a night-club where people are getting drunk," that Staton could not expect "people to still respect her as an example of religious piety."[68]

Dawud, Staton, Malcolm, and Muhammad were having these arguments in an echo chamber. In the eyes of immigrant Muslims practicing Sunni Islam, neither movement was truly Muslim. The public conflict between the Muslim Brotherhood USA and the Nation gained unwanted attention from Naeem's former mentor from *jam'iat-ul-falah*, Dr. Maulana Muhammad Fazl-ur-Rahman Ansari, and the Egyptian Dr. Mahmoud Youssef Shawarbi, both with the World Federation of Islamic Missions, a Pakistani missionary organization. Both men expressed concern about the notion of continuous

FIGURE 3.1A Dakota Staton washing dishes at home in *Jet*, April 19, 1962, p. 18. Johnson Publishing Company.

*Pointing to **Mecca on map**, singer studies **Islamic teachings** with husband. Home is filled with African, Oriental art.*

FIGURE 3.1B Dakota Staton and Talib Dawud together at home in *Jet*, April 19, 1962, p. 19. Johnson Publishing Company.

prophecy—and the rejection of Muhammad ibn-Abdullah as the seal of prophets—central to both the Nation and the Ahmadiyya's teachings.[69]

At some point during this conflict between the Nation and the Muslim Brotherhood USA, Lawson and the UANM abandoned their alliance with the Nation and sided with the Dawuds. The reasons for this schism are unknown, but Lawson had always been controlling of the organization and of individual members within the organization. For example, in April of 1961,

Africa Freedom Day was nearly canceled when a UANM member named James Logan decided to affiliate with another group.[70] In 1961, when UANM hosted a reception for President Touré and his wife, it banned Nation leaders from attendance, hoping to show the Tourés a representation of "true Islam" in the United States.[71] The fight between the two sects escalated to the point that when Dawud was assaulted with acid in front of his store in Harlem and a bomb threat was made on the Ahmadiyya mosque in Philadelphia, it was strongly implied by both Dawud and the media that the Nation was responsible.[72] This was never proven definitively and was vehemently denied by Malcolm weeks later.[73] Regardless, the fight for the ear and attention of African leaders was a matter that ultimately seems to have only concerned Dawud and Muhammad. There is no record of African leaders like Touré or Nkrumah taking sides in their conflict, or in debates about which organization was more authentically Muslim. Furthermore, as evinced by Nasser's general invitation to Black nationalist and Black Muslim leaders, African and Afro-Asian leaders were not monogamous. They were willing to cast their nets widely for any support they could muster from Black people in the United States.

The fact, thus, that the Muhammads were ostensibly granted access to Mecca despite the protestations of much of the Muslim community was a critical piece of evidence that was marshaled by Muhammad to prove the sect's legitimacy. Although he arrived in Mecca too late to complete hajj, Muhammad made sure that the Black media was aware of his success in accessing the holy city and completing *umrah*. In January 1960, immediately upon his return, he sent notes about his trip to Mecca to several newspapers.[74] In a column that was syndicated in multiple publications, he boasted that "Mecca is the only city on our planet that is divinely protected and made sacred and inviolable ... On entering that holy and magnificent place, [the guide] proceeded with us to the court where stands the Kaaba ... There were between five to ten thousand Muslims inside the court of the mosque. Such a prayer service I have never witnessed before being with these thousands of sincere worshipers of God, His religion, and Muhammad His Prophet."[75] In his notes, Muhammad reported performing other Muslim rites, including *wudu*, or ritual purification of the body before salat (prayer), and performing salat in Arabic. This was marshaled to negate reports that the religious rites of the Nation did not align with those of other Muslims. Muhammad had found some way to perform the prayers and rituals to the satisfaction of his guides and the judges at Mecca. However, despite his attempts to do so, the truth was that the Nation's prayers did not align with standard Islamic prayer protocols. Despite Naeem's assurances that the Nation was on the brink of beginning widespread prayer instruction in 1957, by the time Malcolm left for his trip to Egypt in July of 1959, this had yet to happen. When Malcolm was on his trip in July, he reported feeling self-conscious and embarrassed because he did not know enough basic Arabic to sufficiently perform Muslim prayers.[76]

Even though Muhammad used his goodwill tour of Africa and Asia as evidence of his legitimacy as an Afro-Asian Muslim leader, the tour itself did little to affect his actual teachings. Nation temples were now referred to as "mosques," but besides that small change, prayer services, rituals, and foundational teachings for the Nation largely remained the same. However, the Nation's commitment to projecting a spirit of Afro-Asian solidarity and anticolonialism was only strengthened by Muhammad's trip. For the remainder of 1960, the Nation's discourse and its public outreach reflected a commitment—as Malcolm had suggested in April of 1959—to realizing Bandung in Harlem.

Mr. Muhammad Speaks to the Ummah in Black and White

Muhammad had toyed with the idea of having his own newspaper and controlling his own image since 1957, when the *Supreme Wisdom*, the first written compendium of the Nation's teachings, was published. The events of 1959 and 1960, however, accelerated Muhammad's exit from the Black press's editorial pages.[77] For one, the Black press, which had previously given Muhammad almost free rein to publish his teachings, began to publish embarrassing and often unsubstantiated reports about him and the Nation. Accusations from mainstream media sources, like the *Hate That Hate Produced*, to radical Black newspapers, like the *New Crusader*, repeatedly questioned Elijah Muhammad's authority to lead a Muslim movement and joined the chorus of voices questioning whether the Nation was Muslim at all. In February of 1960, the *Chicago American* ran an article characterizing the Nation as illegitimate, unrecognized by Sunni Muslims, and perhaps most inflammatorily, "frighteningly similar to the techniques used by Hitler to bring the world to the brink of disaster."[78] This media blitz was responsible for a dramatic uptick in the Nation's membership, but it also evinced to Nation leaders that they could no longer rely on Black media outlets to spread their message.[79]

Accounts of Muhammad's trip abroad were published in the *New York Amsterdam News*, the *Los Angeles Herald-Dispatch*, and the *Pittsburgh Courier* in early 1960, but by this time, Malcolm was already brainstorming ideas for the Nation's own organizational newspaper. It wouldn't be their first attempt.

Previously, the Nation had unsuccessfully attempted to launch several magazines, *Mr. Muhammad, Salaam, The Messenger, Muhammad Speaks to the Black Man*, and the *Islamic News*, but in May of 1960, Malcolm X spearheaded the Nation's official newspaper, *Mr. Muhammad Speaks*. The publication was renamed *Muhammad Speaks* in December of 1961.[80] The other magazines and newspapers the Nation had tried to launch over the years had not enjoyed a wide readership, but *Muhammad Speaks* took off, serving as the central clearinghouse for the Nation's teachings, projects, fundraising, advertising, discourse, and solidarities.

Muhammad Speaks served several purposes.[81] First, a national newspaper with Malcolm X at the helm served as a way for the Nation to both control and monetize its image. The Black press had proven to have fickle loyalties. Now, the Nation would be able to control its own image, and thus be able to consistently reflect itself in the most positive light, and they would also reap the exclusive profits of the sales.[82] The success of the newspaper vis-à-vis the previous projects that the Nation had attempted was due to the pyramid-like structure of *Muhammad Speaks*'s sale and distribution. Each Nation mosque was required to sell a certain number of newspapers. In order to do this, men from the Fruit of Islam, the Nation's paramilitary auxiliary for men, were required to purchase a set number of newspapers from their local mosque at the cost of fifteen cents per copy and resell them on the open market. In order to break even, they would hit the streets each week to sell the newspapers. This meant that every single copy of the newspaper that came off of the presses was purchased. Whether it was eventually distributed was not the concern of the organization.[83]

Second, *Muhammad Speaks* was intended to express the tenets and teachings of the Nation's Islamic practice, and to understand it in relationship to the global freedom struggles taking the African diaspora by storm. In other words, *Muhammad Speaks* was published with the intention of inscribing Black Muslim people into a larger anticolonial, Muslim, and third world geography. As the public fight between Dakota Staton, Imam Talib Dawud, Elijah Muhammad, and Malcolm X demonstrated, the chief battle for all Black Muslims in the United States was to claim authenticity and assert authority over followers and potential converts.[84] To be sure, *Muhammad Speaks* contained plenty of instruction about the Nation's specific interpretation of Islam. Every issue of the newspaper contained reprinted speeches from Elijah Muhammad and articles from contributors reinforcing the Nation's teachings on the inferiority of "blue eyed devils," the beauty of being Black, the status of Elijah Muhammad as the messenger of Allah, strict gender roles,

Black Muslim education, and building Black business (including selling *Muhammad Speaks* itself). The paper heavily instructed followers on the beliefs and rituals of their particular *'asabiyah*, or tribe. However, the newspaper also served as an affirmation of the Nation's Islamic identity and of its belonging to the ummah. Through articles and editorials instructing believers in the Nation's theology and rituals, *Muhammad Speaks* assisted Nation leaders in imagining themselves as part of a larger transnational Muslim community.[85] This project had been ongoing since the end of World War II, but with the birth of a new form of nationally (and eventually internationally) distributed print media, these ideas could spread to all corners of the globe virtually simultaneously.[86] As the 1960s wore on, Naeem returned as a representative of the Afro-Asian world regularly to both justify the Nation's tribal practices and to ease them more concretely into the Islamic world.

Third, and most critically, since the interwar period, Nation leaders had carefully constructed a geography of imperial resistance that located Islam as a powerful corrective to white supremacy and the subjugation of people of color. As the nations of Bandung attempted to construct a geopolitical and diplomatic jetty for themselves through the Third World, the Nation imagined itself as part of this space, warring alongside Black and Muslim nations against white imperialism. In late 1959, Malcolm and Muhammad's goodwill tours of the Muslim World evinced a commitment to building out the contours of these intellectual alliances, and with the pace of decolonization quickening, they had plenty of allies to choose from. As the United Nations' Afro-Asian bloc grew to forty-six by 1960, the mainstream press noted the frequency with which the United States and Europe found themselves on the minority side of resolutions concerning decolonization, and were often anxious about the bloc's "obsession" with colonialism and large-scale refusal to take sides in the burgeoning Cold War conflict.[87] The first issues of *Muhammad Speaks*, thus, coincided with a growing Western anxiety about the rise of third world political power. The Nation reveled in this anxiety, using it as a proof of the prophesied downfall of white supremacy and colonialism.

The publication of *Muhammad Speaks* was a way for the Nation to outline the contours of the Atlantic Crescent by discursively repeating its teachings on internationalism, visually crafting connections between the decolonization struggles of countries in Africa and Asia by putting them in physical proximity to one another on the printed page, and doctrinally mobilizing Islam as key to Black independence and sovereignty. The newspaper, facilitated by a robust distribution network, allowed the particulars of this formation to more forcefully reach into the homes of Muslim and non-Muslim Black people than had previously been possible. *Muhammad Speaks* helped to visualize and delineate this geography not only through the content it printed on decolonization, imperialism, and African American subjugation but also through the way that editors arranged the articles and photographs regarding independence and revolution in the Afro-Asian world. This was done in two ways. First, the editors intertwined the struggle for independence in Africa, Asia, and eventually the Circum-Caribbean with Muhammad's demands for separate land for Black people. Since 1958, Muhammad had published articles in the *New York Amsterdam News* and the *Pittsburgh Courier* advocating for a separate autonomous state for Black people.[88] Muhammad and the Nation had steadily built their real estate profile during the preceding decade, but they had done nothing to suggest that they were actually ready for secession from the United States. With the publication of *Muhammad Speaks* in 1960, however, this point became repeatedly emphasized through the publication's content and layout. At first, Muhammad conceived of an autonomous Black state carved out of the existing land mass of the United States and given back to Black people for their free labor during slavery.[89] In this way, it would resemble the Native American reservations but would be much larger in area.[90] The newspaper made it easy to repeat these demands month after month, and to intentionally emphasize the Nation's previous teachings on Afro-Asian solidarity. The publication was not, as Manning Marable argued in his 2012 biography of Malcolm X, "schizophrenic," but rather constructed with an eye toward building the parameters of this anti-imperial geography.[91]

From the first issue in May 1960 until 1962, Muhammad's demands for separate land were scattered throughout the newspaper. On some occasions, as in September of 1960, they would be front and center, in large capital letters, directly under the masthead defining the newspaper as a "Militant Monthly Dedicated to Justice for the Black Man."[92] This idea of militant and unapologetic Blackness united the domestic battle for autonomy as reflected in the headline "Muhammad Steps Up Crusade for Separate Black States," with the international focus at the top of the page. Immediately above the masthead, the publication promised a story on the ongoing revolutions against Britain and France sweeping through the African diaspora.[93] Three pages later, the editors delivered on their promises, further emphasizing the visual and ideological connection between these freedom struggles by placing a full story explaining Muhammad's ill-defined plan for autonomy with several articles on the ongoing revolutionary trends in Africa and the Caribbean.[94] The bulk of the visual space was taken up by an article on the ongoing crisis in Congo when the province of Katanga seceded from the country with the support of Belgium, and the Belgian army refused to leave Congo during the violence that ensued. The article discussed how Congo's newly elected president, Joseph Kasa-Vubu, and prime minister, Patrice Lumumba, beseeched the United Nations for help abating Belgian aggression.[95] The issue would occupy not only the United Nations General Assembly but also every edition of *Muhammad Speaks* for the next year until Lumumba's assassination by the Belgian army in 1961.[96]

Where Congo was not directly the focus, the changing balance of power in the United Nations was. Here, Malcolm and the editorial staff of *Muhammad Speaks* would repeat the same motif, linking the freedom work to be done in the United States with articles and photographs extolling the progress made by the newly admitted Afro-Asian nations in the United Nations General Assembly and reporting on the pace of nationalist movements in Asia and Africa.[97] For example, in the inaugural issue of *Muhammad Speaks*, in the middle of a round-up article breaking down the status of multiple African countries, editors included a photograph of Muhammad's daughter and granddaughter poring over a map of the African continent depicting the route taken by Muhammad and his sons on their world tour. The caption of the photograph suggests that the women were discussing the nature of American Muslim interest in the African continent with Sandford Alexander, the editor of the *Los Angeles Herald-Dispatch*.[98]

After publishing only two issues in 1961, *Muhammad Speaks* returned the next year with a new conception of Black separatism.[99] When the newspaper was born, it was largely the brainchild and responsibility of Malcolm X.[100] But in 1962, Malcolm was asked to cede editorship of *Muhammad Speaks* to Muhammad's son, Herbert. The paper's internationalist perspective continued and adapted with Herbert at its helm.[101] It became increasingly clear, however, that the organization would never obtain sovereign land in the United States. Instead, Muhammad began to float the Garvey-esque idea of creating a sovereign Black American state somewhere else. Muhammad suggested that if the Nation was unable to fulfill his initial vision of obtaining land inside the United States, then the bond of purpose Black Americans had with their brothers on the "vast continent[s] of Asia and Africa" would prompt these populations to welcome "every Lost-Found Muslim in America to share with them."[102] It is unclear if Muhammad actually believed this could be successful, but if he did, he had paid no attention to the historical realities of the violence and hostilities that had erupted during attempts to establish similar settlements in Liberia.[103] Moreover, he showed no awareness of the problematic civilizationist assertions that he was endorsing, including the idea that American Blacks could, should, or were uniquely positioned to, colonize Africa and Asia.

In accordance with Muhammad's shift away from the United States and toward Africa or Asia as the geographical home of his sovereign Black state, Herbert Muhammad continued to make visual connections between African American sovereignty and Afro-Asian decolonization. *Muhammad Speaks* continued with bold headlines linking Black freedom and the rising tide of third world Muslim power abroad and mixing articles on separation with reports on independence.[104] On pages otherwise singularly focusing on international events, the editorial staff inserted demands for sovereignty, territory, and self-governance at the foot of the page. In January 1962, for example, as Algerian rebels continued to fight for their independence from France, *Muhammad Speaks* published an article highlighting Algerian premier Ben Youssef Ben Khedda's accusation of French genocide in the country. Next to this article appeared a piece denouncing BBC News for its coverage of Nigerian independence and self-government, calling it slanderous. Immediately below, the editors blocked off the words "We Must Have Some Land!"[105] In the next issue, editors placed the words "We Must Control Our Neighborhoods!" at the bottom of a page with articles on statements of mutual support by Afro-Asian leaders for nations and populations actively fighting for their independence.[106] Using a larger and bolder font and exclamation points, these arrangements drew the reader's eye, emphasizing these transnational and pan-Islamic connections.[107]

In July, the organization's demands for land, jobs, and neighborhood control were concentrated in a section titled "The Muslim Program."[108] Beginning in August of 1963, this section appeared on the last page of the newspaper, bookending the bold headlines and accusatory headlines on the front of the newspaper.[109] In the "Muslim Program," the demand for separate land was one of nine other points that were repeated at first monthly; bimonthly after July 1962; and, in response to growing popularity, weekly after January 1965. After this point, the editors shied away from the pull-quote method to emphasize the connections between European imperialism and the violence of Jim Crow in the United States. However, they continued to place articles on African decolonization and the trials and triumphs of nationhood with the ongoing violence of Jim Crow. In the August 15, 1962, issue of *Muhammad Speaks*, the editors placed these events visually side by side by placing a set of articles dealing with the ongoing oppression of African Black people by white imperialists in Namibia and Mali on a page opposite a set of articles on the ongoing battle to maintain Jim Crow segregation in Alabama.[110] These formatting decisions were intentional. In April 1962, Elijah Muhammad contracted with Naeem to edit a pull-out "magazine-like" section of the newspaper dealing with international political and religious issues. In contracting with Naeem, who would, as he had done with *Moslem World*, solidify the Nation's Muslim geography of imperial resistance, Muhammad envisioned that Naeem would make the "paper one that the entire world will admire and respect for its clean and fresh news of our people's life, work and their political and spiritual conditions throughout the world."[111] At this point, Naeem was hired as a foreign correspondent for the newspaper.[112] This role of "foreign correspondent" aligned with Naeem's other business and professional goals, including his foray into travel planning through Shalimar International.[113] Shalimar's offices hosted a rotating cast of international Afro-Asian and Muslim dignitaries, including on at least one occasion the Nigerian ambassador to the United Nations and the United Arab Republic consul general.[114]

Adapting the Nation's Muslim Geography of Anti-Imperial Resistance

It didn't matter for Malcolm, Muhammad, or Naeem for that matter, that Congo was not a majority Muslim country. Similarly, as the editors and writers of *Muhammad Speaks* celebrated the forward progress of decolonization throughout the Caribbean, it was unimportant that the populations demanding autonomy in Jamaica, Trinidad, Bahamas, or Grenada, for example, were largely Christian.[115] The Nation had long identified all nonwhite people as Black and all Black people as a natural part of the Muslim community, no matter their self-identification. Occasionally, however, a country or leader would surface that challenged the Nation's geopolitical imaginary and forced the organization to adapt it. These examples illustrate how the Nation pieced together its geography of anti-imperial resistance, and the ways that this geography changed over time. Here, the example of Cuba and its president, Fidel Castro, exemplifies how the global geopolitical landscape demanded that the Nation make intellectual and discursive adaptations to its anti-imperial Muslim geography. Moreover, a reading of the treatment of Cuba and Castro in *Muhammad Speaks* provides an example of the thought process by which various nations and populations made their way into the Nation's constructed anti-imperial ummah.

In September of 1960, fourteen African and Asian countries attended the United Nations General Assembly for the first time as new member states. These fourteen countries increased the United Nations' growing Afro-Asian bloc to forty-six, nearly half of the UN's total membership of ninety-nine. This "fundamental transformation" in the world organization did not escape the attention of the Nation and other Black organizations in Harlem. This, in addition to the Soviet bloc and a few neutral European countries, like Sweden, presented an immense challenge to the United States and to the European countries that had previously enjoyed nearly unbridled power and control of the labor and resources of the majority of the globe. As the date of the UN General Assembly approached, Malcolm X and other Harlemites, including the UANM's James Lawson, made plans to accommodate and welcome the onslaught of African dignitaries who would inevitably make their way up to Harlem. These leaders created a Welcoming Committee for Harlem's 28th Precinct that would be charged with greeting representatives from any country that could loosely be classified as African.[116] This included the actual continent of Africa as well as countries from Asia and the Caribbean, both of which had previously fallen into the Nation's Black Muslim geography.

Castro and his delegation had experienced myriad issues securing appropriate accommodations in New York. At the behest of the State Department, the Cubans had been denied lodging at the majority of hotels in Midtown Manhattan.[117] This was due to burgeoning tensions between the United States and Cuba after Castro's successful revolution and ouster of United States–backed dictator Fulgencio Batista in 1959.[118] The United States had already instituted an arms embargo on Cuba in 1958, but after Castro seized foreign investments and assets and nationalized private property, the United States severed all diplomatic ties and tightened its embargo. In 1960, Congress banned all trade between the United States and Cuba with the exception of food and medicine.[119] Cuba increasingly began to rely on assistance from the Soviet Union, stoking fears for the United States government that a Soviet satellite state could exist a mere ninety miles off the coast of Florida. The Cubans finally found accommodations at the Shelburne Hotel in Midtown East but decided to leave due to what they described as a general "climate of inhospitality" from the Shelburne's management—the owner decided to fly an enormous American flag in front of the hotel especially for the occasion, asked for an additional $10,000 security deposit, and denied the delegation the right to eat in the dining room alongside other hotel guests.[120]

The situation seemed bleak for the Cubans until the Welcoming Committee stepped in and helped them secure more suitable arrangements uptown. In the early hours of September 20, 1960, the Cubans traveled six miles uptown to settle into their new accomodations over four floors of Harlem's Hotel Theresa. Soon after their arrival, Malcolm arrived at the hotel with a reporter from the Black press and a photographer in tow.[121] The photographs of the two men taken on that night show them at times laughing riotously and smiling like old friends and at other moments with their heads tilted toward each other in intimate conversation (figures 3.2a and 3.2b). Indeed, Malcolm had played a critical role in helping Castro and his delegation obtain their rooms at the Hotel Theresa. Even before their arrival, Malcolm had suggested to Cuban diplomats that the delegation stay at the Hotel Theresa—at that moment a center of Afro-Asian internationalism and Black radical organizing in Harlem—instead of in Midtown Manhattan. As the late historian Ralph Crowder has argued, Malcom and Castro did this intentionally. They knew that the Cuban delegation's ill treatment and subsequent relocation to Harlem would "focus the press and international community upon American racism and Cuba's allegations of American imperialism."[122] After their relocation, Castro emphasized the connections between Cuba and the Afro-Asian world. He played up the warm welcome he received in Harlem and called Cuba and all African and Latin American nations "African Americans."[123]

Whereas Castro fully and publicly embraced the idea of brotherhood with African Americans, Malcolm expressed some hesitancy to publicly and fully embrace Castro in this moment. During their thirty-minute meeting, Malcolm was reported to have praised Castro, saying that "usually when one sees a man whom the United States is against, there is something good in that man" and that "any man who represented such a small country that would stand up and challenge a country as large as the United States must be sincere."[124] When asked about his visit to Castro's room after the meeting, however, Malcolm stated that he only visited in his role as a representative of the Welcoming Committee and denied that the meeting was prearranged. Rather, Malcolm made it seem that he had only gone to see Castro because no other member of the committee was available at the time, a claim that seems specious given the fact that Malcolm maintained an office inside the Hotel Theresa. Furthermore, Malcolm expressed some reservations about Castro's politics and disavowed any connection with Castro or Cuba, stating that because the Nation was a religious organization, it could not be "affiliated with Communism since it is atheistic."[125] Weeks later, Malcolm would resign from the Welcoming Committee over what he characterized as the press's repeated accusations of alignment with Castro and of communist sympathies.[126] Even so, even at the late hour that the Cubans arrived, Malcolm showed up with three other members of the Nation, two journalists, and one photojournalist, indicating some coordination, even if quite last minute, and a desire to document the occasion for the public.

FIGURE 3.2A Malcolm X and Fidel Castro laughing together at the Hotel Theresa on September 20, 1960. Photograph by Carl Nesfield.

FIGURE 3.2B Malcolm X and Fidel Castro in conversation at the Hotel Theresa on September 20, 1960. Photograph by Carl Nesfield.

Malcolm's fervent disavowal of any relationship between himself and Fidel Castro is curious given the Nation's internationalist and anti-imperialist rhetoric at this moment, and it deserves further examination. Cuba should have been in all ways immediately part of the Nation's anti-imperial Muslim geography. Under normal circumstances, the example of a nonwhite population rising up against an American-backed dictator serving the interests of imperialists would be quick fodder for the Nation, and quickly incorporated into the organization's geography of resistance. The fact that the island was non-Muslim would have made little to no difference. Like Jamaicans and Trinidadians, Cubans should still, given previous precedents, have been openly hailed as African brothers and fellow Muslims. But in the early days of the Cold War, given Cuba's alignment with the Soviet Union—as opposed to the nonalignment espoused by the other populations in the Nation's geography—it was difficult for the Nation to immediately place the country into its imagined third world versus West binary. Indeed, Castro's dalliance with the Soviet Union and implementation of a communist government was the piece that, at least at first, produced palpable ambivalence for Nation leaders. This ambivalence was evident in the way that Malcolm characterized this meeting with Castro in September 1960.

After the United States' failed attempt to invade Cuba and depose the Castro regime in April 1961, it systematically began to pressure Cuba's Latin American and Caribbean neighbors to isolate the country economically and diplomatically. In January 1962, the Americans called an emergency meeting of the Organization of American States where they narrowly obtained the votes necessary to sanction Cuba, remove it from the organization, and embargo any trade in arms.[127] By February, the Kennedy Administration barred all imports from Cuba and recommitted itself to its embargo on all exports except certain foods, medicines, and medical supplies.[128] Cuba characterized this as an act of economic aggression.[129] By October, the United States instituted a naval blockade on any ships delivering offensive weapons to Cuba.[130]

By the time these Cuban–American hostilities peaked, however, Malcolm was no longer the editor of *Muhammad Speaks*, and in his capacity as the new editor in chief, Herbert Muhammad began to express a new organizational attitude toward Castro and Cuba. By late 1962, *Muhammad Speaks* emphasized Cuba's large population of people of African descent and began to include the country in its geography of imperial resistance in the same way it had done with Vietnam, Congo, Kenya, and other countries that had experienced direct or indirect European or American aggression. In November 1962, as the American blockade took effect, Afro-Asian nations expressed "grave concern" that these actions would lead to a "third world war" or a "holocaust of atomic bombs that could destroy civilization" and sought to use their power in the United Nations to thwart this.[131] In an article alleging that Afro-Asian nations had "pulled [the] world [back] from [an] H-Bomb precipice," a writer for *Muhammad Speaks* argued that Afro-Asian nations were concerned about Cuba being used as a "pawn on the international chessboard of power politics."[132] Here, the article suggested that it was not Cuba's choice to be aligned with the Soviet Union, but rather that it was an outcome of an imperialist war between the United States and the Soviet Union. This article was also the first to begin to suggest a racial connection between African Americans and Cubans based on shared African descent and repeatedly referenced a comment by Nigerian prime minister Jaja Wachuku that he "would not like to hear one of these days that an atomic bomb has been dropped on Cuba, nor that, from Cuba, someone had sent a rocket to the United States. We have people of African descent there ... therefore we have an interest."[133] This comment, suggesting a racial brotherhood between the two populations, was quoted or referenced three times in the short article.[134]

This idea of a blood brotherhood of Black Cubans and African Americans was only further solidified as the 1960s wore on and the diplomatic situation between Cuba and the United States continued to degenerate. In July 1963, on the tenth anniversary of the beginning of the Cuban Revolution, editor Herbert Muhammad and *Muhammad Speaks* correspondent Charles Howard visited Cuba as guests of the Cuban government. Howard and Muhammad joined six hundred other international leaders and journalists, including four other Black writers, for a Cuban government trip and set of celebrations.[135] In a two-issue, multi-article report on their visit to Cuba, Howard further sketched out the contours of Cuba's inclusion in the Nation's version of the Black Muslim world when he outlined a vision of Cuba as a racially progressive country where Black Cubans led alongside white Cubans.[136] Under his first installment of Howard's report from inside Cuba, Herbert Muhammad placed a reprint of Castro's speech professing solidarity with the American "Negro." In this speech, Castro identified racial capitalism and imperialism as the drivers of inequality and oppression in both the United States and Cuba.[137]

Of course, Howard's reports in *Muhammad Speaks* only offer a very simplified view of Cuban racial politics that ignores the presence of multiple inconsistencies in Cuba's execution of its antiracist policies. It is true that after Cuba's revolution, Fidel Castro acknowledged the legacy of slavery in marginalizing and subjugating the Afro-Cuban population. Castro felt that the presence of this discrimination and racism was contrary to his socialist and

Marxist ideals and launched an "unprecedented assault on racism," outlawing discrimination and segregation in public spaces. He also took hiring decisions out of the hands of private individuals, allowing only the Ministry of Labor to distribute jobs according to family and economic need. Castro also nationalized private schools and expanded access to literacy programs and adult education. These reforms benefited Afro-Cubans most of all, as they were among the poorest and most marginalized on the island.[138]

These changes, however, came slowly and not immediately, as Castro claimed. Within two decades of Cuba's revolution, Black and white people had achieved equivalent levels of education, literacy, life expectancy, and maternal outcomes, even though they still experienced widespread social discrimination.[139] However, Castro claimed that he had achieved these benefits as early as three years into his regime, alleging that because capitalism and imperialism were the source of racism that these were no longer a problem in Cuba. Discussion of race and inequality became taboo, making Cubans reluctant to talk about race and racial discrimination but not eliminating the issue from Cuban institutions.[140] In fashioning a new Marxist-Leninist Cuban citizen, authorities limited the practice of traditional Afro-Cuban culture, including religion. In particular, Afro-Cuban religions like Santería were depicted in official government publications as counterrevolutionary, regressive, primitive, selfishly individualistic, and "ridiculous," anti-scientific "nonsense."[141] Although it was not illegal to practice these religions, their members were highly surveilled and associated with "high level[s] of social dangerousness and a predisposition to commit crimes" and as refugees for "bandits, counterrevolutionaries, and thieves."[142] They disproportionately found themselves in front of courts and tribunals facing accusations of murder and violent behavior.[143] Thus, despite the Nation's vocal support of Castro, Islam would not have been accepted by the Cuban government, and its practitioners would have likely been subject to the same accusations of ritualism, cultish behavior, and criminality as other religious traditions on the island.

It was obviously Cuba's intent to obscure these contradictions. The event that Howard and Muhammad attended served as a nationalist celebration of Cuba's bloody six-year revolution. Like any national holiday or celebration, the commemoration of the Cuban Revolution would have been a "meticulously contrived" spectacle intended to connect Cuba's past to its present and future.[144] This was a present and future that had, according to the revolutionary government, broken with its racist past. Likewise, the events, tours, and individual Cuban citizens presented to these international guests would have been screened, coordinated, and cleared by the Cuban government. Thus, when

Howard promised to give readers the "real story" on Cuba in his two-issue report, it is unclear whether he, himself, received the "real story" of Cuba's postrevolutionary government and its people.

By 1963, the Nation was actively searching for allies against the United States and Europe, and ultimately, it would stretch the boundaries of its anti-imperial geography in order to include these nations. To be sure, Muhammad was in no way a communist or a socialist. The Nation's message of "do for self" was actively capitalist and steeped in notions of a Black middle-class politics of respectability tied to the accumulation of wealth. However, in the geopolitical context of the Cold War, the Nation returned to its post–World War II formulation of international solidarity. Its allies included all of the United States' critics and sworn enemies, communist or unaligned, especially if they expressed direct support for the African American civil rights movement. Malcolm developed his own socialist Muslim internationalism alongside the Nation's internationalist discourse, later forming the Organization of Afro American Unity and the Muslim Mosque, Inc. in 1964, after his break with the Nation.

In August 1963, Chairman Mao Zedong issued a statement expressing China's support for Black Americans in their fight against racial discrimination and condemning racially motivated colonialism and imperialism.[145] By November 1963, Muhammad had begun to soften on Mao's China. That month, he admonished a member who had reacted negatively to a call he received from Robert Williams, a former NAACP chapter president then exiled in Cuba. Williams called to ask whether Muhammad or his representatives would be interested in visiting Peking, as the Chinese government was extremely interested to know more about the Muslim movement in the United States. This member, who is unnamed in the report, replied that he did not think Muhammad would be interested because the Nation was "not affiliated no way [sic] with the communist world and ... not seeking to be affiliated with them." Elijah Muhammad had a different take, however, and was upset that this member had not consulted him before he expressed these views to Williams. Instead, Muhammad put forth a more inclusive vision of solidarity and intellectual openness. It was irrelevant that the Chinese were communist. Islam could still reach them, give them wisdom, and solidify a sense of international brotherhood.[146]

Conclusion

For the remainder of the 1960s, the Nation, the United States, and the Afro-Asian world underwent a dramatic set of changes. In February 1965, Malcolm

X was assassinated as he spoke on behalf of the Organization of Afro American Unity at the Audubon Ballroom in Harlem. Three years later, in April of 1968, cities across the United States and the African diaspora exploded into uprisings after the assassination of Malcolm's political foil, Dr. Martin Luther King Jr. Throughout this, the Nation maintained its view on the critical importance of international engagement and solidarity in the fight for civil and human rights and continued to center Islam as the key in this struggle.

From September 1969 to March of 1975, Nation political cartoonist Eugene Majied rendered a vision of Muhammad's idea of his role in forging Afro-Asian solidarity on the front page of *Muhammad Speaks*. At the top of the page, centered above the headline, Majied depicted two Black men dressed in traditional white Muslim robes, standing over the continents of Africa and Asia. In the middle, these men clasped their hands in brotherhood over the United States, representing not only the importance of African and Asian solidarity but also America's key role in this relationship. The sun set behind the United States, projecting a sunset in red, gold, black, and green, reflecting the colors of Pan-Africanism (figure 3.3).[147]

By the time Muhammad wrote to Abdul Basit Naeem in April of 1962 expressing his desire that *Muhammad Speaks* become an international publication, the newspaper had already, in some respects, achieved this milestone. As early as 1960, with the very first issues of *Muhammad Speaks*, the publication found itself on the shores of the diminutive island of Bermuda, brought in by cruise and cargo ship workers that regularly frequented the island. Clearly, the Messenger wanted either a larger, or a more widespread, circulation throughout the world. By 1962, in addition to the Bermuda mosque, *Muhammad Speaks* enjoyed readers in British Guiana, Canada, Costa Rica, Egypt, Honduras, Ghana, Guatemala, Jamaica, Mexico, and the United Kingdom, although the extent of the circulation in these places is unclear.[148] By 1968, individual international mosques in Mexico, Bermuda, and Bahamas were well organized enough with sufficient members and resources to send delegations to the Nation's annual Saviour's Day convention in Chicago.[149]

The Nation's international expansion provided an opportunity to test the strength of the organization's Pan-African and anticolonial rhetoric. Muhammad had argued that African Americans in America's urban centers were suffering under the same mechanisms of colonial oppression and imperial exploitation as their brothers throughout the Afro-Asian world and, by the 1960s, the Circum-Caribbean world. For Muhammad, Islam was the way that Black and Brown people could break from the chains of mental slavery and

FIGURE 3.3 Eugene Majied, *Messenger Muhammad's Idea, Muhammad Speaks*, December 18, 1970, p. 1. Cartoon by Eugene Majied.

economic and political exploitation, whether that was in the United States, in Jamaica, or in Indonesia.

The letters that poured in each week to *Muhammad Speaks* from all over the world reflected in some way that the Nation's message and Muhammad's authority served some utility for those in the places he highlighted week after week. But like Majied's rendering, Muhammad's message was American-centered and American-focused—an Atlantic Crescent from the perspective of the United States. Aside from highlighting his vision of how much people throughout the Afro-Asian world—Nation boosters like Naeem included—were allegedly inspired by his message, Muhammad regularly ignored the perspectives of with whom he professed solidarity. How then, given the American-centered nature of Muhammad's Islam, did the followers he boasted elsewhere translate his message to their own needs and historical circumstances? In other words, how did the people who Muhammad talked about repeatedly—those experiencing processes of decolonization and fighting for their own independence—hear, interpret, understand, and use Islam in ways that were meaningful to them given their own specific experiences?

INTERLUDE

Transitions, Crises, and Choices

In the late summer or early fall of 1977, former Bermudian Nation of Islam member Michelle Khaldun and her husband, George, received a phone call at their East Elmhurst, New York, home. George picked up the phone in the kitchen, and Michelle, in her second trimester with the couple's third child, leaned against the doorframe with the long, spiraled phone cord from the next room tautly stretched across her swelling belly. As George spoke, Michelle listened quietly, her facial expressions and thoughts cycling between doubt, confusion, and internal conflict. The mystery caller was Louis Farrakhan.[1]

Farrakhan called the Khalduns as part of his campaign to test the temperature of former Nation members and his most loyal friends and followers.[2] In February 1975, Elijah Muhammad died, and his son Wallace took over the organization. But Wallace was determined to transition his flock from the Nation's particularist practice to one he felt was more firmly rooted in a mainstream Sunni Muslim practice. Tension broke out between the two men. Frustrated, Farrakhan resolved to restore himself to the leadership of a resurrected Nation.[3] He was on the brink of going public, but first, he needed to secure his support base. One of his first calls, thus, was to two of his previously most loyal supporters, Michelle and George Khaldun.

During the early 1970s, during Elijah Muhammad's leadership, the Khalduns were active members of the Nation and of Farrakhan's inner circle in New York. George was an assistant minister, and Michelle taught University of Islam classes for children. George came to the Nation in a more or less typical way. As a member of a gang in Corona, New York, George met Malcolm X while he was still a prominent leader in the Nation. The Nation's teachings and Malcolm's in-the-flesh example of salvation and redemption represented the possibility of a new life of Black self-love, community care, and self-sufficiency. Michelle, on the other hand, came to the Nation through her political involvement with Bermudian independence and Bermuda's version of the Black Panther Party, the Black Beret Cadre (BBC). At the age of seventeen, Michelle left Bermuda to explore greater opportunities and to see the world. After graduation, she told her mother she was going to visit colleges in the United States, but it would be decades before she permanently returned home to

Bermuda. It was then, after her arrival in New York, that she would walk into Farrakhan's mosque—the famed Nation of Islam Harlem Temple No. 7.[4]

Farrakhan maintained a close professional and personal relationship with George and Michelle throughout the 1970s. After Michelle and her best friend, Wanda Perinchief, arrived in New York in 1971, Farrakhan took the girls under his wing, finding accommodation for Michelle, Wanda, and three other women at his aunt's home in Queens. In 1972, Farrakhan set Michelle and George up on their first date, knowingly permitting Michelle to go unchaperoned in violation of the Nation's policy against co-ed mingling. When police raided Harlem Temple No. 7 in 1973, Michelle was initially missing from the hordes of Nation members gathered on the sidewalk, and Farrakhan came back into the building to retrieve her. When he found her inside trying to find the children from her University of Islam class, he screamed at her to get out of the building as a baby-faced police officer, no more than eighteen years old, Michelle figured, pointed a gun in her face.[5]

It was logical, therefore, that Farrakhan would bank on his close relationship with the Khalduns when attempting to recruit old loyalists. But he made one critical error. As Wallace Muhammad ascended to his father's position as Supreme Leader of the Nation, Farrakhan pledged allegiance to Wallace, promising to support his vision.[6] In the meantime, Muslims like George and Michelle were beginning to accept Sunni mainstream teachings under the ministry of Muhammad, who had begun referring to himself as an imam in accordance with the Sunni Muslim tradition. Under Imam Muhammad, these Muslims had discovered a new way of thinking Islamically and politically, while still centering their identities as Black people in the Atlantic world. By the time Farrakhan called, Michelle and George were in the midst of a transformation. As he set down the receiver, George was excited, but apprehensive, about the possibility. Michelle, on the other hand, was firm. In her mind, Farrakhan already had the chance to lead his own movement, and that moment had passed.[7]

Michelle and George, like so many other Black and Muslim people like them, had real choices to make about the future of their religio-political identities. They had real decisions to make about how they would shape their relationship to race and Islam in the late twentieth century. How would they apply and shape the Atlantic Crescent in their own lives? And how would the discourses that they had absorbed, of their identities as members of a universal Muslim third world and coalition against white supremacy and imperial violence, impact how they saw their role in global racial liberation as the world continued to change around them?

In part I of this book, I examined the ways that Black and Muslim organizations and elites from the Moorish Science Temple of America, the Ahmadiyya Movement in Islam, the Nation of Islam, the Muslim Brotherhood USA, and Sunni Muslim movements, developed a geography of imperial resistance centering Islam as a unifying mechanism for far-flung oppressed populations suffering under the yoke of colonialism and white supremacy. Standing at the intersection of three overlapping early twentieth-century diasporas—African American, Afro-Caribbean, and South Asian—I argued that these leaders intellectualized, negotiated, and acted on their religio-racial identities. Reaching out transnationally, while still interpreting and making sense of their specific geographical and historical realities, these leaders made sense of their shared oppression and the role of Islam in ameliorating suffering and violence.

But the Atlantic Crescent was shaped not only by leaders and elites, like Elijah Muhammad, Abdul Basit Naeem, Imam Talib Dawud, Malcolm X, and Louis Farrakhan—men who imposed their vision on a hungry and willing population—but also by rank-and-file practitioners who adopted Islam because of the impact they hoped it would have on their lives. These men and women—like George and Michelle—heard these sermons and pored over the newspapers that these movements produced, letting the words resonate in their ear drums and hearts, and the inky words from the newspapers produced by these movements smudge onto their fingers.

Thus, in part II, I explore the ways that these rank-and-file members translated the messages of men associated with the Nation of Islam, like Elijah Muhammad, Wallace Muhammad, and Louis Farrakhan, in ways that made sense for them. As adherents experienced various internal and external crises, they made decisions about which movements spoke most clearly to them. Many of these discussions were centered around conversations about the continued existence of imperialism and colonialism in the Circum-Caribbean region, whether in its classical form or as a function of the United States' neo-imperial drive for Cold War domination, and the ways that Islam could provide a path forward for Black people continuing to live under colonial and imperial subjugation. For this reason, the three chapters in this section focus on the mid-Atlantic and Circum-Caribbean regions and the ways that the Black liberation struggles in these places were united discursively.

To this end, two of the three chapters in part II focus on the island of Bermuda, highlighting the experiences and choices that men and women, like Michelle Khaldun, made. Bermuda, which is off of the coast of Charleston, South Carolina, in the middle of the Atlantic Ocean, is not geographically in the Caribbean. However, I argue that Bermuda is nevertheless a discursive part of the Caribbean, sharing the same political, intellectual, and cultural influences. This is reflected in both British Foreign Commonwealth Office documents, which read the political and religious activities of Bermudians against the backdrop of the larger Circum-Caribbean region, and by Bermudian people themselves.

Bermuda's Atlantic Crescent provides a critical case of how Black Muslim anticolonial and anti-imperial discourse was translated to action by real Muslims like George and Michelle. In Bermuda, Black Muslims from Elijah Muhammad's Nation transposed his imagined geography of imperial resistance to their colonized island. From there, they translated this discourse to practice and adapted it to their own unique circumstances and lived experiences. Through the Nation's international outreach, which in no small part included *Muhammad Speaks*, individual people throughout the African diaspora identified even more strongly with certain portions of Muhammad's message. The Nation's geography placed Islam at the center of the global quest for freedom from white supremacy and subjugation. For this reason, Muhammad and the editors of *Muhammad Speaks* focused largely on decolonization and its aftermaths, watching with equal parts anxiety and delight as African, Asian, and eventually Caribbean nations attained independence from Europe. But largely, African Americans were not seriously demanding their own sovereign territory. Instead, the African American freedom struggle was based on enfranchisement, equity of opportunity and resources, freedom from racial violence, and the right to control Black neighborhoods; it did not attempt to take control of the United States as a sovereign nation for the use of African Americans. Bermudians, by contrast, were discussing their sovereignty and freedom from British imperial rule. The Nation's message, thus, had to be translated to the Bermudian experience, which was defined by classical imperialism and British colonialism. This resulted in a much different manifestation of political Islam in Bermuda than in the United States, one that saw Black liberation, decolonization, primary and secondary education, and the island's labor movements as united in purpose.

The third chapter in this section focuses on rank-and-file members of the Nation under Louis Farrakhan, in the era after Farrakhan's phone call to George and Michelle. It examines how Muslims associated with Farrakhan's Nation responded to the increasing militarization of the American inner city during the United States' War on Drugs, and how they understood it as part of a larger fight against American neo-imperialism in the Americas more broadly. Like the chapters on Bermuda, I examine how imperial fears of regional instability affected Black and Muslim people at home and how they intellectualized and understood larger local and international politics and attempted—through Islam—to transform their environments in response.

All three of these chapters focus on the Nation or its descendants, and this choice is an intentional one. I choose the Nation because of the importance that my Black and Muslim subjects, like Michelle, gave it in recollecting their personal political and religious journeys. In the sources, which include newspapers, interviews, personal writings, their own memories, and their private collections, Black and Muslim people overwhelmingly express their indebtedness to the Nation's anticolonial discourse and global worldview in shaping their own religio-racial understandings of the world, the boundaries of their Atlantic Crescent, and the rich political lives they undertook and continue to engage in.

Part II
Translations

CHAPTER FOUR

Bermuda Crescent
*Black Muslim Resistance and
Decolonization in Translation*

On December 13, 1965, police officer Gary Perinchief was directing traffic at the intersection of Front Street and Queen Street in Bermuda's capital city of Hamilton. A relatively new police officer and a young Black man from Back-a-Town, a largely impoverished area of Hamilton set back from the tourist-saturated avenues, Perinchief joined the police force in 1962 with a vision to just "do better" than the "white colonists" who dominated the British policing system.[1] Pre-emancipation, numbers of Black and white people in Bermuda were roughly equal, but by 1837, white Bermudians plummeted to less than half of the population.[2] In Bermuda's 1960 census, this number stood at just over 37 percent of the population.[3] This white minority, however, economically and socially dominated all Bermudian institutions, including the police force. In 1965, white men comprised the bulk of Bermudian police officers. These officers pledged to uphold the colonial system, answering directly to Britain's Scotland Yard. The pledge of loyalty to the British colonial system and the skewed racial balance of the police force were concerns for Perinchief and other young Black men. However, when the police force began to desegregate in 1959, the promise of a stable salary, good benefits, and the potential to make a change attracted him and other Black police officers to the job.[4]

As he directed traffic, Perinchief stood in the "birdcage," a raised gazebo-like structure that provided an improved vantage point for surveilling the largely flat coastal area up to Hamilton's docks, which were constantly bustling with cruise ships and cargo vessels. As Perinchief languished in the birdcage, bored with what was proving to be an otherwise routine day, he heard a disturbance break out at the docks. His friend, an Afro-Bermudian named Milton Hill, had arrived to collect a mail-order package from customs that innocently contained a crib and bassinet for his soon-to-arrive first child. Hill's shipment was from Eaton's, a Canadian catalog-order department store, but he was directed to the wrong ship. Instead of the postal vessel, Hill was led to the *Ocean Monarch*, a cruise ship that carried tourists, commercial goods, and illegally smuggled copies of the Nation's *Muhammad Speaks* newspaper to the island from New York City.[5]

Hill was one of the earliest members of the Bermudian branch of the Nation, and the authorities—the "white colonists" who Perinchief spoke of—were well aware of his religious and political leanings. When Hill reached the *Ocean Monarch*, he was immediately confronted by a white police officer who suspected him of conspiring to obtain an illegal shipment of *Muhammad Speaks*. As the police officer menacingly approached him, Hill elbowed him in the solar plexus, and in one swift motion the officer flew backward.[6] Perinchief arrived at the docks just in time to see his colleague's head firmly lodged in a fence and his friend being carted away by police officers.[7] In Hill's memory, seventeen officers tried to subdue him, placed him in a squad car, and hauled him into the Hamilton jail that day to be booked. Hill would not wait for his arraignment alone, however. Joining him in his holding cell were several other Nation members who were also accused of distribution and possession of *Muhammad Speaks*. Hill reported that approximately fifteen to twenty Black Muslims were in jail with him at the same time. While it is possible that there were other Muslims incarcerated simultaneously, the number was most certainly much lower than Hill remembers. In 1966, the British Foreign Commonwealth Office observed that there were only about fifteen regular members of the Nation. Regardless, Hill's memory is significant because it indicates his perception of the relatively large number of Nation of Islam members in jail for *Muhammad Speaks*-related offenses vis-à-vis their numbers, and the general perception of government persecution.

Hill never served any time for the charges related to *Muhammad Speaks*. A young attorney named Lois Browne—a woman who would later become one of the island's most progressive politicians—was able to cut a deal. Instead, Hill languished in jail for a month for assault on the police officers.[8] He was wrongly accused of possession of the newspaper, but his experiences with the Bermudian criminal justice system in the mid-1960s indicated that in the eyes of the colonial authorities, Islam in Bermuda posed a substantial threat to the white-supremacist, imperial order and the stability of the British government on the island. Just a few months prior, in July, the Bermudian Executive Council banned the sale, distribution, and mere possession of *Muhammad Speaks* under the Prohibited Publications Act, identifying it as subversive, antiwhite, anticolonial, "racial propaganda."[9] Prior to the ban, some twelve thousand copies of the newspaper had been imported by Muslims into Bermuda, a significant number for an island of fewer than forty-three thousand inhabitants.[10] The government ban itself indicated that the paper was being circulated in large enough numbers to, as the government and white public feared, profoundly influence Black youth on the island.[11] In the atmosphere of rapid decolonization sweeping through the Atlantic world by 1965, British authorities were anxious about the effect of these ideas and of American Muslim publications, like *Muhammad Speaks*, on decolonization and Black liberation movements on the island.[12] These anxieties were typical of British colonial administrators as they navigated the new political realities of the Cold War, and were informed by their experience in their other Caribbean colonies. During the 1950s, the Pan-Africanism and Black nationalism preached by religions like Rastafarianism, for example, were taken by colonial administrators to be a fundamental threat to colonial order and a harbinger of growing communist sympathies. The solidarities that these religions, which would include Islam, promoted among working-class colonial subjects and the conversations about Black sovereignty and power that they promoted were quite real, and they became particularly troubling for colonial administrators.[13] The ban on *Muhammad Speaks* fits into this general pattern of repression, anxiety, and paranoia. In the aftermath of the ban on *Muhammad Speaks*, the government stepped up harassment and surveillance on Black Muslims in Bermuda, raiding homes in the hopes of finding secret stashes of the newspaper, chasing adherents carrying piles of newspapers in their arms, and arresting members for mere possession of the publication's incendiary political cartoons.[14]

Through *Muhammad Speaks*, Elijah Muhammad and the Nation had reified an anti-imperial geography that placed Islam at the center of the quest for freedom from white supremacy and subjugation in the Atlantic world. Outside of the United States, Islam and Black nationalism served to ground decolonization movements throughout the Atlantic basin, as Black people found within Muhammad's message powerful lessons that drove their demands of freedom from white supremacy and imperial rule.[15]

In Bermuda, Islam served a central role in the island's civil rights and anti-colonial movement. It is normally the geometrical shape of the triangle that defines Bermuda's impact on the Atlantic space surrounding it—from Bermuda to Florida to the Eastern Caribbean. Here, it is the Atlantic Crescent that drives our study of Bermudian Islam, reaching outward to the African diaspora and inward back to the island of Bermuda itself, reflecting specific Black Bermudian lived realities and experiences of colonization and oppression through white minority rule.

Bermuda's Atlantic Crescent is an ideal case study to explore how real Black and Muslim people, who were living under colonialism, translated Black and Muslim anti-imperial and anticolonial discourse into action. There, Muslims associated with the Nation read *Muhammad Speaks* and listened to Elijah Muhammad's and Louis Farrakhan's audio recordings in order to transpose their imagined geography of imperial resistance to their colonized island and lived experience. Bermudian Muslims paid close attention to the focus in *Muhammad Speaks* on decolonization and its aftermaths, watching with equal parts anxiety and delight as African, Asian, and eventually Caribbean nations attained independence from Europe. But largely, African Americans were demanding the right to vote, access to employment and social advancement, and the ability to control their own neighborhoods and livelihood. They were not seriously demanding or making strides toward—at least not in any meaningful way—acquiring their own separate sovereign territory. Bermudians, by contrast, were living under British imperial rule. Thus, in Bermuda—far away from central leadership in the United States—the Nation's religious politics took on a different character than in the United States, intertwining with the island's independence, civil rights, and labor movements.

The Origins of Islam in Bermuda

The twenty-one-square-mile island of Bermuda lies 876 miles due east of Charleston, South Carolina, at the northeastern node of an imagined geographical section of the Atlantic Ocean referred to variously as the Devil's Triangle, or the Bermuda Triangle.[16] In 1616, four years after the island was settled permanently, the first group of enslaved Africans were forcibly transported to Bermuda to support the lucrative agricultural, pearl-diving, whaling, fishing, and ship-building industries. Although Africans typically arrived via other islands in the West Indies or the Circum-Caribbean, on the infrequent occasions that enslaved people came directly from Africa, Gambia and the Guinea Coast—both heavily Muslim areas of West Africa—were prime slaving targets.[17] In the absence of records indicating religious practice, it is impossible to know how many Muslim slaves were among those brought to Bermuda. However, it is likely that, as in other places throughout the Americas, African slaves brought their Indigenous religious traditions, which included Islam, with them to Bermuda. Given the heavy representation of Muslim West Africa in Bermuda's slaving ventures, it would be highly unlikely that Islam would not be represented among these religious practices.[18] But by 1789, Bermuda had halted its practice of importation of African slaves. And, as elsewhere in the African diaspora, maintaining African cultural practices through a connection to the continent became exceedingly difficult. As African-born enslaved people in Bermuda died, they left their children and grandchildren to piece together a patchwork quilt of the cultural and religious expressions that they had been taught in secret.[19] Over time, these connections ruptured, and the majority of Black people in Bermuda adopted Anglicanism, the British state religion.

In the mid-1950s, when a young Black man named Dilton Matthews packed his bags and left Bermuda for New York, there was no known community of Muslim believers in Bermuda. But misfortune followed Matthews, and he found himself in Harlem homeless, hungry, freezing cold, and lured by the warmth and tantalizing aromas of an Ahmadiyya-run soup kitchen. It was there that the Caribbean intersected once again with African America, South Asia, and the African diaspora. At the soup kitchen, Matthews met an Eritrean man named Ibrahim Goula who, as he had no doubt done countless times before, introduced this poor, young, Black man to Islam. Matthews took the name Sayeed Ramadan, symbolically shedding his old identity and joining himself to the global Muslim community.[20]

Ramadan was Bermuda's first-known Muslim convert of the twentieth century.[21] In 1957, he returned to Bermuda and attempted to spread the message of Ahmadi Islam, but no matter how hard he tried—in contrast to the Black neighborhoods of Chicago and Detroit—Ramadan's message did not translate to the Black Bermudian community. Perhaps, as some who knew Matthews have suggested, it was the island's deeply entrenched Anglicanism that proved to be an insurmountable barrier.[22] But more likely, the political climate was not yet ripe. The frustration and rage that would soon characterize the island's civil rights movement had not yet reached its boiling point. And so, Islam did not present itself as a viable alternative to Christianity until two years later, when the island was engulfed in racial tension and civil rights protests.

For people of color throughout the Atlantic world, World War II sparked conversations about rights, racial subjugation, and independence. Bermuda was no exception, and throughout the 1940s, Black Bermudians were demanding the right to vote, to hold gainful employment, to have equal protection under the law, to be represented in government, and to live free from poverty. These efforts were organized primarily through Bermuda's labor unions, the largest of which, the Bermuda Industrial Union (BIU), was formed in 1947.[23] By the 1950s, however, there had been few changes in the legal and social status of the island's Black majority, who still would not "dare to look a white man in the face."[24] This was the Bermuda that Ramadan left when he went back to the United States in early 1959.[25]

This time, Ramadan's destination was Chicago, a target of the Great Migration and a city that by the end of the decade had become a hotbed of Black Muslim radicalism and the headquarters of the Nation. Ramadan arrived exactly at a moment when the Nation was at the front and center of the Black and mainstream media, and he was in the perfect city to be completely immersed in Elijah Muhammad's message. Ramadan himself was the ideal convert to the Nation's vision of Islam. He had already been primed by the Ahmadi message, and now young, Black, poor, colonized, and attuned to conversations about Black rights and freedom, he was ready for the Nation's particularist Islamic practice.[26]

This time, when Ramadan returned to Bermuda in late 1959, he was in luck. In the summer and fall of 1959, two events transformed Bermudian racial politics. The first was a boycott forcing the island's theaters to desegregate. And the second was a strike of 320 mostly Black workers on the white-owned stevedoring firms that employed the workers who loaded and unloaded the cargo ships that were the foundation of Bermuda's economy.[27] Although less explicitly about race than the theater boycott, the dock strike of 1959 was about the triumph of Black working-class labor over white financial interests, and it weakened the position of the white oligarchy. The success of these movements was minimized by Americans as a "mild and happy revolution," but in truth there was nothing "mild" about the theater boycott or the dock strike.[28] These two events were together the spark that kicked off an intense period of racially motivated political activity in Bermuda and the kindling that allowed for Ramadan's teachings to finally take root.[29]

After the boycott, Ramadan's small group of Muslims began to organize themselves in Hamilton and, sometime in 1960, began selling *Muhammad Speaks*. Although the authorities would soon become aware of the newspaper, there is no government record that any white government official knew about, or was in any way threated by, distribution of *Muhammad Speaks* in 1960. At this point, they most likely had no idea that the newspaper was on the island, or that it was being brought by the crews of the cruise ships that docked in Hamilton's port—and that were supporting the island's tourist industry by the late 1950s. These employees were often the American relatives of Bermudian Muslims who transported the message of Black nationalist Islam in neat stacks next to their socks and uniforms. The newspapers were then distributed across Bermuda to followers and fellow travelers by Sayeed Ramadan and the small, but loyal, cadre of Muslims he had amassed.

In addition to the Nation, the Ahmadiyya movement was active on the island during this period. In April of 1960, its presence first came to the attention of the FCO, which noticed distribution of a pamphlet from the Ahmadiyya sect the Muslim Brotherhood USA, titled *The Negro: Man or Myth?*, from a local bookstore. The writers of the pamphlet beseeched the reader to join the organization, which it described as one "dedicated to the spread of Islam and to the elevation of the Black man in America—so that once more he will be able to hold his head up, standing shoulder to shoulder with the rest of mankind."[30] Bermudian and British authorities mistakenly attributed these pamphlets to the Nation.

Catalyzed by the theater boycott's success, in 1960, the matter of universal franchise came into mainstream conversation. Until the early 1960s, Bermuda's franchise had not explicitly excluded Black Bermudians but had vested the right to vote exclusively in the hands of landed property owners. This, by default, excluded the vast majority of Black Bermudians from the polls. With parallel conversations about voting rights taking place in the United States, Black middle-class politicians unsuccessfully began to enter into a series of conversations with Parliament to convince them to extend the franchise to all.

By September of 1960, frustrated by these failures, a group of Black working-class men led by Roosevelt Brown, who had been educated in the United States at Howard University, formed a coalition called the Committee for Universal Adult Suffrage (CUAS).[31] Gramophone recordings of Louis Farrakhan's "A White Man's Heaven is a Black Man's Hell" were regularly played at the organization's private meetings, providing in a sense, a soundtrack for their political activities.[32] Although it is not clear that CUAS and the Nation shared membership, it is evident that the Nation's ideas influenced CUAS's campaign for full citizenship and political representation. Its efforts were only partially successful; by 1962, Parliament eliminated the requirement of real property but allowed freeholders an additional vote.[33]

The promise of universal suffrage paved the way to the creation of political parties for the first time in Bermuda's history. Bermuda's Nation was part of early conversations to establish a politically active group of Black Bermudians. These attempts were tied to the island's labor movement and were solidified in the creation of a short-lived political party called the Bermuda United Workers Party (BUWP), which was controlled by members of the Nation and the British Communist Party. This relationship between labor radicalism, communism, and the Nation of Islam is extremely unusual, and there is no evidence that these dynamics have been replicated anywhere else in the world. As an institutional position, the Nation was actively capitalist and supported the building of Black business, the accumulation of wealth, and the cultivation of Black self-sufficiency as a way to overcome white supremacy and attain spiritual salvation. Communism and Marxism were antithetical to these goals. Even when presented with leaders of formerly colonized countries who were openly anti-American but communist—like Fidel Castro, for example—the Muhammad and the Nation often struggled to place them within their geography of imperial resistance.

While there is no evidence that members of the Nation adopted or espoused communist or socialist ideologies, the mere fact that they saw themselves in solidarity with communists is instructive. This unique relationship is a result of the structure of Bermuda's economy and the high concentration of working-class Black people in the island's trade unions. In addition, even though Nation members may not have been reading Marx, Bermudian and British authorities observed that, together with communists in the BUWP, Nation members appeared to be preparing themselves for violent action. Reports were regularly received by the British Police Services' Special Branch in Bermuda that BUWP members, including those who held membership in the Nation, had begun instructing their ranks in the use and manufacturing of explosive devices and had discussed the deployment of these incendiary devices on private property.[34] It is unclear how credible these reports were.

By August of 1963, at the very latest, the BUWP was defunct. In its place, the less radical Progressive Labour Party (PLP) rose to prominence and became the island's first officially recognized political party in February 1963. The PLP identified its agenda as one that was intended to serve the interests of ordinary, working-class, liberal Bermudians. At its founding, 98 percent of the PLP's membership identified as Black, and it continued to be supported by almost exclusively Black Bermudians throughout the 1960s and 1970s.[35] Black Bermudians used the PLP together with labor radicalism, Black nationalist Islam, and militant Black Power to attack the racial hierarchies entrenched in Bermudian social and political structures. Together these organizations, and their members, worked to achieve a shared vision of Black Bermudian freedom and colonial independence. This vision was articulated for the first time publicly in January 1967, when the PLP published fifteen key points of their platform in the *Bermuda Recorder*. The party members who drafted this statement identified their mission as one to "transform Bermuda into a place where . . . the enlightened spirit of the Common Man replaces the rank odour of Corrupt Materialism."[36] This metaphorical stench of oppression and racial capitalism would only be eliminated by implementing universal health care, affordable housing, living wages, and eliminating import duties on groceries and other necessities, in addition to Bermuda's full independence from Great Britain.[37] Together, these would result in an environment in which Bermuda would "flourish to its maximum" economically, politically, and socially. In response, the opposition in Parliament created the United Bermuda Party (UBP), representing the conservative interests of the ruling class.[38]

Amid these social and political developments, Ramadan had absconded from Bermuda. In September 1962, he stowed away on the *Queen of Bermuda* cruise ship—perhaps assisted by the same crew members who smuggled *Muhammad Speaks* on board—and illegally entered the United States. He was subsequently discovered and imprisoned by American immigration authorities.[39] But even without Ramadan, Islam held on. During the two years of Ramadan's absence, Black Bermudian Muslims met in their homes, largely out of the government's gaze. For this reason, the government recorded small numbers of active Muslims, and their presence in official papers appears equally diminutive. Nevertheless, during the entirety of Ramadan's absence, the Bermudian colonial government anxiously observed the Nation and its burgeoning connections with the island's labor movement.

The Nation of Islam, Radical Labor, and Black Power

In 1964, after serving out his sentence for illegal entry into the United States, Ramadan was deported home to Bermuda. He returned at a critical inflection point in Bermuda's Black freedom movement, and Bermudian authorities were terrified about what his release from prison portended. The four years that Ramadan spent in prison were during the peak of the American civil rights movement, an era when America's growing prison population included civil rights and Black Power activists.[40] Increasingly, they also included converts to the Nation of Islam. Imprisoned together, these prisoners shared ideas, discourses, and tactics, as they had in decades prior.[41] The official government documents on the Nation in Bermuda do not tell us much about where Ramadan was imprisoned or who he was with at the time. The people who knew and followed him have not mentioned any impact of his incarceration on his political ideology. But an experience like incarceration in the United States, during this era in world history, must have had some impact on his leadership, his ideas, and his worldview.[42] At home as well, robust conversations about racial equality and equal rights were being forced in Parliament by the PLP. During this period, under Ramadan's leadership, the Nation increased in visibility, even if not in membership, becoming a primary preoccupation of the colonial authorities.

In 1965, British and Bermudian authorities finally took notice of the sale of *Muhammad Speaks* by Ramadan and his associates.[43] Public consciousness and general fear of the Nation began to grow as its visibility increased. In this year, articles and opinion pieces on the Nation's activities regularly appeared in Bermuda's newspaper of record, the *Royal Gazette*. The vast majority of concerns from the white public and Bermudian and British colonial governments dealt with the possibility that *Muhammad Speaks* contained "hate speech," a strong anticolonial message, "racial propaganda," and the potential for inciting race riots.[44] The governor of the colony, in a report to the secretary of state for the colonies, averred in no uncertain terms that the Black Muslims were "a danger to the peace and harmony of [Bermuda]" and vowed to carefully monitor their activities.[45] In July 1965, in response to growing anxiety over the growth of the Nation's membership and the fear that racial uprisings might break out, the government banned *Muhammad Speaks* under the Prohibited Publications Act.[46] This was the beginning of a prolonged campaign of persecution against Bermuda's Nation members for their religious beliefs, anti-imperial stance, and political activism.

In the immediate months following the ban of *Muhammad Speaks*, government officials reported that there had been "little public reaction" in the form of open protest, and that Black Muslims had "accepted quietly the banning of their newspaper ... [and] intended to abide by the order and to destroy copies of the paper in their possession."[47] Despite the ban, however, papers continued to flow into Bermuda, smuggled by sea, air, and even accidentally by mail, belying the government's observation of disinterest among Black Bermudians. Through some bureaucratic glitch, former Nation member Norwood Salaam—then Norwood X Dowling—continued to openly receive *Muhammad Speaks* via post until its last issue in 1975. He was a special case (figure 4.1).[48] Most Muslims were not so lucky to have the newspaper delivered to their doorstep. Instead, an underground market began to develop as the same distribution networks that were open before the ban—mostly cruise ships like the *Ocean Monarch* and the *Queen of Bermuda*—continued to operate surreptitiously, often through their international crews. Occasionally, members would take extended trips to the United States, and instead of souvenirs, they would bring back suitcases filled with *Muhammad Speaks* newspapers. Scarcity made the papers nearly as valuable as currency.[49]

Although access was possible, sale and possession of the newspaper were criminal offenses by jail time, as the case of Milton Hill's arrest at the Hamilton Docks demonstrates. Similarly, one of Ramadan's first converts, Kenneth Castle Muhammad, fled from police holding an armful of the newspapers he was offering for sale. Castle knew that he had to dispose of the contraband or risk jail time, so he jettisoned the newspapers by throwing them into an active construction site and kept running.[50] Gary Perinchief left the police force five years after he witnessed Hill's arrest and assault at the docks and joined the Nation. After obtaining newspapers via cruise ship distribution networks,

FIGURE 4.1 A stack of *Muhammad Speaks* newspapers (2015) mistakenly delivered to Norwood Salaam.

Perinchief hid them under the floorboards of his attic.[51] Even Salaam, who had no problems acquiring the newspapers, dared not be seen with them in public or non-Muslim private spaces. He rented a storage space down the street from his home where he kept the papers out of prying eyes.[52] As all these men knew very well, jail time was a real possibility for those found with *Muhammad Speaks* in their possession. But despite this danger, members of Bermuda's Nation kept importing them, selling them, distributing them, reading them, and saving them. Forty years later, there are members who possess every copy they hid during the darkest days of the ban.[53] These small acts of defiance in enjoying and spreading Islam were ways of deploying their religio-racial understanding of the world in order to slowly chip away at the Bermudian racial hierarchy and the British system of institutionalized subjugation. This was a system in which the British, and the oligarchy via the UBP, were deeply invested in preserving.

Labor Radicalism, Islam, and Independence

By the time the Bermudian government was in active panic over the Nation's rise in Bermuda, other British dependencies had already gained sovereignty.

Trinidad and Tobago and Jamaica achieved independence in 1962; and Barbados and British Guiana in 1966. Bermuda, however, remained firmly in the grasp of the British Crown. As the Bermudian colonial government recognized the nexus between the growth of pro-independence politics, Black radicalism, and dissatisfaction with the censorship of *Muhammad Speaks*, Nation members repeatedly appeared in FCO documents. These actors were in the thick of politically charged discussions regarding Bermudian independence, the effects of government censorship, and the role of the labor movement on the island.[54]

By 1967, Bermuda's Nation had established itself in its first permanent mosque on Angle Street in Hamilton and, according to the intelligence community, had usurped the leadership of the Bermuda Dock Workers Union (BDWU), a division of the BIU that had grown to be the strongest and most influential union on the island. Intelligence officials observed that the BDWU was "under Black Muslim leadership," with three Nation members at its helm, in control of other BIU subsidiaries, or wielding considerable influence in some way. Nation members Albert Johnston and Carlton Burchall were president and vice president, respectively, of the BDWU in 1967. In 1968, Burchall was elected president of the Longshoremen's Division of the BIU. Kenneth Castle Muhammad, who was already on the radar of law enforcement for his visible and flagrant violations of the propaganda laws, was an extremely active member of the union, even though he did not hold office in the BIU. For years prior to the founding of the mosque on Angle Street, Castle and Burchall had fought a more moderate faction of the BIU for control of the union. This moderate faction pledged to work with the existing government, including UBP members.[55]

Every aspect of Bermuda's economy and culture is related to the sea, and thus, the maintenance of the commercial enterprises and labor that extract resources from the ocean are of critical importance to the nation's leadership. Thus, at this moment, when Burchall, Johnston, and Castle rose to leadership in the BIU, the government, still smarting from the dock strike of 1959, began watching closely. In 1967, when 30 percent of the union's active membership supported a petition circulated by Castle and Ramadan to lift the government's ban on *Muhammad Speaks*, the Bermudian government immediately began to map out how deeply the Nation had penetrated the ranks of the BIU.[56] BIU leadership denied that it supported, endorsed, or had any knowledge of Burchall and Castle's petition, but given the fact that these men were themselves high ranking, this is unlikely. Burchall was both vice president of the BDWU and one of the key sources for Nation information on the island, and it was Castle who had recruited Burchall and Johnston to the Nation earlier in the decade. Beginning in 1965, Burchall was responsible for the importation of Nation books and broadcasts and was the key point of contact between the Bermudian Nation of Islam and the United States.[57] In June 1968, he was personally responsible for the importation of forty-eight copies of the Nation publication, *Message to the Blackman*.[58]

It wasn't just Castle and Burchall's petition that was fanning the flames of the government's anxieties. In June, the Longshoremen's Division of the BIU absorbed all of the members of the BDWU, effectively giving the union the ability to cripple the entire economy of the colony with coordinated labor strikes.[59] The BDWU was also on the cusp of issuing a statement officially supporting the PLP, and thereby a fully democratic and independent Bermuda, a prospect that the governor defined as "ominous ... and alarming."[60] Under the leadership of Burchall, Johnston, and Castle, the BIU and the BDWU became deeply allied with the PLP and remained under Nation control for the remainder of the decade and into the early 1970s.[61]

Ultimately, efforts to have the ban lifted on *Muhammad Speaks* were ineffective. The UBP-led government enacted the ban with the stated purpose of keeping racial tension at bay. Of course, the actual causes of racial tension—unemployment, racial discrimination, police violence, and disenfranchisement—went unaddressed, and tension continued to brew. As a result of the government's unwillingness to address the structural causes of racial tension in Bermuda, a series of racially and politically motivated uprisings swept the island in April 1968.

On April 25, the island hosted its annual Floral Pageant, an event for tourists featuring elaborate displays of flowers adorning a parade of floats. After the pageant, a group of Black youths attempted to gain entry to the Fair of All, a separate charity event held at a municipal building in Hamilton. After being denied entry to the fair by a white police officer on the grounds that the hall was at full occupancy, the officer admitted several white people. When two of the Black youths forced their way inside, they were met with physical violence, forceful ejection from the premises, and arrest. Later that day, when a Black police officer admitted a Black man, the man was nonetheless asked to leave and, when he refused, was assaulted and subsequently arrested by a white police officer. In response, a crush of Black youths—who had been attracted to the main tourist throughfare, Front Street, because of the pageant and the fair—stormed the police station, kicking off a two-day-long uprising by approximately three hundred young Black men who threw Molotov cocktails and glass bottles at law enforcement and set ablaze public and private property. These men were held off by police wielding riot shields, truncheons, and tear gas.[62] In response, the governor responded by deploying the police, calling a state of emergency, setting an eleven-day curfew, and requesting security backup for the British.[63]

Of the 141 people arrested for violating curfew and other "related offenses" during the Floral Pageant Uprisings, two were identified at the time as known members of the Nation. In a report issued four years later in 1972, however, the FCO noted that "several members of the Nation... were leaders of riots in 1968," although the report did not indicate who.[64] In 1968, the core membership of the organization was recorded by the FCO as approximately fifteen. This number may have been an underestimate, but nonetheless, the actual number of people the intelligence community was talking about may have not been more than a handful. At minimum, this observation by the FCO goes to the government's perception—and perhaps even the reality—of the disproportionate role of Nation members in stoking the uprisings.

The Floral Pageant Uprisings of 1968 took place a mere three weeks after the assassination of Dr. Martin Luther King Jr. rocked the United States and stoked urban rebellions from Washington, DC, to Paris.[65] The FCO did not cite the assassination of King as an instigating factor, but it is difficult to believe that given the long history of communication and the extent to which Bermuda's civil rights movement was in solidarity with, and inspired by, the American Black freedom movement, that this tragedy did not bring Black Bermudians to a boiling point. It is equally unbelievable that the infectious nature of America's freedom movement, which the colonial authorities had cited several times, and the proliferation of uprising and revolution globally, were not on the government's mind as it responded to these uprisings with police violence and arrests.[66] As Bermudians often say of the ease with which ideas pass from the United States to their island in the middle of the Atlantic, "When America sneezes, Bermuda catches a cold."[67]

Black Power and Black Islam

In the aftermath of the Floral Pageant Uprisings, the British maintained a façade of utter surprise at the events of April 1968. They maintained that the uprisings appeared to have no real racial or political motivation, even though Bermudians clearly expressed the opinion that the immediate cause of the uprisings was a combination of police brutality and the banning of the *Muhammad Speaks* newspaper.[68] In addition to these opinions, PLP members blamed the uprisings on larger institutional and structural issues, like colonialism and the lack of educational facilities for Black Bermudians.[69] After temperatures had slightly cooled and the governor was confident that "order" had been restored, the FCO, at the urging of the Bermudian government, convened a panel into the April "disturbances."[70] The panel, headed by Afro-Barbadian lawyer and politician Hugh Wooding, was tasked with inquiring into the causes of the civil disturbances, reporting its findings, and making appropriate recommendations. The words "disturbance" and "disorder" appear repeatedly throughout the commission's report. This language is commonly used in British legal texts when describing policy recommendations after racially based uprisings, but it indicates an extremely narrow and racialized conception of "social order," which can be easily "disturbed" by any instance of nonwhite people challenging their placement in the racial hierarchy.[71]

When the Wooding Commission issued its findings, it came to a completely different conclusion than that initially reached by the British. It cited clear racial and political motivations for the uprisings and noted two contributing factors—the presence of Black Power on the island and the ban on *Muhammad Speaks*. These two elements, Black Power and Black Islam, were viewed as inextricably intertwined, and nearly synonymous, in the eyes of the British FCO and Bermudian Intelligence. The Wooding Commission had ultimately concluded that racial tension had been "arrested" and that there was "no need for fear."[72] Despite this, surveillance documents indicate that neither the British nor the Bermudian colonists were prepared to "Keep Calm and Carry On."[73] They began to closely monitor this relationship between Black Power and Black Islam in Bermuda, searching for a way to prevent these "disturbances" from reoccurring without making any structural changes within the country.

The push for structural change from the bottom, however, continued. In 1969, plans for a Black Power Conference were discussed among members of the PLP and spearheaded by Roosevelt Brown—as an elected Parliamentary representative and member of the PLP—and the PLP's Youth Wing. The PLP had appealed to Nation members because of its strong pro-Black, pro-independence, anti-British message, and the conference, which was restricted to Black participants only, held the same pull.[74] The appeal was not one-sided. There was much cross-pollination and mixing between the PLP and the Nation. Many members of the PLP, including Brown, had long been influenced by the Black nationalist, separatist message of the Nation, even if they did not join the organization. Young Black Bermudians, in particular, were drawn to the Nation, and the government viewed them as particularly vulnerable to the message of radicalized Black Islam.[75] These young Black people, therefore, were seen by the government and by the Nation as a key demographic that could potentially topple the colonial order.

In preparation for the meeting, which was scheduled for July of 1969, Brown traveled throughout the Circum-Caribbean and to the United States, Mexico, and Canada in order meet with both prominent Black nationalist and Black Muslim leaders.[76] On Brown's trip to the United States, he intended to meet with a Black nationalist and Black Muslim named Abu Ahmed, or James Harvey Thomas. There is no further information available on Ahmed, and we do not know which movements he was affiliated with, but Brown's attempts to contact him are indicative of his internal thinking on the matter. In Brown's mind—as in the minds of FCO and Bermudian government officials—Black Power and Black Islam were connected. In addition, the African diasporic perspective was crucial to Brown as he planned the conference.[77]

In Bermuda, Brown often held forums for PLP Youth Wing members on the subject of Black Power. Out of two hundred attendees, approximately twelve to fifteen members of the Nation were in attendance. According to official records, this was a substantial part of the membership of the organization at the time, as average recorded regular mosque attendance was only about six as of January 1969.[78] However, this small number may have been due to increased government surveillance and the desire of Nation members to remain out of the government's eye. Even Brown's associations outside of the context of the Black Power Conference indicate this nexus between Black Power and Black Islam, and he often used his social and political clout on the island to affect these relationships. In the late 1960s or early 1970s, in response to his belief that the political education of Bermuda's youth was at stake, Brown brought Catherine X, a woman associated with the Nation's Philadelphia mosque, to teach at Sandy's Secondary School in the southwestern portion of the island.[79] Brown had previously made previous comments the island was being made into a "garbage dump" for elementary and secondary school teachers who had been in the colonial service and that such "garbage dumping should be stopped" immediately. Redirecting the colonial narrative in education was a principal concern of not only Brown but also the PLP more generally throughout the 1960s and 1970s.[80]

As conference plans solidified in mid-1969, Bermudian government anxieties rose.[81] Citing previous violence during Black Power events on other Caribbean islands, the possibility of irreparable damage to "tourism and race relations"—in that order—and fears that the Black Power Conference would produce "nothing but trouble," Bermuda beseeched the British government to find any loophole it could to prevent or delay the conference. At a minimum, Bermuda requested that Britain ban particularly subversive international Black Power leaders from entering the island.⁸² The British could find no legal means of doing so, and therefore, despite extensive government attempts to frustrate it, the Black Power Conference took place from July 10–13, 1969.⁸³ In response, the Bermudian government launched an extensive surveillance operative with Black informants and undercover agents posing as sympathetic or curious conference participants. British troops were installed, at Bermuda's expense, to maintain order and prevent a reprise of the previous year's uprisings.⁸⁴

The conference, with panels on Black economics, religion, politics, and psychology, was positioned by those who organized it as a smashing success.⁸⁵ The numbers alone seem to support some level of success in reaching interested Black Bermudians. Approximately one thousand unique people were admitted to conference events in total, and daily attendance fluctuated from between three and six hundred attendees with the sessions on Black history and religion attracting the largest audiences. The closing plenary session alone was attended by over four hundred people, including a significant number of high-profile scholars and activists, like British Marxist historian C.L.R. James, who was one of 110 foreign participants.⁸⁶ The British, on the other hand, argued that the numbers had been inflated by people who were curious of, but not committed to, the cause of Black Power.⁸⁷ In the aftermath of the conference, Governor Lord Martonmere argued that the conference had left "scars" on the island and widened the chasm between Black and white Bermudians.⁸⁸

For Black people, however, the synergies between the PLP Youth Wing and the Nation continued, and members of these organizations maintained close contact with each other. In September 1969, for example, Woodrow Wilson, a Nation member and the nephew of Sayeed Ramadan, gave a speech at PLP headquarters to a group of approximately twelve youths instructing them on methods for making Molotov cocktails, just like they had during the Floral Pageant Uprisings.⁸⁹ In the face of government interference, instead of circumscribing their liberation activities, Black Bermudians chose to build new movements and strengthen existing connections, and this included the relationship between Black Islam and Black Power, which grew ideologically and geographically closer in the summer following the Black Power Conference of 1969.

The Left Door or the Right Door?

In the summer of 1969, a group of young Bermudians between the ages of sixteen and thirty gathered under the leadership of John Hilton "Bobbie" Bassett Jr. to form the Black Beret Cadre (BBC), an organization modeled on the American Black Panther Party (BPP).[90] The youth who gathered under the banner of the BBC were from diverse socioeconomic backgrounds, but they all experienced a political awakening that convinced them that revolution was the only means forward for Black Bermudians and that this revolution should be obtained through "peace if possible," but ultimately seized by "any means necessary."[91] Like the American BPP, the BBC had a multi-point program that it adapted to its unique historical and political circumstances. BBC members demanded freedom, sovereignty, housing, education, jobs, an end to police brutality, and justice. Indeed, the message of the BBC was incredibly similar to that of Bermuda's Nation, with two key exceptions. One, the BBC eschewed religion and "religious escapism" by Black Bermudians. Second, the BBC's revolution involved the elimination of the racial capitalism it believed was intimately linked with the colonization of Bermuda and the subjugation of its Black population.[92] Nevertheless, the unity of purpose was great enough that some Nation members elected to send their children to the BBC's Malcolm X Liberation School in addition to their standard public or parochial school education.[93] Meeting on Saturdays between 10:30 A.M. and 12:15 P.M., children were taught general Black global history, self-defense, in addition to receiving instruction on the realities of environmental racism, police violence, and colonial oppression.[94]

The BBC and the Nation shared an ease of ideological cross-pollination that was facilitated through not only by their ideological proximity but also their geographical closeness. In 1969 and 1970, the Nation and the BBC shared a meeting space in a building in Downtown Hamilton called the Bassett Building. Upon walking up to the building stairs, the entrant had two choices—to either walk through a door to the left or to the right (figure 4.2).[95] In the lefthand meeting space, BBC members heard an American Black Power–inspired message of Black liberation, anti-capitalism, and anticolonialism.[96] On the right, Nation adherents heard a spiritually grounded message that taught that Islam was the way out of colonial subjugation and white oppression. Thus, any Black person who was dissatisfied with their subjugated status in Bermuda needed only to go to the Bassett Building and choose which door, and which movement, spoke most clearly to them. Using the words and memories of former Bermuda Nation members, this section elaborates on how the Nation—over the BBC—became a powerful means by which Afro-Bermudian people navigated their identities as Black, colonized, and African diasporic subjects.

With a clear similarity of purpose and shared disdain for Bermuda's colonial government, families and friends often found themselves at odds over

FIGURE 4.2 The Bassett Building (2015) showing the left and right doors that the Nation of Islam and Black Beret Cadre used to use.

their exact vision of what a revolution in Bermuda would entail. Radical and expansive change to the Bermudian racial hierarchy was, of course, one of the reasons that Bermudians found themselves at the Bassett Building. But with two options that promised to effect racial liberation, the question became: How did Black Bermudians make a choice to go left or right? Even though Nation members had been deeply involved with Bermudian politics for a decade before the founding of the BBC, Black Bermudians who converted to Islam through the Nation remember their choice as one between religious nonviolence and political radicalism. Approximately fifty years later, as they recounted these stories, the choices that Bermuda's Nation members made between violence and nonviolence likely seem much more black and white than they were at the time. Nation members did openly advocate the use of explosive devices like Molotov cocktails, were engaged in physical altercations with the police, and actively participated in uprisings.

Nevertheless, the promise of a nonviolent revolution driven by religion and spirituality was the primary factor that prompted Bermudians to walk through the Bassett Building's righthand door and up the stairs to the Nation's meeting space. Milton Hill, for example—whose assault by the Bermudian police begins this chapter—had been a Nation member since the early 1960s. A shipbuilder by trade, Hill was born in 1943, as labor radicals organized the island's overwhelmingly Black workers against white industrialists.[97] As a sixteen-year-old on the brink of adulthood, Hill was witness to the desegregation of Bermuda's public spaces as a result of the theater boycott and dock strike of 1959. Like the Bermudians who drove the theater boycott, Hill recognized that Black capital and labor were expropriated under British colonialism in order to support the island's economy. As a shipbuilder, he knew that his physical labor was used to build the vessels that supported Bermuda's maritime economy, and the ships coming into the harbor on a daily basis were for him a constant reminder of the exploitation of "black labor to build white wealth."[98]

As a young man and into adulthood, Hill carried with him a lesson that his father taught him—that he could never expect to "get justice when the devil's the judge." The question still remained, however: Could justice ever be served for Black Bermudians? Despite the success of the theater boycott and the dock strike, Black Bermudians were "subservient to people in [their] own country," and a mere glance at their passports served as a reminder that they carried the credentials of subjects, not citizens.[99] Hill looked to the United States for inspiration. And given the intensified push for civil rights in Bermuda, Hill and others who fell in line under Ramadan's leadership of the

Nation recognized that Islam provided a plausible blueprint to an "aggressive," but nonviolent, "way to bring about the revolution," a revolution that would transform the subjugated status of Bermuda's majority Black population and see it gain independence as a sovereign nation. For Hill, it was the Nation, and not the BBC, that could accomplish this. It wasn't that he wasn't aware of the organization or its message. To the contrary, Hill knew about the BBC and often saw its members linger on the sidewalk outside of the Bassett Building. However, in his eyes, the BBC's radical political and social agenda lacked a religious and spiritual element. Even as his neighbors and friends tried to convince him to listen to Bassett speak about fomenting an anticolonial and racial revolution in Bermuda, Hill was never motivated to attend a BBC meeting. The Nation's religio-political platform provided him with personal fulfillment, and its social teachings led to financial gain—he was lucky enough to own a lucrative Muslim restaurant, called a "Steak and Take," which he opened with two other partners in 1971. In 1973, after personality conflicts with the Bermudian Nation's leader, Byron Philip, Hill was excommunicated from the organization. He left the religion entirely and never returned to Islam.[100]

The small number of men who had converted to Islam under Sayeed Ramadan in the early 1960s were less likely to experiment with the BBC than vice versa. Early members Kenneth Castle Muhammad, Carlton Burchall, and Albert Johnston, all contemporaries of Hill, do not appear to have been swayed by the message of the BBC, at least not in any meaningful way. This loyalty to the Nation may have to do with several factors, not least of which include their age at the time of the founding of the BBC in 1969. Hill was about twenty-six when the BBC was founded, and he certainly had more responsibilities than the average BBC teenager. He was a married man with a stable family life, including a wife and children, by the late 1960s. The Nation supported this vision of the strong Black family, and although the BBC also emphasized the importance of a healthy Black family, its overall message advocated radical tactics to bring about a revolution, including armed insurrection if necessary. Older Bermudians seemed to balk at the BBC's tactics, even those who, in theory, supported the BBC's right to form their own vision of Black freedom in Bermuda. Even the more radical members of the PLP who had organized and supported Bermuda's Black Power Conference were among this contingent. Roosevelt Brown, for instance, did not join the BBC, but he believed that the members who were severing ties with the PLP's Youth Wing were engaging in a legitimate "programme of militant activity designed at breaking the [established] power structure."[101] In addition, the age of these older Nation members likely made them less attractive as recruits to the BBC, as the organization "tightly controlled" who they admitted, were not "anxious to increase their numbers[,] and [were] selective over who they accepted for membership."[102] The organization openly balked at influence from the political establishment or from "adults," thus making the adults who had converted to the Nation early on very unlikely BBC targets.

Unlike older adults like Hill, the Bermudian teenagers and young adults who sought revolutionary change were not monogamous as they explored the best methods for bringing Bermuda to the brink of revolution. Often the conversations they had with themselves as they parsed out which movement to associate themselves with had to do with what they wanted to become culturally, politically, and racially. Najiyyah Shamsiddeen, for instance, looked at her choice between the BBC and the Nation as a decision over whether she wanted to be a "cultural nationalist, a [political] revolutionary, or a Muslim."[103] Shamsiddeen grew up in Warwick parish, centrally located east of Hamilton, as the daughter of a politically active and Black-conscious business owner. Shamsiddeen's father committed himself fully to civil rights both in Bermuda and elsewhere in the African diaspora. In August of 1963, he was among the more than 250,000 people who gathered at the historic March on Washington and heard Dr. Martin Luther King Jr. deliver his famed "I Have a Dream" speech. In May 1968, after the elimination of additional votes for freeholders in Bermudian elections, Shamsiddeen's parents' living room served as the staging ground for a massive voter registration drive. As Black Bermudians came to register and cast their votes, Shamsiddeen physically carried their ballots and registrations to the polls. It was an easy transition, thus, to the PLP's Youth Wing. After she graduated from high school, Shamsideen spent six months in New York and New Jersey, where she nurtured her African roots and identity through spending time at the National Dance Theater, sporting an afro, and designing African-inspired clothing. She also fed her revolutionary spirit dodging bullets at the Black Panther Party office in New Jersey.

By 1970, Shamsiddeen found herself in a romantic relationship with Bassett and a member of the BBC, but her romantic commitment to Bassett would not keep her from exploring the Nation and its religious and spiritual means of affecting political change. One day, around 1970, she allowed herself to be convinced to attend a Nation meeting by the Fruit of Islam who milled about in front of the Nation and BBC's shared meeting space fishing for converts. In retrospect, she had, in a way, grown up with Elijah Muhammad's teachings all along. Her father brought home a copy of Muhammad's *Message to the Blackman* and displayed it prominently in their home. Before 1970,

Shamsiddeen's strategy for Black liberation was purely and expressly political. But her visit to the Nation forced her to have a serious conversation with herself about exactly how she wanted to participate in Bermuda's political transformation—culturally, politically, or religiously? Like Milton Hill's distinction between violent revolution through the BBC and nonviolent revolution through the Nation, Shamsiddeen's choice between cultural nationalism, revolutionary politics, and Islam likely seems much starker in retrospect than it was at the time. More than anything, the Nation's doctrinal teachings were part of what Shamsiddeen defines as a new avant-garde consciousness that transformed her life and ushered her into a politically inflected Islam. At the end, her choice was between the secular and the spiritual.[104] She chose the Nation's religio-political message over the purely political.

Like Shamsiddeen, her younger cousin Michelle Khaldun found herself a prominent and vocal member of the BBC through the PLP's Youth Wing. As a teenager, Michelle immersed herself in Frantz Fanon's *The Wretched of the Earth*, *The Autobiography of Malcolm X*, and Martin Luther King Jr.'s "Letter from Birmingham Jail." Through these authors and theorists, Michelle sought out a connection to Black pride and diasporic identity that had eluded her in Bermuda. As the biracial daughter of a Black woman and Bermudian white man, Michelle read the intellectuals of the African diaspora to make sense of the racially dystopian world in which she lived. It was a world where she, her Black mother, her white father, and her Black and white siblings were all treated differently because of their races and skin tones. It was a world in which even after legal desegregation, the Black side of her family would be forced to sit behind their white relatives at their neighborhood Anglican church.[105]

By the time she reached the age of fifteen, however, Michelle was prepared to challenge the Bermudian racial hierarchy, the oligarchy, and white hegemony. In the summer of 1969, Michelle transitioned from the PLP's Youth Wing to the BBC. Like Najiyyah, she was attracted to the anticolonial, pro-Black, and Black internationalist message of the BBC as well as its social uplift programs for the Bermudian Black community, which included the children's liberation school, political education, a legal defense fund, daycare, and prison outreach.[106] As a BBC member, she was visible and vocal, often speaking at rallies and leading marches. In 1970, however, Michelle too found herself persuaded to skip a BBC meeting by her parent's friend, "Uncle Sy," or early Nation member and Molotov cocktail virtuoso Woodrow Wilson. The scores of handsome, clean-cut, Black men outside of the Bassett Building didn't hurt Wilson's elevator pitch, but Khaldun followed him to the Nation's meeting space because of the intimate connection they shared as neighbors and friends on a small island. Inside the mosque, Michelle discovered a message that combined religion, spirituality, and politics, driven by what she perceived as Elijah Muhammad's "lack of fear of the establishment." This message kept her coming back week after week and prompted her to get her X—or to become an official member of the Nation—later that year.[107]

Immediately upon discovering the transformative potential of the Nation, Khaldun began to do her own fishing for converts and brought over her best friend, Wanda Perinchief. Wanda had plenty of reason to stay in the BBC—her older brothers Phil and Jerome were prominent members. Instead, Wanda joined the Nation and began to recruit her own family members, including her brother Gary, who retired from the police force in 1970 or 1971 to join the Nation, and Gary's wife, her sister-in-law, Edna.[108] This period also saw other "hard-core" BBC members, many of them women, attracted to the Nation.[109] With Wanda, Michelle, and Najiyyah among the ranks of the Muslim Girls Training (MGT), the women's auxiliary, the mosque now had a critical mass of young, unmarried women who left the BBC for the Nation, and they found themselves among a growing number of Muslims on the island.[110] Many of these women eventually left Bermuda to explore the world, finding themselves on the African continent, in the United States at the Nation's Mosque No. 7 in Harlem, and in the United Kingdom.

The ranks of the Nation, however, did not flag with the departure of these young women. By 1972, Nation membership had increased from the fifteen members the FCO cited in 1968 to at least 150 members. This prompted British Intelligence to change its opinion that the Nation was generally harmless, albeit bothersome, to a conviction that the organization "could constitute a threat to *international* security" if its membership continued to grow at the same rate.[111] Many of these new members included families and married couples who were initially less drawn by the political aspects of the religion and more compelled by the messages of "doing for self" and the centrality of the Black family. When reflecting on the reasons that they joined the Nation, these individuals were less likely to cite political or revolutionary reasons. However, this does not mean that they did not engage in political and social activism. Often, the nature of this activism revolved around combating the colonial political education of their children and reducing bullying on religious and racial grounds in educational settings.[112] Through this activism, these parents sought to reconfigure the processes by which their children thought of their national, religious, and racial identities. As we will see in the next chapter, these values would drive subsequent battles in religious education for Muslim children in Bermuda through the 1970s, 1980s, and 1990s.[113]

Winning the Battle for Hearts, Minds, and Souls

The young women who converted to Islam at the beginning of the 1970s, including Wanda, Michelle, and Najiyyah, are representative of a phenomenon that became commonplace in Bermuda. Families, friends, neighbors, and lovers often found themselves split over the best practices for fomenting revolution. The reasons that Bermudians picked one organization over the others were largely personal, and often Nation and BBC members continued to work with each other, indicating that their conflicts were minimal. In 1970, for instance, 150 BBC members intended to conduct a demonstration during which they would intentionally sell banned *Muhammad Speaks* newspapers. This demonstration does not appear to have ever happened, but the reason for this was likely that a large shipment of papers was temporarily unavailable via the usual cruise ship smuggling circuit.[114] Indeed, the BBC saw the aims of the Nation as aligned with its own and was "willing to strive hard, working hand in hand with programmes that the Muslims and [BBC] have sincerely established for the benefit of" Black people.[115]

Nevertheless, due to a combination of factors, including a change of leadership for the Nation and increased government persecution for the BBC, this was a battle that ultimately the Nation won. The Nation's initial period of growth at the beginning of the 1970s coincided with new leadership focused on bringing Bermuda's Nation in line with Elijah Muhammad's international standards. American-Bermudian Byron Philip, a man who had spent time in the United States studying under Elijah Muhammad, assumed the position of leader of the Bermudian Nation. With the assistance of Wali and Umm Salamah Muhammad, who had studied in Chicago, and others, Philip introduced a barrage of changes aligning Bermuda's temple with international expectations, including revamping the FOI, MGT, and women's General Civilization Classes.[116] Members began attending conventions by 1972 and wore uniforms tailored by Shamsiddeen.[117] With this larger organization, the Nation entered an era of prosperity and financial stability. In 1971, the Nation opened two bakeries and began to purchase plots of land for agricultural and business use. In 1972, the members opened two "Steak and Take" Muslim restaurants.[118] To manage this new influx of funds, the mosque created the position of treasurer-secretary, held by member Robert Hunt.[119] This dramatic growth in Muslim business resulted in the Bermudian government anxiously concluding that the "N.O.I. is highly organized and extremely well situated financially," adding that its ongoing "financial campaign [in the form of donations and tithing from members] is obviously designed to obtain financial independence and thus far a great deal has been achieved."[120]

Whereas the Nation exhibited a larger level of organization by 1972, the BBC's leadership was in shambles. In September 1972 and 1973, Bassett and his comrade Ottiwell Simmons Jr. were forced to leave Bermuda after a series of murders rocked the island.[121] In September 1972, police commissioner George Duckett was murdered at his home. Six months later, in March of 1973, the newly appointed governor John Sharples, his aide-de-camp, and Sharples's Great Dane, Horsa, were assassinated. Despite no evidence indicating that the BBC was involved in these murders, police brought BBC members in for questioning, detaining some for days.[122] Given the high level of surveillance and persecution of the BBC during 1973, neither Simmons nor Bassett believed he would be able to receive a fair trial in Bermuda.[123] Ultimately, two men only loosely associated with the BBC, Erskine "Buck" Burrows and Larry Tacklyn, were found responsible for the murders of Sharples and his deputy and were arrested in September of 1973.[124] Even after the arrest of Burrows, the premier of Bermuda related that the police were still under the belief that Burrows had simply been "used by well known revolutionaries," mentioning Simmons by name.[125] The increased surveillance and persecution of the BBC pushed them farther underground, reducing their public presence.[126] By contrast, the Nation continued to grow and to publicly engage in civil rights and anticolonial activism. This position of increasing power would form the basis of a new religio-political reading of the world, which adherents used to make sense of their identities as Black, Bermudian, and colonized subjects in the Atlantic world.

Conclusion

By 1975, Bermuda's Nation boasted a stable core of at least 280 members who regularly attended meetings. Some observers suspected that the FCO's estimates were artificially low and that the Nation in Bermuda may have been as large as five hundred by 1975, indicating significant growth over the decades.[127] This growth did not come without stress on the organization. Philip's domineering personality led to internal conflict and clashing egos. Conflicts abounded over the use and management of income and charitable contributions.[128]

In February of that year, Bermuda's Nation members took their annual pilgrimage to the Nation's Saviour's Day Convention in Chicago. As usual, the air crackled with excitement.[129] That year, however, instead of Muhammad coming out to greet them and the rest of his adoring followers, they were met with a somber announcement. Just hours prior, Elijah Muhammad had taken his last breath and was dead at the age of seventy-seven. In a surprise move that shocked the organization, Muhammad left the leadership of the Nation not to Louis Farrakhan, the charismatic young calypso singer who had ascended to the helm of Malcolm X's old Harlem Temple No. 7, but to his son Wallace D. Muhammad.[130]

Elijah and Wallace had long had myriad conflicts. Wallace had been exiled from the organization numerous times for criticizing his father's slowness to embrace Sunni Islam and the mainstream Muslim tradition, only to be welcomed back into his father's fold again and again. However, with Elijah now gone, Wallace was free to implement the changes he had long craved. By November, *Muhammad Speaks* had changed its name to the *Bilalian News*, meant to symbolize the connection between Black Muslims in the United States and the birthplace of Islam. The name Bilalian referred to one of the Prophet's first converts, an Ethiopian man named Bilal ibn-Rabbah.

Across the African diaspora, these changes created deep fissures in the organization as mosques and members split over the issue of the pace of the congregation's Islamization. In Bermuda, the Nation's mosque, calling itself the World Community of al-Islam in the West by 1976, was at odds with Byron Philip's refusal to implement Muhammad's changes. On one side, former Nation members held fast to Muhammad's old rituals and teachings. On the other, a new contingent of dissenters arose who took the opposite view. They felt it was taking far too long to transition to Sunnism and sought to involve leadership at the highest levels.[131] The organization eventually split into three separate entities, and lingering tensions exist almost four decades later.[132]

The story of institutional change, tension, and rupture after Wallace's ascension to leadership is one that was likely repeated numerous times throughout the Afro-Atlantic world in mosques from New York to Accra. As these Muslims sought to reestablish their faith and activism in the ashes of the Nation's demise, they would bring with them the legacy of Muslim protest and activism. In doing so, they continued to hold close the internationalism that had fueled their movements from the earliest days of their conversion and molded their Atlantic Crescent to their local and contemporary realities.

CHAPTER FIVE

The Bold Muslims We Were
Gender, Education, and Anticolonial Islam

The photographs have long gone missing. Perhaps they are crushed into the bottom of file cabinets and suitcases in attics and basements. Maybe over the decades, they succumbed to the mildew brought by Bermuda's humid winter air. But whether they were in black and white, sepia, or color, there are no remaining photographic representations of the protest that Bermuda's Masjid Muhammad Sunni community organized in front of Bermuda's Cabinet Building in 1983. No mention of it can be found in any of the island's newspapers. But despite the lack of archival evidence, every elder sister at Masjid Muhammad today has the same memory. Holding placards and hand-painted signs attached to long wooden planks, the sisters marched on government land dressed in modest leg-covering skirts and hijabs, demanding that the Ministry of Education approve their application to officially open a Muslim elementary school on the grounds of their mosque.[1] This would not be the only demonstration either. Masjid Muhammad's sisters remember that throughout the 1980s, the mosque held a series of protests at the Ministry of Education, but none of these protests made it into the public record. The sole place they live is etched into the memories of the women—and men—who made these demands to the Bermudian government.

From 1981 until 1989, Masjid Muhammad fought the Bermudian government to open a Muslim parochial school. Citing numerous concerns, including the inability of their children to maintain their Islamic identity and practice in Bermuda's public and private schools, the Muslims of Masjid Muhammad launched an eight-year jihad of words for the survival of their community and way of life. In 1981, when this fight began, most of the community's members were former members of the Nation of Islam. In 1975, upon the death of Elijah Muhammad, these Muslims experienced the community's transition to Sunni Islam under Wallace's leadership. Soon, Wallace adopted the name Warith Deen Muhammad, signaling his new role as a renewer of his father's religion. He also became political and religiously liberal. His followers would embrace their American identity. The white man would not longer be a "devil." The community would look toward the Middle East for theological guidance, all the while asserting its identity as Black North

American Muslims. In the United States, these changes resulted in Imam Muhammad's followers taking on a new, moderate, and less radical political stance.

Despite Imam Muhammad's revisions and reinterpretations, however, in Bermuda Masjid Muhammad remained politically radical as it moved into its next phase of religious practice. Their status as British colonial subjects and their identities as Black men and women in the late-twentieth-century Atlantic world continued to inform their politics and their religious practice. Throughout the 1980s, this radical political vision was channeled into the battle to open the Clara Muhammad–Bermuda Muslim (CMS-Bermuda) parochial school. In 1989, after Masjid Muhammad finally opened CMS-Bermuda, their vision of an immersive Muslim education free from colonial influence was reflected in everything from the choice of uniform to the curriculum and textbooks. The Muslims of Masjid Muhammad saw the battle to open Bermuda's Muslim school as anticolonial at its core. Both race and Islam were part and parcel of their jihad of words and a central part of the anticolonial theory that drove their nearly decade-long battle.

As a British overseas territory, Bermuda was—and still is—subject to the same educational philosophy and standards as the other colonies, territories, and protectorates throughout the British Empire. In the British Empire, Christianity has historically played a central role in educating and maintaining control over colonial subjects. In the middle of the twentieth century, even though the British government outsourced school planning to religious missionaries in their colonies, it made explicit recommendations that colonial governments should "plainly declare their moral and material support for deep and sincere [Christian] belief as the basis of all education."[2] The challenge, however, was exactly how authorities could supplant Indigenous beliefs and educational practices with "sound" Christian religious training and values. In places like West Africa, for example—where Islam is an Indigenous religious tradition—this resulted in a sharp decline of Islamic educational systems where Qur'an and hadith could be fully integrated into all aspects of a pupil's education.[3]

Writers and theorists living under the yoke of colonial rule have articulated their own experiences of the ways that colonial educational systems—in their attempts to create docile, disciplined, and loyal colonial and national subjects—configured racialized and religious others. As Frantz Fanon argued in *The Wretched of the Earth*, colonial educational systems have historically served to reinforce respect and obedience to an established order that "create[s] around the exploited person an atmosphere of submission and of inhibition."[4] These experiences were acutely felt by Indigenous colonized populations on the ground. Historically, colonized populations across the globe resisted British attempts to erase their systems of educating youth and instructing them religiously. As these populations resisted, the British lamented this trend, writing without self-reflection or self-awareness in 1953 that they had gone to great length to discover the root of this animus and how to circumvent—but notably, not to prevent or soothe— it.[5]

The efforts of Muslim parents at Masjid Muhammad are consistent with long-standing efforts by Black and Muslim colonial subjects across the British Empire to keep their traditions alive. A Muslim school allowed children to be educated with Indigenous values and without the overarching colonial mandates of Bermudian society. For the Bermudian government and the British FCO, however, the Muslim fight for a school presented a threat to the integrity of British Empire and the stability of Bermudian society.[6] This was because this school and its curriculum rejected the Bermudian government's standard ways of educating and socializing children and its preferred methods of replicating, subjugating, and disciplining colonial subjects. Instead of creating good, loyal Bermudians, CMS-Bermuda would imbue Muslim children with a particular geographical and religio-racial understanding of themselves as British subjects and citizens of the larger Atlantic world, and it tasked children with shaping their own Atlantic Crescent and their roles in it. This view would result in speedy rejections for Muslim schools in Bermuda throughout the 1980s.

The archival record documenting Masjid Muhammad's fight to open CMS-Bermuda is scattered, uneven, and in many instances, nonexistent. The limitations of colonial archives, and the silences that they produce around subaltern, vulnerable, oppressed, and female populations, are problems that historians have been grappling with for the better part of the last decade.[7] The case of Masjid Muhammad and CMS-Bermuda—Black, Muslim, and located in the middle of the Atlantic Ocean—is no different. There are some events, like the 1983 protests, that have been completely erased from this historical record. There are also incidents for which the record is incomplete, emphasizing the participation of the most vocal male members of the community and erasing the contributions of women in public (attending official meetings and debating government officials) and private (interacting with teachers, meeting debating government officials) advocacy. To be clear, all members of the Masjid Muhammad community—those with children in school and those without, new members and elders, men and women—participated in the fight to open CMS-Bermuda and the process of building CMS-Bermuda as an educational institution. But the role of Muslim women in CMS-Bermuda's fight to open a parochial school cannot be overstated, precisely because their presence is almost completely erased from the textual record.

Masjid Muhammad's 1983 protest in front of the Bermuda Cabinet—the event with which I begin this chapter—and the subsequent memories of it, present one avenue through which to investigate the significance of Sunni Black and Muslim women in anticolonial protest in the African diaspora and, particularly, the role of memory in excavating that history. Although the archival record of Masjid Muhammad's 1983 protest no longer exists, I take its existence as fact. I make this evidentiary leap because the memory of the protest lives in too many elder members of the community, and particularly in women who were pregnant during that protest (and therefore acutely aware of time and space) to have been misremembered.[8] This protest was a significant memory for the Muslims of Masjid Muhammad, both men and women, because it represented for them the manifestation of the radical roots they developed in the Nation throughout the 1960s and 1970s projected onto a Sunni Muslim future for the 1980s and 1990s.[9] Their past with the Nation, its role in the Bermudian Black freedom struggle, and the geographical solidarities it promoted, drove their ideas, their values, and their need to open CMS-Bermuda. In this chapter, memory is a critical avenue for the recovery of the past. It is a way that the unevenness of the power of archives becomes evident and the exaltation of documentary evidence as "truth" breaks down. And it is the only way that the critical role of women in the political process—both public and private—of building a Muslim school and developing an anticolonial curriculum for the education of Muslim children comes to light.

Background

By the 1983 protest, the Muslims of Bermuda—just as Muslims of African descent elsewhere in the African diaspora—had undergone several schisms, fractures, and crises. After the death of Elijah Muhammad in February 1975, his son Wallace transitioned the Nation to Sunni praxis.[10] In March 1975, Wallace declared that he would act as a *mujeddid*, just as modernist Islamic thinkers, like Mirza Ghulam Ahmad, had done in the Muslim world in the late nineteenth and early twentieth centuries.[11] Although he promised to uphold his father's teachings, Wallace alluded to the imminent evolution of the community from a "baby" Nation that needed to remain under the "private care of its mother until it [was] strong enough to go out into the broad world of" the Muslim community.[12] To this end, Wallace began to roll back the Nation's open condemnation of white people, stating that he would deemphasize the mistreatment that the Black man had received in America, stop calling the white man a "devil," allow financial contributions by whites to the organization, and seek partnerships with Arab Muslims.[13]

Wallace justified these changes by arguing that they were a logical stage in the development of the organization as a mature Muslim community. Now, however, it had come to a point where an emphasis on racial separation was "no longer necessary."[14] This marked the Nation's emergence into the "wider [Muslim] community with a clear desire to have a psychological, inspirational, and organizational impact on the entire community."[15] This statement was accompanied by a new theological direction for Wallace's Muslim community. In November, *Muhammad Speaks* ceased production and was replaced by the *Bilalian News*.[16] This shift was also meant to emphasize a symbol of Blackness that was easily recognizable by the mainstream Muslim community and was a signifier that Wallace would begin teaching directly from the Qur'an, would emphasize Islamic history, and would align the organization with his interpretation of Sunni Islam.[17] By 1976, the organization changed its name from the Nation to the World Community of al-Islam in the West (WCIW), nominally signifying its break from the past and its intention to move solidly forward into the Muslim ummah. The next year, Muhammad changed his title from supreme minister to chief imam, reflecting his role as a guide to the community rather than a supreme, infallible leader.[18] That same year, three hundred WCIW followers descended on Mecca to perform hajj as guests of the Saudi government, a marked turn from their previous ostracization by the larger Muslim community.[19]

Politically, the WCIW organizationally abandoned the Black radicalism that the Nation had practiced under the leadership of Elijah Muhammad. While Wallace Muhammad interpreted the Qur'an and the Sunnah in light of the Black experience in the West, he did not reject American identity.[20] By 1976, Wallace began to actively encourage his followers to participate in American politics, and to emphasize their identity as Americans.[21] In a departure from his father's teachings, Imam Muhammad encouraged his followers to vote. In July of 1978, a flying American flag was proudly displayed on the front page of the *Bilalian News*, and followers were encouraged to celebrate July 4th, which the newspaper called "New World Patriotism Day."[22] Together, followers were encouraged to participate in a joint recitation of the Pledge of Allegiance, positioned by Imam Muhammad as "another great and significant move in the reformation and transformation of the [WCIW's] membership into outstanding examples of model American citizens."²³ In addition, members of the community developed direct business relationships with the United States government, abandoning the Black nationalist, separatist trappings of Elijah Muhammad's Nation. For example, in 1979, Salaam International, a company run by followers of Wallace Muhammad, contracted with the United States Department of Defense to provide food service to the military.²⁴

Muslims who were in the Nation at the time of Elijah Muhammad's death and Wallace's ascension to leadership experienced an overwhelming sense of crisis. This partially stemmed from the nature and pace of the changes. For some, these changes happened too rapidly. These Muslims needed more time to think about how Islam squared with their Black, Western, colonized identities. Some had no desire to practice Sunni Islam, preferring instead the Black particularist message of the Honorable Elijah Muhammad's teachings. Many members began to protest, and others left entirely, when Wallace adjusted the Nation's policies on white membership and began to revise its religious teachings.²⁵ Others were simply tired of the internal fighting and confusion.²⁶ This sense of crisis, and the precipitous drop in membership, is reflected in the number of paid subscriptions to the *Bilalian News* in 1977, two years after the transition. In 1975, *Muhammad Speaks* boasted 900,000 paid weekly subscriptions. By 1977, paid subscriptions had depreciated by 85 percent, dropping to 132,000. The financial consequences were dire, resulting in a deficit of $150,000 per week, and nearly leading to a complete shutdown of the newspaper in April 1977.²⁷ Many of these displeased Muslims saw the transition as an opportunity to assert their own power and to coordinate their own movements.

In Bermuda, as in the rest of the African diaspora, members of the Nation grappled with whether they wanted to implement Imam Muhammad's recommendations, continue to follow Elijah Muhammad's teachings, or leave the religion. No matter which direction they elected to go, these Muslims made serious and personally intimate decisions about the type of Islam that worked for them. For those who remained with Imam Muhammad, it would be the community's location at the junction of Atlantic trading routes and as a prominent site of cruise tourism that would facilitate their transition to Sunni Islam. Indonesian Muslims working on cruise and freight ships were instrumental in the community's process of learning the Sunnah, or the ways and practices of the Prophet Muhammad, and taking *shahadah*, or declaration of faith, in the last half of the 1970s.²⁸ As in decades past, overlapping diasporas of people and ideas facilitated the transition to Sunni Islam for Bermuda's Nation members.

Sunni Muslims and Political Participation

In 1977, the Muslims following Imam Muhammad's *tafsir*, or interpretation of the Qur'an, changed their mosque's name to Masjid Muhammad and settled into their current location, a former convent located at 26 Cedar Street in Hamilton (figure 5.1).[29] I focus on Masjid Muhammad in this study because it is the oldest, largest, and most visible Muslim community on the island of Bermuda. In 1989, the community was estimated at approximately 500 with a "stable core" of between 150 and 300 members who regularly attended services.[30] Muslims are a micro-minority in Bermuda, and throughout the 1980s constituted such a small portion of the Bermudian population that they are not specifically listed among the island's religious groups. Instead, they are collapsed into the "other" category.[31] Nevertheless, in the 1980s, as in the 1960s and 1970s, Bermudian Muslims had a disproportionate political impact given their small numbers.

The masjid building itself is physically visible and located at the intersection of two major streets in the center of Hamilton. It is also the most politically active. The island boasts three other Muslim communities in addition to Masjid Muhammad, including the Nation; Masjid al-Quba, led by a Trinidadian imam named Ashmead Ali; and the Orthodox Brotherhood of Islam in Bermuda, now Salafi influenced and known as the Islamic Center of Bermuda. However, aside from Masjid al-Quba, which engaged in a brief fight for a Muslim burial ground in the 1990s, Masjid Muhammad is the only community that has repeatedly inserted itself into Bermudian political life.

As in the United States, Wallace Muhammad's revised guidance on political participation and patriotism made it possible for the members of Masjid Muhammad to embrace political participation as they reconciled their belief system with their identities as Bermudian subjects. The Muslims of Masjid Muhammad, however, never abandoned the anticolonial and anti-imperial concerns that animated their political activism as members of the Nation during the 1960s and 1970s. This legacy allowed them to continue to be "bold [and] Muslim" politically.[32] Although they embraced their identities as Bermudians, they rejected their status as British colonial subjects. Thus, for those who chose to remain under the ministry of Imam Muhammad, their politics presented as anticolonial, occasionally subversive, and driven by an understanding that their religion demanded freedom and self-determination. Again, as in the case of Bermuda's Nation in the 1960s and 1970s, the local Muslim community translated relevant discourse from movement leaders into grassroots political action that made sense for it given its geographical

FIGURE 5.1 Masjid Muhammad, 26 Cedar Street, Hamilton, Bermuda, in 2015.

realities. It remained influenced by their past as it dealt with the realities of their present.

In January 1982, Masjid Muhammad took on its first public political cause as a community—gaining government approval to build a Muslim school on the grounds of the masjid.[33] Building a school had been a long-standing goal of the community, surfacing at least once during the previous decade during the height of the Nation's popularity.[34] Although it had been discussed as early as 1971, in 1974 then Nation leader Minister Byron Philip applied to Bermuda's Ministry of Education for a grades 1 through 12 University of Islam school.[35] University of Islam schools were the Nation's means of educating children at the primary and secondary school levels from the 1950s to the 1970s. They taught standard subjects like math, science, and language arts along with theology, Black-oriented history, and Arabic.[36] In the sole surviving document submitted by Bermuda's Nation to the Ministry of Education, a letter dated August 29, 1974, Philip made explicit promises that the school would not discriminate on racial lines despite the Nation's Black supremacist teachings.[37] Nevertheless, the ministry rejected the application, citing three concerns. First, that the Nation had "specific racial denotations surrounding it." Indeed, as described in detail in the preceding chapter, the Bermudian government had heavily surveilled, censored, and attempted to repress the Nation during the 1960s and 1970s because of its dissemination of antiwhite propaganda. Second, that any increase in the number of private or parochial schools on the island would "negate attempts by the Ministry to produce sound educational planning."[38] There was no explanation or definition of "sound educational planning" in this memorandum. And third, that perhaps allowing the Nation to establish a school would prompt other groups to make similar requests in the future."[39]

In the past, the Ministry of Education had denied applications to both the Catholic Church and the Seventh Day Adventist Church, citing similar concerns about the expansion of the private school system.[40] These churches are, and were at the time of Philips's application, minority religions in Bermuda, with substantially smaller memberships than the British state-run Anglican church, to which the majority of Bermudians belong.[41] However, despite the government's stated desire to ban the opening of all religious schools entirely, it had no legal authority under which to effect this policy. In attempting to impose this ban, the government relied on an anachronistic statute titled the Schools Act of 1926 that was intended to expire decades earlier. Moreover, the Schools Act only gave the Ministry of Education limited authority to deny individual school applications, not to implement a ban on parochial schools entirely.⁴² Critically, these conversations surrounding legality do not seem to have arisen supporting the Catholic Church or the Adventist Church's application. Only the Muslim application triggered governmental anxiety around the opening of religious schools.⁴³ Similarly in the United States, jurisdictions throughout the country launched lawsuits to halt the operation of the Nation's University of Islam schools. In Detroit, for example, Nation leaders and teachers were arrested for contributing to the delinquency of minors when they persisted in sending their children to the Nation's schools despite the Board of Education's ban.⁴⁴

Soon after the ministry dashed the Nation's hopes of opening its own University of Islam, the organization fell into crisis with the death of Elijah Muhammad and the ascension of Imam Muhammad to leadership. Although Imam Muhammad was directing the organization toward Sunni Islam, Philip refused to take part, preferring Elijah Muhammad's particularist message. The mosque split into factions, with some supporting Philip, others holding that the process of Islamization was too slow, and others leaving Islam altogether.⁴⁵ In the years following the transition to Sunnism, Philip appears to have dropped the issue of the University of Islam, likely because he was occupied with his tenuous grip on power and his opposition to the changes in theology and praxis. These tensions came to a head in 1977, when Philip was ousted from the mosque after a visit from Imam Muhammad's administration.⁴⁶

From 1975 to 1981, there is no public record of any conversations between the Bermudian government and members of Masjid Muhammad regarding opening a Muslim school. The Bermuda Ministry of Education also appears to have dropped the issue of implementing a ban on parochial schools, perhaps because the masjid was no longer publicly pushing the issue. With the knowledge that the Schools Act gave the ministry little authority to institute a ban, the ministry acknowledged that it needed to write a new policy on private and religious schools.⁴⁷ However, it never did so. There would be no further mention of any policy preventing the opening of private or parochial schools on the part of the Bermudian government until Masjid Muhammad reignited the fight for its own school in December 1981. This does not mean, however, that Masjid Muhammad was not involved in expanding its educational programs and shaping its vision of schooling for Muslim children in Bermuda. As early as 1979, however, Masjid Muhammad operated a nursery school on the premises of the masjid.⁴⁸ In 1980, after a $10,000 gift from a Saudi sheikh—reflecting the masjid's increasing communication with, and guidance from, Muslims from the Middle East under Imam Muhammad—the masjid began to discuss actively expanding its educational programs.⁴⁹ In October of 1981, armed with these new funds, Masjid Muhammad applied to open a Clara Mohammed primary school at the masjid for the 1982–83 academic year. The school, which would only temporarily cater to grades 1 and 2, would educate students in all subjects required by the Bermuda Ministry of Education and include modules on Arabic language, Islamic practice, and Qur'an.

For the Muslims of Masjid Muhammad, having their own school was critically important because of their faith. The community universally held that as Muslims, there was no education system that could provide a "better education for a Muslim child than a Muslim school."[50] This was because Islam was all encompassing, not only as a system of faith but also as a way of life. The imams who led the community through this battle reflected this in their public statements. Imam Dawud Nasir stated, "Islam is not just a religion that you remember once a week, but it is a total way of life. It's the way you walk. The way you talk, the way you breathe, the way you think, the way you were born and the way you will die. Your every action in Islam should be a form of worshipping the creator."[51] Education, even at the primary school level, was a manifestation of this reverence for Allah.[52] It was, indeed, a matter of keeping faith. In July 1982, newly elected Imam Cromwell Shakir echoed Nasir's comments in a strongly worded memorandum to education minister William Cox. He wrote that the school was a necessity for the perpetuation of their Muslim community and that "without educating [their children they] would never survive as a force on this island. The culture and [their] religion would die."[53]

As Masjid Muhammad members recalled their struggle to open CMS-Bermuda over three decades later, they reflected many of the same sentiments that imams Nasir and Shakir expressed at the time. In an interview in 2015, former imam Cromwell Shakir used the same language he used in his memorandum to Minister Cox. He stated, "In our religion, we're supposed to educate ourselves and we know that. We were going to fight for it. I think that's a natural fight. That's a fight that God wanted every human being to have, the fight to have what is rightfully ours, the freedom to be educated in the best manner.... I didn't find it as a mission. I found it as a natural process."[54] Zakiyyah Shakir, principal of the Clara Mohammed School since its founding, reflected that the rationale behind opening the school is that it provided the best for Muslim children "Islamically speaking."[55] Although the community does not believe that the public schools are educationally insufficient, it was also critical for Muslim children to be educated with certain values. Indeed, "God-consciousness," an aspect of the Islamic educational process that Muslim children could not get in the public schools, was at the forefront of the community's need for an Islamic school.[56]

The drive to open CMS-Bermuda, however, did not only come from masjid imams like Dawud Nasir and Cromwell Shakir but was also reflected in the desires and concerns of Bermudian Muslim parents as well. Many of these parents, despite working full time, volunteered their time to the CMS-Bermuda Educational Advisory Committee, which was tasked with navigating the issues of integrating the state's required curriculum with a holistic Muslim education. Parents who elected to send their children to CMS-Bermuda were influenced by the appeal of total Islamic immersion. Ameenah Abdul-Hadee, a former teacher at CMS-Bermuda and a member of the Educational Advisory from the 1980s until 2014, revealed that she sent her son to CMS-Bermuda because she "saw the value of him being in an environment with people who had the same values." Muslim education, thus, perfectly tied together Muslim family life and masjid life. It was constantly reinforcing, "confirming and strengthening" the education her son received at home.[57]

As a structural matter, parents and community leaders were incredibly concerned that Bermuda's public schools were not set up to allow for Muslim education and practice. In addition to religious education, Masjid Muhammad parents, educators, and leaders indicated that they were motivated to separate themselves from the Bermudian educational system because of lack of prayer spaces for Muslim children, the style of the school uniforms (which for boys included the island's namesake knee-length shorts and for girls skirts at the knee), the lack of halal meals, compulsory Christian prayers, and the omnipresence of "temptation" in mixed-sex environments.[58] Parents believed that Christianity had colonized the Bermudian school system, and that this reality was unacceptable. Arifah Madyun, also a member of the Educational Advisory, sent her youngest son to CMS-Bermuda because she was dissatisfied with the idea that Christianity was the default religious tradition on the island. There were many Christian rituals and holidays, like Christmas and Easter, that Madyun and her husband were concerned would eclipse the importance of Muslim holidays like Ramadan for their son.[59] Safiyyah Salaam, a member of the Educational Advisory until 2015, reflected that avoiding reinforcement of Christian values was, indeed, a major motivator for many parents and for the larger Masjid Muhammad community."[60]

For better or worse, being Muslim marked students as different from their peers. As early as the 1970s, during the height of the Nation's popularity, Muslim children experienced harassment and bullying from adults and children alike. Shame, deployed by both teachers and classmates, was commonly used to force Bermuda's Black Muslim students to conform to Bermudian tradition. Muslim parents, reflecting on their children's school experience in the 1980s, recalled hearing disparaging comments about the Sunnah directed to them or their children. For example, after Zaheera Shakir made an application for her daughter to wear longer pants, sleeves, and a hijab instead of shorts and a T-shirt in physical education, a teacher commented that she simply could not understand why.[61] Safiyyah Salaam recalled that after her family changed their last name from Bean to Salaam in the 1980s, her youngest daughter's teacher mocked their chosen surname, which means "peace" in Arabic, calling her "Salami."[62] Whether the teacher knew as well that salami is haram, or prohibited for consumption in the Muslim religion, is unclear. But fear of this type of bullying, or worse, made many parents believe that the mindset of the average Bermudian teacher or administrator would be detrimental to their children's education. As Safiyyah Salaam noted, "Bermuda being small, twenty-one square miles, sometimes you think people's mindset is twenty-one square miles. Narrow. We don't accept somebody different, something different. We're so used to [the idea that] everybody should be Christian, [and] if you're Muslim you shouldn't be," and should adapt to fit the standard mores of Bermudian society.[63] These women, their children, and their families sought to challenge this colonial frame of mind through religious education, and to shape their understandings of religion, race, and political engagement in the Atlantic Crescent for another generation.

Education against Empire

The Documentary "Facts"

If we examine the archival record, the following series of events come to light regarding the masjid's fight against colonial education: In December of 1981, the Ministry of Education denied the masjid's application to open CMS-Bermuda. Without further explanation, the ministry cited the existence of an alleged policy against opening new religious schools and its need to provide "sound educational planning" within an "integrated educational system."[64] In January 1982, the masjid launched what would become a seven-year battle to challenge the government's determination. In a public statement echoing the spirit of the Nation from decades prior, Imam Nasir declared that the community would defy the government's prohibition. Nasir argued that the masjid had a right to open a school under the Bermuda Constitutional Order of 1968, which prohibits the government from preventing or hindering any religious community or order from providing religious education to its members.[65] The ministry immediately requested several legal opinions on the matter but repeatedly maintained that Masjid Muhammad had no constitutional right to open a school.[66]

On January 25, 1982, Minister Cox invited Imam Nasir and several other Muslims, including the public relations officer Takbir Sharrieff and two unnamed "female Muslims," to a meeting.[67] The meeting was a failure. Frustrated at the government's unwillingness to compromise, Nasir, Sharrieff, and their female colleagues walked out.[68] Later, Sharrieff declared that the Muslims would not resume talks with the government until they were prepared to "intelligently" discuss the matter.[69] In addition, Sharrieff accused Minister Cox of lying about the policy in question, noting that the ministry could not produce the policy prohibiting the opening of new religious schools precisely because it did not exist.[70]

By February 1982, the government had very slightly adjusted its position, conceding that Masjid Muhammad did have a constitutional right to open its own school. Regardless, the Constitution did not give the masjid the right to force the government to register the school as required by the Education Act of 1954.[71] Privately, however, the government acknowledged the weakness of its position. Those at the highest levels of government, and legal counsel, doubted the minister of education's legal basis to deny religious private school applications.[72] The matter received widespread attention through 1982 in the international Muslim community.[73] The controversy also made it to the WCIW headquarters. WCIW officials in Chicago were in touch with Minister Cox in order to express their support in early February 1982.[74]

As support poured in from across the African diaspora, the community began to discuss taking their case before Bermuda's newly formed Human Rights Commission.[75] At the end of February, the Bermudian government sent a request to Imam Nasir asking the masjid to explain why the island's existing schools could not cater to Muslim children. In response, on March 8, 1982, Imam Nasir wrote a letter on behalf of the masjid reiterating the Muslims' belief that the minister's denial of their application amounted to a violation of human and constitutional rights. In the meantime, they appeared to gear up to open their school with or without governmental approval. In March 1982, in open defiance of the government's ban, the masjid began taking out advertisements for teachers qualified in early childhood and elementary school education in the *Royal Gazette*.[76] The choice of newspaper is particularly salient. The *Royal Gazette* is the newspaper of record in Bermuda. It is conservative leaning, widely read, and the only daily newspaper in the country. Everyone in Bermuda would see Masjid Muhammad's advertisement. Thus, the placement of this ad in this particular newspaper can be read as a direct challenge to the government.

In June 1982, the government noted a lull in Masjid Muhammad's petitioning, press conferences, and meeting activity. Wrongly, they assumed that the Muslims were "backing off" of their effort to open CMS-Bermuda.[77] This lack of activity, however, was most likely a result of an internal leadership transition. In 1982, Imam Nasir stepped down and was replaced by Cromwell Shakir. Imam Shakir aggressively reembarked on the masjid's campaign to open the school and resubmitted an application to Minister Cox on August 25, 1982.[78] By September, Cox had doubled down on his position, arguing that the opening of a Muslim school would be a "retrograde step for the future of education in Bermuda."[79] Despite insistence that the school would open with or without government approval, the school did not open in September, allegedly due to renovations to the space and delays in appointing teachers. Imam Shakir vowed, however, to keep fighting and in a hopeful bid for support, Shakir finally submitted a petition to the Bermuda Human Rights Commission in March of 1983.[80] But the school didn't open the following year, or the year after that. From mid-1983 until 1988, Masjid Muhammad was quiet about the Muslim school in public. In 1989, Amir Shakir, who succeeded Cromwell Shakir as imam, only briefly mentioned in April that the masjid still had interest in opening a primary school.[81] The textual record ends there.

Memories of Protest

If we were to take the textual record at face value, we would take away the idea that except for the two unnamed Muslim women who walked out of Minister Cox's office on February 25, 1982, that only men were involved in the political undertaking to gain approval for CMS-Bermuda. Articles in Bermuda's main newspapers, the *Royal Gazette*, the *Bermuda Sun*, and the *Mid-Ocean News*, along with Bermuda Annual Reports from 1982, indicate that Masjid Muhammad imams Dawud Nasir, Cromwell Shakir, Amir Shakir, and a host of male advocates, including public relations officer Sharrieff, were involved in the government petition. These men are on the record sitting in meetings with Premier John Swan and Minister of Education Cox. They repeatedly publicized their demands by utilizing the press. One female member of Masjid Muhammad, Zaheera Shakir—then head of the CMS-Bermuda Educational Advisory Committee—was named in a single article during this time period, and then only to reiterate the community's interest in opening the school.[82]

Oral testimonies, however, and the memories of the members of Masjid Muhammad who lived through this period reveal that both brothers *and* sisters developed a concern for the education of their children over the 1970s and 1980s. Both men and women actively participated in the political process of obtaining school approval, but it is critical to focus on the women who took part in this fight because of their erasure from the textual record. Interviews universally reveal a group of mothers who acted as fierce advocates for their children in both private and public forums. In the case of Muslim women in the Caribbean and Atlantic world, more specifically, scholars have uncovered women's active political lives through examination of their participation in internal and largely private masjid politics. In these cases, women's participation comes into focus by looking behind the scenes, at the committees and caucuses in which women argued and debated with one another and with the men in the community. From there, these women would privately influence their husbands on political matters.[83]

Since we do not immediately see the women of Masjid Muhammad participating in Bermudian politics in public, examining their participation in internal matters away from the public eye is a logical place to begin. Indeed, Masjid Muhammad women engaged in private meetings with public and private school principals and teachers. These women often tried to circumvent the erasure of their culture that was reflected in the emphasis on Christian holidays and instruction and the shame that resulted from bullying by students and teachers. Naturally, this resulted in additional, unpaid, often unacknowledged labor by these women. Zaheera Shakir recalls that she proactively prepared an educational packet during Ramadan each year with information on fasting and prayer for teachers. Shakir's hope was that this knowledge would lead to respect for the religious obligations that her six children were required to undertake during this month of fasting, prayer, and reflection.[84] In addition to this affective labor, women took active roles in the parent-teacher associations of their children's schools. To drive these conversations, women like Zaheera served in leadership roles. Shakir served as president of Purvis Primary School, located in Warwick, for several years during the 1980s while her children were in attendance. Although other women did not serve as parent-teacher association officers, they remained an integral part of the battles for religious accommodation during the 1980s. Indeed, the majority of the battles for modification of school uniforms, school meals, and dedicated prayer space were waged through these associations.[85]

For many Muslim families, their piecemeal wins on uniform, prayer, and nutrition were simply not enough. A Muslim school was still necessary for the education of their children and the perpetuation of their community. While the Bermudian press virtually erased the participation of Muslim women in discussions with Minister Cox and Premier Swan, the elder sisters and brothers of Masjid Muhammad have an entirely different memory. Muslim women, particularly Zaheera Shakir, Edna Sharrieff, Safiyyah Salaam, and Zakiyyah Shakir, regularly attended meetings with the government throughout the early 1980s. In January 1982, when public relations officer Sharrieff accused the government of lying about a written policy barring the opening of new religious schools, he was able to do this because of the meticulous legislative research that Zaheera Shakir had done on the matter. In 1983, during a series of meetings with the Bermuda Human Rights Commission, the Ministry of Education, and the masjid, Zaheera asked the government's attorney three times when the masjid would receive a copy of the government's written policy for their review. Eventually, after Zaheera's relentless questioning, the government's counsel was forced to concede that the policy in question did not exist and was simply a verbal agreement that members of the government had made among themselves to disallow the licensing of additional schools.[86] In public, as well as in private, men and women worked together to open CMS-Bermuda for the benefit of their children and their community. This not only included meetings with government officials but also public protest. One of the most vivid memories of public protest and activism in the community is in the form of the 1983 protest with which this chapter begins. The men and women of Masjid Muhammad gathered on government land to demand that the government license CMS-Bermuda. They were prominent and visible with their protest placards and signs, sartorially marked as Muslims in hijabs and skullcaps.[87] Some members of the community attended—and were proud to do so—despite their advanced pregnancies.[88]

The publicity that surrounded Masjid Muhammad's battle for CMS-Bermuda alienated some non-Muslim neighbors and colleagues. These non-Muslims often used shame in order to coerce the members of the Masjid Muhammad community to fall into line. They questioned how these men and women could dare to be out in public petitioning, marching, and openly defying the government. For these Muslims, they continued to engage in this activism because of the "bold Muslims they were."[89] Because of their historical roots in the Nation, these Muslims found themselves unafraid of censure or legal sanction. They had no anxiety about the idea that they could lose their jobs or that there could be social consequences. The issue was a much larger one. Through Islamic education, parents hoped to instill the same assertiveness and confidence through which they found themselves navigating the world around them. They sought to create in Bermuda Islamically educated and nurtured leaders for the future.[90]

Masjid Muhammad would never get official approval from the government. However, through Zaheera Shakir's meticulous legal research and persistence, the Bermudian government was forced to acknowledge that they had no legal way to prevent the opening of the school. Given this, Premier John Swan gave the masjid his unofficial approval "in principle" to proceed and shifted away from a very publicly driven fight to a scramble to put together the infrastructure necessary to educate Masjid Muhammad's children Islamically. The masjid and its Educational Advisory would stay in the background for the next six years until CMS-Bermuda finally opened in 1989.[91]

An Islamically Inspired Curriculum

Much of the work necessary to transform CMS-Bermuda from a nursery school to a primary school revolved around the development of an appropriate curriculum that would satisfy the Ministry of Education's basic requirements while providing a holistic Muslim education. For Masjid Muhammad, curriculum development was both a transnational and local project. Locally, the masjid's Educational Advisory Committee, consisting entirely of women, bore the brunt of the project of curriculum development. As a transnational matter, they undertook this task in consultation with other members of Imam Muhammad's movement from the United States, including Ameenah Abduh-Hadee, one of the first teachers at Masjid Muhammad's nursery school and an American by birth.[92] Abdul-Hadee left Bermuda for the United States for two years, right at the critical moment of CMS-Bermuda's opening for the 1989 academic year. She remained engaged in CMS-Bermuda's curriculum development from abroad, however, regularly staying in contact with the CMS-Bermuda Educational Advisory and the staff of the Clara Mohammed School.[93]

Beginning in the early 1990s, the Educational Advisory and teachers of CMS-Bermuda attended annual three- to four-day conferences led by the Northeast Region of the WCIW. For the most part, these conferences took place in the United States, but in September 1990, a conference was held in Bermuda. Over these three or four days, seasoned Muslim educators would discuss the Clara Mohammed School model and best practices for educating children as Muslims and as global and local citizens. This process involved emphasizing a thematic approach to teaching in which the Qur'an served as the basis for teaching every subject. This meant that not only would students be given compulsory units in Arabic language and Islamic theology but that Islam would permeate into every subject taught to students.

A how-to guide written by Atlanta's Clara Mohammed School and Warith Deen Muhammad High School for the 1992 Islamic Education Conference elaborates more fully on the Qur'anic integration approach. The document, titled "How to Integrate the Holy Qur'an into the Classroom," indicates that the primary objective of Qur'an-based education is to demonstrate that "all knowledge comes from Allah," and "whatever is true, is true without conflict with the revelation of Al-Qur'an."[94] In practice, this is done through fully incorporating the message of the Qur'an using the textual revelation itself, Qur'anic concordance by scholars, Arabic and English dictionaries, and hadith. This is then combined with the information contained in "so-called secular textbooks."[95] For example, a lesson on the effect of the rotation of the Earth around the Sun on the calendar might be accompanied by an analysis of Qur'an 10:5. This *Surah* states, "It is He who made the sun to be a shining glory and the moon to be a light (of beauty), and measured out the stages for it, that ye might know the number of years and the amount (of time)."[96] A lesson on metric weights and measures might use Surah 55:7–9, "and the Firmament has He raised high, and He has set up the Balance (of Justice), In Order that ye may not transgress (due) balance. So establish weight with justice and fall not short in balance."[97] A fully integrated thematic Qur'anic curriculum would include units on social science (*'umma*-tology); science (*'ilm*); language arts and communications (*bayaan mubeen*); health and safety (*tayyib*, halal, and *amin*); and mathematics, including judgment (*mizan*).[98]

In pursuit of this goal of a completely Qur'anically integrated curriculum, the CMS-Bermuda Educational Advisory began to labor over curriculum and syllabi beginning in 1989, integrating the Qur'an as fully as possible into each of the six grades of primary education represented at the school. In addition to the guides provided at the Islamic Educational Conferences, such as the 1992 "How to Integrate the Qur'an into the Classroom," materials were borrowed from Muslim educators at Clara Mohammed Schools throughout the United States and from the Muslim Teachers College in Virginia. For a number of months, an imam from the Center for Islam and Cultural Awareness in Fort Myers, Florida, 'Abd al-Haqq Muhammad, lived at the masjid and helped the Educational Advisory with educational logistics and curriculum planning.

Even though the Islamic Educational Conferences introduced universal best practices for educating Muslim children, educators acknowledged that each mosque and community would adopt a slightly different approach. This approach respected the unique local, geographical, and historical circumstances of each individual Muslim community. And naturally, this would result in different uniforms, content, and textbooks, all of which would need to be tailored to the specific locality. In Bermuda, the Educational Advisory needed to adhere to University of Cambridge Primary curriculum guidelines on educating children so that when their students left CMS-Bermuda, they would be prepared to transition to a fully secular education in the British system. Nevertheless, the Educational Advisory rejected the use of British textbooks, which are the standard in Bermuda's public and private schools. Instead, they chose to use American textbooks published by Harcourt Mifflin and Compass Learning.[99] This represented a conscious decision by the masjid to destabilize the primacy of British colonial educational materials and content in a Black Muslim classroom and to consciously define what it meant to be a Bermudian Black Muslim person.

The sisters of Masjid Muhammad describe the process of fighting for CMS-Bermuda and educating their children Islamically as a labor of love bolstered by Islamic obligation and a general feeling that it was the "right thing" for the community. From opening the school itself to developing curriculum, there have been challenges at every turn for CMS-Bermuda. Aside from Principal Shakir and the handful of full-time teachers employed at CMS-Bermuda, the masjid's Educational Advisory is made up of a mostly female volunteer force. These women balance their unpaid work for CMS-Bermuda with their jobs, family lives, and their general services to the masjid community.

Conclusion

Masjid Muhammad's fight to open CMS-Bermuda represents their continued attempts to carve out an identity at the intersection of race and Islam relevant to its members' experiences, and histories as Black Bermudians living under colonialism. But it also reflects how the enduring legacies and memories of the past continue to affect and guide the actions of practitioners throughout their lives. For the women of Masjid Muhammad, membership in the Nation of Islam, with its critical lens against colonialism and its association with communism, labor, and Black Power in Bermuda, engendered a type of radicalism. Their adaption of Islam were both parts of a spiritual journey and ways to facilitate lives free of racial violence and colonial domination. In Bermuda, which remained under the control of the British, these motivations did not falter, even as their religious beliefs adapted to be in line with mainstream Islamic practices. For the Muslims of Bermuda, their insistence on opening Masjid Muhammad was not simply about educating their children Islamically but about opposing a system of colonial education that failed to uplift their children as Black and Muslim people.

The story of the fight to open CMS-Bermuda is also about how we know what we know, and how that information is preserved for the consumption of future generations. Historians of the African diaspora have long had to grapple with the absence of archival evidence about the lives, particularly the internal lives, of Black people. In this chapter, I have presented a case of how we can get a more holistic picture of not only the existence of the fight to open CMS-Bermuda, but the meaning of that struggle for Black and Muslim people continuing to live under white supremacy and colonialism. In this case, comparing the archival record with the memories of those who took part in the struggle provides this critical missing piece.

CHAPTER SIX

Who You Gonna Call?
Islam, American Neo-Imperialism, and Dopebusting in the Inner City

On a late April day in 1988, as a local high school band played "Battle Hymn of the Republic," local politician and Nation psychologist A. Alim Muhammad approached a platform set up in the center of the Mayfair Mansions housing project in Washington, DC.¹ On that day, hundreds of residents of northeast Washington gathered together to celebrate a new anti-drug program launched by the Nation only a few days prior.² The Tenants Association of Mayfair Mansions, populated by a cross-section of the largely Black apartment complex, had requested the assistance of the Nation's paramilitary arm, the Fruit of Islam (FOI), earlier in April.³ Beleaguered by crack-related drug trafficking and violence in the area, residents of Mayfair Mansions felt that the local Washington, DC, police had failed to sufficiently address the issue and eliminate the presence of drugs and the attendant gang violence in the community.⁴ In fact, many members of the Mayfair Mansions community maintained that instead of working to eliminate drugs in the complex, the police were "directly involved" in drug trafficking efforts.⁵ FOI patrollers, dubbed "Dopebusters" by a local Black newspaper, took up a vacant third-floor apartment in Mayfair Mansions, adorning the door of their office space with a plaque indicating that these were "Officers' Quarters."⁶ A flag bearing the star and crescent moon, the symbols of Islam, flew proudly over the complex as soldiers patrolled the grounds, intimidated drug dealers, and sought to restore the "order" that the "law" seemed to be at best unable, and at worst unwilling, to do.

By April of 1988, the Mayfair Mansions community, like many other Black communities in the United States, was tired and frustrated. By the time of Dr. Muhammad's Dopebusters rally, they had already suffered through seven years of Ronald Reagan's systematic expansion of the carceral state, an environment in which citizens and subjects are controlled and pacified not only by formal prison buildings but also by surveillance, borders and walls, and security checkpoints. This expansion was made possible through what historian Heather Ann Thompson calls the "criminalization of urban space," a "process by which increasing numbers of urban dwellers—overwhelmingly men and women of color—became subject to a growing number of laws that not only regulated bodies and communities in thoroughly new ways but also subjected violators to unprecedented time behind bars."[7]

The effects of American policing on spatial control and the subjugation of people of color were not just visible on a national level. After World War II, the US imperial project continued to grow like a cancer over the Third World. These dual processes of internal and external occupation were connected, both theoretically and in execution.[8] Looking back on these policies and their effects, historians have begun making connections between these national and international spheres; however, the people who were subjected to these regimes theorized about them and developed practical solutions in the moment. As these top-down processes took hold for American urban residents, they engaged in a dialectic through which they responded to these new laws and policies.[9] Black people developed intellectual frameworks that made sense of the increasing militarization of the inner city, the larger connections to American imperialism and war-making abroad, and the prescription of religio-political solutions to these crises. They also created organizations, networks, and frameworks, like Dopebusters, to combat them.

For the Nation, the use of the military would come to be seen as particularly salient. As the Dopebusters responded to Mayfair Mansions' request for protection not only from drugs but also from the police, they homed in on the increasing militarization of local police forces and appropriated the language and symbolism of Reagan's War on Drugs to indicate that they were engaged in a countermilitarization and an Islamic jihad against law enforcement, the US government, and drugs themselves. They did not view this American military campaign, however, as a solely domestic problem. The growth of the American carceral state and the resulting uptick in the incarceration of Black bodies was a logical result and critical component, they argued, of American expansion abroad.

In this chapter, I investigate how the rank-and-file members in Louis Farrakhan's Nation of Islam understood the increasing criminalization of urban space happening in America's inner cities during the War on Drugs. To do this, I first discuss how Louis Farrakhan, leader of the Nation during this time, articulated his critique of American neo-imperialism in the Circum-Caribbean region, linked this to the suffering of Black Americans in America's inner cities during the so-called War on Drugs, and positioned Islam as a corrective against this. I then explore how rank-and-file members at the grassroots level—some of them writing through the Nation's press organ, the *Final Call*—and others associated with the Dopebusters army described at the beginning of this chapter, understood their role as Black and Muslim people in the fight against imperialism, white supremacy, and racial violence.

In 1977, two years after he pledged his loyalty to Wallace Muhammad, Farrakhan broke with Wallace's Sunni Muslim movement. He took a small group of followers with him and reconstituted the Nation, reviving its original teachings under Elijah Muhammad.[10] Farrakhan's goal, however, was not just to promote himself as a religious leader but also to assert his relevancy as a political leader. Thus, along with claiming himself to be the recipient of a continuing Islamic revelation and prophecy, Farrakhan sought—as Elijah Muhammad had in the decades prior—to mobilize Black people globally through activism to improve their social and political circumstances. The way this would look in 1977, however, would be different than it had at the beginning of the Nation's founding in 1930 or at the dawn of its eventual foray into national and international publishing in 1960. This was because the world itself had undergone marked changes to its geopolitical composition, making it a dramatically different place than the world that Muhammad and Malcolm X contended with in the pages of *Muhammad Speaks*.

When *Muhammad Speaks* was launched in 1960, it focused heavily on the evils of European colonialism in Southeast Asia and Africa and looked jubilantly at the pace at which these countries were breaking free of this oppression. In the first five years of publication, from 1960 to 1965, the world saw twenty-eight new countries in Africa and Asia become independent. Fourteen of these attained sovereignty in 1960 alone.[11] These countries were incorporated into the Nation's Muslim geography of imperial resistance, which identified Islam as the driver of liberation and freedom for people of color throughout the world. Even where the countries undergoing processes of independence were not Muslim majority, as in the case of Cuba, the editors and writers of *Muhammad Speaks* still included these countries in their geography. By contrast, in the last five years of *Muhammad Speaks*'s publication, from 1970 to 1975, only thirteen nations achieved independence, and at a much slower pace. From 1970 to 1974, more specifically, only six nations achieved independence. The remaining seven gained sovereignty in 1975.[12]

The last push for African, Asian, and Caribbean independence in the 1970s meant that the majority of the world's Black, Brown, and Muslim population was, at least on paper, living in sovereign, independent nations. The anticolonial spirit that the Nation possessed from the 1950s to the early 1970s, however, did not disappear but instead changed its character. The Cold War between the United States and the Soviet Union increased in intensity from the mid-1970s until the official demise of the Soviet Union in 1991. During this time, both the United States and the Soviet Union engaged in their own expansion of empire.[13] In this race for influence, the Nation's anticolonialist discourse shifted its attention away from Europe as the primary antagonist and toward American imperial activity in Latin America, Africa, and the Middle East. This neo-imperialism was different in character. Instead of directly and openly controlling these territories, the United States treated these countries, and their populations, as proxies. Military invasion was always on the table, but instead of openly sending troops to depose troublesome leaders, the United States preferred the strategy of manipulating the people themselves to influence elections. Some of the tactics used by the American government during this time included funding and training counterrevolutionaries, rigging elections, and installing America-friendly dictators. By the time Farrakhan ascended to leadership, all eyes were on the United States and the Soviet Union on the global stage, and the Nation read America's interference in the Third World as an attempt to re-enslave and recolonize populations of color globally.

In public, using both speeches and the newspaper of his resurrected Nation, the *Final Call*, Farrakhan adjusted and adapted the Nation's geography of imperial resistance for a new age. Here, he positioned Islam and the Third World as a united front against the expansion of American empire. To do this, Farrakhan imagined himself in solidarity with leaders in North Africa, Latin America, and the Caribbean who resisted the United States' attempts to intervene in their militaries, economies, and political parties. Like Elijah Muhammad, Farrakhan developed friendships, intimacies, and economic entanglements with these leaders. These friendships had little effect on the people who followed Farrakhan as a matter of quotidian life, but they were powerful in sketching out an evolving geographical understanding of Black Muslim world power.

By the 1980s, the Nation viewed increasing American intervention in the Circum-Caribbean, particularly in Grenada, Nicaragua, and Panama, as a "practice round" for an imminent military occupation of America's majority Black inner cities in response to Ronald Reagan's War on Drugs and expansion of the carceral state.[14] Accordingly, in the *Final Call* and in the streets, men and women in the Nation articulated their understanding of the War on Drugs and its connections to a larger political project. Eventually, in response to a lack of effort by state and local leaders to ameliorate what eventually became a real drug crisis in the American inner city, Farrakhan launched his own army of Muslim men from the ranks of the Nation's paramilitary FOI. Modeled on the successful, yet controversial, drug patrols of former Nation member and Sunni imam Siraj Wahhaj of Brooklyn, this army was tasked with eradicating drugs from Black communities to prevent the "spiritual sickening" that drug distribution and addiction caused. These men articulated their project clearly. Their intention was both to save their brothers and sisters from moral blight and eternal damnation and to remove any pretext for law enforcement authorities to invade Black inner-city communities, staving off—as countries throughout the Third World had done—imperial occupation. These programs were far from perfect. Often Dopebusters would create tension and prompt violence, even as they sought to diffuse it. Because of this, they were regularly compared by the Black press to vigilantes. However, these programs were indicative of the larger way in which ordinary Black people intellectualized the greater domestic and international implications surrounding Reagan's so-called War on Drugs and developed a toolbox of solutions in this context. Dopebusters, and these discourses surrounding it, served as a return to the local, and the inward-facing, reflective face of the Atlantic Crescent, and a way that the rank-and-file understood, made sense of, and acted on the larger anti-imperial discourses pressing on them from above.

Geographically Expanding the Nation of Islam's Anti-Imperial Rhetoric to the Circum-Caribbean

In 1978, Louis Farrakhan began to give speeches rallying new and old followers to his revived Nation of Islam. From the beginning, Farrakhan realized the need to globalize and internationalize his teachings on imperialism, colonialism, and racism, and he delineated the parameters of his version of the Nation's anti-imperial geography. In a speech given in the early years of the Nation's revival, Farrakhan preached that the use of the word "minority" had negative effects on Black and Latino people because it instilled the idea of Black physical and numerical inferiority. This, according to Farrakhan, was "debilitating." Rather, Black and Brown people should "take the world as a whole" in order to place the white man in the minority. This was a problem of discourse for Farrakhan, and he argued that it was a conscious strategy on the part of white leaders to rob Black people of their ability to come together, to develop international ties, and to properly equip themselves to deal more effectively with their problems. When this perspective shifted, these problems became remarkably similar.[15] The solution for Farrakhan, as it had been for Elijah Muhammad, was Islam, which Farrakhan argued had the unique ability to unite people globally because it was "equivalent to truth, righteousness, freedom, [and] justice."[16]

In May 1979, Farrakhan made the first attempts to relay his message in writing by launching the *Final Call*.[17] Most of these early articles contain vague pronouncements of unity and solidarity with the Third World, but in 1982, three years after the first issue of the *Final Call*, Farrakhan began to engage the domestic realities of urban Black people and connect them with the global suffering of people of color globally.[18] While the Nation's imperial antagonist—and leadership—had both changed, Farrakhan imagined the starting point of his geographical formulation to be the unity of people of color globally, particularly as it related to African-descended people in the Americas and the rest of the Third World.

The Nation had expanded its anti-imperial rhetoric to non-Muslim-majority countries in the past and found ways to incorporate them fully into its anti-imperial geography. After the independence movements of the 1960s, the Circum-Caribbean was rife with them. Although the Nation had mosques in several locations throughout Latin America and the Caribbean, including in Panama and Jamaica, it does not appear that Farrakhan maintained ongoing relationships and exchanges with any Latin American or Caribbean leaders. While he would occasionally embark on a speaking engagement, and vice versa, there are no markers of the physical, economic, and ideological closeness that was present even in Nasser's 1959 invitation to Elijah Muhammad to visit Egypt. Still, Farrakhan marshaled the way that Latin American and Caribbean leaders resisted American imperial power repeatedly. This resistance was critical in expanding the boundaries of his version of the Atlantic Crescent. Indeed, both the geographical and metaphorical proximity of these countries to the United States, and therefore to the circumstances of African American urban populations, provided Farrakhan with a strong basis for comparison. As the US government's so-called War on Drugs ravaged American inner cities, the example of Latin America and the Caribbean would serve as a powerful example of what could happen if positive community action was not taken.

The Circum-Caribbean initially became a part of the Nation's alternative mapping of the anticolonial Muslim world by, strangely, a reference to the Iranian revolution. Farrakhan and the editors of the *Final Call* believed that there was a real possibility that the "success" of the Iranian revolution could be replicated in Latin America. Throughout the 1980s and 1990s, the Nation understood the United States' attempts to control Latin America and the Caribbean—which included supporting regime changes and providing military support to various nations—as part and parcel of an attempt to prevent a repeat of the 1979 Iranian revolution. Citing an exposé written by investigative journalist Bob Woodward, the *Final Call* identified the ultimate goal of America's Latin America policy from the 1980s to the 1990s to be the prevention of the rise of the next Ayatollah Khomeini, "a man coming up that could lead the angry masses."[19] This was the first, and one of the only, times that the Nation cited the Iranian revolution, despite the fact that it was a perfect historical example of a successfully implemented revolutionary Islamic state. However, the way the Iranian revolution was used is indicative of the way that the Nation viewed the foreign policies of the Reagan, and eventually Bush, administration. These policies were identified as emerging from the same need to control the Third World and prevent mass revolution contrary to US interests. Throughout the 1980s and 1990s, the Nation understood this potential alliance of the "oppressed" to be the United States' chief concern.

Beginning in 1985, in response to what the *Final Call* characterized as United States–backed bombings in Lebanon, Farrakhan began to geographically expand his anticolonial discourse to some of these non-Muslim countries by citing American interference in the affairs of nations in the Circum-Caribbean.[20] In January 1986, in response to the election of Jamaican prime minister Edward Seaga, the *Final Call* accused the United States of orchestrating the election. Seaga, an extremely light-skinned man of Lebanese, African, Indian, and Scottish ancestry, was the Reagan administration's "great white hope" in the West Indies, "expected to create a showcase of free market prosperity after the socialist policies of his predecessor [Michael Manley] had ended in political and economic turmoil."[21]

The bulk of Farrakhan's ire about Reagan's policies in Latin America and the Caribbean, however, was reserved for condemnation of the US government's attempts to destabilize the Sandinista revolutionary government in Nicaragua. The Sandinista National Liberation Front (*Frente Sandinista de Liberación Naciónal* [FSLN]), formed by Carlos Fonseca, German Pomares, and Tomas Barge, began as a guerilla organization in 1961. Its focus was to topple the forty-three-year-old pro-American Somoza dynasty, a dictatorship instituted in 1936 by Anastasio Somoza Garcia. By the time the FSLN was formed, the United States had in some form occupied or influenced Nicaraguan politics since 1909, including a physical occupation from 1912 to 1933. The FSLN, joined by the popular support of the masses—including some bourgeoisie and the Catholic clergy—gained strength throughout the late 1970s, eventually leading to a war of liberation. This civil war culminated in the defeat of Somoza's army and the success of the Nicaraguan revolution in 1979.[22] In 1984, the Sandinistas held their first elections for both president and National Assembly. Running as the FSLN's candidate, Daniel Ortega and his running mate, Sergio Ramírez, won.[23]

The rise of the Sandinista government, however, presented a problem for the United States. The Sandinista government was nationalist, deeply religious, and, most troubling for the United States, openly Marxist or Marxist-Leninist. It was, therefore, feared by Nicaragua's middle and upper class and by Washington, which was suspicious of the rise of another Fidel Castro. After Reagan was elected president of the United States in 1980, the US government embarked on a campaign to destroy the Sandinistas, which included disseminating propaganda, enacting an embargo on trade with Nicaragua, and funneling financial and military support through covert cover agencies to anti-Sandinista forces, or *Contras*.[24] From 1986 until the fall of Ortega's Sandinista government in 1990, the Nation criticized what it perceived as the United States' unjust policies aimed to topple the Sandinista government, concentrating on the political, social, and economic aspects of American interference.

After the Americans imposed an embargo on Nicaragua, Nicaragua became fully incorporated into the Nation's anti-imperial geography, and its battle was positioned as key in the fight against "colonialism and neo-colonialism." As such, the Nation called on "socialist countries, non-aligned and OAU League, [and] ... liberation movements," as it had done throughout the era of European decolonization, to line up behind Ortega and speak out against the United States' actions.[25] Turning the use of the term "terrorism" on its head, the *Final Call* repeatedly defined Reagan's attempts to overthrow the democratically elected Sandinista government as "acts of terrorism" and the Contras as "mercenary pawns under Reagan's CIA, waging a war against the Nicaraguan people."[26] In 1986, when it came to light that the Reagan administration had been illegally funding Contra operations, the *Final Call* cited the World Court's decision of June 27, 1986, which stated that this project violated international law and Nicaraguan sovereignty. Using racialized language usually reserved by elites, law enforcement, and politicians, the *Final Call* referred to Reagan and the CIA as a "bunch of thugs" with absolutely no regard for international peace or order.[27]

Race was a key factor in including the Sandinistas in the Atlantic Crescent and within the boundaries of their anti-imperial geography. Much like Fidel Castro, a phenotypically white leader of a majority Black country, including Ortega in the Atlantic Crescent wasn't a given. However, the collective impact of the United States' strong-arm policies, including a trade and import embargo on the country, emphasized the racialized nature of American neo-imperialism. The economic toll of the US embargo was disproportionately felt by those in poor, rural regions, the overwhelming majority of whom were Black. The US embargo increased inflation and poverty. As a result, simple over-the-counter medicines like aspirin became unsustainably expensive, beans and milk were unobtainable, and children in rural districts were forced to leave school. When the *Final Call* emphasized these inequalities, it was in concordance with generally held views by scholars and economists on the effect of American policies after the Nicaraguan revolution. These policies created severe shortages of imported goods and machinery and a reduction in social services and quality of life.[28] This amplified the already racialized nature of empire itself.

Ortega and the Sandinistas were a problematic inclusion into the Nation's anti-imperial geography. The Nation had skirted around issues of the racial identity and appearance of leaders before—for example, in the very similar incorporation of Fidel Castro into its anti-imperial geography and in inscribing Cuba into the boundaries of the Atlantic Crescent in the 1960s. What it should not have been able to get around, however, is the fact that despite their Marxist-Leninist ideas, socialist framework, and widespread public support, Sandinista policies did not always align with the interests of Black Nicaraguans. There were several communities of African-descended "Creole" Nicaraguans concentrated along the Caribbean coast of the country who openly contested the Sandinista regime. These communities were never mentioned or acknowledged by the Nation in any of its articles about the American occupation of Nicaragua.[29] This is another example of how the Nation's imaginary often elided realities, tensions, and individual community identities. Despite claims to the contrary, Black people were not a singular, undifferentiated category, and Blackness had different meanings depending on historical circumstance.

Nicaragua received a lot of attention, but it was not particularly special. To the contrary, the Nation identified Nicaragua as simply the most recent manifestation of a number of linked instances of imperial aggression on the part of the United States throughout Latin America and the Circum-Caribbean. In 1984, Farrakhan began to make a series of connections between the history of American invasions of sovereign nations in the Circum-Caribbean. The first in this chain was the island of Grenada. In October of 1983, President Reagan ordered an invasion of Grenada, citing inflated reports that there had been an influx of Cuban combat troops on the island, deliveries of Soviet and Cuban arms, and documents indicating that a Cuban military occupation was imminent.[30] The Nation positioned this as an intentional action meant to create a chain reaction in the region, citing reports from "Washington insiders" positing that the invasion had simply been a "dress rehearsal" for a future invasion of Nicaragua.[31]

Three years later, in February of 1986, Reagan confirmed this "chain of events" theory. During a visit to Grenada to celebrate the success of the 1983 American invasion, Reagan gave a speech saying that he would "never be sorry" for ordering the invasion and that he would not be "satisfied until all the people of the Americas have joined us in the warm sunshine of liberty and justice."[32] Justifying the invasion of the island through reference to American lives, Reagan used the opportunity to call for "law and order" in the Americas and to make the case for a potential invasion of Nicaragua.[33] The *Final Call* covered this speech and, the next month, emphasized these connections with a political cartoon depicting Reagan carrying a machine gun and creating a splash in Grenada while stepping into Nicaragua in spiked combat boots (figure 6.1).[34]

Nicaragua, however, was not the only Latin American country that became a target of the Nation's anti-imperial geography, even if it was the most frequently discussed throughout the mid-1980s. Beginning in 1988, the *Final Call* switched from its focus on Nicaragua to the United States' attempts to oust the head of the Panamanian state, Manuel Noriega, despite regional support for his rule.[35] The "Noriega problem" defined the final year of Reagan's presidency and the start of George H.W. Bush's presidency in January 1989. Throughout the 1980s, the United States saw Noriega as an ally. He backed the Nicaraguan Contras by providing them with arms and providing intelligence to officials in Managua and Washington, and he collaborated with Reagan's efforts to oust the Nicaraguan Sandinista government. During this same period, however, Noriega began a lucrative trade in smuggling guns and drugs for the Colombian Medellín family cartel and initiated money-laundering schemes to disguise his participation. When the United States became aware of his activities in the mid-1980s, the Reagan administration actively ignored it because Noriega was its only regional support in bolstering the Contra offensive.[36]

After middle-class protest increased in 1987, making continued support of Noriega an embarrassment, the Reagan administration made a decision to oust him. In 1988, the Reagan administration attempted to force Noriega's resignation by indicting him in federal court on narcotics smuggling and money-laundering charges and imposing widespread economic sanctions on Panama. When Bush assumed the presidency in January 1989, he sparred with Noriega for months, until he had a legitimate reason to use open military force. In December 1989, several US soldiers were fired upon by the

FIGURE 6.1 A political cartoon of Reagan stepping into Grenada with combat boots in the *Final Call*, April 27, 1986, p. 9. Cartoon by Robert Muhammad.

Panamanian Defense Force. In response, President Bush ordered a full-scale invasion of the country.[37]

Although the Nation initially criticized Noriega for acting as an informant for the CIA, it still placed the United States' interest in Noriega squarely within the realm of American expansion, questioning whether he was the monster depicted by the United States or simply another victim of American imperialism.[38] When the United States invaded Panama during what it nicknamed "Operation Just Cause," the Nation placed the invasion of Panama squarely in the context of America's lust for the growth of her empire and the control of her surrounding unaligned nations.[39] The *Final Call*'s editor, Wali Muhammad, wrote, "Will the darker peoples of the earth be allowed to rise up from the ashes of imperialism, colonialism, racism and the grip of superpower hegemony, or will a newly emerging US government psychosis to militarily re-establish her empire, coupled with the apparent alliance of the white world powers, pronounce a declaration of war on the 'Third World' and the aspirations of the smaller nations of this earth to be independent and self-determining?"[40] Up to this point, Wali Muhammad had run several articles in the *Final Call* condemning the growth of the US military empire in Nicaragua, Libya, and the Caribbean. These contradict Muhammad's assertion that this was a "newly emerging US government psychosis" to control the Third World.[41] However, the Nation, Farrakhan, and Wali Muhammad continued to make broad connections between the past and the present.

Echoing an artistic rendering of Reagan invading Nicaragua from Grenada, a January 29, 1990, cartoon emphasized the connection between US military expansion into the Caribbean and Bush's then-current war on Panama.[42] Here, the Nation placed Panama squarely within its internationalist anti-imperial discourse and challenged the United States' stated reasons for invading Panama. The Nation, through the *Final Call*, challenged the United States' assertions that the invasion was about restoring democracy to Panama and bringing General Noriega to justice for alleged drug trafficking and money laundering. Instead, it maintained that the invasion was an attempt to secure the United States' control of the Panama Canal, which would revert to Panamanian jurisdiction in 1999.[43]

Again, the American invasion of Panama was important not only in the specific context of the dangerous expansion of American empire but also as a global Black problem. Criticizing American Black leadership for not having the "courage" to condemn President Bush's policy with regard to Panama, the Nation painted the American invasion as a "war against Blacks," identifying the myriad horrors of the invasion. When American forces dropped bombs on the countryside surrounding Panama City, and on the capital's "Blackest" neighborhood, El Chorillo, the *Final Call* condemned it as a "murderous" assault by noting the frequency with which—even during targeted bombings—Black, Mestizo, and Indigenous communities who supported Noriega's Panamanian Defense Forces lost their lives.[44]

Contradicting US reports that the number of Panamanian dead totaled 220, Wali Muhammad alleged that the total death toll was in the thousands, and that the majority of those dead were from nonwhite communities.[45] Conjuring images that visually contrasted the dark-skinned regional supporters of Noriega with the white American-installed leadership of Guillermo Endara, Wali Muhammad suggested that the "hidden" reasons for the Panamanian invasion and its assault on the Black and Brown people of the world were exposed by examining

> the black, brown and red faces of youth being handcuffed in the streets of Panama under the guns of U.S. soldiers; the many dark skinned faces behind the barbed wire in the "refugee camps," a euphemism for detention centers or concentration camps; the white faces in designer jeans and T-shirts chanting in the streets of Panama amidst high-rise apartments

and shiny automobiles when General Noriega left the Vatican Embassy; and the replacement of the black diplomats of the Noriega regime with the white diplomats of the U.S.-installed Guillermo Endara regime at the United Nations (UN) and Organization for American States (OAS).[46]

The installation of Endara as president of Panama, therefore, and the removal of Noriega's Brown cabinet, was a visible attempt by the United States to extend white control over the hemisphere. The racial insult of Endara's ascension was further emphasized by reference to his connections to the wealthy Eleta Almarán family, proprietors of Harinas de Panamá, S.A. On April 6, 1989, the head of the corporation, Carlos Eleta Almarán, was arrested for conspiring to import over 600 kilos of cocaine to the United States and using Harinas de Panamá as a front to launder money connected to this illegal enterprise.[47] Simultaneously, while installing a person proximate to the distribution of cocaine to lead the Panamanian government, the Bush administration was cracking down mercilessly on African Americans in America's inner cities during what Reagan had dubbed the "War on Drugs."

The bombing of El Chorillo and Colón by the American military in January of 1990 prompted accusations by Farrakhan and the Nation that the government had declared a "War on Blacks." The Bush administration's official position was that the invasion, nicknamed "Operation Just Cause," was designed to protect American citizens living in Panama, to stop the spread of drug trafficking into the United States, to protect the integrity of the Panama Canal, and to defend democracy in the Western Hemisphere. By 1990, these alleged designs to preserve "law" and "order" over unruly populations across the globe had enjoyed over a hundred years of support by American presidents and legislators. But these were also the reasons given to oppress Black, Brown, Asian, and Indigenous people domestically as well. The inherent unruly nature and ungovernability of Black and Brown people were oft cited reasons for the imposition of Jim Crow laws after Reconstruction, for the maintenance of de facto and de jure segregated neighborhoods and facilities, and for the brutal use of law enforcement in Black neighborhoods.

American Empire Comes Home: Intellectualizing the War on Drugs and the Carceral Crisis

Presidents Reagan and Bush made ample use of "law and order" rhetoric in order to justify their domestic and international strong-arm tactics. Building on an increasing focus on disorder, lawlessness, and moral decline in Black communities, Bush and Reagan built on nearly twenty years of American domestic policy involving the federal government in local law enforcement. Beginning with the Johnson administration, liberal and conservative American politicians on the federal and state level evidenced a commitment to supporting local police departments in their efforts to control and surveil inner-city communities through funding and legislation.[48] Under this regime, police acquired new discretion in obtaining confessions without a Miranda warning; expanded electronic surveillance by allowing assistant attorney generals or any state or local district attorney to plant a bug or tap a phone if the crime carried a sentence of at least one year; and disqualified any individuals convicted of a felony committed during a riot from receiving federal assistance or holding federal employment. Beginning in 1968, police departments became eligible to seek up to $400 million in federal funds through block grants to state agencies with very few restrictions.[49] At the constitutional level, the rights of citizens under the Fourth Amendment's prohibition against "unreasonable search and seizure" were further eroded, giving police officers broad discretion to engage in stop and frisks without probable cause that a crime had been committed or was in process.[50]

These legislative changes continued on the state level throughout the 1970s. The state of New York was at the forefront in enacting laws imposing harsh penalties for drug possession. In 1973, under Governor Nelson Rockefeller, the state of New York passed a series of harsh drug laws. For example, these laws mandated "mandatory minimum sentences of 15 years to life for possession of four ounces of narcotics—about the same as a sentence for second-degree murder."[51] In 1978, Michigan followed suit and passed the "650 lifer" law. This law mandated a life sentence, with no possibility of parole, for anyone convicted of intent to deliver 650 grams or more of any mixture containing cocaine.[52] Black neighborhoods would bear the brunt of these increased police searches, arrests, and convictions.[53]

When he ascended to the presidency, Reagan built on this "law and order" push by bringing race-neutral language that played the interests of white Americans against the interests of Black Americans.[54] Black people disproportionately received social services like Supplemental Security Income, food stamps, and emergency cash assistance. Therefore, when Reagan attacked "welfare queens" and criminal "predators" who exploited the welfare system, the public understood these people as Black. After his inauguration in January 1981, Reagan implemented regulatory changes and legislation that codified into law these coded associations.

Within the first year of his presidency, Reagan's attorney general, William French Smith, appointed a task force to create a role for the federal government in combating "violent crime."[55] In August 1981, the task force issued a final report to the Department of Justice. In the report, the task force made several recommendations that would alter involvement of the federal government in local and state law enforcement; make military resources available for the containment and prosecution of drug offenders; abolish parole; restrict the writ of habeas corpus; give greater rights to the victims of crimes; allocate additional funds to state and local prisons; and allow federal jurisdiction over juvenile offenders in some cases. In other words, the federal recommendation was that the carceral system be revised and expanded to ensure maximum control over greater numbers of offenders at an increasingly younger age.[56] The number of people in prison would increase exponentially, and the task force anticipated this. In its recommendations, it suggested that abandoned military bases be made available for use as correctional facilities by states and localities.[57] The task force's view of violence was also incredibly restricted and narrowly defined to capture crimes associated with Black and Brown people—drug use and distribution and organized gang activity.[58] As Reagan's war on crime increased the number of Black bodies in US prisons, both the Black community and Farrakhan's Nation took note. In response, the Nation used its geography of imperial resistance to understand why this War on Drugs was happening and how to push back against it.

Prisoners Fight the War on Drugs from Behind Bars

In October 1982, Reagan officially declared a war on drugs.[59] Even prior to this official declaration, Farrakhan was well aware that, as a result of Reagan's legislative and policy changes, the number of incarcerated Black men and women had increased in the United States. He in no way, however, supported drug use or distribution. The Nation's teachings strictly prohibited the use of intoxicating substances, and their use was grounds for exile from the community. However, despite the true threat that drugs and alcohol presented, Farrakhan was concerned about the increase in poverty, single-parent households, physical and mental illness, and general instability in the Black community that would result from Black mass incarceration. Through the *Final Call*, ordinary Muslims in the Nation attempted to understand the realities of mass incarceration, articulated these understandings, and enabled each other to act out against them.

In 1984, the *Final Call* ran a recurring series called "Black Nation behind Bars." This series, which lasted from July 1984 until at least July 1985, made visible incarcerated Muslims by publishing letters they wrote to the publication via postal mail.[60] After July 1985, the publication still published letters from prison, but they were not consolidated under the title "Black Nation behind Bars." Instead, they were published as regular "Letters to the Editor."[61] These letters, although filtered through the institutional prerogatives of Farrakhan and the Nation, give us a window into the thoughts, motivations, theorizations, and ideas of protests of average, non-elite Muslims at the grassroots level and how they applied them to their quotidian existence.

In the first installment of "Black Nation behind Bars," a Muslim named Jonny Anderson promised to report "first-hand information" on his life in an unnamed prison. Anderson gripped his readers' attention with a provocative first sentence proclaiming that it was no "coincidence that Black people in America are only 12% of the total population but over 75% of the inmates of American penal institutions."[62] Noting the connections between poverty, inadequate legal representation, and long prison sentences, the letter proclaimed that "most of the blacks in prisons [are] the victims of a political system that has nothing at all to do with justice."[63] Instead, lamenting that Black women would have nowhere to go to "find hope and fulfillment with their men being destroyed," Anderson concluded that prisons were "a weapon used by the system to again rob the Black race of its male population."[64] Prisons were just another tool in the arsenal of calculated genocide against Black people in America.

A letter published in the second installment of "Black Nation behind Bars" echoes Anderson's concerns about genocide. There, an anonymous inmate at Trenton State Prison in New Jersey wrote to the newspaper in a panic over the existence of an unaddressed AIDS epidemic at the prison. According to this prisoner, several people had died of AIDS at Trenton State since the beginning of the year, and he pleaded for the state of New Jersey to simply educate prisoners about AIDS and HIV.[65] Although the letter reveals many misconceptions about the spread of AIDS and HIV common to the early 1980s, such as the idea that it can be spread through contact with food that an infected person has handled, the focus of this letter was to plead for the preservation of the integrity and health of the Black body both inside, and outside, of prison. This inmate argues that prisons, by ignoring AIDS and HIV, acted as though Black people in prison had been sentenced to "extermination by the Department of Corrections." People were dying because of the Department of Corrections' willful ignorance, but it wasn't simply about the people *inside* prison. As the anonymous prisoner noted, presumably most prisoners would be "returning to the community and the public one day."[66] Therefore, this "disease [presented] a serious threat to [their] well-being and that of [their] famil[ies] and loved ones."[67] The epidemiological effects of deadly prison outbreaks would reverberate in the community at large. This anonymous prisoner, thus, made a connection between the public health consequences of ignoring disease outbreaks and the long-term effects on the Black community.

Prisoners who wrote to "Black Nation behind Bars" did so with an eye to exposing the ineffective and inhumane machinations of the criminal justice system and highlighting Black Muslim political protest. In the same way their predecessors engaged in organized activism in prison in the 1940s, 1950s, and 1960s, Farrakhan's Muslims continued this legacy.[68] In July 1985, a death row prisoner named James E. Smith revealed that a group of prisoners in his cell block had written motions to the court requesting that their pending death row appeals be dismissed and that their sentences be carried out without delay.[69]

Smith's motion was, effectively, a request to quickly end his own life. This seems, initially, like a strange form of protest—particularly for a Muslim in the Nation, a movement that had zealously promoted the increase of the Black population.[70] However, a closer reading of the letter reveals two motivations. One of these motivations is Smith's desire to minimize torture and inhumane conditions while inmates languish, in some cases, for more than a decade. Smith continues to highlight, as previous prisoners had, the shocking and dehumanizing conditions within prisons.[71] Two, Smith reveals the prisoners' collective desire, even in a situation in which their liberty is circumscribed, to exercise agency and control over their lives and deaths. Death in prison, Smith argues, is a money game in which the appeals process only benefits lawyers, judges, and legislators, who are ultimately enriched by this process. By refusing to appeal their sentences, these inmates made a statement that they refused "to be involved as *objects* of legal maneuvers which serve no other purpose but to line [the] pockets of the legalists at the expense of our dehumanization for years while they get rich, and then executed when they can no longer make money off of us." Smith pled, "If we are to be executed, do it now and be done with it. Don't keep us under psychological and physical stress for years."[72] By writing this letter, Smith revealed his desire to assert himself as a human being and to end further attempts at his dehumanization through refusing to engage with a rigged legal system.

"Black Nation behind Bars" gave voice to Black Muslim prisoners who were otherwise silenced by their exile from society and the circumscription of their liberty. While it revealed the inner lives and concerns of male prisoners, it often fell short on highlighting the female experience both inside and outside of prison. In the entire year-long run of "Black Nation behind Bars," only one letter came from a female prisoner. Part of this lack of representation has to do with the Nation's focus during this time. Farrakhan was fixated on the vacuum caused by the lack of Black men in urban communities. This was consistent with the Nation's long-standing belief that Black men needed to take on the role of providers and protectors of Black women and the Black family, roles they had been robbed of because of slavery and Jim Crow. To the extent that he was concerned about women, his concerns related to how they would be affected by the absence of Black male leadership, control, and guidance. The majority of the testimonials from "Black Nation behind Bars" gives a skewed perception and an almost entirely Black male view of the effects of mass incarceration. Women often factor into these analyses only in terms of how men *believed* women would be affected by the absence of Black men in the community.

There is one notable exception. In July 1985, over a year after "Black Nation Behind Bars" began, three women wrote a joint letter to the *Final Call*. These women, Jacqui Lopes, Deborah McCants, and Susan Johnson, were inmates at a women's correctional facility in Framingham, Massachusetts. The letter, unlike previous missives written by male inmates, does not show incarcerated women as political beings, nor does it share their experiences in prison. Instead, the letter focuses on these women's submission to Allah and on their acceptance of the Nation's teachings on the appropriate gender roles for Black men and women. Lopes, McCants, and Johnson wrote, "The Black Woman must be restored to her proper place as The Mother of all nations and the Black Man must return to his responsibility as head of the house.... There is a way to stop this deliberate and systematic destruction of our people—genocide, for Islam is not only a religion, but it is a way of life: the proper way for the Black Man and Woman."[73] These women, thus, focus on execution of a proper Muslim way of life, and how the gender balance that it promoted was disrupted through these genocidal practices. This type of doubling down on the Nation's strict gender roles is not uncommon among the Nation's female adherents, and it reflects, as Ula Taylor argues, a power in the message of patriarchy and the promise of protection for Black women that Black nationalist organizations like the Nation promoted.[74] Black women like Lopes, McCants, and Johnson often found themselves at the intersection of a promise of protection, adoration, and support located within the Nation's message, and the blatantly misogynist discourse about a woman's inferior position in the family and community hierarchy.[75] Although these three women publicly toed the line of the Nation's gender teachings, it is impossible to tell what kind of internal conflicts and reservations they may have had. Moreover, the editors of the *Final Call* likely chose to publish letters that reflected their own gender teachings—men's letters considering the social and political consequences of their incarceration, and women reflecting on the way that Islam could remedy the removal of a strong Black male head of household. We do not know how many letters arguing the opposite, or representing women as political thinkers in their own right, were thrown in the trash.

Self-Fulfilling Prophecies: Islam's Role in Fighting the Crack Epidemic and the War on Drugs

In October 1985, the Reagan administration started a media campaign targeting crack cocaine.[76] When Reagan started his war on drugs in 1982, crack was not in the legislative or executive imaginary. It had not yet been introduced to the drug market and was not widely available until late 1985, three years after Reagan's War on Drugs began. Changes to the carceral system preceded the appearance of crack cocaine in the United States, but crack's appearance provided a convenient excuse to legitimize the sweeping changes to American drug policy. In June of 1986, *Newsweek* declared crack to be a story on par with the Vietnam War, the fall of the Nixon presidency, and the civil rights movement, and pledged to cover it with the same frequency.[77]

Crack certainly presented a convenient excuse to wage a drug war, but that does not minimize the reality that its presence caused a true crisis in the Black community. The mainstream media widely reported on the effects of crack in the inner city, often publishing sensationalist stories stoking white middle-class fears. In June and July 1986 alone, immediately after the drug came to the attention of politicians and the media, the *New York Times* ran at least fifteen stories on crack cocaine.[78] But the Black Muslim press also wasted no time reporting on what was to become a legitimate crisis in the Black community. These stories concentrated on highlighting the experiences of former and current members of the Nation, both incarcerated and free. In addition, these articles identified crack as a genocidal tool against the Black community and identified Islam as the only way to overcome this plot.

For the remainder of this chapter, when discussing the Black response to the threat of crack cocaine use, distribution, and the attendant increase in Black-on-Black violence, I will use the term "crack crisis." I use this term instead of the term "crack epidemic," commonly used in the press in the 1980s and 1990s. This is because, as historian Donna Murch notes, the term "crack epidemic" denotes a state-sponsored discourse mobilizing fear, anger, and disorientation to justify the growth of the carceral state in Black communities. "Crack crisis," on the other hand, addresses the fact that members of the Black community, like the Nation, recognized the unprecedented threat of crack and sought solutions.[79]

The *Final Call* picked up stories centering the crack crisis in August 1986, after the mainstream media sensationalized its emergence. By August, however, the newspaper noted that crack had already led to devastating consequences for the Black community. The drug was so powerful that it was ravaging the Black community and leaving "twisted, dehydrated human frames in its wake."[80] When the *Final Call* ran its first story on crack cocaine, the author, Lamont X Curry, used the lives of four residents of Harlem to center his article. All of these individuals were at that time addicted to crack, had recovered from their addiction, or had family members who had been afflicted by an addiction to crack. At least two of these individuals were associated with the Nation.

In this article, Curry takes his readers on a visual and textual journey through the crack dens of Harlem guided by a man named Blondie. Early in the article, we learn that Blondie used to be a part of the Nation but was no longer a member. This is evident when he and Curry approached a crack house on 142nd Street, between Amsterdam Avenue and Broadway. As the door creaked open, Blondie proudly introduced Curry and the freelance photographer joining them as journalists from the *Final Call*. Moreover, he asserted his Muslim identity to the bouncer. He proudly confessed, "I'm a Muslim. I was in the Nation and I'm going back."[81] We don't know the reason for Blondie's absence from the Nation of Islam, but there is a good chance it has to do with his drug use. Although he claimed to be on the road to recovery from crack cocaine addiction, he admitted that he still occasionally smokes a "wuda," a crack cocaine–spiked marijuana joint.

Blondie's story, while satisfying the reader's voyeuristic tendencies and curiosity, gives us an incredibly humanizing picture of the crack crisis. He described the feeling of taking crack cocaine, but he also emphasized the human toll that the drug was taking on the Black community in Harlem. Blondie lamented, "They find so many bodies on 144th street that they don't even chalk around the bodies anymore. 'X' marks the spot and that's it. There were 28 bodies taken out of here last month, man."[82] Here, Blondie emphasized the sheer number of victims of the crack crisis in Harlem in 1986 and expressed his exasperation with the inability of even these shocking numbers of dead Harlemites to make an impact on the environment around them—whether visually through a chalked outline on the sidewalk or materially by serving as a warning and stopping future deaths.

Curry concluded his exposé by recounting the experience of recovered addict and current Nation member Eugene 12X Butler. As he sat on the porch of an abandoned building on 148th Street, Butler's father wove in and out of Curry's vision turning rapidly in circles, high on crack, chasing what he described as an invisible "cloud." Butler revealed that crack caused him to lose everything in his life. He confessed, "Crack did to me in one year what speedballs (heroin mixed with cocaine) couldn't do in 17.... When I moved into this block I had a wife, children, a Cadillac, a job. Crack took it all."[83]

Butler emphasized, like Blondie, the human impact of the crack epidemic. While the mainstream media reported on the statistics and public policy implications of crack cocaine, Curry's feature—through Butler and Blondie—focused on the lived experiences of people in the Black community in Harlem during the late 1980s. They are, of course, meant to be a cautionary tale for the *Final Call*'s readers, emphasizing the devastation that crack had wrought on the Black community and that it could wreak on a person's life. But they also propose that Islam is the solution to saving the Black community from this scourge. Blondie and Butler demonstrate this through their own words. At the beginning of Curry's story, when Blondie convinced the guard at the crack house to allow them to enter, Blondie chastized the guard for his reluctance to let them in, reasoning, "You'll let them whites come through here with cameras and (bleep) and they don't mean you no good. These brothers want to help our people."[84] By the end of the journey, Blondie and Butler still believe that the Nation had a critical role in tempering the crisis of crack cocaine in the Black community. Both expressed, in their own words, the sentiment that "in a little while the only thing standing in America will be the Nation, because only Allah can deal with crack."[85] The story concludes with hope brought by the Muslim religion. Both Butler and Blondie changed their lives, making substantial steps toward recovery and rebuilding their lives. We discover at the end of the article that Blondie was able to make amends with his wife and children. Butler moved to Long Island, got a new job, regained custody of his children, and was heading toward reconciling with his wife. He reported, "Allah has blessed me brother. He is ever merciful. I will have my new car in a minute. I'm working on a house and will soon go get Silvia (his wife). She'll make it all complete."[86]

A Practice Round for the Inner City

In 1986, crack cocaine was widely available on the streets of American cities, and the US military secretly armed counterrevolutionary armies in Nicaragua against the Marxist-Leninist Sandinista government. The Nation reported on these two events simultaneously and, after the American invasion of Panama in 1988, began to link American imperial expansion and the militarization of the police in American inner cities. The *Final Call*'s preoccupation with Nicaragua took up the bulk of the decade, but the treatment of Panama beginning in 1988 allowed for a fuller connection between the rise of American military aggression in the Circum-Caribbean and its connections to the American inner city. It would be these connections that eventually birthed the Dopebusters movement, which placed Muslim men in charge of policing and redeeming their own communities.

Farrakhan had warned that the US government had a plan to commit genocide against Black people since at least 1978. He had spoken on the increase in mass incarceration of Black men as early as 1983, of an actual crack epidemic in the Black community as early as 1986, and of the war on drugs repeatedly as a war on Black freedom. However, when Farrakhan began to talk about a "deep" and "diabolical" plot to use military force against Black youth in the inner city, he was reflecting on current events, including the mobilization of the US military to assist local law enforcement in the federal government's growing national War on Drugs.

In 1989, Congress earmarked $300 million of the defense budget to curtail the flow of illegal drugs into the United States through surveillance and interdiction outside of the country.[87] In March of 1989, the federal government revisited the possibility of using both active and abandoned military prisons for inmates convicted of drug crimes, citing overcrowding in civilian jails as the justification. In March and April of 1989, the Department of Defense approved the release of $40 million in funds to National Guard militias across the United States and to local police departments. The stated purpose of the money was to aid local law enforcement in surveillance and tracking of drug smugglers, to assist with customs searches of shipping containers, and to lend equipment to local law enforcement, including infrared goggles, helicopters, military-grade arms, and bulletproof vests.[88]

For Farrakhan and the journalists of the *Final Call*, one of the most disturbing parts of this systematic expansion of the federal military into the inner city was the response of liberal Black leadership. By 1986, when the mainstream media regularly started reporting on the "crack epidemic," Black leaders across America's cities acknowledged that crack was making a negative impact on their communities.[89] Black leaders were sharply divided, however, on whether to support the harsh government response. Some leaders saw the militarization of the police as simply another way to subjugate and pacify Black bodies. These voices advocated for drug treatment, job training, and a focus on social services as opposed to boosting law enforcement. Others, however, felt that the threat presented by crack cocaine was the greater one to the Black community and needed to be stopped at all costs. These leaders focused on the crack crisis and the increase in gang violence in order to justify the growth of the carceral state and militarization of the police.[90] Farrakhan and the Nation fall into the former category.

In an editorial published in July 1989, *Final Call* editor Wali Muhammad criticized mainstream liberal Black leaders when he noted that the NAACP and the Urban League had remained silent in the face of widespread civil liberties violations connected to drug raids in Los Angeles and Florida.[91] In September 1989, Muhammad wrote that the US government was setting up Black leaders to sanction the invasion and colonization of the Black community by the US military. Specifically, liberal Black leaders like John Jacob of the Urban League and Reverend Jacob Lowery of the Southern Christian Leadership Conference were practically begging for an increased law-and-order response to drugs in the Black community.[92] According to Muhammad, these leaders were misled by their myopic vision.

Muhammad argued that Jacob, Lowery, and other Black leaders had failed to recognize the explicit connections between American neo-imperialism and the drug problem in the inner city. He wrote, "We must ask the right questions. Who brings the drugs into our country? Who makes the guns; where do they come from?"[93] Drugs came from abroad, Muhammad wrote, from foreign elements supported by the United States like the Contras. More troublingly, none of the voices who "stridently call for a war on drug dealers ... [had] raised [their voices] with indignation at Mr. Bush for his part in the Contra drug schemes, which brought illegal drugs on U.S. planes into this country; drugs which ultimately found their way into the pockets of those drug dealers [they want] to make war on."[94]

In anticipation of the December 1989 invasion of Panama, Muhammad asked, "Will U.S. troops invade Panama under the guise of arresting General Manuel Noriega for drug charges, and claim the Panama Canal?"[95] More importantly, would Black leadership be used as pawns to allow a silent invasion of the Black inner city? As Muhammad painted a war scene, where "fires rage, bullets tear through flesh and metal, grenades explode, tear gas permeates, and blood soaks the streets of the inner city," he asked whether Black leadership will later cry out that they "only wanted to get rid of the drugs."[96] By the end of 1989, this exact scenario seemed imminent as Black congressman Major Owens entered into discussions with New York governor Mario Cuomo to permit the National Guard to back up New York Police Department forces

FIGURE 6.2 A political cartoon of Reagan and Bush fused together and stepping into Nicaragua. The word "Next?!" questions where American empire will next go. In the *Final Call*, January 29, 1990, p. 12. Cartoon by Robert Muhammad.

"overwhelmed with drug-related violence."⁹⁷ In January 1990, as discussions of allowing the National Guard to invade Brooklyn were taking place between Governor Cuomo and Owens, the Nation responded to the December 1989 invasion of Panama, making connections between the American invasion and the death of marginalized Black and Brown people.⁹⁸

The War on Drugs was part of a chain of events that led American presidents from one Black space to another. Echoing an earlier political cartoon from April 1986 in which Reagan stepped from Grenada into Nicaragua wearing combat boots (figure 6.1), a political cartoon published on January 29, 1990, emphasized the connection between US military expansion in the Caribbean and Bush's then-war on Panama. In political cartoonist Robert Muhammad's vision, presidents Reagan and Bush were fused together as conjoined twins, representing Bush's continuation of Reagan's pro-imperialist policies. Reagan, with a smoking gun in his hand, placed one foot in Grenada as he and Bush stepped together into Panama. Bush's foot hovered mid-step, as the word "Next?!" questioned where would be the next logical place over which American Empire would extend (figure 6.2).⁹⁹

For the Nation, what was logically "Next" was an invasion of the inner city justified by the War on Drugs and assisted by a global expansion of the American military apparatus. Just as the United States had used drugs to demonize and remove Noriega in order to reassert imperial control over the Panama Canal, the War on Drugs in the United States was positioned as a mere farce intended to cover the government's intention to pacify and subjugate the Black community. Muhammad elaborated that "the alleged *War on Drugs* ... has been the Trojan horse smuggling extra police officers, sheriffs, FBI agents, and soon National Guardsmen into the inner cities of America resulting in legions of black youth being locked up in America's prisons and jails."[100] He then plainly stated, "Panama was just practice for the real thing; urban warfare in the United States against black people."[101]

Muhammad's language was inflammatory, but it was not an unsubstantiated conspiracy theory. Since World War II, American police had been used as security experts by the US military and State Department to maintain law and order and prevent the spread of communism and anti-American interests abroad. This process necessarily reinforced American and imperial racial hierarchies. As these police and security officers cycled through their tours of duty, they applied the lessons they took from counterinsurgency prevention abroad and used them to maintain racial hierarchies and social control at home.[102] Thus, the Nation's discourse about Panama as a "practice round" for the militarized racial oppression on the horizon for American Black people was not conjecture or conspiracy theory, but took stock of these realities and used them in order to promote its message of community control, self-reliance, and Muslim religious redemption.

Dopebusting and the Search for Productive Solutions

If the War on Drugs was a farce, it stood to reason that it was not designed to help or rehabilitate the Black community, but instead to subject it to more suffering. Thus, in addition to exposing the actual harm the War on Drugs would do to the Black community, the Nation expressed the reality that the War on Drugs was simply ineffective. Not only was this ongoing siege actually contributing to unemployment, poverty, death, and alienation in the Black community, but it was also largely ineffective at stopping the sale, use, and distribution of drugs. Moreover, it did nothing to address the root causes of gang activity and Black participation in the illicit drug economy.[103]

All of this went back to the expansion of empire. Drugs themselves were simply an imperialist political "tool of the colonizer" designed to "destroy the productive capacities of youth."[104] These frustrations with the failure of the drug war led Nation members to take matters into their own hands at the government level. In May 1990, an article in the *Final Call* announced the candidacy of three Washington, DC, Nation members for public office. This article was accompanied by a striking photographic representation, expressing the candidates' exasperation with the government's response against crack cocaine. The photograph showed the three candidates surrounding a display-sided report card, grading President Bush's drug czar, William Bennett, on his progress on the War on Drugs. The results of the Nation's assessment were scathing. In six out of seven categories, which included drug abuse, crime prevention, community relations, drug rehabilitation, drug interdiction, and keeping promises, Bennett was given an "F." The sole aberration in Bennett's failing score was the mark given to him regarding his rhetoric. On that category, the report card assigned a mark of "I" for incoherent.[105]

It was in response to the types of frustrations reflected by the "Report Card" on the War on Drugs that the Nation's Dopebusters program was born in April of 1988 when A. Alim Muhammad stood on the dais in front of the Mayfair Mansions community, with the star and crescent moon flying at full staff over the complex. Modeled on successful Black Muslim drug patrols in Bedford-Stuyvesant, Brooklyn, led by former Nation member and Sunni imam Siraj Wahhaj, the Nation mobilized Muslim and non-Muslim men to patrol the grounds of several housing complexes in the Washington, DC, area.[106] They homed in on the increasing militarization of local police forces and the language of "war" circulating in the media to launch a countermilitarization and Islamic jihad against law enforcement, the government, and drugs themselves.[107] FOI used intimidating tactics, and violence where necessary, to discourage drug dealers from entering the grounds of complexes they patrolled. One of the first incidents involved Dopebusters assaulting a man who allegedly pulled a sawed-off shotgun and a camera crew recording the events.[108] This resulted in largely negative initial media attention for the Dopebusters program.[109]

Despite these negative reports, however, the Nation maintained that the program had made quick progress in reducing the visible presence of drug-related activity at Mayfair Mansions. Although it is unclear whether these claims are empirically true, testimonials by some individuals interviewed for the Nation, national mainstream, and international publications do indicate that at least some members of the community expressed positive responses to the presence of the Dopebusters immediately after they began their patrols.[110] For example, in an interview in *Time* magazine, the property manager of Mayfair Mansions, Glenn French, indicated that he was delighted by the Dopebusters, stating that the Dopebusters' presence had caused "something good [to happen] here."[111] Community politicians and non-Muslim religious leaders also publicly thanked the Dopebusters. Councilman H. R. Crawford said, "We need the Muslims and we applaud them.... We do support their efforts to stabilize our communities."[112] Reverend Ernest Gibson, identified by the Nation as a prominent religious leader in the community, said that he "deeply appreciated the effort to rid the community of drug traffic and violence."[113] Gibson also shrugged off the Dopebusters' initial altercation, blaming the incident on the man who drew the gun. He explained, "A shotgun is violence; once you have drawn it, the violence has started."[114]

The patrolling system was only one part of the Dopebusters effort, however. From the beginning, the Nation recognized that drug dealers and traffickers were simply supplying a product in relation to the community's demand. Therefore, in order to truly eradicate drugs, the community's "appetite for illegal drugs" needed to be addressed.[115] This hunger was fueled by a "spiritual sickening" to which the Nation and the Dopebusters would tend.[116] Part of that project was treating addiction at the source by providing treatment and counseling services for those addicted to crack cocaine and other drugs.

In January 1989, Farrakhan held a press conference to announce that the Dopebusters anti-drug program would expand again to include a methadone-free drug rehabilitation facility. The clinic, named the Abundant Life Clinic, was introduced in response to a request by Muslims in the community for drug treatment for an afflicted community member. From there, the program expanded to become a permanent fixture at Mayfair Mansions. The treatment plan would include medical withdrawal counseling as well as psychological therapy and support by three Nation members who had themselves overcome drug addiction.[117] Although the program was technically open to all residents regardless of religious affiliation, there is strong evidence that the psychological counseling included instruction in the Nation's key teachings and constituted a form of Islamic *da'wah*. In addition to therapy, the program included "manhood and womanhood training."[118] It is not clear what exactly that instruction entailed in the context of drug rehabilitation, but it can be assumed that this reiterated the Nation's gendered teachings and provided a practical opportunity for Farrakhan to increase his visibility and embeddedness in these communities.

The Dopebusters program, however, was envisioned to lie at the intersection of religious duty and military mobilization. It was both a countermilitary exercise and a jihad against drugs as a tool of the colonizer. As the historian Garrett Felber argues, this response to the discipline of the state was accomplished with members' own discipline—of body, of soul, and of community—and constituted a "dialectics of discipline."[119] In this particular instance, this dialectic presented itself through the performance of military pomp. First, the Nation coordinated Dopebusters activities through its paramilitary branch, the FOI. These men looked and acted like soldiers. Although they carried walkie-talkies and not weapons, they were regularly trained in self-defense and martial arts techniques, and wore uniforms embellished with the symbol of their nation—the star and crescent moon. At Mayfair Mansions, these "soldiers" took up space in the complex, demarcating their space with a plaque indicating that these were, indeed, "Officers' Quarters."[120] A flag bearing the star and crescent moon flew proudly over the complex as FOI patrolled the grounds, intimidated drug dealers, and sought to restore the "order" that the "law" seemed to be at best unable, and at worse unwilling, to do.[121] When Dopebusters went on their patrols, they carried the Nation's flag with them like a battle flag.[122]

Second, the Nation symbolically reinforced the association between the Dopebusters program and a religious military expedition. This was evident in the performances, including the music, that surrounded the unveiling of the Dopebusters program itself. For example, as indicated at the beginning of this introduction, at the first Dopebusters rally, the choice of the song "Battle Hymn of the Republic" positioned the activities of the FOI as the instruments of truth and redemption for their nation and their God.[123] Third, the language that the Nation used to describe the environment into which it was intervening often used the language of war, violence, and battle. In an article describing the alleged successes of the Dopebusters program, a *Final Call* journalist described Mayfair Mansions before the Dopebusters' intervention as a "war zone, complete with nightly and daily gun battles."[124]

During the Dopebusters program, Farrakhan and other Dopebusters officials emphasized that they were compelled to wage this jihad against drugs because of their Muslim faith. Repeatedly, Farrakhan and Dr. Alim Muhammad, who ran the Abundant Life Clinic, emphasized the immense sacrifice of the Dopebusters soldiers. Part of that sacrifice was economic. Dr. Muhammad noted that some Dopebusters volunteers were so dedicated to their patrols that they had stayed up all night and either missed work or arrived late. But there was also an immense physical risk to the bodies of the Dopebusters soldiers. These threats emerged not only from drug dealers but also from the police.

Often, the FOI came under intense police scrutiny, and members found themselves in verbal and physical altercations with law enforcement. In August 1989, twenty-five Fruit of Islam members patrolling an area of downtown Washington, DC, known for prostitution and drug sales alleged that they were assaulted by DC Metropolitan Police and Secret Service agents wielding revolvers, blackjacks, and nightsticks. While the details of this altercation are unclear—as is the matter of why the Secret Service would be involved—photographs published in the *Final Call* showed that three FOI members were left substantially bloodied after the interaction.[125] In Los Angeles, Dopebusters soldiers alleged that they were repeatedly harassed, physically assaulted, and even killed by the police.[126] Thus, while Dopebusters was born out of ideas about Islam and its power as an anticolonial, counteroppressive force, this discourse served a real purpose. It sustained the men who embarked on these patrols as they risked their bodily safety to ensure the safety of the Black community.

Conclusion

Whether the Dopebusters and Abundant Life actually reduced crime or cured addiction in the neighborhoods they patrolled is a difficult question to answer given the available sources. Local police agencies often refused to comment on the effectiveness of the Dopebusters.[127] And by the Nation's own accounts, the Dopebusters were—of course—incredibly successful. From the program's founding in 1988 into the 1990s, the *Final Call* published pieces on the Dopebusters filled with laudatory quotations from local politicians, from residents and staff of the housing complexes they patrolled, and from Black newspapers and magazines.[128] These sources, however, must be viewed with a critical eye as they were designed to boost the Nation's visibility and reputation. Moreover, these reports were intended to emphasize the Islamic duty that Dopebusters engaged as they participated in these grassroots countermilitary campaigns. They conjured images of FOI men marching into crack dens to intimidate drug dealers while holding their ideals, the flag of their nation, and their belief in Allah aloft.

Outside of these self-serving narratives, however, there is mixed evidence of the Dopebusters' effectiveness, and their commitment to faith and community over notoriety and financial gain. In February 1989, the *Washington Post* reported that the Nation had started asking for $5,000 "donations" to provide the Dopebusters service and openly questioned whether the service was for the public good.[129] Other publications went further, equating the request for such a large sum of money from impoverished Black communities with few other options to extortion.[130] Nation officials insisted that the donations were necessary because they had been "deluged" with requests from communities under siege.

Whether it was "extortion" or not, communities continued to pay the $5,000 donations and actively petitioned their local governments to pay the Nation to patrol their neighborhoods. Through these acts, residents indicated that they saw immense value in the Dopebusters service.[131] Some residents, especially the elderly, spoke to mainstream journalists and credited the Nation's patrols with a reduction in crime and an overall calm and "blissful" environment.[132] At Ocean Towers, a New York state-financed housing project, the management company credited the Dopebusters with reducing vacancies from fifty in 1993 to five by 1996.[133] Young people had a mixed response, sometimes protesting the Dopebusters' presence.[134]

Perhaps for many, Dopebusters was a selfless endeavor, but it was also a money-making enterprise. While official FOI patrols were originally free or donation based, by the mid-1990s, Nation members had incorporated at least eight for-profit security corporations in Maryland, Pennsylvania, New York, Illinois, and Washington, DC.[135] These corporations actively competed for and successfully won security contracts to police public and federally subsidized apartment complexes. The value of these contracts ranged from tens of thousands to millions of dollars.[136] In early 1995 alone, Nation corporations held nine contracts worth approximately $10 million. Another fifteen contracts had expired or had been terminated.[137] This capitalist project is in line with the Nation's Black nationalist roots and its emphasis on "doing for self" through Black-owned business. The evidence is also consistent with the assertion that Black communities actively lobbied for the presence of Dopebusters in their neighborhoods and saw immense value in these security services. Whether they were paid a $5,000 donation or signed a multi-million-dollar contract, by the mid-1990s, it was clear that Dopebusters was in demand.

In 1994, these Dopebusters corporations gained unwanted attention from the Department of Housing and Urban Development (HUD), which accused them of improper licensing, filing false tax information, and discriminatory hiring practices. By November 1995, after an investigation, HUD canceled all Nation security contracts in federal housing projects.[138] Cancellation of contracts at the state and local levels soon followed, with some jurisdictions alleging that the cancellation was due to the Dopebusters' propensity to disseminate "anti-Semitic propaganda."[139] As these contracts were terminated by state and federal agencies, residents threatened to vote with their feet by saying that if the Dopebusters left, they would leave as well.[140]

For Dopebusters, HUD's investigation was the beginning of the end. In June 1995, the Nation of Islam Security Agency, Inc., filed for voluntary bankruptcy protection, citing unpaid federal and state taxes in excess of $240,000 and other debts.[141] In September 1996, the Internal Revenue Service froze the assets of Dr. Muhammad's Abundant Life Clinic, alleging that it owed $43,000 in taxes.[142] By the end of the twentieth century, most of these corporations were involuntarily dissolved by local secretaries of state, or fell into bad standing due to failure to file relevant statutorily required forms.[143] After that, they fall out of the historical record with regard to the suppression of drug use and distribution in Black inner-city neighborhoods.

WHILE THE ULTIMATE SUCCESS, or failure, of the Dopebusters is unclear, what is evident is that Dopebusters was a practical solution implemented in response to a sixteen-year-long process of intellectual production about the growth of American empire abroad, and the subjugation of Black bodies at home through drugs, surveillance, and police brutality. When the US empire expanded into the Circum-Caribbean, resulting in the incursions into Grenada, Panama, and Nicaragua, the Nation understood these invasions as part of a logical chain of events and condemned the United States' actions. As Reagan's War on Drugs bulked up local police department arsenals and coffers, amending federal laws to do so, Farrakhan and the Nation's writers interpreted these events as a manifestation of white supremacy intimately connected to America's military aggression in the Circum-Caribbean. Both of these processes involved the use of the military and violence to subjugate and dominate Black people and resources.

The Nation did not do much in practice to broker peace in the Circum-Caribbean region, but it drew a firm line at sitting idly by when it came to the protection of its own "nation within a nation." Motivated by years of creating a discourse that understood mass incarceration and drugs as genocide, Nation members absorbed the anti-imperial discourse that Farrakhan and the editors of the *Final Call* created, applied it to their own life circumstances, and took action at the grassroots level to eradicate drugs, violence, and addiction from their communities. While imperfect, the Nation's activism through Dopebusters represents how rank-and-file members of the Nation translated Farrakhan's religio-political discourse and intellectual production into practice in order to shape their own understanding and practice of Islam in the African diaspora, and to mold their own vision of the Atlantic Crescent.

EPILOGUE

The Bow, the Arrow, and the Crescent
Blackness and Islam in the Past, Present, and Future

In February 2016, over four decades after he converted to the Nation of Islam in an American prison, Mustapha Rasheed joined me in the middle of a construction site in St. George, Bermuda, to reflect on the totality of his identity as a Muslim, Black, and Bermudian man. In the 1980s, Rasheed transitioned to Islam under the ministry of Imam Warith Deen Muhammad; began to observe the Sunnah, the body of sayings and practices of the Prophet Muhammad that guide the lives of Sunni Muslims; started to derive his religious practice from the Qur'an itself; and rejected Elijah Muhammad's teachings that the white man was the devil. One thing that he never abandoned, however, was the idea that Blackness and being a colonized Bermudian subject were both of critical importance to his religious practice and identity. Even though Rasheed practices Sunni Islam today, this racial and religious positioning remains an integral part of his beliefs and the reason that he elected to follow Imam Muhammad, specifically. According to Rasheed, to be Black and Muslim in the Atlantic world is to understand the nature of Islam and the place of race in systems of historical oppression. He summarized the process as follows: Race and "ethnicity [are] the bow [but] the arrow is Islam."[1]

This is how Rasheed defined his Atlantic Crescent, his own Muslim religio-racial identity at the intersection of his understanding of his own experience and his interpretation of discourses about global racial injustice, white supremacy, and colonial domination. For Rasheed, as he imagined himself to be part of a locally specific and globally engaged articulation of Islam, he rooted himself firmly in his Afro-Bermudian experience while engaging Islam as a transcendent and universal religious tradition.

Rasheed is only one of many Black and Muslim people whose testimonies, papers, writings, and experiences form the archive that I used to write this book. Over the preceding six chapters, I have argued that Black and Muslim people from World War I until the end of the twentieth century used Islam to dream of a world free from white supremacy, anti-Black racism, and colonial domination. In some cases, I have demonstrated that these groups, communities, and individuals went beyond the realm of discourse and used these ideas to implement concrete plans to fight against colonialism, resource extraction, and labor expropriation; to build their own anti-imperial educational systems; to form their own community policing bodies inspired by their anticolonial worldview; and to create their own transnational intellectual, religious, and political communities. In these processes of thinking about and organizing their relationship to both Islam and Blackness, these Black and Muslim people used these imagined geographies of imperial resistance along with the framework, doctrines, practice, and ethics of Islam to develop a new religio-racial identity and religio-political orientation, an imagined space I call the "Atlantic Crescent."

I situate the history of Black Islam in the twentieth-century Atlantic world at the intersection of three overlapping diasporas—African Americans from the Southern United States during the first part of the Great Migration (1915–30), African-descended people from the Anglophone Caribbean (1900–37), and South Asian migrants (1900–30). At the same time as these diasporas were moving across space and coming into contact with each other, nationalist and anticolonial movements from Southeast Asia to the African continent began to gain steam. As these discourses flowed across oceans, carried by new forms of media and by the people who experienced them, they created solidarities between themselves and other populations living under the yoke of white supremacy and racial violence. At the intersection of these overlapping diasporas, and in the context of these political and cultural movements, Black and Muslim people leaned on Islam to unite themselves with far-flung populations, to feed their radical imaginaries, and to make sense of their histories in global context. In this way, these Black and Muslim thinkers became able to discursively reconfigure their social and political status. Instead of minorities, they were united together as a global majority.

Part I of this book explores the ways that Black and Muslim elites and intellectuals, in the Venn diagram of these diasporas, created, adapted, and modified their geographies of imperial resistance and used these geographies to craft their own internationalist Muslim movements. Chapter 1 begins in the second decade of the twentieth century and examines the rise of two early Black and Muslim movements, the Moorish Science Temple of America (MSTA) and the Ahmadiyya Movement in Islam (AMI). I argue that these movements, and their leaders, used Black nationalism, Black internationalism, and Afro-Asian discourses to create an Islam that would appeal to the resettled African American communities of the Great Migration. These discourses were forged through discursive and physical encounters with ideas and people from the Black Anglophone Caribbean (through Marcus Garvey and the UNIA) and the Indian subcontinent (through the Ahmadiyya). Chapter 2 uses the life of a Pakistani Muslim immigrant named Abdul Basit Naeem, his travels, his dynamic philosophies, his experience with decolonization, and his relationships with African American and Afro-Caribbean immigrants to examine how Naeem's journalism contributed to the Nation's internationalist discourse and religious teachings during the 1950s and 1960s. Chapter 3 explores the use of print media, in particular the newspaper, as a medium that was used by Black and Muslim people to inscribe themselves within a larger Muslim ummah. In particular, this chapter looks at the ways that Elijah Muhammad, Malcolm X, and the imam of the Muslim Brotherhood USA, Afro-Antiguan Talib Dawud, used print media to make claims to authenticity and to further their inclusion in a Black and Muslim anti-imperial geography.

Part II incorporates the perspectives of rank-and-file Black and Muslim people in the United States and in the Anglophone Caribbean. All of these practitioners and theorists were associated at some point with the Nation and continued to be influenced by it throughout their activist lives. Part II's primary preoccupation is the ways that regular Black and Muslim people interpreted institutional directives, using them to take control of their own salvation and liberation. In doing so, these practitioners often created a living Islam much different from that articulated by the leaders at the head of their movements, and responsive to their own local, geographical, cultural, and historical circumstances. To this end, two of the three chapters in this section focus on the island of Bermuda. There, far away from central leadership, Bermudian people were able to craft a politically inflected Islam linked to Black Power, labor radicalism, and communism. Chapter 4 uses a case study to examine how Black and Muslim activists translated the anti-imperial geographies developed by Elijah Muhammad into action in the Bermudian context. I explore the involvement of Nation members in the island's Black Power movement, in the labor radicalism movement, in the movement for independence, and in the communist party. These dynamics were markedly different from the way that Nation of Islam practitioners manifested their religious and political practice anywhere else in the world and were adapted to Bermuda's unique circumstances. Chapter 5 continues to look at the Bermudian Muslim community, this time after its transition to Sunni Islam under the leadership of Imam Warith Deen Muhammad. Comparing the documentary archival record with the memories and oral testimonies of the female members of this community, I examine their central role in the building of the island's Muslim parochial school, a feat they identified as critical to their survival as Black and Muslim people living under empire. In constructing this school, these women engaged their history in the Nation, identifying it as the source of their radicalism. Chapter 6 takes us back to the United States and examines the ways that members of Louis Farrakhan's Nation of Islam intellectualized and acted on a growing militarization of the American inner city during the 1980s and 1990s. Connecting the United States' so-called War on Drugs with the expansion of military aggression in the Circum-Caribbean region, these Black and Muslim people used Farrakhan's internationalist discourse to figure out real solutions to mass incarceration, crack cocaine, and the devastation affecting their communities.

AS A WORK OF HISTORICAL SCHOLARSHIP, *Atlantic Crescent* has elucidated the dynamics and intellectual foundations of Black and Muslim liberation movements in the twentieth century. I chose to begin this monograph in 1913, with Noble Drew Ali's founding of the Canaanite Temple in Newark, New Jersey. I elected to end in the late 1990s, with the rise and fall of the Nation's Dopebusters security organization and its origins during a period of increasing American military aggression in the Circum-Caribbean and police activity in the American inner city. But my decision to limit this study to these years was born out of a complex web of reasons and considerations, including disciplinary conventions, archival limitations, page limits, and the pesky—but omnipresent—reality of my readers' limited time and attention span. None of what I have written in this book should be construed to mean that Black and Muslim internationalism, political solidarity, or intellectual community lived and died in those years alone. Nor should my words be taken to argue that this was a phenomenon confined exclusively to the past.

As I began the steady march toward finishing this book, I've heard the constant echo of Mustapha Rasheed's words in my head—his assertion that Blackness is the bow, or the tool, that he used to orient and direct the arrow of his interpretation and practice of Islam. I thought about his claim that to be Black and Muslim is to have a unique relationship to systems of racial and colonial oppression. And then I reflected on the direction and orientation of Black Islam's arrow so far in the twenty-first century, and where it is going in the future.

In the second decade of the twenty-first century, Black and Muslim liberation movements have continued to focus on the connections between local, national, and international subjugation as a vestige of colonialism, imperialism, and slavery. These connections between the suffering of far-flung nonwhite populations are not new but, as I've shown in this book, were developed, cultivated, and adapted over the course of the twentieth century. Just as Black and Muslim internationalism changed over the twentieth century in response to local and global events, it continues to shift today. Today, solidly in the third decade of the twenty-first century, the flash point for Black and Muslim solidarity in the Americas is firmly focused on how the treatment of Palestinian people by the state of Israel and the subjugation of Black people by a growing and expanding militarized local and international police force are part and parcel of the same oppressive mechanisms.[2]

How did this become the case? In the summer of 2014, two seemingly unrelated events thousands of miles away solidified the intellectual, political, and spiritual relationship between the movement for Black lives and the movement for Palestine liberation. First, for fifty-one days in July and August 2014, the Israeli Defense Forces launched their most intense air and ground assault since 2006 in the Gaza Strip, razing apartment buildings, private homes, hospitals, schools, mosques, refugee camps, power plants, and water treatment facilities. This military assault, dubbed "Operation Protective Edge," was an effort by the Israeli state to further destabilize Hamas, which had won representative control of Gaza in Palestine's legislative elections of 2006. Despite claims that it was not targeting civilians, and only Hamas, Israel sealed Gaza's borders, concentrating its population of nearly two million people and enhancing the devastation. At the end, according to the United Nations, over 1,500 Palestinian civilians were killed, including 538 children. By contrast, Hamas attacks killed five civilians. Across the West Bank, Palestinians protesting the violence were brutally repressed by Israeli Defense Forces.[3]

In the midst of this violence in Gaza, on August 9, 2014, eighteen-year-old Black teenager Michael Brown was shot dead by the Ferguson, Missouri, police officer Darren Wilson. Brown, who was unarmed, was shot a minimum of six times in the upper body, including once through the eye socket, once in the head, and four times in the right arm.[4] Refusing to move with haste, Wilson and the Ferguson Police Department left Brown's body to rot in the Missouri summer heat for four-and-a-half hours. When Brown's parents arrived to identify their son's body, Ferguson police staved them off with dogs and guns.[5] In a city already beleaguered by tensions between a mostly Black population and an overwhelmingly white police force, the Brown incident was the proverbial straw that broke the camel's back. Immediately after Brown's body was removed, Ferguson residents erected a makeshift memorial to Brown, laying out photographs, flowers, and stuffed animals. But after police disrespected the memorial several times—one officer allowed his dog to urinate on it—Black people in Ferguson were taken to their breaking point.

The next day, on August 10, 2014, Ferguson exploded into uprisings.[6] Protesters were immediately met with the tools of a militarized police state that the Muslims in this book, most notably Louis Farrakhan, had repeatedly warned of. Tanks with mounted semiautomatic weapons rolled through the streets of Ferguson. Helicopters flew overhead. Police deployed truncheons, rubber bullets, and tear gas. One hundred and seventy-two people, overwhelmingly Black, were arrested, most charged with the crime of failure to disperse.[7]

The level of devastation in Ferguson was not on par with what was going on in Gaza, but the sentiments that animated these movements reflected similar frustrations and desires. And people on both sides of the Atlantic Ocean—in Gaza and in Ferguson—continued to see their plights as linked and as part of the same long-standing pattern of subjugation, pacification, and white supremacist violence against colonized subjects.

Brown's death was just the latest in a series of killings of Black people. Just two weeks prior, Staten Island resident Eric Garner was murdered after New York Police Department officer Daniel Pantaleo put him in an illegal chokehold. Pantaleo approached, subdued, and felt the life drain out of Garner because he was merely suspected of illegally selling loose cigarettes.[8] Two years prior, seventeen-year-old Trayvon Martin was killed by George Zimmerman in his Sanford, Florida, community. Zimmerman, who was on neighborhood watch, saw Martin in a hooded sweatshirt and perceived him as an unwelcome and threatening interloper in the community. He was later acquitted by a jury which held that Zimmerman acted in self-defense.[9]

Many activists, religious leaders, and intellectuals engaged with the events in Gaza and in Ferguson through their identities as Black and/or Muslim people. Farrakhan, in a speech given in Chicago on August 17, 2014, explicitly linked these two events together in front of his congregation, engaging his long-standing geography of imperial resistance and his belief in the intimate connections between the global suffering of Black and Brown people under colonialism and imperialism. Speaking of the "anguish" he felt by the bombing of Gaza, and the plight of the "helpless Palestinians against the armed might of Israel with weapons given to them by America," he asked—just as the Nation had asked of President George H.W. Bush during the War on Drugs—"who [is] the real 'terrorist'?"[10] Condemning the Muslim world for failing to come to the aid of the Palestinian people, Farrakhan then turned to the situation in Ferguson. Ferguson is a "microcosm of the macrocosm," he argued, the global reality of the systematic oppression of people of color. And in Ferguson, as in Gaza, the people had finally said, "enough is enough ... Suffering conditions, injustice, brings about a response."[11] Of course, Farrakhan did not fail to take advantage of the opportunity to promote Islam and convert listeners. He argued that he had been elevated by Elijah Muhammad to his current position to warn people of these connections and to lead Black and Brown people to liberation through his Islamic message, proclaiming, "The message of Elijah Muhammad and the prophets is not for cowards."[12] He also linked the people of Ferguson and Gaza together as victims of a sustained campaign of American imperialism and military domination in the service of white supremacy.

For many Black and Muslim people, these solidarities were emphasized, as they had been in generations past, by newly widespread technologies. This time, in addition to newspapers, it was Twitter, Facebook, and other forms of social media that created an overlapping diaspora of ideas, images, and strategies. As images from Ferguson were broadcast across the world, Palestinian activists with ample experience evading technologies of subjugation took to Twitter to give advice to Black activists in Ferguson. They taught them how to wash tear gas out of their eyes with milk or Coca-Cola, to stay close to the police to make it difficult to deploy tear gas canisters, and to jump upwind to evade tear gas clouds. They also made conscious connections between the use of the same technologies, many manufactured in the United States, to suppress protest against state violence in both Gaza and Ferguson.[13]

Since 2014, these solidarities have been repeatedly engaged by both Black and Muslim activists in the United States and across the world. For Black activists, these connections have been critical in understanding their own projects and aims. Black Lives Matter, which was founded in 2013 after Zimmerman's acquittal, made explicit connections between the oppression of Black people and Palestinians when it endorsed the Boycott, Divestment, and Sanctions movement in 2016, and explicitly condemned Israeli policy on Palestine as "genocide" and characterized Israel as an "apartheid state." The Movement for Black Lives, a coalition of fifty Black and Brown activist organizations, including Black Lives Matter, also made connections between Israeli policy and genocide and accused the United States government of complicity in its 2016 Six Point Platform.[14] For Palestinian and Arab Muslim activists, these connections are also critically important. As human rights lawyer Noura Erakat has demonstrated, secular and Muslim Palestinian activists have personally articulated how they have intellectualized the connections between police brutality and state repression in America's inner cities and Israeli state policy against the Palestinian people.[15]

Through observation and photographic analysis, we can also see ordinary people at these protests making these connections between global and local oppression as well. In 2020, a series of global protests were sparked by the police killings of George Floyd—who was killed after Minneapolis police officer Derek Chauvin knelt on his neck for a minimum of eight minutes and fifteen seconds—and Breonna Taylor—who was shot after Louisville, Kentucky, police officers stormed into her home.[16] At these actions, protesters from London to Paris could regularly be seen waving the Palestinian flag and carrying signs engaging Islamic identity and praxis. At one London protest in Trafalgar Square, a protester held aloft a sign proclaiming that "Pigs are Haram," referencing both the Muslim prohibition against eating pork and condemning religiously motivated and racialized state violence by the police, who are referred to colloquially as "pigs." In Paris, protesters stood on top of the statue at the *Place de la Liberté* waving a Palestinian flag.[17]

As historians have recently demonstrated, the types of solidarities articulated by activists like Black Lives Matter and the Movement for Black Lives, and Muslims like the Nation of Islam, are not new but are continuations of the types of internationalist sentiments, imaginaries, and actions that I explore throughout this book.[18] In the aftermath of the Second World War, Black Americans had an ambivalent relationship to the formation of the Israeli state and to the Zionist movement. But beginning in the 1960s, the tide of opinion began to turn. As early as 1964, Malcolm X expressed his opinion that Jewish settlement in Palestine was a form of European colonialism and a result of the unbridled expansion of capitalism.[19] This was in line with the long-standing, and constantly developing, anti-imperial geographical imaginary that I outline extensively in this book. But it was in 1967, with Israel's defeat of Arab forces and the annexation of the Gaza Strip, West Bank, Golan Heights, and portions of the Sinai Peninsula that turned Black radical opinion on Palestine for good.[20] Beginning with the Student Nonviolent Coordinating Committee's article the "Palestine Question," Black radical groups began to develop what Alex Lubin calls an "intercommunal political imaginary" that linked the struggles of African Americans, Palestinians, and even Black and Arab Jews inside of Israel together.[21]

Not only do activists look to the past; they shape the present as they look to the future. I have previously called this process of looking back into the past while being attentive to the social and political context of the present and looking to the future "historical Sankofa." Borrowing a concept from the Akan funerary tradition of Ghana, the Sankofa is a symbol of our relationship to our ancestors, to our present moment, and to our future trajectory. It is symbolized as a bird standing in place, with its feet pointing forward and its beak reaching back to grab the wisdom of the past, represented by an egg, from its back.[22] The story of how Black and Muslim people built the Atlantic Crescent through their historical activism, identity building, internationalism, and discourse is an important example of the ways that ideas of solidarity and internationalism can translate into real political projects. But it is a snapshot of the middle of an ongoing process; a process that is happening all around us and that continues to the present day.

Activists around the world are continuing to organize around the intertwined issues of Black subjugation and the enduring legacies of colonialism and slavery, and trying to build a more just future. In doing so, they not only continue to shape the Atlantic Crescent in the present and for the future, but they do so through deploying the process of historical Sankofa. Although anecdotal, I have seen this in my own experience and capacity as a professor in the American university system. In April 2024, student activists in the United States began to erect encampments in the centers of their campuses. These encampments, building on a common activist strategy popularized during the civil rights movement, were responses to an ongoing military bombardment of Gaza by Israel. On October 7, 2023, Hamas soldiers broke through the barrier separating Gaza from Israel, launched rockets into Israeli airspace, infiltrated towns, killed 1,200 Israelis, and took 251 hostages. In response, as it did in 2014, Israel launched a relentless aerial bombardment and ground invasion of Gaza. As of April 2024, when these encampments were erected, official numbers indicated that 34,000 Palestinians had been killed.

In erecting these encampments, student organizers—who came from a variety of backgrounds but who were overwhelmingly Black, Latinx, Arab, and/or Muslim—joined with other universities across the country to force university administrators to reckon with Israel's ongoing assault on Gaza, their own financial investments in technologies of war, and the connection of Israel's campaign with their own subjugation as people of color in the United States. At the University of Southern California (USC), where I am currently employed, students calling themselves "Divest from Death" joined in a mass action to "disrupt" the university in order to force administrators to answer community and international calls for "full divestment from the Zionist entity [Israel], and all of the industries that sustain it."[23] Characterizing Israel's response to Hamas as a genocide, Divest from Death made six demands. Four of these demands related to withdrawing university investments in Israel, the United States military, and weapons manufacturers; engaging in an academic boycott of Israel; protecting free speech on campus for pro-Palestinian students and faculty; and publicly calling for a ceasefire in Gaza. The final two made explicit the connections between the oppression of Black, Brown, and

Muslim people in the United States and the subjugation of Palestinians in Gaza. Divest from Death demanded that USC stop "all land grabs, whether in South Central Tongva territory [where USC sits], or Palestine," and to "provide reparations, and support housing for low-income South Central [Los Angeles] residents." They also spoke out against the harassment of "black, brown, and Palestinian students and their allies on and off campus," citing concerns about actions taken by campus security, including USC's Department of Public Safety, and by the Los Angeles Police Department. These demands were publicized through USC's Student Coalition Against Labor Exploitation (SCALE) via its Instagram page (@uscscale).[24]

On April 24, 2024, as the Israelis prepared for a ground invasion of Rafah, Divest from Death began an occupation of USC's Alumni Park in the center of campus. Within hours, they were met with a response by USC's Department of Public Safety and then the Los Angeles Police Department in riot gear.[25] Ninety-three people, including faculty, were arrested, mostly on charges of misdemeanor trespassing and failure to disperse. After the arrests, these students rebuilt their encampment and continued to demand an audience with college administrators. They held daily programs of yoga, teach-ins about camping safety, movie screenings, and ceramics workshops. In the aftermath of their arrests, they continued to use their academic work to make connections between their silencing and the use of state tools of control, surveillance, the violence they experienced at the hands of the police, and the historic subjugation and oppression of Black and Brown people through colonialism in Los Angeles, in Palestine, and throughout the world.[26] The encampment was dismantled permanently in the early morning hours of May 5, 2024.[27]

While many of these students are Black and Muslim, they have not gone as far as the Black and Muslim people in this book. They have not mobilized Islam specifically to make sense of the events in Gaza and the subjugation of Black people in the inner cities of the African diaspora. But Black and Muslim groups have. On November 4, 2024, as Israel ramped up its military assault on Gaza, Bermuda's Muslim community held a solidarity march with Palestine in Hamilton, titling their action a "Walk for Peace" and demanding that Israel "Stop the Genocide."[28] In February 2024, Farrakhan stood in front of his followers at the Nation's annual Saviour's Day conference to repeat much of what he had said in 2014 during Operation Protective Edge. Again, he condemned the Muslim world for not coming to the aid of the Palestinian people, and while lamenting the loss of Jewish life during the October 7th attacks, asked them to "stand up to the genocide that is happening to our Palestinian family."[29] In an article published in the *Final Call* two weeks after Farrakhan's speech, *Final Call* editor Naba'a Muhammad used Farrakhan's speech to sustain the imagined geographies that fueled the Nation's anti-imperial discourse decades prior. This time, Muhammad argued that this wickedness was driving the word toward its ultimate end. He wrote, "The slaughter in Gaza is driving the world closer and closer to the final war of Armageddon, which will engulf the planet. Rulers of the current world are failing. America is unraveling. Warning is mercy if it is heeded in time."[30] That warning would allow the faithful to come to Islam, to be in "God's presence," and to "win" the war being waged against the world's people of color.

This epilogue should not be taken to mean that Palestine is the only thing that occupies the attention of Black and Muslim people, or that it will continue to captivate them forever. This begs the question: Where will the bow of Blackness launch Islam's arrow in the future? If the past informs our understanding of human nature and priorities, Black and Muslim activists, practitioners, and leaders will continue to look at their past alliances, discourses, and strategies to sustain them. As Black and Muslim people before them, they might look to Japan, to the Caribbean, to Latin America, to the Aborigines of Australia, or to oppressed populations in Europe. Wherever they do look, they will continue to create imagined geographies of resistance, linking themselves to other populations across the globe, and they will persist in shaping their understandings of how religion and race intersect to inform their identities, their politics, and their understanding of the world. The trajectory of the bow and the arrow of Islam will continue to shape the Atlantic Crescent.

Acknowledgments

As a scholar of the African diaspora, there is a particular way that you end up living a diasporic existence. As I traveled to the archives and libraries that housed the documents that became the basis for this book, I found myself at the intersections of overlapping diasporas. Like my subjects, I navigated oceans and crossed mountains in search of the histories that I present in these pages. Along the way, like the subjects who populate these pages, I amassed an enormous transnational community of people, institutions, and organizations who helped me make what had been a long-standing dream into a reality.

Acknowledgments are, unfortunately, an imprecise and incomplete art. In the process of trying to categorize some of the most important people in my life, I've realized that my community has become intersectional. Mentors have become friends. Students have taught me as much as I've taught them. And cohort-mates have—in a stroke of the best luck—become colleagues. I wish I could dedicate a chapter to each of you, but in the interest of brevity, I only mentioned each person's contributions briefly. Equally regrettably, there are people who have helped me immensely who are not mentioned here. To all of you who helped this book see the light of day, please know that I am indebted to your contributions.

This would truly have never been possible without the assistance, support, and faith of the University of North Carolina Press, the anonymous reviewers who pushed my argument further, my editor Mark Simpson-Vos, and editorial assistant Thomas Bedenbaugh. Thank you as well to the entire editorial and production team who made everything from the cover art to the most precise footnote edits happen. Especially to Mark—you are an absolute gem, and I am so happy we decided to put our faith in each other. Thank you as well to Beth Berhane, who proofread this book.

There are so many people whose advice, critique, and interest in my life have made both my career as an academic and the production of this book possible. At Rutgers University, it was James W. Jones and Karla Jackson-Brewer who supported my earliest ambitions in the academy. Katherine Franke's courses and mentorship at Columbia Law School served as a constant reminder that I was an academic and scholar in mind and heart. As a young litigator, Christine Riley kept me sane and protected. My advisors at New York University, Michael Gomez, Zvi Ben-Dor Benite, Aisha Khan, Michelle Mitchell, and Andrew Needham, spent hours reading drafts, discussing literature, and molding me into a historian. Thank you as well to the other formal and informal mentors and advisors I've had over the years, including Jennifer Brody, Keisha Blain, Sylvia Chan-Malik, Nathan Connolly, Edward Curtis, Alice Echols, Katherine Gin Lum, John Kieschnick, Lon Kurashige, George Sanchez, Ula Taylor, and Francille Wilson.

The following people have, in some way, made this book better over the years. These people either read drafts, discussed secondary literature with me, workshopped my chapters and articles, helped me find sources, or simply listened to me rant until I began to make sense. My gratitude goes to: Anthony Andersson, Alex Aviña, Edward Ball, Alice Baumgartner, Lisa

Blaydes, Laura Briggs, James Cantres, Zakiyyah Collier, Joshua Cohen, Emilie Connolly, Louis DeCaro, Shane Dillingham, Erin Durban, Brent Hayes Edwards, Jeannette Estruth, Garrett Felber, Joan Flores-Villalobos, Sarah Gualtieri, Anasa Hicks, Sherman Jackson, Dominique Jean-Louis, Chris Johnson, Miranda Joseph, Mélanie Lamotte, Camilo Lund-Montaño, Maddox, Beth Manley, Gwynneth Malin, Yannis Mahil, David Mills, Sarah Molinari, Emma Otheguy, Jason Glenn, Josh Goldstein, Nathan Perl-Rosenthal, Helena Ribeiro, Steve Ross, Ahmad Shokr, Masha Solomon, Rachel Afi Quinn, Adam Warren, Alex Winder, Aro Velmet, and Elliott Young.

Thank you to my friends, colleagues, students, and staff at New York University, Stanford University, and the University of Southern California. I am also particularly grateful to the Abbasi Program in Islamic Studies, the African~Diaspora Forum at New York University, the Association for the Study of the Worldwide African Diaspora, the Center for the Study of African and the African Diaspora at New York University, the History Workshop at the University of Southern California, the Humanities Center at New York University's 2016–17 cohort, and my graduate cohort in the History Department at New York University.

As a result of being awarded the Islam in America Postdoctoral Fellowship at Stanford University's Department of Religious Studies and Abbasi Program in Islamic Studies and an ACLS/Ford Foundation Fellowship at the New York Public Library's Schomburg Institute for Research in Black Culture, I was given the gifts of time to write and of interdisciplinary communities of like-minded scholars to workshop and refine my ideas. Over the years, I have also received material support from the American Historical Association, the Marcus Garvey Memorial Foundation, the Mellon Foundation, and the Social Science Research Council, which allowed me to travel to archives around the world, interview subjects, and conduct the research at the core of this book.

Archives are at the heart of what we do as historians, and without the archivists and librarians who helped me over the last decade, my work would have been exponentially more difficult, if not impossible. I would like to give a special thank you to the archivists who went above and beyond the call of duty: Kenisha Shakir at the Bermuda National Library; Rossy Mendez at the New York Municipal Archives; and Maira Liriano, A. J. Muhammad, and Auburn Nelson at the Schomburg Center. Where the archives were silent or quiet, the oral testimonies and personal papers of several people were invaluable to creating a rounded picture of the scope of Islam and anticolonial thought in the Atlantic basin. Thank you to Ameenah Abdul-Hadee, Wayne Brown, Milton Hill, Michelle Khaldun, Arifah Madyun, Student Minister Clive Muhammad of Jamaica's Nation of Islam, Student Minister Hilary Muhammad of the United Kingdom's Nation of Islam, Kenneth Castle Muhammad, Basim Muwwakkil, Mustapha Rasheed, Hasaan Salaam, Norwood Salaam, Safiyyah Salaam, Dyab Seifuddin Stowe, Najiyyah Shamsiddeen, Cromwell Shakir, Zaheera Shakir, Zakiyyah Shakir, Takbir Sharrieff, and Khalid Wasi for taking the time to let me interview them, sometimes more than once. Thank you to Ronald X. Stewart for being open to sharing his experience through email. Particular thanks to Shahid Naeem, Norwood Salaam, Zakiyyah Shakir, and Edna Sharrieff for providing photographs and documents from their personal archives.

Thank you as well to the libraries, estates, and archives that allowed me to reprint or republish material in this book, including the Archives and Regional History Collection at Western Michigan University. Parts of chapter 6 originally appeared as Alaina M. Morgan,

"A Practice Round for the Inner City: Circum-Caribbean Occupation, Crack Cocaine, and Religious Duty in Louis Farrakhan's Nation of Islam," *Journal of African American History* 108, no. 2 (Spring 2023): 244–72. It has been reprinted with the permission of the *Journal of African American History*.

My somewhat nomadic research life would have been incredibly lonely if not for the hospitality of many people who shared their homes, families, friend circles, and associates with me. In Bermuda, thank you to Michelle and Fanon Khaldun who opened their home at Serenity Rock to me and introduced me to their community at Masjid Muhammad and in the larger community. Thank you as well to Radell Tankard who shared documents, connections, and social networks with me. In Jamaica, thank you to old family friends Russell and Carole Bell who helped me connect with my ancestral roots in my mother's birthplace. In the Bay Area, I owe an unpayable debt to Zack and Clare Al-Witri, who basically adopted me—feeding me, housing me for more than a few stretches, and becoming my lifelong friends. In London, I am grateful to Zainab Abbas, who generously put me up in her home in Fulham, brought me into her community of Black British radicalism, and became my "British mum."

Of course, there are a host of other people who have been, and who have become, part of my emotional support system. This community sustained me when I was grieving, anxiety ridden, and doubting whether I could make it to the finish line. They supported me when I needed to vent and when I needed to cry. They buoyed me with hugs, cheers, and jokes. Thank you from the bottom of my heart to Toni Agajanian, Alice Baumgartner, Fiori Berhane, Clare Al-Witri, Zack Al-Witri, Jeannette Estruth, Brianne Gungoll, Joan Flores-Villalobos, Katherine Marino, Lydia Mendoza Mosser, Kelly Murphy, Vicky Poumpouridis, Nicole Beliveau Sheff, Carla Small, Conchita Valenzuela, Juan M. Valles de Noriega, Aro Velmet, and Lisa Zivkovic.

My family has been incredible throughout this entire process. My grandparents, living and in the realm of the ancestors, made immeasurable sacrifices without which I would not be able to do the work I do and make the choices I make. I am also incredibly grateful for the strength and support of my immediate family, who I am sure most of the time had no idea what I was doing. My brother, Devin, was always ready to distract me with a joke. My sister-in-law, Audra, kept us grounded and centered. My niece, Kyla, and my nephew, Brooks, enchanted me with their wonder, hilarity, and absolutely adorable faces. My godmother, Renee—whom I have known since I was only a few hours old—has a love for me that is remarkable not only because it has endured so long but because we are family by choice, not by blood. In the midst of the COVID-19 pandemic, I introduced a new member to my family: my dog, Ozzy. Don't ask him about anything going on in my professional life—he cares only about cuddles, scritches, and freeze-dried toppers, but he made the process of writing this book much easier simply by warming my lap as I typed. I'd like to think that, in some way, he knows how important he was to the process. And finally, my father, Ron—one of the kindest and most loving people I know—how do I thank him? He has been my fearless protector, my champion, and my model for how to be a good citizen. Thanks for being a great Dad.

My village has had their work cut out for them. The road leading up to the publication of this book has not been easy, and I endured numerous personal difficulties on the road to publication. In April 2021, my family suffered a devastating loss when my maternal grandmother, Veronica, passed away at nearly 101 years old. She was our matriarch and the rock of our family. Then, in late 2023, as I was completing this manuscript, my mother Lorna was diagnosed with a terminal illness. As this book goes into production, she continues to put up a brave fight. This book is dedicated to the two of them—both the strongest and most beautiful women I have ever known. I inherited their intellect, their resilience, and their way of looking at the world creatively and analytically; of seeing barriers and thinking of the most interesting ways to leap over them. They taught me not only to be a woman who was strong and self-sufficient, but to deeply embed myself in my community and in networks of care. Mom and Gaga—thank you. This is for you. I can only hope that I make you a fraction as proud of me as I have been of both of you.

Notes

Abbreviations

BIC	Bermuda Intelligence Committee
BIR	Bermuda Intelligence Records
BNA	Bermuda National Archives (Hamilton, Bermuda)
BOSSI	NYPD Bureau of Special Services and Investigations
BPM	Black Power Movement
BT	Board of Trade
CMS	Clara Mohammed School (Hamilton, Bermuda)
CO	Colonial Office
CPF	Central Policy Files
CSO	Cabinet Secretary's Office
FBI	Federal Bureau of Investigation
FCO	Foreign Commonwealth Office
KJV	King James Version of the Bible
LIR	Local Intelligence Report
MSTA	Moorish Science Temple
NARA	National Archives and Records Administration (College Park, Maryland)
NCJRS	National Criminal Justice Records Service
NOI	Nation of Islam
NYDS	New York Department of State
NYPD	New York Police Department
RG	Record Group
SAC	Special Agent in Charge
SCRBC	Schomburg Center for Research in Black Culture (New York)
TNA	The British National Archives (Kew Gardens, UK)

Introduction

1. Elijah Muhammad, "Evil Spreading Far and Wide!," *Muhammad Speaks*, March 25, 1966, 1; Eugene Majied, "The World Serpent," *Muhammad Speaks*, March 25, 1965, 13–14.

2. Majied, "World Serpent," 13–14.

3. Majied, "World Serpent," 13–14. The verse reads, "The great dragon was cast out, that old serpent, called the Devil, and Satan, which deceiveth the whole world: he was cast out into the earth, and his angels were cast out with him," Rev. 12:9, KJV.

4. Majied, "World Serpent," 13–14.

5. Diouf, *Servants of Allah*, 70; Gomez, *Exchanging Our Country Marks*, 60.

6. Gomez, *Exchanging Our Country Marks*, 60.

7. Gomez, *Exchanging Our Country Marks*, 60–68; Diouf, *Servants of Allah*, 68–70.

8. Diouf, *Servants of Allah*, 37–55.

9. Diouf, *Servants of Allah*, 36–37.

10. Diouf, *Servants of Allah*, 68–70; Gomez, *Exchanging Our Country Marks*, 80.

11. Diouf, *Servants of Allah*, 19; Gomez, *Exchanging Our Country Marks*, 80–82.

12. Gomez, *Exchanging Our Country Marks*, 80–82.

13. Diouf, *Servants of Allah*, 71–97; Gomez, *Black Crescent*, 183.

14. Georgia Writers' Project, *Drums and Shadows*, 169–170. See also Gomez, *Exchanging Our Country Marks*, 81.

15. Marks, *Farewell—We're Good and Gone*, 1, citing Bureau of the Census, *Current Population Reports*, Special Studies Series P23, No. 80 (1978), 15; Berlin, *Making of African America*, 154.

16. Kusmer, *A Ghetto Takes Shape*, 157–234; Berlin, *Making of African America*, 165–66, 175–84; Marks, *Farewell- We're Good and Gone*, 145–50.

17. Gomez, *Black Crescent*, 207–8; Weisenfeld, *New World A-Coming*, 1–27.

18. Dannin, *Black Pilgrimage to Islam*, 26; Weisenfeld, *New World A-Coming*, 1–21; Turner, *Islam in the African American Experience*, 73–75.

19. Gomez, *Black Crescent*, 207–10.

20. Lewis, "To Turn as on a Pivot," 765–87.

21. See table 4, "World Region and Country or Area of Birth of the Foreign-Born Population, with Geographic Detail Shown in Decennial Census Populations of 1930 or Earlier: 1850 to 1930 and 1960 to 2000," in Gibson and Jung, "Working Paper No. 81," 109–10. In February 2006, a working paper by the US Census Bureau updated the estimated statistics on foreign-born populations in the United States from 1850–2000. The numbers in this report differ from the actual numbers represented by historical censuses because they correct for sampling and nonsampling errors by census takers. For example, the original 1930 census estimates the Indian, or "Hindu," population at 3,130, whereas the 2006 working paper estimates the Indian population at 5,850. See table 3, "Urban, Rural-Farm, and Rural-Nonfarm Population of the United States, by Color, Nativity, and Parentage," in Gibson and Jung, "Working Paper No. 81," 2; in US Census Bureau, *1930 Census; Population: Volume II*, 27. See also Watkins-Owens, *Blood Relations*, 3–4; Taylor, *The Veiled Garvey*, 19.

22. Watkins-Owens, *Blood Relations*, 3–4.

23. Turner, *Islam in the African American Experience*, 80–90.

24. Turner, *Islam in the African American Experience*, 78–80.

25. Weisenfeld, *New World A-Coming*, 17.

26. Gibson and Jung, "Working Paper No. 81," 109–10, table 4; US Census Bureau, *1930 Census*, 27, table 3.

27. An Act to Execute Certain Treaty Stipulations Relating to the Chinese (Chinese Exclusion Act), 22 Stat. 58, Ch. 126 (1882); An Act to Regulate the Immigration of Aliens to, and the Residence of Aliens in, the United States (1917 Immigration Act), 39 Stat. 874, Ch. 29 (1917); An Act to Limit the Number of Immigrants Allowed Entry into the United States, and for Other Purposes (Johnson-Reed Act), 43 Stat. 153, Ch. 190 (1924). See also Lee, *At America's Gates*, 77–103; Ngai, *Impossible Subjects*, 17–55; Haney-López, *White by Law*, 37–39.

28. Gibson and Jung, "Working Paper No. 81," 109–110, table 4; US Census Bureau, *1930 Census*, 27, table 3.

29. Chinese Exclusion Act (1882); 1917 Immigration Act (1917); Johnson-Reed Act (1924).

30. Bald, *Bengali Harlem*, 49–93.

31. Gomez, *Black Crescent*, 209. For more on prevailing anti-imperial and nationalist movements of the time, see Emerson, *From Empire to Nation*; Hourani, *Arabic Thought*;

Anderson, *Imagined Communities*; Dawisha, *Arab Nationalism in the Twentieth Century*. For more on prevailing Black nationalist movements of the time, see Pinkney, *Red, Black, and Green*; Moses, *The Golden Age of Black Nationalism*; Van DeBurg, *Modern Black Nationalism*; Blain, *Set the World on Fire*.

32. Weisenfeld, *New World A-Coming*, 42–55; Gomez, *Black Crescent*, 219–22.
33. McKittrick, *Demonic Grounds*, xiv, xx.
34. McKittrick, *Demonic Grounds*; Gilroy, *Black Atlantic*.
35. McCloud, *African American Islam*, 3–5.
36. McCloud, *African American Islam*, 3–5.
37. I imagine the term "freedom realities" as the counterpart to Robin D. G. Kelley's concept of "freedom dreams" in the Black radical imagination. Kelley, *Freedom Dreams*.
38. Weisenfeld, *New World A-Coming*.
39. Edwards, *Practice of Diaspora*, 13.
40. Edwards, *Practice of Diaspora*, 13–16.
41. von Eschen, *Race against Empire*; Makalani, *In the Cause of Freedom*; Lubin, *Geographies of Liberation*; Blain, *Set the World on Fire*; Edwards, *Practice of Diaspora*.
42. McCloud, *African American Islam*; Curtis, *Islam in Black America*; Weisenfeld, *New World A-Coming*; Gomez, *Black Crescent*; Turner, *Islam in the African American Experience*.
43. See Felber, *Those Who Know Don't Say*; Jeffries, *No Higher Than Its Women*; Taylor, *Promise of Patriarchy*.
44. Diouf, *Servants of Allah*; Greewal, *Islam Is a Foreign Country*; Turner, *Islam in the African American Experience*; Chan-Malik, *Being Muslim*.
45. Azaransky, *This Worldwide Struggle*; Bedasse, *Jah Kingdom*.
46. Turner, *Soundtrack to a Movement*.
47. Marsh, *From Black Islam to Islam*, 41–66; Curtis, *Islam in Black America*, 45–106.
48. Haddad and Smith, "Introduction," in *Mission to America*, 1–22.
49. Robinson, *Muslim Societies in African History*, 27–59, 91–196.
50. For more on Abdul Basit Naeem, see Felber, *Those Who Know Don't Say*, 31–35; DeCaro, *On the Side of My People*, 149–64.
51. Felber, *Those Who Know Don't Say*.

Chapter One

1. "List of Manifest of Alien Passengers for the United States Immigration Officer at Port of Arrival, S.S. Haverford," Passenger Lists of Vessels Arriving at Philadelphia, Pennsylvania, January 24, 1920–February 15, 1920, NARA, RG 85, Series T840, Roll 135; "Ahmadiyya Mission News," *Review of Religions*, July 1921, 242–44.
2. 1917 Immigration Act.
3. For more on the racial position of South Asian and Arab immigrants to the United States during this period, see Gualtieri, *Between Arab and White*, 52–80; Haney-López, *White by Law*, 68–92.
4. Mufti Muhammad Sadiq, "One Year's Moslem Missionary Work in America," *Moslem Sunrise*, July 1921, 12; "America's Intolerance: Our Missionary in the Detention House," *Review of Religions*, April and May 1920, 158–60.
5. "Ahmadiyya Mission News," *Review of Religions*, July 1920, 240–41.
6. Sadiq, "One Year's Moslem Missionary Work in America," 12–13.

7. "Brief Report of the Work in America," *Moslem Sunrise*, July 1922, 112; Mufti Muhammad Sadiq, in *Moslem Sunrise*, 1923, January 1923, 1. For more on the city of Chicago, race, and inequality in the 1920s, see Balto, *Occupied Territory*, 26–55.

8. "True Salvation of the American Negroes: The Real Solution of the Negro Question," *Moslem Sunrise*, October 1923, 266–67.

9. Mufti Muhammad Sadiq, "Press Notices: 'Moslem Mullah in Mission to Chicago,'" *Moslem Sunrise*, April and July 1923, 195, reprinted from "Moslem Mullah in Chicago," *Chicago Herald & Examiner*, March 11, 1923.

10. Cronon, *Black Moses*, 44; Grant, *Negro with a Hat*, 164–65.

11. "Brief Report of the Work in America," *Moslem Sunrise*, January 1923, 167; "New Converts," *Moslem Sunrise*, April and July 1923, 191.

12. Marks, *Farewell—We're Good and Gone*, 1, citing Bureau of the Census, *Current Population Reports*, Special Studies Series P23, No. 80 (1978), 15; Berlin, *The Making of African America*, 154; Mufti Muhammad Sadiq, in *Moslem Sunrise*, January 1923, 1.

13. Gomez, *Black Crescent*, 209.

14. Gomez, *Black Crescent*, 209.

15. McCloud, *African American Islam*, 10–11; Turner, *Islam in the African American Experience*, 92; Gomez, *Black Crescent*, 206.

16. Wilson, *Sacred Drift*, 17; Turner, *Islam in the African American Experience*, 92.

17. Gomez, *Black Crescent*, 215–60; Turner, *Islam in the African American Experience*, 90–97.

18. Gomez, *Black Crescent*, 203–4; Turner, *Islam in the African American Experience*, 90.

19. Gomez, *Black Crescent*, 203.

20. Gomez, *Black Crescent*, 204–5.

21. Gomez, *Black Crescent*, 204.

22. Gomez, *Black Crescent*, 205.

23. Wilson, *Sacred Drift*, 15.

24. Dorman, *Princess and the Prophet*, 22.

25. Dorman, *Princess and the Prophet*, 78. See also Turner, *Islam in the African American Experience*; Gomez, *Black Crescent*, 206; Wilson, *Sacred Drift*, 16.

26. Hoganson, "Cosmopolitan Domesticity," 55–83; Bald, *Bengali Harlem*, 16–20.

27. Dorman, *Princess and the Prophet*, 77–78, 83–84.

28. Bald, *Bengali Harlem*, 23.

29. Bald, *Bengali Harlem*, 19–24, 32.

30. Bald, *Bengali Harlem*, 14–16.

31. Mumford, *Newark*, 20.

32. Anderson, *This Was Harlem*; Makalani and Baldwin, *Escape from New York*; Weisenberg, *New World A-Coming*.

33. Makalani and Baldwin, *Escape from New York*; Edwards, *Practice of Diaspora*.

34. Watkins-Owens, *Blood Relations*, 3–4; Turner, *Caribbean Crusaders*.

35. Cronon, *Black Moses*, 14–15; Grant, *Negro with a Hat*, 28–33.

36. Marcus Garvey, "The British West Indies in the Mirror of Civilization," *African Times and Orient Review*, October 1913, 158–60. For more on Dusé Mohamed Ali and his Pan-Islamism, see "African Times and Orient Review; Dusé Mohamed Ali," November 1917, TNA, CO 554/35; "Letter from S. Hall to the Earl of Leitrum re: the African Times and

Orient Review," October 21, 1917, TNA, CO 554/35. See also Grant, *Negro with a Hat*, 38–41.

37. Grant, *Negro with a Hat*, 49.

38. Cronon, *Black Moses*, 16, quoting *Philosophy and Opinions of Marcus Garvey*, 126.

39. See, for example, Letter from Marcus Garvey to Travers Buxton, Secretary, Anti-Slavery and Aborigines' Protection Society," in Hill, *Marcus Garvey and the UNIA Papers* (Volume 1), 52–54.

40. Cronon, *Black Moses*, 45; Grant, *Negro with a Hat*, 135–38.

41. Cronon, *Black Moses*, 45; Grant, *Negro with a Hat*, 138.

42. "Speech by Marcus Garvey," January 29, 1922, in Hill, *Marcus Garvey and the UNIA Papers* (Volume 5), 467. See also Turner, *Islam in the African American Experience*, 88; Martin, *Race First*, 65.

43. For example, see Dusé Mohamed Ali, "Foreign Affairs," *Negro World*, May 6, 1922, 4; Dusé Mohamed Ali, "Foreign Affairs," *Negro World*, May 20, 1922, 4; Dusé Mohamed Ali, "Foreign Affairs," *Negro World*, June 3, 1922, 4; Dusé Mohamed Ali, "Foreign Affairs," *Negro World*, June 10, 1922, 4; Dusé Mohamed Ali, "Foreign Affairs," *Negro World*, June 17, 1922, 4; Dusé Mohamed Ali, "Foreign Affairs," *Negro World*, July 1, 1922, 4; Dusé Mohamed Ali, "Foreign Affairs," *Negro World*, July 8, 1922, 4; Dusé Mohamed Ali, "Foreign Affairs," *Negro World*, July 15, 1922, 4.

44. Ford, *Universal Ethiopian Hymnal*.

45. Ford, "Allah-Hu-Akbar" in *Universal Ethiopian Hymnal*, 26; Sheet Music: Arnold J. Ford, Hymns Composed by Arnold J. Ford and others (Hymns), 1922, Sheet Music, SCRBC.

46. Ford, Hymns, 1922, Sheet Music, SCRBC.

47. Ford, "God Bless Our President," in *Universal Ethiopian Hymnal*, 34; Ford, Hymns, Sheet Music, SCRBC.

48. Ford, "Potentate's Hymn," in the *Universal Ethiopian Hymnal*, 32; Ford, Hymns, 1922, Sheet Music, SCRBC.

49. Ford, "The Password," in the *Universal Ethiopian Hymnal*, 36; Ford, Hymns, 1922, Sheet Music, SCRBC.

50. J.A. O'Meally, "Crescent or Cross?," *Moslem Sunrise*, October 1923, 263. A note at the bottom of the article indicates that this was reprinted from the *Negro World*'s August 4, 1923, issue; however, I have found no such article in that edition.

51. O'Meally, "Crescent or Cross?," 263.

52. O'Meally, "Crescent or Cross?," 263.

53. Leonard Smith to Marcus Garvey, September 19, 1927, in Hill, *Marcus Garvey and the UNIA Papers*, vol. 7, 82; Marcus Garvey to Leonard Smith, September 21, 1927, in Hill, *Marcus Garvey and the UNIA Papers*, vol. 7, 92. See also Gomez, *Black Crescent*, 226–27; Turner, *Islam in the African American Experience*, 107.

54. Mortimer J. Davis, *U.S. v. Black Star Line, Inc.*, Summary Report, November 1922, FBI Monograph on Marcus Garvey (Part 5 of 12).

55. McDuffie, "Chicago, Garveyism," 133.

56. Letter to director, Bureau of Investigation, Department of Justice, Washington, DC, from Department of Justice, Bureau of Investigation, Philadelphia, PA, September 12, 1931, FBI Monograph on the MSTA. See also McDuffie, "Chicago, Garveyism," 137; Moses, *Golden Age of Black Nationalism*.

57. "Noble Drew Ali Returns after Long Visit South," *Chicago Defender*, November 19, 1927, 5. See also McDuffie, "Chicago, Garveyism," 129–45.

58. Martin, *Race First*, 77, citing Benjamin W. Jones, secretary of the Philadelphia UNIA to Joseph B. Keenan, assistant attorney general, May 21, 1935, NARA, RG 60, 39-51-821.

59. Turner, *Islam in the African American Experience*, 92; Gomez, *Black Crescent*, 206–8.

60. Ali, *The Holy Koran of the Moorish Science Temple of America* (1927), 3, MSTA Collection, SCRBC.

61. Ali, "Chapter XLV. The Divine Origin of the Asiatic Nations," 1, in *Holy Koran of the Moorish Science Temple of America*, MSTA Collection, SCRBC. But see Gomez, *Black Crescent*, 228–29, providing an alternative possibility that Drew may have been referring to his own *Circle Seven Koran* in his reference to the "Holy Koran of Mecca."

62. Ali, "Chapter XLVII. Egypt, the Capital Empire of the Dominion of Africa," *The Holy Koran of the Moorish Science Temple of America*, 57–59, MSTA Collection, SCRBC.

63. Genesis 9: 21–22, KJV.

64. Genesis 9: 22–25, KJV.

65. Robinson, *Lost White Tribe*, 60.

66. Genesis 9–10, KJV.

67. Robinson, *Lost White Tribe*, 62–63.

68. Moses, *Afrotopia*, 97.

69. Moses, *Afrotopia*, 97.

70. Moses, *Afrotopia*, 136–68.

71. Ali, "Chapter XLVII. Egypt, the Capital Empire of the Dominion of Africa," *The Holy Koran of the Moorish Science Temple of America*, 57–59, MSTA Collection, SCRBC.

72. Weisenfeld, *New World A-Coming*, 45.

73. Wegener, *Origin of Continents and Oceans*. See also Frankel, *Continental Drift Controversy*, 50–61; Greene, *Alfred Wegener*, 239–85.

74. "Think Land Linked Europe to America," *New York Times*, November 2, 1925, 19.

75. Ali, "Chapter XXV. A Holy Covenant of the Asiatic Nation," *The Holy Koran of the Moorish Science Temple of America*, 35–36, MSTA Collection, SCRBC.

76. Ali, "Chapter XLV. The Divine Origin of the Asiatic Nations," *The Holy Koran of the Moorish Science Temple of America*, 56–57, MSTA Collection, SCRBC.

77. Ali, "Chapter XLVII. Egypt, the Capital Empire of the Dominion of Africa," *The Holy Koran of the Moorish Science Temple of America*, 57–59, MSTA Collection, SCRBC.

78. Ali, "Chapter XLVIII. The End of Time and the Fulfilling of the Prophesies," *The Holy Koran of the Moorish Science Temple of America*, 59–60, MSTA Collection, SCRBC.

79. Mufti Muhammad Sadiq, "Brief Report of the Work in America," *Moslem Sunrise*, January 1923, 166.

80. "Cobb Whips Hilltop Fan for Insults," *New York Times*, May 16, 1912, 12; "Detroit Baseball Club on Strike," *New York Times*, May 18, 1912, 1.

81. "200 Diners Boost Cobb and Mates," *Detroit Free Press*, May 21, 1912, 1.

82. For more on the history of missionaries in Africa and Asia, see Sharkey, *Cultural Conversions*; Hardiman, *Healing Bodies, Saving Soul*; Tom Hiney, *On the Missionary Trail*.

83. Bob White, "Talk about School," 9–25; Diouf, "Cultural Resistance to Missionary Schools," 26–35; Haddad, *Cultures Colliding*; Fitzgerald, "Jumping the Fences," 175–92.

84. Turner, *Islam in the African American Experience*, 111; Friedmann, *Prophecy Continuous*, 15.

85. Friedmann, *Prophecy Continuous*, 4–10; Turner, *Islam in the African American Experience*, 110–11. For more on the consolidation of British rule in India, see Bender, *1857 Indian Uprising*.

86. See Charles Kurzman, "Introduction: The Modernist Islamic Movement," in Kurzman, *Modernist Islam, 1840–1940: A Sourcebook*, 3–30; Hourani, *Arabic Thought in the Liberal Age*, 67–244.

87. Friedmann, *Prophecy Continuous*, 4–10.

88. Friedmann, *Prophecy Continuous*, 24–31.

89. Turner, *Islam in the African American Experience*, citing "Religion of Islam—Spread of the Faith in This Country," *The Sheffield Evening Telegraph*, November 29, 1913.

90. For Ahmad's positive views on the British Empire, see Ahmad, *Tohfa-e-Qaisariyyah (A Gift for the Queen)* (originally published in 1897); Ahmad, *Sitara-e-Qaisarah (Star of the Empress)*, Sharmeen Butt, trans. (originally published in 1899).

91. *Moslem Sunrise*, October 1921, 1; *Moslem Sunrise*, Fourth Quarter 1948, 1.

92. "Empress Mary," *Moslem Sunrise*, July 1921, 17–18.

93. This phrase was first attributed to Earl George Macartney in his 1773 *Account of Ireland*, 55.

94. Mirza Mahmud Ahmad, "Greetings!," *Moslem Sunrise*, July 1921, 3.

95. Ahmad, *Star of the Empress*, 11–12; Ahmad, *Tadhkirah*, 483. For more on the premodern expansion of the Islamic empire, see Hoyland, *In God's Path*.

96. Ahmad, *Tadhkirah*, 327 (fn. 374). For a synthesis of the Ahmadiyya religious beliefs, see Friedmann, *Prophecy Continuous*; Turner, *Islam in the African American Experience*, 112–13.

97. Sadiq, "One Year's Moslem Missionary Work in America," 12.

98. "Notes and News," *Review of Religions*, October 1920, 352.

99. Green, *Terrains of Exchange*, 215.

100. GhaneaBassiri, *History of Islam in America*, 135–50.

101. Untitled photograph, 1921, in *Moslem Sunrise*, October 1921, 30; "Seed of Islam Finds No Root," *Detroit Free Press*, D3. See also Turner, *Islam in the African American Experience*, 121.

102. Mufti Muhammad Sadiq, "Some of My First Impressions," *Moslem Sunrise*, July 1921, 24.

103. *Mirza Ahmad F.L. Anderson*, 1921, in *Moslem Sunrise*, October 1921, 1; *Mr. James I.D. Sodick*, 1921, in *Moslem Sunrise*, October 1921, 42; *Ralph Totten (Bashir)*, 1921, in *Moslem Sunrise*, October 1921, 45; *Mr. R.J.H. Rochford*, 1922, in *Moslem Sunrise*, April 1922, 77; *Mr. Denzel Carr*, 1923, in *Moslem Sunrise*, January 1923, 163.

104. Mufti Muhammad Sadiq, "Dr. Sadiq," *Review of Religions*, September 1922, 350–51; "Seed of Islam Finds No Root," D3. See also Turner, *Islam in the African American Experience*, 124–25.

105. *Four American Moslem Ladies*, 1923, in *Moslem Sunrise*, January 1923, 165.

106. Mufti Muhammad Sadiq, "True Salvation of the American Negroes: The Real Solution of the Negro Question," *Moslem Sunrise*, April and July 1923, 184.

107. Mufti Muhammad Sadiq, "The Only Solution of Color Prejudice," *Moslem Sunrise*, October 1921, 41.

108. Mufti Muhammad Sadiq, "Press Notices," *Moslem Sunrise*, April and July 1923, 194.

109. Sadiq, "True Salvation of the American Negroes," 184.

110. Muhammad Sadiq, "Brief Report of the Work in America," *Moslem Sunrise*, April and July 1923, 190.

111. "Moslem Mollah in Mission to Chicago," *Chicago Herald & Examiner*, March 11, 1923; Mufti Muhammad Sadiq, "Press Notices," *Moslem Sunrise*, April and July 1923, 194.

112. *Sheikh Ahmad Din*, in *Moslem Sunrise*, July 1922, 119; "Moslem Priest in Chicago Wins 700 to His Faith: Says Mohammedanism Is Cure for Race Problem," *Moslem Sunrise*, January 1924, 45–46.

113. "Greetings!," *Moslem Sunrise*, July 1921, 3.

114. "Dr. Sadiq," *Moslem Sunrise*, January 1924, 45.

115. "New Converts," *Moslem Sunrise*, January 1923, 169–71.

116. "List or Manifest of Alien Passengers Arriving for the United States Immigration Officer at Port of Arrival, Boston, MA, S.S. Ausonia, March 17–27, 1923," Passenger Lists of Vessels Arriving at Boston, Massachusetts, 1891–1943, NARA, RG 85, Series T843, Roll 276; Maulvi Muhammad Din, "B.A.," in *Moslem Sunrise*, April and July, 1923, 183; "Brief Report on the Work in America," *Moslem Sunrise*, April and July 1923, 190; *Moslem Sunrise*, October 1923, 1.

117. J. A. O'Meally, "Crescent or Cross?: A Negro May Aspire to Any Position under Islam without Discrimination," *Moslem Sunrise*, October 1923, 263.

118. Friedmann, *Prophecy Continuous*, 34–38.

119. *Afternoon 'Id Gathering at the Mosque Ahmadia*, 1923, in *Moslem Sunrise*, October 1923, 256.

120. For more on Muslim nationalism and Indian independence, see Dhulipali, *Creating a New Medina*; M. Reza Pirbhai, *Fatima Jinnah*.

121. Maulvi Muhammad Din, "Our Loyalty to Our Principle," *Moslem Sunrise*, January 1924, 7.

122. Din, "Our Loyalty to Our Principle, 7.

123. Din, "Our Loyalty to Our Principle," 7.

124. "Al Din 'Aitanaquu al Islam Hadithan (Newly converted to the Islamic faith)," *Moslem Sunrise*, April 1924, 74.

125. Maulvi Muhammad Din, "To Our Subscribers and Patrons," *Moslem Sunrise*, April 1924, 73.

126. Turner, *Islam in the African American Experience*, 132.

127. "Al Din 'Aitanaquu," *Moslem Sunrise*, 74.

128. "Names and Descriptions of British Passengers, Cunard Steamship Line, HMS Berengaria, August 13–19, 1924," TNA, BT 25, Piece 778, Item 3.

129. "Activities of the Ahmadiyya Moslem Mission," *Moslem Sunrise*, July 1930, 11.

130. *Moslem Sunrise*, Second and Third Quarter 1947, 1.

131. "Activities of the American Ahmadiyya Moslem Mission," *Moslem Sunrise*, December 1930, 23. See also Turner, *Islam in the African American Experience*, 131–36.

132. Beynon, "Voodoo Cult," 906.

133. Gomez, *Black Crescent*, 278; Clegg, *An Original Man*, 70–71; Taylor, *Promise of Patriarchy*, 2.

Chapter Two

1. Naeem Family Photograph, circa late 1950s. Courtesy of Shahid Naeem. The Naeem family would eventually include six children. Naeem email, August 19, 2024.

2. DeCaro, *On the Side of My People*, 149–64.

3. According to Erdmann Beynon, a University of Michigan sociologist who is responsible for publishing the first academic study of the Nation of Islam in 1938, W. D. Fard Muhammad was most often known as Mr. Wali Farrad or Mr. W. D. Fard. Less frequently, he used the name Professor Ford, Mr. Farad Muhammad, or Mr. F. Mohammed Ali. See Beynon, "The Voodoo Cult," 894–907.

4. Sister Denke Majied (née Mrs. Lawrence Adams), interview by Erdmann Beynon (circa 1938) in Beynon, "The Voodoo Cult," 894–96. See also Gomez, *Black Crescent*, 279.

5. Bald, *Bengali Harlem*.

6. Gomez, *Black Crescent*, 276.

7. At least one early convert did allege that Fard originated from Morocco, but there is no evidence that he ever asserted this. This is likely a conflation of Arab and Islamic identity with Moorish origination as seen in earlier movements like the Moorish Science Temple. See, for example, Taylor, *Promise of Patriarchy*, 23, citing "Voodoo Slayer Admits Plotting Death of Judges," *Detroit Free Press*, November 22, 1932, 2.

8. Beynon, "The Voodoo Cult," 900, 902. See also Taylor, *Promise of Patriarchy*, 19; Turner, *Islam in the African American Experience*, 151.

9. Taylor, *Promise of Patriarchy*, 22.

10. Sister Carrie Mohammed (née Mrs. Carrie Peoples) and uncited "others," interview by Erdmann Beynon (circa 1938) in Beynon, "The Voodoo Cult," 897; Elijah Muhammad, *The Supreme Wisdom: Solution to the So-Called Negroes Problem*, 1st ed. (Newport News, VA, 1957). See also Clegg, *An Original Man*, 64–67; Turner, *Islam in the African American Experience*, 151; Gomez, *Black Crescent*, 279; Taylor, *The Promise of Patriarchy*, 19–22; Curtis, *Black Muslim Religion*, 11.

11. These teachings were codified into a text titled *Teaching for the Lost Found Nation of Islam in a Mathematical Way*, which consisted of thirty-four mathematical problems. A two-part teaching titled *The Secret Ritual of the Nation of Islam* was transmitted orally. Beynon, "The Voodoo Cult," fn. 17. As Beynon's text was published four years after Fard's disappearance, and makes use of oral interviews with members who allege to have been recruited by Fard, I use this article as both a primary and secondary source.

12. These three teachings were reorganized and published into several texts, *Student Enrollment, Actual Facts, English Lesson No. C1 (Part 3)*, and *Lost-Found Muslim Lessons Nos. 1 and 2*. See, Gomez, *Black Crescent*, 310. In 1957, these teachings were published into a volume titled *The Supreme Wisdom: Solution to the So-Called Negroes' Problem*.

13. Beynon, "Voodoo Cult," 906. For more on the connections between Garveyism, the Moorish Science Temple, and the Nation of Islam, see Gomez, *Black Crescent*, 278; Clegg, *An Original Man*, 70–71; Taylor, *Promise of Patriarchy*, 2.

14. Beynon, "Voodoo Cult," 906.

15. Gomez, *Black Crescent*, 278; Evanzz, *The Messenger*, 402–7.

16. Beynon, "Voodoo Cult," 897, 904, fn. 10. Nation of Islam officials estimated their membership at 8,000. The Detroit Special Investigation Squad estimated membership at

5,000. In 1930, the Black population of Detroit was approximately 120,000. By 1940, it had more than doubled to over 300,000. Gomez, *Black Crescent*, 279; Bureau of the Census, "Table 1. Characteristics of the Population, by Census Tracts: 1950," in *1950: United States Census of Population*, 7.

17. Beynon, "Voodoo Cult," 896–97.

18. Evanzz, *The Messenger*, 400. For FBI records on Fard's origins, see "Office Memorandum to SAC from SA Edwin O. Raudsup," Case No. 100–43165, March 8, 1965, in FBI Monograph on Wallace Ford Muhammed; "Records Los Angeles Police Department on Wallei Ford," March 6, 1965, FBI Monograph on Wallace Fard Muhammed. Evanzz's book on Elijah Muhammad must be read carefully given its bias against the Nation and overreliance on government documents. In this circumstance, and in all circumstances in which Evanzz is cited in this volume, his facts have been cross-checked with other sources or he has provided compelling evidence that his conclusions are correct. For more on the process of race-making for South Asian and Middle Eastern immigrants to the United States, see Bald, *Bengali Harlem*; Bayoumi, "Racing Religion," 267–93; Gualtieri, *Between Arab and White*.

19. Evanzz, *The Messenger*, 411.

20. Sultana, "Ethnicity and Healing Rituals," 170; Bhatt, *The African Diaspora in India*, 13–25, 45.

21. There is no evidence that this money was ever paid. SAC Memorandum from SA Edwin O. Raudsep to SAC, Subject Wallace D. Fard, Case No. 100–43165, March 8, 1965, FBI Monograph on Wallace Fard Muhammed; Elijah Muhammad, "Beware of Phony Claims," *Muhammad Speaks*, August 16, 1963, 1, 3.

22. Wesley Muhammad, "Master W. Fard Muhammad and FBI COINTELPRO," *Nation of Islam*, accessed August 29, 2024, http://www.noi.org/fard-muhammad-fbi-cointelpro.

23. Beynon, "Voodoo Cult," 896, 906–7.

24. Taylor, *Promise of Patriarchy*, 8.

25. Taylor, *Promise of Patriarchy*, 8, citing Sahib A. Hatim, *The Nation of Islam*, master's thesis, University of Chicago, 1951.

26. Clegg, *An Original Man*, 16; Taylor, *Promise of Patriarchy*, 8, citing Chicago FBI Report on Allah Temple of Islam (9/11/42), September 11, 1942, 11, NARA, RG 65, and noting that the 1930 United States census reported Elijah Poole (Muhammad) was unemployed. See United States Census Bureau, "Fifteenth Census of the United States: 1930, Population Schedule—Detroit, Wayne, Michigan, Ward 9, Block no. 528."

27. Taylor, *Promise of Patriarchy*, 8, citing Best Efforts, Inc., Archives, Department of Police, Detroit, Michigan, Bureau of Identification, document number 21177; Clegg, *An Original Man*, 17.

28. Taylor, *Promise of Patriarchy*, 15, citing Hatim, "Nation of Islam," 92.

29. Clegg, *An Original Man*, 17, citing Hatim, "Nation of Islam," 92.

30. Taylor, *Promise of Patriarchy*, 15–16, citing Hatim, "Nation of Islam," 91–93, 126. For numbers of Nation members in the 1930s, see "Voodoo Slayer Admits Plotting Death of Judges," *Detroit Free Press*, November 22, 1932.

31. Beynon, "The Voodoo Cult," 903–4. See also Taylor, *Promise of Patriarchy*, 23–24; Clegg, *An Original Man*, 31–32.

32. Taylor, *Promise of Patriarchy*, 23–24; Clegg, *An Original Man*, 33.

33. "Pastors Decry Growth of Cult Practices Here: Negro Leaders Pledge Support to Wipe out Voodooism," *Detroit Free Press*, November 28, 1932. See also Taylor, *Promise of Patriarchy*, 27–28; Clegg, *An Original Man*, 36–37.

34. Beynon, "Voodoo Cult," 906–7. See also Taylor, *Promise of Patriarchy*, 70; Clegg, *An Original Man*, 37.

35. Taylor, *Promise of Patriarchy*, 70, citing Chicago FBI Report on Allah Temple of Islam (9/18/42), 10, NARA, RG 65; Clegg, *An Original Man*, 89, citing Hatim, "Nation of Islam," 172.

36. Taylor, *Promise of Patriarchy*, 57.

37. Taylor, *Promise of Patriarchy*, 61–63.

38. Case Report on Allah Temple of Islam, File No. 100–9129, September 30, 1942, FBI Monograph on Wallace Fard Muhammed.

39. Memorandum to Director; FBI, December 18, 1942, FBI Monograph on Wallace Fard Muhammed.

40. Taylor, *Promise of Patriarchy*, 66–67.

41. Subject Report from FBI, File No. 25–8786, October 9, 1943, FBI Monograph on Wallace Fard Muhammed; Statement of [Redacted], September 20, 1942, FBI Monograph on Wallace Fard Muhammed.

42. Subject Report from FBI, File No. 25–8786, October 9, 1943, FBI Monograph on Wallace Fard Muhammed.

43. "FBI File No. 100–12899," October 18, 1943, FBI Monograph on Wallace Fard Muhammed. See also, Subject Report from FBI of [Redacted], File No. 25–8786, October 9, 1943, FBI Monograph on Wallace Fard Muhammed.

44. Taylor, *Promise of Patriarchy*, 36.

45. Clegg, *An Original Man*, 95.

46. Clegg, *An Original Man*, 96.

47. Clegg, *An Original Man*, 91, 95–96.

48. Taylor, *Promise of Patriarchy*, 72–73. Taylor revises previous scholarly suggestions that it was primarily Clara Muhammad who held the Nation of Islam together during Elijah's incarceration by asserting that it was most likely a "tag team" between Muhammad and Behar.

49. It is unclear how many people were on record as Nation of Islam members nationally before the FBI raid; however, membership of the Detroit headquarters peaked at approximately eight thousand by the early 1930s. Taylor, *Promise of Patriarchy*, 73.

50. For a more thorough discussion of the dramatic impact of World War II on African American political engagement with anticolonialism in the African diaspora and Asian Third World, see von Eschen, *Race against Empire*; Horne, *Facing the Rising Sun*; Frazier, "Afro-Asia and Cold War Black Radicalism," *Socialism and Democracy* 25, no. 1 (March 2011): 257–65.

51. For examples, see James, "Playing the Russian Game," 509–34; Abou-El-Fadl, "Neutralism Made Positive," 219–40.

52. von Eschen, *Race against Empire*.

53. For more on the role of print media and nationalist sentiment, see Anderson, *Imagined Communities*.

54. Passenger and Crew List of Vessels Arriving at New York, New York, 1897–1957, NARA, RG 85, Series T715, Roll A3461, p. 78.

55. *Brown and Gold* (1948), 95, 148, Western Michigan University Archives and Regional History Collections; *Brown and Gold* (1949), 98, Western Michigan University Archives and Regional History Collections.

56. *Brown and Gold* (1949), 49, Western Michigan University Archives and Regional History Collections.

57. Naeem, "Current Topics," 227.

58. *Brown and Gold* (1952), 107, Western Michigan University Archives and Regional History Collections.

59. "Has Magazine for Moslems," *Iowa Quest*, June 1955, 7; List of Outward Bound Passengers (United States Citizens and Nationals), SS "City of Madras," June 13, 1953, Passenger and Crew Lists of Vessels and Airplanes Department from New York, New York, 07/01/1948–12/31/1956, NARA, RG 85, Series A4169, Roll 218.

60. "Shereen Naeem," in *California Birth Index*; "Shahid Naeem," in *California Birth Index*.

61. "Professor Abdul Basit Naeem Leaves for the United States," *Voice of Islam*, December 1953, 78.

62. "Professor Abdul Basit Naeem Leaves," 78; "Aims and Objects of the Jam'iyat-ul-falah, Karachi," *Voice of Islam*, October 1952, 1; "Contents," *Moslem World & the U.S.A.*, June–July 1956, 3.

63. *Voice of Islam*, October 1952; Maulana Fazlullah Khan, "The Jamiyat-ul-Falah: Its Aims and Activities," *Voice of Islam*, October 1952, 6–7; Hon'ble Maulana Tamizuddin Khan, "Missionary Needs of Islam and the Jam'iyat-ul-Falah," *Voice of Islam*, 44.

64. "Professor Abdul Basit Naeem Leaves," 78; List of Outward Bound Passengers (United States Citizens and Nationals), SS "City of Madras," June 13, 1953; Passenger Manifest, Transworld Airlines, Inc., Flight No. 967/14, Passenger Vessels Arriving at New York, New York, 1820–1957, December 14, 1953, NARA, RG 36, Series T715.

65. "Professor Abdul Basit Naeem Leaves," 79.

66. "Has Magazine for Moslems," 7.

67. Office Memorandum from director, FBI to SAC Philadelphia, April 30, 1954, FBI monograph on Malcolm X.

68. DeCaro, *On the Side of My People*, 149–64.

69. Walter Kolarz, "The Soviet Regime and Arabic Culture," *Voice of Islam*, November 1953, 52–53; Mostafa Mohsin Afifi, "Moscow Versus Mecca," *Voice of Islam*, November 1953, 63; Sufi Nazir Ahmad, "Resolving the World-Crisis in General and the Crisis in Asia in Particular: A Scheme for Third Block," *Voice of Islam*, February 1954, 169–74; William Banks, "Kremlin's Threat to the Muslim World," *Voice of Islam*, April 1954, 232–34.

70. "Professor Abdul Basit Naeem Leaves," 78. See also Turner, *Islam in the African American Experience*, 64.

71. "Luck Finally Changes for Naeem," *Des Moines Register*, January 1955.

72. Wilford, *America's Great Game*, 113–27.

73. Wilford, *America's Great Game*, 118, citing NSA 10/2, June 18, 1948.

74. Wilford, *America's Great Game*, 118–20; Felber, *Those Who Know Don't Say*, 32, fn. 107.

75. "Has Magazine for Moslems," 7.

76. Aouney Wafa Dejany, "What Is Islam?," *Moslem World & the U.S.A.*, January 1955, 5–8; Mahmoud F. Hoballah, "Institutions of Marriage, Divorce, and Inheritance in Islam," *Moslem World & the U.S.A.*, January 1955, 9–18.

77. Arnold J. Toynbee, "Pakistan—As an Historian Sees Her," *Moslem World & the U.S.A.*, January 1955, 19–20, 41.

78. Turner, *Islam in the African American Experience*, 110–14; Gomez, *Black Crescent*, 250–51.

79. "New 'Pilgrims' Fail in Propaganda Mission: Appearance of Two U.S. Moslems at Mecca Is Reds' Undoing," *Moslem World & the U.S.A.*, January 1955, 28–30, 33.

80. "Only Three Decades Ago," *Moslem World & the U.S.A.*, January 1955, 44.

81. "Press Round-Up: Communism and the Future of the Moslem World," *Moslem World & the U.S.A.*, February–March 1955, 37–39, 43.

82. "Only Three Decades Ago," 44.

83. Editor, "On to Madinat-Asslam," *Moslem World & the U.S.A.*, April–May 1956, 2. For a discussion of the effects of white flight on racial and ethnic diversity in Brooklyn after World War II, see Osman, *Making of Brownstone Brooklyn*, 43.

84. Abdul B. Naeem, "On to Madinat-Asslam," *Moslem World & the U.S.A.*, April–May 1956, 2; Abdul B. Naeem, "Our Third Year, Second Volume," *Moslem World & the U.S.A.*, October–November–December, 4.

85. Abdul Basit Naeem, "March on Moslems!," *Moslem World & the U.S.A.*, June–July 1956, 4; "Keep It Up, Algeria!," *Moslem World & the U.S.A.*, August–September 1956, 4–5.

86. Naeem, "March on Moslems!," 4.

87. "Is Islam a So-Called Negro Religion," *Moslem World & the U.S.A.*, October–November–December 1956, 15.

88. "Islam Is Misunderstood, and Why?," *Moslem World & the U.S.A.*, August–September 1956, 8–10; "The Black Man and Islam," *Moslem World & the U.S.A.*, August–September 1956, 11–12.

89. "The Black Man and Islam," 11–13.

90. Kamil Abdul Rahim, "Independence Is Their Goal," *Moslem World & the U.S.A.*, June–July 1956, 12–14; "Nationalists' Representative in New York City Warns against 'Internationalization' of Algerian Conflict," *Moslem World & the U.S.A.*, June–July 1956, 39; "Keep It Up Algeria!," 4–5.

91. "Moslems in the U.S.S.R.," *Moslem World & the U.S.A.*, August–September 1956, 6–7; Dr. Muhammad Fazlur-Rahman Ansari Al-Qaderi, "Manifesto of the World Federation of Islamic Missions," *Moslem World & the U.S.A.*, May–June 1957, 23–26.

92. Naeem, "March on Moslems!," 4.

93. Dannin, *Black Pilgrimage to Islam*, 62–65.

94. Abdul Basit Naeem, "On to Madinat-Asslam," *Moslem World & the U.S.A.*, April–May 1956, 2.

95. Dannin, *Black Pilgrimage to Islam*, 63–65.

96. "Contents," *Moslem World & the U.S.A.*, April–May 1956, 3; "Contents," *Moslem World & the U.S.A*, June–July 1956, 3; "Contents," *Moslem World & the U.S.A*, August–September 1956, 3; "Contents," *Moslem World & the U.S.A*, October–November–December 1956, 3; "Contents," *Moslem World & the U.S.A.*, March–April 1957, 3; "Contents," *Moslem World & the U.S.A.*, January–February 1957, 2; "Contents," *Moslem World & the U.S.A.*, May–June 1957, 3.

97. Abdul B. Naeem, "The South Chicago Moslems," *Moslem World & the U.S.A.*, April–May 1956, 22–23.

98. Elijah Muhammad, "The Supreme Wisdom: The Black Nation, the Original People of Our Planet," *Moslem World & the U.S.A.*, August–September 1956, 15–17; "We Arose from the Dead," *Moslem World & the U.S.A.*, August–September 1956, 24–27, 36; Elijah Muhammad, "The Teachings of Mr. Elijah Muhammad," *Moslem World & the U.S.A.*, 18–35.

99. Felber, *Those Who Know Don't Say*, 33.

100. Muhammad, "The Supreme Wisdom," 15–17; "We Arose from the Dead," *Moslem World & the U.S.A.*, August–September 1956, 24–27, 36; Muhammad, "The Teachings of Mr. Elijah Muhammad," 18–35.

101. "Mr. Elijah Muhammad and *Moslem World & the U.S.A.*," *Moslem World & the U.S.A.*, Oct.–Nov.–Dec. 1956, 8–9. There is no evidence that Naeem was under contract with the Nation of Islam at this time; although by 1957, he was engaged in a host of editorial and promotional activities, and according to a NYPD BOSSI report, was contracted by the Nation of Islam to produce his 1957 special brochure on the Nation of Islam's Saviour's Day Convention. See Evanzz, 183, citing NYPD BOSSI report on Malcolm X.

102. Abdul Basit Naeem, "American Moslems of African Descent," *Moslem World and the U.S.A.* 2, nos. 5–6 (May 1957): 7.

103. Abdul Basit Naeem, "Introduction," in Muhammad, *The Supreme Wisdom*, 4.

104. Naeem, "Introduction," 4.

105. Abdul B. Naeem, "Moslem World & the U.S.A. Editor-Publisher's Brief Address at the Moslem's Convention," *Moslem World & the U.S.A.*, March–April 1957, 23–25.

106. "Is Islam a So-Called 'Negro' Religion?," 15.

107. "The Black Man and Islam," *Moslem World & the U.S.A.*, August–September 1956, 11–13.

108. Naeem, "Introduction," *The Supreme Wisdom*, 5.

109. SAC New York, "Malcolm X; Security Matter—Nation," April 23, 1959, FBI Monograph on Malcolm X.

110. SAC New York, "Malcolm X; Security Matter—Nation."

111. SAC New York, "Malcolm X; Security Matter—Nation."

112. SAC New York. "Malcolm X; Security Matter—Nation.

113. Makalani, *In the Cause of Freedom*, 23–44; Watkins-Owens, *Blood Relations*, 1–10; Edwards, *The Practice of Diaspora*, 1–8.

114. von Eschen, *Race against Empire*, 8.

115. "UN Starts Move Today to East River Building," *New York Times*, August 18, 1950, 8.

116. Plummer, *In Search of Power*, 33.

117. "African Meet Sets Regular Friday Talks," *New York Amsterdam News*, April 14, 1951, 33.

118. "United African Nationalists to Hold Conference," *Atlanta Daily World*, May 11, 1955, 1; "Ethiopian Press Attaché Speaks at UANM Meet," *New York Amsterdam News*, June 2, 1956, 16; "Three African Countries Hail Independence," *New York Amsterdam News*, February 16, 1957, 4.

119. Plummer, *In Search of Power*, 34.

120. "African Group to Demonstrate at UN," *Afro-American*, September 21, 1957, 3.

121. "African Nationalists Alarmed at U.S. Stand," *New York Amsterdam News*, February 1, 1958, 15.

122. "Moslem World & the U.S.A. Publisher Addresses United African Nationalists on Suez," *Moslem World & the U.S.A.*, October–November–December 1956, 59.

123. "Be a Charter Subscriber to The African-Asian World," *The Moslem World & the U.S.A.*, October–November–December 1956, 58, emphasis in original.

124. "News From the United States," *Moslem World & the U.S.A.*, May–June 1956, 29.

125. "News From the United States," 29.

126. Abdul Basit Naeem, "Random Notes," *Muhammad Speaks*, April 1962, 7.

127. "Photograph: Greeting in Peace," *Muhammad Speaks*, May 1962, 6; Felber, *Those Who Know Don't Say*, 34, reprinting photograph of Abdul Basit Naeem, Muhammad Ngileruma, Malcolm X, Issa Serag, others at Shalimar International, c. 1962, Robert Haggins Collection, SCRBC.

128. "Letter from Elijah Muhammad to Abdul Basit Naeem," April 12, 1962, Malcolm X Papers, Box 11, Folder 4, SCRBC.

129. Stewart email.

130. "Abdul B. Naeem," in US Phone and Address Directories.

131. Naeem email, April 24, 2024.

Chapter Three

1. Untitled Photograph, 1959, at *Elijah Muhammad Speaks*, accessed August 30, 2024, https://www.elijahmuhammadspeaks.com/pakistani-view-of-messenger-muhammad.

2. "Mr. Muhammad Speaks," *Pittsburgh Courier*, June 9, 1956, B3. According to an issue of *Moslem World & the U.S.A.*, the circulation of the *Pittsburgh Courier* in late 1956 was approximately 200,000. "Mr. Muhammad Speaks," *Moslem World & the U.S.A.*, October–November–December 1956, 7. For more on the Nation of Islam's early publishing in Black newspapers, see Wilson, "Get off the Cross and Get under the Crescent," 494–506.

3. "The Teachings of Mr. Elijah Muhammad," *Moslem World & the U.S.A.*, October–November–December 1956, 18.

4. "The Islam World," *New York Amsterdam News*, July 27, 1957, 7.

5. SAC New York, "Malcolm Little; Security Matter—Nation," April 30, 1958, FBI Monograph on Malcolm X.

6. Jane Krieger Rose, "Close-up of the Afro-Asian Bloc," *New York Times*, December 17, 1961, 19, 33; "Will the UN Catch Up?," *U.S. News and World Report*, October 2, 1961, 41; Nawaz, "Afro-Asians and the United Nations."

7. Complaint Report, BOSS #102-M, June 29, 1956. NYPD Intelligence Records, Box 28, F.5, New York Municipal Archives.

8. Letter from commanding officer, BOSSI to chief inspector. Subject: Visit of Muslim Cult of Islam to This City on June 30, 1956, July 2, 1956, NYPD Intelligence Records, Box 28, F.5, New York Municipal Archives.

9. Scholars have mistakenly claimed that Sukarno, the president of Indonesia and one of the architects of Bandung, was present at Abyssinian Baptist Church during this meeting. SAC New York, "Malcolm Little; Security Matter—Nation," April 30, 1958, FBI Monograph on Malcolm X. In addition, the FBI file cites an article from the July 20, 1957, issue of the *Pittsburgh Courier* titled "Moslems Help Welcome Leaders from Indonesia," which does not appear to exist. See *Pittsburgh Courier*, July 20, 1957.

10. SAC New York, "Malcolm Little; Security Matter—Nation," April 30, 1958, FBI Monograph on Malcolm X.

11. "Mister Muhammad's Message to African-Asian Conference!," *Pittsburgh Courier*, January 18, 1958, 9. See also Clegg, *An Original Man*, 122; Felber, *Those Who Know Don't Say*, 30.

12. "Mister Muhammad's Message to African-Asian Conference," 9.

13. "Mister Muhammad's Message to African-Asian Conference," 9.

14. Al Nall, "700 Attended Moslem Program," *New York Amsterdam News*, January 11, 1958, 14.

15. "Nasser Answers Muhammad Cable," *New York Amsterdam News*, February 15, 1958, 17.

16. Evanzz, *The Messenger*, 185, citing NYPD BOSSI file on Malcolm X, memorandum dated July 23, 1959.

17. SAC New York, "Malcolm X; Security Matter—Nation," April 23, 1957, FBI Monograph on Malcolm X.

18. The root of these suspicions lay in the Nation's growing anti-Zionist and pro-Arab rhetoric. These issues were taken up directly at a conference celebrating Third Pakistan Republic Day in April of 1958. Although the conference named Pakistan directly, it also focused heavily on the tenth anniversary of the state of Israel. See Evanzz, *The Messenger*, 181–87.

19. Dannin, *Black Pilgrimage to Islam*, 58.

20. Chan-Malik, *Being Muslim*, 283.

21. Dannin, *Black Pilgrimage to Islam*, 61; Turner, *Soundtrack to a Movement*, 115; Chan-Malik, *Being Muslim*, 283.

22. Dannin, *Black Pilgrimage to Islam*, 61; Turner, *Soundtrack to a Movement*, 115.

23. Chan-Malik, *Being Muslim*, 285–85.

24. Talib Dawud, "Part I: In Struggle for Africa: Christianity vs. Islam," *Pittsburgh Courier*, August 24, 1957, B6.

25. Talib Dawud, "Part II: In Struggle for Africa: Christianity vs. Islam," *Pittsburgh Courier*, August 31, 1957, A4.

26. Dawud, "Part II," A4.

27. Ahmad Jamal, "Letter to the Editor: Talib Dawud Articles Win Praise in Chicago," *Pittsburgh Courier*, December 7, 1957, B8.

28. Yusuf Ahmad, "Letter to the Editor: Is 'Mr. Muhammad' a Fake?," *Pittsburgh Courier*, August 18, 1956, A6. These critiques were commonplace, but for every letter blasting the publication for its unbalanced perspective, there were far more praising Muhammad's teachings and their effectiveness for building racial pride and promoting Black salvation. "Voice of the People—What Courier Readers Think: Thoughts on 'Muhammad,' Pro and Con," *Pittsburgh Courier*, August 18, 1956, A6; "What the People Think... Voice of the People: Atlanta Readers Go for Mr. Muhammad," *Pittsburgh Courier*, July 21, 1956, 12; "Voice of the People—What Courier Readers Think: They Are Still Reading Muhammad," *Pittsburgh Courier*, September 1, 1956, A6.

29. Office Memorandum from director, FBI to SAC Philadelphia, April 30, 1954, FBI monograph on Malcolm X.

30. SAC New York, "Malcolm K. Little; Internal Security—Nation," November 19, 1959, FBI Monograph on Malcolm X.

31. SAC New York, "Malcolm K. Little; Internal Security—Nation," November 17, 1959, FBI Monograph on Malcolm X, quoting "Malcolm X Calls for Bandung Conference of Negro Leaders," *Los Angeles Herald-Dispatch*, April 23, 1959.

32. As early as February 1959, the FBI had information that Muhammad intended to go to Egypt in April of that year but had made no other plans besides acquiring the passport application. Muhammad never went on this trip. Federal Bureau of Investigation, "Elijah Muhammad; Internal Security-Nation," February 5, 1959, FBI Monograph on Elijah Muhammad.

33. Evanzz, *The Messenger*, 193, citing BOSSI File on Malcolm X.

34. Hajj is one of the five pillars of Islam, required once in a lifetime for all Muslims who are physically and financially able to undertake it. The ritual involves travel to the Holy City of Mecca, located in Saudi Arabia, and performance of several ritual reenactments of events from the lives of Abraham, Hagar, and Ishmael. Hajj takes place every year during the month of *Dhu al-Hijah*, the twelfth and final month of the Islamic calendar. The Islamic calendar is lunar, and therefore, when converted to a solar calendar system, like the standard Western Gregorian calendar, *Dhu al-Hijah* shifts back approximately one month each year. In 1959, the month fell between June 7 and July 6, 1959. For a simple explanation of hajj, see "Hajj," in Esposito, *The Oxford Dictionary of Islam*, 103–4.

35. Evanzz, *The Messenger*, 193 citing BOSSI File on Malcolm X.

36. The FBI repeatedly placed stops on passport applications by Muhammad and his family members in connection with their trip to Egypt and Saudi Arabia. FBI Chicago Office, "Office Memorandum from SAC, Chicago to Director, FBI; Subject: Nation of Islam IS-Nation," May 26, 1959, FBI Monograph on Elijah Muhammad; FBI Field Office Chicago, "Memorandum from Director, FBI to SAC, Chicago," June 3, 1959, FBI Monograph on Elijah Muhammad; FBI Washington Field Office, "Office Memorandum from SAC, Washington to Director, FBI Re: Elijah Muhamad, aka IS-Nation," June 19, 1959, FBI Monograph on Elijah Muhammad; FBI Chicago Field Office, "Office Memorandum from SAC, Chicago to Director, FBI. Subject: Elijah Muhammad aka Internal Security—Nation," July 9, 1959, FBI Monograph on Elijah Muhammad.

37. FBI, "Elijah Poole, also known as Elijah Muhammed," July 15, 1959, FBI Monograph on Elijah Muhammad; FBI Chicago Field Office, "Internal Security—Nation," August 27, 1959, FBI Monograph on Elijah Muhammad.

38. FBI Washington Field Office, "Office Memorandum From SAC, WFO to Director, FBI. Subject: Elijah Poole aka IS-Nation," July 15, 1959, FBI Monograph on Elijah Muhammad.

39. SAC, Washington Field Office, "Airtel from SAC, Washington to Director, FBI re: Malcolm K. Little; Internal Security—Nation," July 27, 1959, FBI Monograph on Malcolm X.

40. In a speech at the St. Nicholas Arena in New York, Malcolm reported that he did not speak with Nasser but that he did see him in Egypt. SAC, New York, "Office Memorandum from SAC, New York to Director, FBI; Subject: Malcolm K. Little; IS-Nation," July 29, 1959, FBI Monograph on Malcolm X. See also, Evanzz, *The Messenger*, 199; Marable, *Malcolm X*, 166.

41. SAC New York, "Office Memorandum from SAC, New York to Director, FBI; Subject: Malcolm K. Little; IS-Nation," July 29, 1959, FBI Monograph on Malcolm X.

42. SAC New York, "Malcolm X; Security Matter—Nation," April 23, 1957, p. 118, reprinting a letter from Malcolm X to [redacted], circa September 1956, FBI Monograph on Malcolm X.

43. "Malcolm X Off to Tour Middle East," *New York Amsterdam News*, July 11, 1959, 18.

44. Malcolm X, "Arabs Send Warm Greetings to 'Our Brothers' of Color in U.S.A.," *Pittsburgh Courier*, August 15, 1959, C1. One of these letters was reprinted in the column "Pulse

of the Public," in the *New York Amsterdam News*. See "Pulse of the Public," *New York Amsterdam News*, August 15, 1959, 10.

45. Marable, *Malcolm X*, 168.

46. SAC New York, "Office Memorandum from SAC, New York to Director, FBI; Subject: Malcolm K. Little; IS-Nation," July 29, 1959, FBI Monograph on Malcolm X.

47. "Muslim Leader Leaves for Mecca," *Philadelphia Tribune*, June 9, 1959, 12.

48. J.A. Rogers, "History Shows," *Pittsburgh Courier*, July 18, 1959, A5.

49. Rogers, "History Shows," A5.

50. Rogers, "History Shows," A5.

51. "Muslim Leader Leaves for Mecca," *Philadelphia Tribune*, June 9, 1959, 12; "He Returns from Visit to Mecca," *New York Amsterdam News*, July 18, 1959, 24. For more on the World Islamic Congress, see Freas, "Hajj Amin al-Husayni and the Haram al-Sharif," 19–51; Roberts, "Making Jerusalem the Centre of the Muslim World," 52–63.

52. John Edgar Hoover, "Memorandum from J. Edgar Hoover to Office of Security and Department of State," November 20, 1959, FBI Monograph on Elijah Muhammad; SAC New York, "Office Memorandum to Director, FBI from SAC, New York; Subject: Nation of Islam," November 23, 1959, FBI Monograph on Elijah Muhammad; SAC, New York, "Teletype from SAC New York to Director and SAC, Chicago," November 21, 1959, FBI Monograph on Elijah Muhammad. See also Evanzz, *The Messenger*, 212.

53. Clegg, *Original Man*, 139–41.

54. Although the trip to Mecca, and its associated rites, can be made at any time, if they do not take place within the month of *Dhu al-Hijah*, they are not considered to constitute a hajj. Instead, the pilgrim is considered to have undertaken an *umrah*, or lesser pilgrimage. For a basic explanation of *umrah*, see "Umrah," in Esposito, *Oxford Dictionary of Islam*, 349.

55. FBI Chicago Field Office, "Elijah Muhammad Internal Security—Nation of Islam," January 13, 1960, FBI Monograph on Elijah Muhammad.

56. Legal Attaché, Madrid, "Office Memorandum to Director, FBI," January 15, 1960, FBI Monograph on Elijah Muhammad.

57. FBI Chicago Field Office, "Elijah Muhammad; Internal Security—Nation of Islam," November 20, 1959, FBI Monograph on Elijah Muhammad.

58. Elijah Muhammad, "Islam, Holy City," *New York Amsterdam News*, January 23, 1960, 6.

59. "He Returns from a Visit to Mecca," *New York Amsterdam News*, July 18, 1959, 24.

60. SAC Chicago, "Elijah Poole; Internal Security—Nation," March 3, 1960, FBI Monograph on Elijah Muhammad; "Muslim Leader Calls Moslem Leader 'Phony,'" *New York Amsterdam News*, October 3, 1959, 11.

61. "Singer Lashes Mike Wallace: Dakota Says There's No Connection 'Tween Her Faith, Muhammad," *Pittsburgh Courier*, August 1, 1959, 6.

62. "Muslim Leader Calls Moslem Leader 'Phony,'" *New York Amsterdam News*, October 3, 1959, 11.

63. Elijah Muhammad, "Mr. Muhammad Speaks," *Pittsburgh Courier*, August 15, 1959, B6.

64. Muhammad, "Mr. Muhammad Speaks," *Pittsburgh Courier*, August 15, 1959, B6.

65. Chan-Malik, *Being Muslim*, 289–92, talking in depth about Staton's *Jet* magazine feature.

66. Chan-Malik, *Being Muslim*, 292–93, citing "Dakota Staton, Hubby File Suit against Muhammad," *New Pittsburgh Courier*, June 9, 1962, 1.

67. Chan-Malik, *Being Muslim*, 294–95.//
68. Malcolm X, "No Compromise," *New York Amsterdam News*, December 1, 1962, 10. For more on Malcolm's response to Dakota Staton, see Chan-Malik, *Being Muslim*, 295–96.
69. "Moslems Denounce US 'Muslims,'" *New York Amsterdam News*, October 22, 1960, 1; "African Muslim Praises Muhammad's Work," *Mr. Muhammad Speaks*, December 1960, 2, 27, reprinting a speech given by Dr. Mahmoud Youssef Sharwarbi at the Nation's Afro-Asian Bazaar in Harlem in April 1960. While an article in the *New York Amsterdam* News alleged that Sharwarbi and Fazl-ur-Rahman Ansari had "denounced" the Nation, Sharwarbi gave a speech at the Nation of Islam's Afro-Asian Bazaar where he denied denouncing the nation of Islam, invited Nation followers to an Islamic Conference in July 1961, and acknowledged the differences in interpretation but characterized Muhammad's movement as "healthy."
70. Letter from Detective William K. DeFossett, # 631 B.S.S.; To: Commanding Officer, BOSSI, April 6, 1961, NYPD REC 0044, Communication Files, Box 10, Folder BSS #87M/1961, New York Municipal Archives.
71. "Harlem Prepares to Greet Sekou Toure," *Baltimore Afro-American*, October 31, 1959, 19; "Mme. Toure Visit Stirs Harlem Fuore," *Cleveland Call and Post*, November 21, 1959, 1C; James Booker, "Lawson Hits Press; Defends His Role," *New York Amsterdam News*, November 21, 1959, 1.
72. "Fete for Touré Noisy, Booing Fiasco: Acid Thrown as 'Moslems' Clash," *New Pittsburgh Courier*, November 21, 1959, 11.
73. FBI, SAC New York, "Malcolm K. Little; Internal Security—Nation," November 11, 1959, FBI Monograph on Malcolm X.
74. Elijah Muhammad, "Muslim Leader Returns from Visit to Mecca," *New York Amsterdam News*, January 16, 1960, 1.
75. Muhammad, "Muslim Leader Returns from Visit to Mecca." See also Evanzz, *The Messenger*, 213–14, quoting, "Muhammad Speaks," *Los Angeles Herald-Dispatch*, January 14, 1960, 13–14.
76. Claude Clegg, *An Original Man: The Life and Times of Elijah Muhammad* (New York: St. Martin's Press, 1997), 124.
77. FBI Chicago Field Office, "Internal Security—Nation," January 27, 1958, FBI Monograph on Elijah Muhammad.
78. FBI Chicago Field Office, "Elijah Poole; Internal Security—NOI," September 6, 1960, FBI Monograph on Elijah Muhammad.
79. Clegg, *An Original Man*, 126, 159.
80. The initial order for *Muhammad Speaks to the Black Man* was 50,000 copies, but it is unclear how many of those were sold. SAC Chicago, "Elijah Poole; Internal Security—Nation," September 2, 1960, FBI Monograph on Elijah Muhammad; SAC New York, "Malcolm K. Little; Internal Security—Nation," November 17, 1959, FBI Monograph on Malcolm X; *Mr. Muhammad Speaks*, May 1960. See also Evanzz, *The Messenger*, 204–6; Clegg, *An Original Man*, 116.
81. *Mr. Muhammad Speaks* and *Muhammad Speaks*, despite the slightly different titles, are virtually identical in format. Therefore, I will refer to both publications as *Muhammad Speaks*.

82. Clegg, *An Original Man*, 159.

83. Clegg, *An Original Man*, 159–60.

84. For more on the issue of authority for Muslims in the United States, see Jackson, *Islam and the Blackamerican*; Greewal, *Islam is a Foreign Country*.

85. For a full-length monograph examining *Muhammad Speaks*, see Curtis, *Black Muslim Religion*.

86. For an exploration of the role of print media in forging national identity, see Benedict Anderson's foundational study of nationalism and community identity. Anderson, *Imagined Communities*.

87. Thomas J. Hamilton, "Colonialism at UN: United States is Again Accused of Lining up with 'Imperialists,'" *New York Times*, December 18, 1960, 9.

88. Elijah Muhammad, "Islamic World," *New York Amsterdam News*, March 1, 1958, 15; Elijah Muhammad, "Islamic World," *New York Amsterdam News*, August 2, 1958, 28.

89. Malcolm X, "Moslems Hold Political Balance of Power," *Mr. Muhammad Speaks*, September 1960, 2, 20–22.

90. For example, "Full Text of Messenger Muhammad's Speech: 'Future of American Negroes . . . ,'" *Muhammad Speaks*, April 1962, 3.

91. Marable, *Malcolm X*, 163.

92. *Mr. Muhammad Speaks*, September 1960, 1.

93. *Mr. Muhammad Speaks*, September 1960, 1.

94. "Muhammad Demands Separate States," *Mr. Muhammad Speaks*, September 1960, 3; "Lumumba Envoy Scores Belgians," *Mr. Muhammad Speaks*, September 1960, 3; "Europeans Congo Trickery Exposed," *Mr. Muhammad Speaks*, September 1960, 3; "Fear Spreads to Northern Rhodesia," *Mr. Muhammad Speaks*, September 1960, 3; "Africans Riot in Southern Rhodesia," *Mr. Muhammad Speaks*, September 1960, 3; "Revolt in West Indies," *Mr. Muhammad Speaks*, September 1960, 3; "All-Africa Army Sought," *Mr. Muhammad Speaks*, September 1960, 3.

For a similar format, see "Problems of Black Man in Africa, Asia, America the Same," *Muhammad Speaks*, December 1961, 1; "What Is Un-American," *Muhammad Speaks*, December 1961, 1; Dan Burley, "Black Man's Problem Same Everywhere," *Muhammad Speaks*, December 1961, 5; "President Sukarno Lays Foundation," *Muhammad Speaks*, December 1961, 5.

95. Gerard and Kuklick, *Death in the Congo*, 27–31.

96. "U.S. Backs Belgians in Congo Against UN," *Mr. Muhammad Speaks*, December 1960, 22; "Nkrumah Speaks in Harlem," *Mr. Muhammad Speaks*, December 1960, 22.

97. "Muhammad Returns Home to Georgia: Demands Land!," *Mr. Muhammad Speaks*, December 1960, 2, 15; "Demand More UN Posts for Africans-Asian Delegates," *Mr. Muhammad Speaks*, December 1960, 15–18; "African Muslim Praises Muhammad," *Mr. Muhammad Speaks*, December 1960, 2, 26; "Nationalism Stirs Asia," *Mr. Muhammad Speaks*, December 1960, 26; "Thousands Hear Muhammad Issue Call for Separation: Says So-Called Negro Is the Biblical Lost Sheep," *Mr. Muhammad Speaks*, Special Edition 1961, 3; William R. Mathews, "South Africa Is Paradise for Whites; but It's 'Hell' for Black Races," *Mr. Muhammad Speaks*, Special Edition 1961, 3; "Back-to-Africa Movement Scores Gains in West Indies," *Mr. Muhammad Speaks*, Special Edition 1961, 3; "News Briefs from around the

World," *Mr. Muhammad Speaks*, Special Edition 1961, 8; "Muslims Plan Freedom Rally in Harlem," *Mr. Muhammad Speaks*, Special Edition 1961, 8.

98. "Africa Moves toward Freedom: Originals Revolt; Colonials Disturbed," *Mr. Muhammad Speaks*, May 1960, 14; "Photograph," *Mr. Muhammad Speaks*, May 1960, 14.

99. One of these issues is labeled a "Special Edition" with no date and only a notation that indicates that it is volume 1, number 6. Based on numerous references to the murder of Patrice Lumumba, and a photograph on page 8 depicting Harlem residents mourning the death of Patrice Lumumba, the issue must have been published after Lumumba's assassination on January 17, 1961. "News Briefs from around the World," *Mr. Muhammad Speaks*, Special Edition, vol. 1, no. 6, 8; "Harlemites Join with Black Nationalists in "Funeral" for Congolese Premier Patrice Lumumba," *Muhammad Speaks*, Special Edition, vol. 1, no. 6, 8.

100. Marable, *Malcolm X*, 163.

101. Marable, *Malcolm X*, 195.

102. "Messenger Muhammad Answers Four Key Questions on Program," *Muhammad Speaks*, May 1962, 7.

103. Clegg, *Price of Liberty*, 77–162.

104. See, for example, "Blood Mixing Death of Races," *Muhammad Speaks*, January 1962, 1, 4; "Dr. Ira A. Reid Says: Rise of Muslims Reality Facing World," *Muhammad Speaks*, January 1962, 1, 10; Special Correspondent, "Independence Awakens Jamaica," *Muhammad Speaks*, April 1962, 2; Dan Burley, "We Must Have Some of this Earth," *Muhammad Speaks*, April 1962, 3; Elijah Muhammad, "Future of American So-Called Negroes," *Muhammad Speaks*, April 1962, 3.

105. "Algerian Premier Charges France with Genocide," *Muhammad Speaks*, January 1962, 7; Staff Correspondent, "Nigerian Youth Unit Raps BBC on Africa News," *Muhammad Speaks*, January 1962, 7; "We Must Have Some Land!," *Muhammad Speaks*, January 1962, 7.

106. "King Saud Calls Muslim World over to Unit," *Muhammad Speaks*, February 1962, 2; Staff Correspondent, "Tanganyika Adds Power to UN's Afro-Asia Bloc," *Muhammad Speaks*, February 1962, 2; Foreign Press Service, "Azikiwe Urges African Unity," *Muhammad Speaks*, February 1962, 2; Special Correspondent, "UN's Afro-Asians Condemn Continued Brutality By French to Algerian Rebels," *Muhammad Speaks*, February 1962, 2; "We Must Control Our Neighborhoods!," *Muhammad Speaks*, February 1962, 2.

107. For more examples of this format, see "Study Muslim Progress: Members Deserting NAACP Fed Up at Getting Nowhere," *Muhammad Speaks*, March 1962, 8; Foreign Press Service, "Singapore Shoe Industry Hails Production Hike," *Muhammad Speaks*, March 1962, 8; Abdul Basit Naeem, "Nigeria to Build $200 Million Dam on Mighty Niger River," *Muhammad Speaks*, March 1962, 8; Foreign Press Service, "Philippine Muslims Visit in the Sudan," *Muhammad Speaks*, March 1962.

108. Elijah Muhammad, "The Honorable Elijah Muhammad: The Muslim Program," July 31, 1962, 3.

109. Elijah Muhammad, "The Honorable Elijah Muhammad: The Muslim Program," *Muhammad Speaks*, July 31, 1962, 3; "On Separate Territory," *Muhammad Speaks*, May 24, 1963, 12; "The Messenger Presents: The Muslim Program," *Muhammad Speaks*, August 16, 1963, 24.

110. "White Supremist Writer Flees Kenya," *Muhammad Speaks*, August 15, 1962, 4; "Radio Ghana Blasts Common Market: Warns Africa Beware of 'Imperialist Club,'" *Muhammad Speaks*, August 15, 1962, 4; "UN Report Rips African Murder," *Muhammad Speaks*, August 15, 1962, 4; "Mali Blocks Plot Hatched by Outsiders," *Muhammad Speaks*, August 15, 1962, 4.

111. "Letter from Elijah Muhammad to Abdul Basit Naeem," April 12, 1962, Malcolm X Papers, Box 11, Folder, SCRBC.

112. "Letter from Elijah Muhammad to Abdul Basit Naeem," SCRBC.

113. Abdul Basit Naeem, "Random Notes," *Muhammad Speaks*, April 1962, 7.

114. Photograph of Abdul Basit Naeem, Muhammad Ngileruma, Malcolm X, Issa Serag, others at Shalimar International, c. 1962, Robert Haggins Collection, SCRBC; "Photograph: Greeting in Peace," *Muhammad Speaks*, May 1962, 6. See also Felber, *Those Who Know Don't Say*, 34, reprinting above referenced photograph of Naeem, Ngileruma, and Malcolm X by Robert Haggins.

115. "Independence Awakens Jamaica," *Muhammad Speaks*, April 1962, 2, 10; "Blacks in Bermuda Jubilant over First Negro Regime; Expect Changes," *Muhammad Speaks*, February 3, 1967, 27; Charles P. Howard, "Whites Keep Strangle Hold on Bahamas," *Muhammad Speaks*, March 19, 1965, 19.

116. FBI New York Office, "Malcolm K. Little; IS—Nation," November 17, 1960, FBI Monograph on Malcolm X. See also Crowder, "Fidel Castro and Harlem," 79.

117. Hall, *Ten Days in Harlem*, 84.

118. For more on the United States and the Cuban Revolution against Fulgencio Batista, see Patterson, *Contesting Castro*; Schoult, *That Infernal Little Cuban Republic*; Benjamin, *United States and the Origins of the Cuban Revolution*.

119. Schoult, *That Infernal Little Cuban Republic*, 74–141.

120. Max Frankel, "Cuban in Harlem: He Balks at East Side Bill and Spurns U.S. Offer on Quarters," *New York Times*, September 20, 1960, 1, 16. See also Hall, *Ten Days in Harlem*, 89; Crowder, "Fidel Castro and Harlem," 79.

121. Frankel, "Cuban in Harlem," 16.

122. Crowder, "Fidel Castro and Harlem," 79.

123. James Booker, "Castro Talks Bar White Press; He Calls Himself African American," *Amsterdam News*, September 24, 1960, 1, 31.

124. New York Office, "Malcolm K. Little; IS—Nation," FBI Monograph on Malcolm X, November 17, 1960.

125. New York Office, "Malcolm K. Little; IS—Nation," FBI Monograph on Malcolm X.

126. Letter from Malcolm X to James L. Hicks, September 30, 1960, reprinted in *Mr. Muhammad Speaks*, December 1960, 21; "Malcolm X Resigns from Harlem Committee," *Muhammad Speaks*, December 1960, 21.

127. "O.A.S. Votes to Deny Cuba Any Inter-American Role; Prohibits Trade in Arms," *New York Times*, January 31, 1962, 1, 10; Max Frankel, "Rusk, Home, Gets Kennedy Praise," *New York Times*, February 1, 1962, 1.

128. "Cuban Embargo Statement and Text," *New York Times*, February 4, 1962, 22.

129. R. Hart Phillips, "Castro Attacks U.S. Import Ban," *New York Times*, February 5, 1962, 1, 13.

130. "Text of Proclamation by the President," *New York Times*, October 24, 1962, 21.

131. "Egypt Is Worried by Threat of War," *New York Times*, October 24, 1962, 25; Juan de Onis, "Brazil's Premier Supports Cubans," *New York Times*, October 24, 1962, 23; Kathleen Teltsch, "Crisis over Cuba Preoccupies UN," *New York Times*, October 24, 1962, 26; "Thant Statement and Excerpts from Debate on Cuba in the Security Council," *New York Times*, October 25, 1962, 23.

132. "How Afro-Asians Pulled World from H-Bomb Precipice," *Muhammad Speaks*, November 15, 1962, 2.

133. "How Afro-Asians Pulled World from H-Bomb Precipice," 2.

134. "How Afro-Asians Pulled World from H-Bomb Precipice," 2.

135. Peter Kihss, "Cuba Asks 15 in U.S. to Castro Anniversary," *Muhammad Speaks*, July 2, 1963, 10; "3 Negro Writers to Visit Cuba during Celebration This Month," *New York Times*, July 4, 1963, 2; "2 Newsmen to Visit Cuba at Invitation of Government," *New York Times*, July 9, 1963, 10; "U.S. Issues Permits to 3 to Visit Cuba," *New York Times*, July 19, 1963, 2.

136. Chas. P. Howard Sr. "First Report from Inside Cuba!," *Muhammad Speaks*, August 30, 1963, 2, 4.

137. "What Castro Said about U.S. Negro," *Muhammad Speaks*, August 30, 1963, 2.

138. de la Fuente, *Nation for All*, 263–79.

139. de la Fuente, *Nation for All*, 318–34.

140. de la Fuente, *Nation for All*, 279–85.

141. de la Fuente, *Nation for All*, 290–92.

142. de la Fuente, *Nation for All*, 292.

143. de la Fuente, *Nation for All*, 292–93.

144. Jon E. Fox, "National Holiday Commemorations: The View from Below," in Tsant and Woods, eds., *Cultural Politics of Nationalism and Nation-Building*, 38.

145. "Message from Mao: China and the World Back Negro Struggle," *Muhammad Speaks*, August 30, 1963, 4.

146. SAC Phoenix to director, FBI, "Nation of Islam; IS—Nation," December 2, 1963, FBI Monograph on Elijah Muhammad.

147. "Messenger Muhammad's Idea," *Muhammad Speaks*, September 25, 1970, 1.

148. "Letters to the Editor," *Muhammad Speaks*, March 1962, 21; "Letters to the Editor," *Muhammad Speaks*, April 1962, 21.

149. Bayinnah Sharrieff, "How the Beauty of Unity Was Apparent in Chicago at the Muslim Convention," *Muhammad Speaks*, March 8, 1968, 10.

Interlude

1. Khaldun interview, March 2, 2016; Khaldun email, April 11, 2016.
2. Khaldun interview.
3. Gardell, *In the Name of Elijah Muhammad*, 102–14, 121; Curtis, *Islam in Black America*, 113–27, 129–30.
4. Khaldun interview.
5. Khaldun interview.
6. Gardell, *In the Name of Elijah Muhammad*, 122; Curtis, *Islam in Black America*, 129.
7. Khaldun interview.

Chapter Four

1. Takbir Sharrieff interview, April 14, 2015.
2. As of 2014, approximately 52 percent of the population of the island identifies itself as Black. "Bermuda: People and Society," CIA World Fact Book.
3. Bermuda Government, "Population," Census of 23rd October 1960, 6–7.
4. Sharrieff interview; Darrell, *Acel'dama*, 20–30.
5. Hill interview, April 30, 2015; Hill interview, February 8, 2016. See also Tankard, *Development of Islam in Bermuda*, 32, noting that the cruise ship industry had a key role to play in the distribution of Muslim literature in Bermuda.
6. Hill interview, April 30, 2015; Hill interview, February 8, 2016.
7. Sharrieff interview.
8. Hill interview, April 30, 2015; BIC Reports, December 1968, FCO 44/213, TNA; Letter from Lord Martonmere, January 1970, Folder: Bermuda: Black Power Activities in Bermuda, Part A, FCO 44/195, TNA; Second Basic Paper on the Nation of Islam (N.O.I.), June 23, 1972, BIR, FCO 63/946, TNA.
9. "Muhammad Speaks Is Ordered Banned," *Royal Gazette*, July 28, 1965, 1, 3. The Executive Council, which was renamed the Cabinet in 1973, consists of senior servants and five or six representatives from the House of Assembly, the elected lower house of the Bermuda legislature. All members are selected by the governor.
10. Second Basic Paper on the NOI. See also Tankard, *Development of Islam in Bermuda*, 30. For statistics on Bermuda's population in 1960, see Bermuda Government, Census of 23rd October 1960.
11. Second Basic Paper on the NOI; Harry Viera, "Letter to the Editor," *Royal Gazette*, July 6, 1964, 4; "Houses of Assembly," *Royal Gazette*, July 8, 1965, 1; "Warning," *Royal Gazette*, July 9, 1965, 1.
12. Airgram from George W. Renchard to the Department of State, October 1, 1963, CPF 1964–1966, NARA, RG 59, Box 1918.
13. Thomas, "Rastafari, Communism, and Surveillance," 63–84.
14. K. Muhammad interview; Castle e-mail; Bermuda, LIR—December 1967, BIR, FCO 44/71, TNA.
15. See MacGregor, "Black Moslems in Bermuda," 154, FCO 1031/4766.
16. Department of Statistics, "Facts and Figures 2018" (Hamilton, Bermuda: Government of Bermuda, 2019), 3.
17. Packwood, *Chained on the Rock*, 1–9, 54–55.
18. See Gomez, *Exchanging Our Country Marks*, 59–87; Diouf, *Servants of Allah*, 20–70.
19. Gomez, *Exchanging Our Country Marks*, 55.
20. Hill interview, April 30, 2015.
21. Hill interview, April 30, 2015; K. Muhammad interview.
22. Hill interview, April 30, 2015.
23. Brown, *Bermuda and the Struggle for Reform*, 19–47, loc. 343–752, Kindle; Philip, *History of the Bermuda Industrial Union*, 63–88.
24. Hill interview, April 30, 2015.
25. Hill interview, April 30, 2015.

26. Turner, *Islam in the African American Experience*, 109–46; Gomez, *Black Crescent*, 250–54; Dannin, *Black Pilgrimage to Islam*, 35–65; Haddad and Smith, *Mission to America*.

27. Hodgson, *Storm in a Teacup*, 26–49. See also Swan, *Black Power in Bermuda*; Philip, *History of the Bermuda Industrial Union*, 94. For a more thorough discussion of the role of organized labor in the Caribbean and West Indies and race, see Alexander, *History of Organized Labor*, 17–20; Moreno, *Black Americans and Organized*, 220–84.

28. Sidney Lafoon, the American Consul General, reported that Dr. Mordecai Johnson, president of Howard University, had stated that the theater boycott was a "mild and happy revolution" resulting in the removal of restrictions on the "colored" population. Foreign Service Despatch from Sidney K. Lafoon to the Department of State, July 31, 1959, RG 59, CPF 1955–1959, Box 3209. See also Foreign Service Despatch from Sidney K. Lafoon to Department of State, July 1, 1959, RG 59, CPF 1955–1959, Box 4458; "End of Discrimination in Colony's Chief Hotels," *Royal Gazette*, June 29, 1959, 1, 10.

29. See Swan, *Black Power in Bermuda*, 16–17, arguing that the dockworkers strike and the theater boycott together "demonstrated that Bermuda's Black masses had the potential power to orchestrate change beyond the halls of Parliament."

30. Letter from J. M. MacGregor, superintendent head for commissioner of police, August 16, 1963, CO 1031/4766, TNA; Second Basic Paper on the NOI. See also Swan, *Black Power in Bermuda*, 19.

31. Brown, *Bermuda and the Struggle for Reform*, 64; Swan, *Black Power in Bermuda*, 18.

32. J. M. MacGregor, "Letter re: Black Moslems in Bermuda," August 16, 1963, CO 1031/4766, TNA.

33. Bermuda Parliament Election Act of 1961. See also Brown, *Bermuda and the Struggle for Reform*, 64–71.

34. MacGregor, "Letter re: Black Moslems in Bermuda." See also Swan, *Black Power in Bermuda*, 20.

35. Foreign Service Despatch from George W. Renchard to Department of State (A-130), May 16, 1963, NARA, RG 59, CPF 1964–1966, Box 1918; Airgram from George W. Renchard to Department of State (A-22), September 12, 1966, NARA, RG 59, CFP 1964–1966, Box 1918; Airgram from George W. Renchard to Department of State, February 16, 1963, RG 59, CPF 1963, Box 3827; Report of the Local Intelligence Committee for the Month of February 1963, March 5, 1963, CO 1031/4766, TNA. See also Brown, *Bermuda and the Struggle for Reform*, 96.

36. "PLP Policy Outlined: Spirit of Common Man vs. Corrupt Materialism," *Bermuda Recorder*, January 27, 1967, 1, 4.

37. "PLP Policy Outlined," 1, 4. See also Swan, *Black Power in Bermuda*, 22.

38. Brown, *Bermuda and the Struggle for Reform*, 93–96.

39. Brown, *Bermuda and the Struggle for Reform*, 93–96; Letter from J. M. MacGregor; See also Swan, *Black Power in Bermuda*, 20.

40. Berger, *Black Prison Organizing in the Civil Rights Era*.

41. Felber, *Those Who Know Don't Say*, 21–27.

42. For more on prison activism during the 1960s, see Berger, *Black Prison Organizing in the Civil Rights Era*.

43. Second Basic Paper on the NOI.

44. Viera, "Letter to the Editor," 4; "Houses of Assembly," 1; "Warning," 1.

45. Letter from Lord Martonmere to the Secretary of State for the Colonies, Document No. 302, July 3, 1965, CO 1031/4766, TNA.

46. "Muhammad Speaks Banned," *Royal Gazette*, July 28, 1965, 1, 3; Letter from Lord Martonmere to the Secretary of State for the Colonies, Document No. 302, July 3, 1965, CO 1031/4766, TNA; Second Basic Paper on the Nation of Islam; Bermuda Parliament, Prohibited Publications Act, 1963.

47. Letter from Lord Martonmere to the Secretary of State for the Colonies, Document No. 453, September 4, 1965, CO 1031/4766, TNA; Letter from Sykes to the Secretary of State for the Colonies, Document No. 278, August 4, 1965, CO 1031/4766.

48. N. Salaam interview.

49. Sharrieff interview; Seifuddin Stowe interview.

50. Muhammad interview.

51. Sharrieff interview.

52. N. Salaam interview.

53. N. Salaam interview.

54. See Swan, *Black Power in Bermuda*, 20, noting in passing connections between the BIU, the Bermuda United Workers Party, and the Nation of Islam.

55. Letter from Lord Martonmere to the Commonwealth Office, Dependent Territories Division, July 6, 1967, FCO 44/71, TNA; Bermuda LIR—July 1967, FCO 44/71, TNA; Cypher from Bermuda to Commonwealth Officer, No. 161, August 8, 1968, FCO 44/71, TNA.

56. Bermuda, LIR—December 1967, FCO 44/71, TNA. See Tankard, *The Development of Islam in Bermuda*, 22, noting that it was Kenneth Castle who recruited Johnston and Burchall to the Nation of Islam.

57. Cypher from Bermuda to Commonwealth Officer, No. 161; Second Basic Paper on the NOI.

58. Bermuda, LIR—December 1967, FCO 44/71, TNA. See Tankard, *The Development of Islam in Bermuda*, 22, discussing the history of Burchall and Johnston's recruitment to the Nation of Islam.

59. Bermuda Local Intelligence Committee's Report—June 1968, FCO 44/71, TNA.

60. Letter from Lord Martonmere to the Commonwealth Office, July 6, 1967. Later in July 1967, the FCO reported that Albert Johnston, another Black Muslim, had been elected president of the Dock Workers Union, and that Johnson's intention was to "clean up" the Union.

61. See Letter from L.S. Price to Miss Terry, et al., June 11, 1968, Bermuda Intelligence, FCO 44/71, TNA; Airgram from Janney to Department of State (A-69), May 27, 1968, RG 59, CPF 1967–1969, Box 1871; Second Basic Paper on the Nation of Islam.

62. Airgram from Manning to Department of State (A-20), April 26, 1969, RG 59, CPF 1967–1969, Box 1871; Bermuda Civil Disorders 1968: Report of Commission and Statement of the Government of Bermuda, paras. 18–42. See also Swan, *Black Power in Bermuda*, 25–27.

63. Letter from Governor Martonmere to FCO, May 16, 1968, Bermuda Intelligence, FCO 44/71, TNA; Local Intelligence Committee's Report, April–May 15, 1968, Bermuda Intelligence, FCO 44/71, TNA.

64. Local Intelligence Committee's Report, May 15, 1968, FCO 44/71, TNA; Second Basic Paper on the Nation of Islam.

65. For more on urban uprisings in 1968 and in the aftermath of King's assassination, see Abu-Lughod, *Race, Space, and Riots*; Elfenbein, Hallowak, and Nix, *Baltimore '68*; Markarian, *Uruguay 1968*; Levy, *The Great Uprising*; Hinton, *America on Fire*.

66. In general, 1968 stands out as a remarkable year for global revolution and uprising. As historian Ruth Wilson Gilmore has noted, 1968 was "a disorderly year, when revolutionaries around the world made as much trouble as possible in as many places as possible." Gilmore, *Golden Gulag*, 24. Regardless, there have been very few scholarly attempts to place these uprisings in conversation with each other. For an exception, see Ross, *May '68 and its Afterlives*; Carey and Andrea, *Protests in the Streets*; Skærlund Risager, Cox, and Mohandesi, *Voices of 1968*.

67. C. Shakir Interview.

68. Letter from Lord Martonmere to the Secretary of State for Commonwealth Affairs, May 16, 1968, FCO 44/71, TNA. See also Swan, *Black Power in Bermuda*, 29, citing interviews conducted with Black Bermudians on their memories of the causes of the Floral Pageant Uprisings.

69. Cypher to Commonwealth Office, Telegram No. 111, October 4, 1968, FCO 44/71, TNA; BIC's Report—September 1968, FCO 44/71, TNA.

70. Wooding, Springer, and Browning, *Bermuda Civil Disorders 1968*, paras. 18–42.

71. See, for example, Scarman, *The Scarman Report*.

72. Wooding, Springer, and Browning, *Bermuda Civil Disorders 1968*, paras. 72–79.

73. Wooding, Springer, and Browning, *Bermuda Civil Disorders 1968*, paras. 234–36. See also Swan, *Black Power in Bermuda*, 27–28.

74. Second Basic Paper on the NOI.

75. Local Intelligence Committee Report, May 15–28, 1968, Bermuda Intelligence, FCO 44/71, TNA.

76. Telegram No. 2 Personal to Governor Bahamas, March 14, 1969, Bermuda: Black Power Activities in Bermuda, Part A, FCO 44/195, TNA; Priority Bermuda to Foreign and Commonwealth Office, Telegram 62, March 14, 1969, Bermuda Intelligence, FCO 44/195, TNA. See also Swan, *Black Power in Bermuda*, 40.

77. Telegram No. 2 Personal to Governor Bahamas, March 14, 1969, Bermuda: Black Power Activities in Bermuda, Part A, FCO 44/195, TNA; Priority Bermuda to Foreign and Commonwealth Office, Telegram 62, March 14, 1969, Bermuda Intelligence, FCO 44/195, TNA

78. BIC's Report—January 1969, FCO 44/213, TNA.

79. Shamisddeen Interview, April 25, 2015.

80. Letter from J. M. MacGregor Superintendent Head for Commissioner of Police re: Monthly Intelligence Report for the Period 1st to 31st August 1963, Document No. 8 of 1963, September 2, 1963, CO 1031/4766, TNA.

81. Letter from Lord Martonmere, May 9, 1969, Bermuda: "Black Power" Activities in Bermuda, Part D, FCO 44/198, TNA.

82. Visits of Black Power Leaders to Bermuda, 1969, Bermuda: Black Power Activities in Bermuda, Part A, FCO 44/195, TNA; Priority St. Lucia to Foreign and Commonwealth Offices, Telegram No. 386, April 1969, Bermuda Intelligence, FCO 44/197; Letter to Mr. Cruchley from L. S. Price, April 9, 1969, Black Power in Bermuda, Part D, FCO 44/197, TNA.

83. Report, October 28–November 24, 1969, Bermuda Intelligence, FCO 44/213, TNA.

84. Letter from the Ministry of Defence to C. S. Roberts, Head of the Caribbean Department, November 2, 1972, FCO 63/945, noting that Bermuda had a long outstanding debt of

£38,724 from deployment of the British military during the uprisings. See also Swan, *Black Power in Bermuda*, 85–86, citing Bermuda: Cost of Britain Troops in Bermuda, June 11, 1969, FCO 44/211, TNA.

85. Report, July 17–August 18, 1969, Appendix C, Regional Conference of Black Power Closing Session, BIR, FCO 44/213, TNA.

86. West Indies and Caribbean Area Monthly Intelligence Summary—Bermuda, August 15, 1969, BIR, FCO 44/213, TNA.

87. Report, October 28–November 24, 1969, FCO 44/213, TNA.

88. Swan, *Black Power in Bermuda*, 209, citing Record of Meetings in Mr. J. C. Morgan's Room, August 18, 1969, FCO 44/202, TNA.

89. Letter from the governor's deputy to the secretary of state for FCO affairs, attaching oral report on Progressive Labour Party Youth Wing Activities, Bermuda, September 24, 1969, CSO, BPM 1/1, Part A, BNA.

90. Swan, *Black Power in Bermuda*, 97.

91. Telegram from Washington UK Mission, New York from FCO, Appendix A, "Aims of the Black Berets," March 25, 1970, CSO, BPM 1/1, Part A, BNA.

92. Black Beret Cadre, Manifesto, December 19, 1970, BPM 1/1, Part C, BNA; *The Black Beret: Voice of the Revolutionaries*, June 1970, CSO, BPM 1/1, Part B, BNA. See also Swan, *Black Power in Bermuda*, 97–107, summarizing the platform of the BBC in depth.

93. Mr. E. E. Wayne, administrative secretary to Reverend George Buchanan, chairman of Race Relations Council, November 17, 1971, Chief Secretary's Office, "Black Power Movement: Malcolm X Liberation School," CSO File No. 1/25, BNA.

94. "Malcolm X Liberation School," March 4, 1971, Chief Secretary's Office, "Black Power Movement: Malcolm X Liberation School," CSO, File No. 1/25, BNA.

95. Khaldun Interview; Shamsiddeen.

96. Draft Telegram to FCO, Appendix A, "The Aims of the Black Berets July 1969," March 25, 1970, CSO, BPM 1/1, Part A, BNA. Shamsiddeen Interview; Khaldun Interview.

97. Ira A. Philip, *The History of the Bermuda Industrial Union*, 13–88.

98. Hill interview, April 30, 2015.

99. Hill interview, April 30, 2015.

100. Hill interview, April 30, 2015.

101. Report (Special Meeting on 24 March 1970), No. 4 of 1970, Appendix A, Basic Paper 19th March 1970—Black Beret Cadre, March 19, 1970, CSO, BPM 1/1, Part A, Bermuda National Archives (BNA).

102. Report (Special Meeting on 24 March 1970), Appendix D, Membership of the Black Beret Cadre and Associated Organisations, CSO, BPM 1/1, Part A, BNA.

103. Shamsiddeen interview.

104. Shamsiddeen interview.

105. Khaldun interview.

106. Khaldun interview. See also Swan, *Black Power in Bermuda*, 105, citing the BBC's various programs.

107. Khaldun interview.

108. Khaldun interview; Sharrieff interview. Radell Tankard, a historian of Islam in Bermuda, pinpoints Gary Perinchief's conversion to Islam in 1972. Tankard, *Development of Islam in Bermuda*. This discrepancy is likely due to the subject's faulty memory forty years

after the fact. Perinchief was recruited by his sister Wanda and her best friend, Michelle Khaldun, who left the island permanently in 1971. Therefore, it is more likely that Perinchief converted prior to their departure. Khaldun interview.

109. Second Basic Paper on the NOI.
110. Khaldun interview; Madyun interview.
111. Second Basic Paper on the NOI.
112. Khaldun interview; Madyun interview.
113. Zakiyyah Shakir interview, February 16, 2016; Zaheera Shakir interview; S. Salaam interview; Abdul-Hadee interview; Madyun interview; C. Shakir interview.
114. BIC Report, March 24, 1970, CSO, BPM 1/1, Part A, BNA.
115. Swan, *Black Power in Bermuda*, 111, citing *Black Beret* (June 1971).
116. Tankard, *Development of Islam in Bermuda*, 41.
117. Shamisddeen interview. See also Tankard, *Development of Islam in Bermuda*, 43.
118. BIC Report 6 September 1972–2 October 1972, No. 9 of 1972, FCO 63/946, TNA; Second Basic Paper on the NOI, June 23, 1972, FCO 63/946, TNA. See also Swan, *Black Power in Bermuda*, 164; Tankard, *Development of Islam in Bermuda*, 43.
119. Tankard, *Development of Islam in Bermuda*, 51 (loc. 49), 68 (loc. 947), Kindle.
120. Second Basic Paper on the NOI.
121. BIC Report, 3 October 1972–7 November 1972, No. 10 of 1972, FCO 63/946, TNA; Cypher from Bermuda to Priority FCO. See Swan, *Black Power in Bermuda*, 163–82, giving a detailed account of the BBC's activities after the murders of Duckett, Sharples, and Horsa.
122. Darrell, *Acel'dama*, 73. See also Swan, *Black Power in Bermuda*, 163–82.
123. BIR 3 October 1972–7 November 1972, No. 10 of 1972, FCO 63/946, TNA; Shamsiddeen interview.
124. Swan, *Black Power in Bermuda*, 163–82.
125. "Record of a Conversation between the Minister of State and the Premier of Bermuda Held at the Foreign and Commonwealth Office," December 20, 1973, FCO 63/1094, TNA.
126. Swan, *Black Power in Bermuda*, 181–82.
127. "BIC Report, 3 October, 1973–6 November, 1973," No. 10 of 1973, FCO 63/1099, TNA; S. Salaam interview.
128. Hill interview, April 30, 2015; Muhammad interview.
129. Zakiyyah Shakir interview, April 2015.
130. Clegg, *Original Man*, 274–77.
131. Brown interview; Wasi interview.
132. Tankard, *Development of Islam in Bermuda*, 68–72.

Chapter Five

1. Zakiyyah Shakir interview, February 16, 2016; Zakiyyah Shakir interview, April 2015; Zaheera Shakir interview, February 26, 2016; S. Salaam interview; Abdul-Hadee interview; Madyun interview.
2. White, "Talk about School," 18, citing *African Education*, 69. *African Education* was a joint study produced by the British Colonial Office and the Nuffield Foundation in 1953.
3. White, "Talk about School," 18, citing *African Education*, 64.

4. Fanon, *Wretched of the Earth*, 38.

5. Fanon, *Wretched of the Earth*, 38; White, "Talk about School," 18, citing *African Education*, 64.

6. See, for example, "BIC Report, July 7, 1971–August 3, 1971," No. 7 of 1971, Bermuda Monthly Intelligence Reports, FCO 44/541, TNA; BIC Report, June 2, 1971–July 6, 1971, No. 6 of 1971, FCO 44/541, TNA; Report, April 30, 1971–June 1, 1971," No. 5 of 1971, FCO 44/541, TNA.

7. Gayatri Chakravorty Spivak, "Can the Subaltern Speak?," in Nelson and Grossberg, eds. *Marxism and the Recreation of Culture*, 271–316; Trouillot, *Silencing the Past*; Chakrabarty, "Postcoloniality and the Artifice of History," 1–26; Stoler, *Along the Archival Grain*.

8. Abdul-Hadee interview; Zakiyyah Shakir interview, February 16, 2016; Zakiyyah Shakir interview, April 2015; S. Salaam interview; Madyun interview; C. Shakir interview.

9. Zakiyyah Shakir interview, February 16, 2016.

10. Wallace D. Muhammad, "Minister's Kit—May 1, 1975, Nation of Islam Collection, Folder 1–10, SCRBC; Munir Um'rani, "W.D. Muhammad Provides New Name for Blacks," *Muhammad Speaks/Bilalian News*, October 24, 1975, 2; W.D. Muhammad, "Special Announcement," *Bilalian News*, November 7, 1976, 1. For more information on the transition from Nation of Islam to Sunni Islam under Wallace Muhammad, see Curtis, *Islam in Black America*, 109; Fraser-Rahim, *America's Other Muslims*, 73.

11. "First Official Interview with the Supreme Minister of the Nation of Islam, the Honorable Wallace D. Muhammad," *Muhammad Speaks*, March 21, 1975, 11; Herbert Muhammad, "New Muslim Leader Tells Why Muslims Bar Whites," *New York Amsterdam News*, April 15, 1975, A1–2. See also Curtis, *Islam in Black America*, 117.

12. Muhammad, "New Muslim Leader Tells Why Muslims Bar Whites," A2. See also Curtis, *Islam in Black America*, 113–17; Gibson, *A History of the Nation of Islam*, 75–78.

13. "New Muslim Chief Toning Down Hate," *Afro-American*, March 15, 1975, 1; "Exclusive Interview with Wallace Muhammad: New Muslim Leader Invites Contributions from Whites," *New York Amsterdam News*, May 30, 1975, A2; "Muslim Chief Downplays Hatred of Whites Theme," *Washington Post*, March 8, 1975, B8; "Muslims Ease Secrecy, Plan to Drop Race Ban," *Afro-American*, June 28, 1975, 1; "Muslim Moves Are Linked to Arabs; Shabazz Replaces Farrakhan," *New York Amsterdam News*, July 2, 1975, A1–2; Roy Wilkins, "An Amen for Black Muslims," *Afro-American*, July 5, 1975, 4; Francis Ward, "Black Muslims Will End Longtime Ban on Whites," *New York Times*, June 17, 1975, 9; Les Matthews, "Muslims to Accept White Followers," *New York Amsterdam News*, June 25, 1975, A1, A10; Caralayne Hunter, "Muslim Leader Urges Whites to Join," *New York Times*, June 30, 1975, 13; Les Payne, "Muslims Welcome 'Blue-Eyed Devils,'" *Newsday*, June 30, 1975, 4, 32; Walter L. Lowe Jr., "Black Skin, White Skin: Wallace Muhammad and a Radical Doctrine," *Chicago Defender*, October 23, 1975, 8; W. D. Muhammad, "Ramadan," *Muhammad Speaks*, August 29, 1975, 15; "Advertisement," *Muhammad Speaks*, October 17, 1975, 3. See also Curtis, *Islam in Black America*, 114.

14. Frances Ward, "Black Muslims Change Name, Direction," *Los Angeles Times*, November 9, 1975, 31.

15. Ward, "Black Muslims Change Name," 31.

16. W. D. Muhammad, "Bilalian," *Bilalian News*, November 14, 1975, 24; Ward, "Black Muslims Change Name," 3.

17. See, for example, Muhammad's Temple No. 2, "Minister's Kit—May 1, 1975"; Muhammad's Temple No. 2, "Minister's Kit—July 1, 1975," NOI Collection, Box 1, Folder 1/11, SCRBC; "Muhammad's Temple No. 2, "Minister's Kit—September 1, 1975," NOI Collection, Box 1, Folder 1/12, SCRBC. See also Curtis, *Islam in Black America*, 115–16; Fraser-Rahim, *America's Other Muslims*, 75–76.

18. Fraser-Rahim, *America's Other Muslims*, 76–77; Curtis, *Islam in Black America*, 116.

19. Samuel Ayyub Bilal, "Servants of the People: Meet the Officials of the World Community of al-Islam in the West," *Bilalian News*, January 7, 1977, 13; Ghayth Nur Kashif, "Servants of the People: Meet the Officials of the World Community of Islam in the West," *Bilalian News*, January 14, 1977, 13; Samuel Ayyub Bilal, "Servants of the People: Meet the Officials of the World Community of Islam in the West," *Bilalian News*, January 23, 1977, 13. See also Curtis, *Islam in Black America*, 115–17.

20. Curtis, *Islam in Black America*, 108.

21. Curtis, *Islam in Black America*, 116.

22. *Bilalian News*, July 7, 1978, 1; Nathaniel Omar, "WCIW Reveals Plans for New World Patriotism Day," *Bilalian News*, July 7, 1978, 7. See also Curtis, *Islam in Black America*, 116.

23. Omar, "WCIW Reveals Plans for New World Patriotism Day," 7.

24. Curtis, *Islam in Black America*, 116; Martha Lee, *Nation of Islam*, 96.

25. Wallace D. Muhammad, "Speech Given at Spiritual Meeting," July 25, 1975, NOI Collection, Box 1, Folder 1/12, SCRBC; Wallace D. Muhammad, "Speech Given at Spiritual Meeting," September 1, 1975, Nation of Islam Collection, Box 1, Folder 1/15, SCRBC.

26. Milton Hill interview, February 8, 2016.

27. Askia Muhammad, "Bilalian News Averts Complete Shutdown," *New Pittsburgh Courier*, April 30, 1977, 1, 5.

28. N. Salaam interview; Brown interview; Abdurrahman, *Historical Roots of Proper Islamic Governance*, 12–13; Wasi, *A Muted Imam*, 126; "Muslim Paper's Claims," *Royal Gazette*, November 5, 1984, 5.

29. Masjid is the Arabic word for mosque. In 1977, Imam Muhammad issued a directive that all former Nation of Islam temples would be called masjids. See Curtis, *Islam in Black America*, 116; Fraser-Rahim, *America's Other Muslims*, 76.

30. "Muslims in Bermuda: Image Problems Challenge a Church," *Mid-Ocean News*, April 14, 1989, 5.

31. "Table 10. Distribution and Rate of Growth of Major Religious Denominations at Census Dates—1991 and 1980," in Bermuda Census Office, *1991 Census*, 22.

32. Zakiyyah Shakir interview, February 16, 2016.

33. "Irate Muslims Defy School Refusal," *Royal Gazette*, January 5, 1982, 1, 2.

34. For more on the Nation's popularity in Bermuda at this time, see BIC Report, 3 October, 1973–6 November, 1973, No. 10 of 1973, BIR, FCO 63/1099, TNA; S. Salaam interview.

35. Zaheera Shakir interview; Memorandum by the Minister of Education, "Muhammad's Temple of Islam—'Black Muslims,'" October 4, 1974, Records of the Cabinet, Cabinet Memo No. 569/74, BNA.

36. Curtis, *Black Muslim Religion*, 154. For more on University of Islam schools, see Curtis, *Black Muslim Religion*, 153–60.

37. "Memorandum by the Minister of Education," October 4, 1974.

38. "Memorandum by the Minister of Education," October 4, 1974.

39. "Memorandum by the Minister of Education," October 4, 1974.

40. "School Rights Superseded by Education Act, Says Minister," *Royal Gazette*, February 1, 1982, 5.

41. "Table 8. Population by Sex and Religion—Town, City, and Parish," in Bermuda Census Office, *Report of the Population Census 1970*, 71.

42. Memorandum by the Minister of Education, October 4, 1974.

43. Memorandum by the Minister of Education, October 4, 1974.

44. Taylor, *Promise of Patriarchy*, 27–29; Evanzz, *The Messenger*, 96–102.

45. Tankard, *Development of Islam in Bermuda*, 51–68, 75–78, citing Zaheera Shakir, interview with Radell Tankard, September 8, 1996; Zakiyyah Shakir, interview with Radell Tankard, December 22, 2002; and Judith Thorne, interview with Radell Tankard, August 26, 1998; Abdurrahman, *The Historical Roots of Proper Islamic Governance in Bermuda*, 12; Wasi, *A Muted Imam*, 39–42; Wasi interview; Brown interview.

46. Tankard, *Development of Islam in Bermuda*, 51–68; Abdurrahman, *The Historical Roots of Proper Islamic Governance*, 12; Wasi, *A Muted Imam*, 39–42; Wasi interview, April 23, 2015; Brown interview.

47. Zaheera Shakir interview.

48. S. Salaam interview.

49. "Mosque gets $10,000 Donations," 3.

50. "Muslim School—A Simple Matter of Keeping Faith," *Royal Gazette*, January 27, 1982, 7.

51. "Muslim School," 7.

52. "Muslim School," 7.

53. Memorandum by the Acting Minister of Education, "Proposed Muslim School," August 27, 1982, RC, Cabinet Memo No. 250/82, BNA.

54. Cromwell Shakir interview.

55. Zakiyyah Shakir interview, February 16, 2016.

56. Zakiyyah Shakir interview, February 16, 2016.

57. Abdul-Hadee interview.

58. Memorandum by the Acting Minister of Education, "Proposed Muslim School," August 27, 1982, RC, Cabinet Memo No. 250/82 BNA; "Muslim School—A Simple Matter of Keeping Faith," 6; "Muslims to Hold Public Forum on Education," *Royal Gazette*, January 1982, 12.

59. Madyun interview.

60. S. Salaam interview.

61. Zaheera Shakir interview.

62. S. Salaam interview.

63. S. Salaam interview.

64. "Irate Muslims to Defy School Refusal," *Royal Gazette*, January 5, 1982, 1, 2.

65. "Irate Muslims to Defy School Refusal," 1, 2.

66. Memorandum by the Acting Minister of Education, "Proposed Muslim School," August 27, 1982, RC, Cabinet Memo No, 259/82, BNA; "Muslims 'No Rights' to School," *Royal Gazette*, January 6, 1982, 1.

67. "Muslim School Meeting Today," *Royal Gazette*, January 25, 1982.

68. "Muslims Walk Out of School Talks," *Royal Gazette*, January 26, 1982, 1; "Monthly Intelligence Reports for the Period 4th January 1982 to 1st February 1982," February 1, 1982, BIR, FCO 44/2465, TNA.

69. "Muslims Walk Out of School Talk," 1.

70. "Muslims Walk Out of School Talk," 1.

71. "School Rights Superseded by Education Act, Says Minister," 1.

72. Letter from Sir Richard Posnett to J. C. Edwards, Esq., "Re: B.I.C. Report June 1, 1982," July 12, 1982, BIR, FCO 44/2465, TNA.

73. "School Refusal Is Headlined by World Muslim News," *Royal Gazette*, February 20, 1982; "Support Mounting for Muslim School," *Royal Gazette*, February 23, 1982, 8.

74. Letter to the Secretary of State for Foreign & Commonwealth Affairs, February 8, 1982, FCO 44/2465; "Support Mounting for Muslim School," 8.

75. "Support Mounting for the Muslim School," *Royal Gazette*, February 23, 1982, 8. See also "Muslims Will Go to Commission," *Royal Gazette*, May 13, 1982, 1, 6; "Muslims May Go to Human Rights Group Over School," *Royal Gazette*, December 29, 1982, 2.

76. "Teachers Required," *Royal Gazette*, March 11, 1983, 23; "Muslims Go Ahead with School," *Royal Gazette*, March 3, 1982, 1, 12.

77. Letter from Sir Richard Posnett to J. C. Edwards, Esq., "Re: B.I.C. Report June 1982," July 12, 1982, BIR, FCO 44/2465, TNA.

78. Letter from Cromwell Shakir to Hon. William M. Cox, August 25, 1982, RC, annexed to Cabinet Memo No. 259/82, BNA.

79. "Muslims Ponder School Rejection," *Royal Gazette*, September 22, 1982, 1.

80. "Muslims Protest to Rights Commission," *Royal Gazette*, March 29, 1983, 2.

81. "Muslims in Bermuda: Image Problems Challenge a Church," *Mid-Ocean News*, April 14, 1989, 5.

82. "Moslem Private School Planned," *Bermuda Sun*, August 19, 1988, 3.

83. Gabrielle Jamela Hossein, "Democracy, Gender, and Indian Muslim Modernity in Trinidad," in Khan, *Islam in the Americas*, 249–68; Rhoda Reddock, "'Up Against a Wall': Women's Struggle to Reclaim Masjid Space in Trinidad and Tobago," in Khan, *Islam in the Americas*, 217–49.

84. Zaheera Shakir interview; C. Shakir interview.

85. Zakiyyah Shakir interview, February 16, 2016.

86. Zaheera Shakir interview.

87. Zakiyyah Shakir interview, February 16, 2016; Zakiyyah Shakir interview, April 2015; Zaheera Shakir interview; S. Salaam interview; Abdul-Hadee interview; Madyun interview.

88. Abdul-Hadee interview.

89. Zakiyyah Shakir interview, February 16, 2016.

90. Zakiyyah Shakir interview, February 16, 2016; Zakiyyah Shakir interview, April 2015.

91. C. Shakir interview; Zaheera Shakir interview.

92. Zakiyyah Shakir interview, April 2015; Zakiyyah Shakir interview, February 16, 2016.

93. Abdul-Hadee interview.

94. Clara Mohammed Elementary School and W. D. Mohammed High School Atlanta, "How to Integrate the Holy Qur'an in the Classroom," Islamic Educational Conference Pamphlet, 1992, CMS.

95. Clara Mohammed Elementary School and W. D. Mohammed High School Atlanta, "How to Integrate the Holy Qur'an," CMS.

96. Clara Mohammed Elementary School and W. D. Mohammed High School Atlanta, "How to Integrate the Holy Qur'an," CMS.

97. Clara Mohammed Elementary School and W. D. Mohammed High School Atlanta, "How to Integrate the Holy Qur'an," CMS.

98. Clara Mohammed Elementary School and W. D. Mohammed High School Atlanta, "How to Integrate the Holy Qur'an," CMS.

99. Zainab Brown, "CMS-Bermuda Strategy," 2015–16, CMS; Zakiyyah Shakir interview, February 16, 2016; Abdul-Hadee interview.

Chapter Six

1. James Rupert, "Muslim 'Dopebusters' to Widen Patrol," *Washington Post*, April 30, 1988, B4; Richard 3X Bryant, "Community Welcomes Muslim 'Dopebusters,'" *Final Call*, May 37, 1988, 3.

2. Rupert, "Muslim Dopebusters," B4.

3. Rupert, "Muslim Dopebusters," B4; Bryant, "Community Welcomes Muslim Dopebusters," 3.

4. Rupert, "Muslim Dopebusters," B4; Bryant, "Community Welcomes Muslim Dopebusters," 3.

5. Rupert, "Muslim Dopebusters," B4. The DC Metropolitan Police Department, of course, vehemently denied these allegations.

6. Bryant, "Community Welcomes Muslim Dopebusters," 3; Lynne Duke, "Big Demand for Drug Patrols Forces Muslims to Face Economics," *Washington Post*, February 12, 1989, B11.

7. Thompson, "Why Mass Incarceration Matters," 706. The term "carceral state" is derived from French philosopher Michel Foucault's carceral archipelago. See Foucault, *Discipline and Punish*, 293–308.

8. Schrader, *Badges without Borders*, 1–26.

9. Felber, *Those Who Know Don't Say*, 2–3.

10. Gardell, *In the Name of Elijah Muhammad*, 123, citing Lawrence Muhammad, "New Farrakhan Thrust. Opposes Muslim Ideology, Still in Skin Game," *Chicago Defender*, December 3, 1977, weekend edition.

11. See Springhall, *Decolonization Since 1945*, xii–xiii.

12. Springhall, *Decolonization Since 1945*, xii–xiii.

13. Zubok, *A Failed Empire*, 29–93, 227–64.

14. A. Alim Muhammad, "Lessons from Panama," *Final Call*, January 29, 1990, 16.

15. Louis Farrakhan, "The Ultimate Challenge," *Final Call*, May 1979, 5, emphasis in original.

16. Farrakhan, "The Ultimate Challenge," 3.

17. Lee, *Nation of Islam*, 105, citing an interview by the author with Abdul Wali Muhammad, *Final Call*, May 23, 1986; *Final Call*, May 1979.

18. See, Elijah Muhammad, "The Fall and Break Up of the Old World," *Final Call* 2, no. 7 (1982): 1, 15, reprinted from *Muhammad Speaks*, April 12, 1968.

19. A. Wali Muhammad, "Thousands Dead; U.S. Invasion Takes Toll on Blacks in Panama," *Final Call*, January 29, 1990, 32.

20. "Arabs Decry U.S.-Backed Terrorist Bombing," 11.

21. "Seaga: Reagan's Carib 'White Hope,'" *Final Call*, February 14, 1986, 15 (reprinted from *Latinamerica Press* as Matthew Kelsey, "Jamaica: Seaga's Popularity Sinks to All-Time Low," *Latinamerica Press*, January 23, 1986, 1–2).

22. Thomas W. Walker, "Introduction," in Walker, *Reagan versus the Sandinistas*, 2–3; David Close and Salvador Martí i Puig, "The Sandinistas and Nicaragua Since 1979," in Close, Martí i Puig, and McConnell, *The Sandinistas and Nicaragua Since 1979*, 2–4.

23. Walker "Introduction," 3; Close and i Puig, "The Sandinistas and Nicaragua Since 1979," 6–7.

24. Walker, "Introduction," 3; Peter Kornbluh, "The Covert War," in Walker, *Reagan Versus the Sandinistas*, 21–22.

25. Karrim Essack, "In Defense of Nicaragua," *Final Call*, May 30, 1986, 12.

26. Abdul Wali Muhammad, "Mr. Ortega—The Revolution Will Not Be Televised, Sir!," *Final Call*, August 30, 1986, 8.

27. Muhammad, "Mr. Ortega," 8.

28. Vanessa Baird, "U.S.-Backed Contras Plague Nicaraguan Poor: Latin American Perspective," *Final Call*, March 19, 1986, 8 (reprinted from the *Latinamerica Press*, as Vanessa Baird, "Food Shortages, Unemployment, Black Market Plague War-Weary Nicaragua," *Latinamerica Press*, January 23, 1986, 3–4). For more on the Nicaraguan economy after the revolution, see Thomas W. Walker, "Introduction," in Walker, *Reagan Versus the Sandinistas*, 8–9.

29. Gordon, *Disparate Diasporas*, 206–27, 231–32, 240–49.

30. Phillip Taubman, "The Reason for Invading," *New York Times*, November 1, 1983, A1; Stuart Taylor Jr., "In Wake of Invasion, Much Official Misinformation by U.S. Comes to Light," *New York Times*, November 5, 1983, Section 1, 20.

31. Abdul Allah Muhammad, "Grenada Defined," *Final Call* 3, no. 5 (1984): 6.

32. Ronald Reagan, "Remarks to Citizens in St. George's, Grenada," February 20, 1986, RRPL, https://www.reaganlibrary.gov/archives/speech/remarks-citizens-st-georges-grenada.

33. Reagan, "Remarks to Citizens."

34. Abdul Wali Muhammad, "Grenada: Stepping Stone to Nicaragua," *Final Call*, March 19, 1986, 2; untitled cartoon in *Final Call*, April 27, 1986, 9.

35. Michele Labrut and Blanche Patrich, "Noriega: Monster or U.S. Victim," *Final Call*, March 19, 1988, 10, 31; Michele Labrut, "Latin American Not Opposed to Noriega," *Final Call*, May 9, 1988, 3, 11.

36. Conniff, *The United States and Panama*, 151–66.

37. Conniff, *The United States and Panama*, 151–66.

38. Labrut and Patrich, "Noriega: Monster or U.S. Victim?," 10.

39. "U.S. Declares War on Blacks," *Final Call*, January 29, 1990, 1.

40. Muhammad, "Thousands Dead," 2.

41. Muhammad, "Thousands Dead," 2.

42. Robert Muhammad, untitled cartoon, *Final Call*, January 29, 1990, 12; Robert Muhammad, untitled cartoon, *Final Call*, April 27, 1986, 9.

43. "Lessons from Panama," *Final Call*, January 29, 1990, 16.

44. Muhammad, "Thousands Dead," 2–3, 12, 26.

45. Muhammad, "Thousands Dead," 2, 3, 12; José Montano, "'What We Have Lived through Is Worse Than a Nightmare': Panamanian Refugees Wait for Aid," *Final Call*, March 21, 1990, 3, 12, 13 (reprinted from *Latinamerica Press* as José Montano, "'What We Have Lived through Was Worse Than a Nightmare': Panamanian Refugees Wait for Aid," *Latinamerica Press*, January 25, 1990, 4); Richard Muhammad, "Panama's Pain: Victims of U.S. Bombing Tell Tales of Horror," *Final Call*, June 22, 1990, 4.

46. Muhammad, "Thousands Dead," 3.

47. *United States v. Castillo-Bourcy*, 712 F. Supp. 927 (Md.Ga. May 3, 1989).

48. Lyndon B. Johnson, "Special Message to the Congress on Law Enforcement and the Administration of Justice," March 8, 1965, APP, https://www.presidency.ucsb.edu/documents/special-message-the-congress-law-enforcement-and-the-administration-justice, available August 30, 2024. See also Flamm, *Law and Order*, 52; Beckett, *Making Crime Pay*, 37.

49. Lyndon B. Johnson, "Statement by the President Upon Signing the Omnibus Crime Control and Safe Streets Act of 1968," June 19, 1968, APP, https://www.presidency.ucsb.edu/documents/statement-the-president-upon-signing-the-omnibus-crime-control-and-safe-streets-act-1968. See also Flamm, *In the Heat of the Summer*, 280–85; Hinton, *From the War on Poverty*, 2.

50. *Brinegar v. United States*, 338 U.S. 160 (1949), defining probable cause.

51. Thompson, *Blood in the Water*, 563, citing Madison Gray, "A Brief History of the Rockefeller Drug Laws," *Time*, April 2, 2009.

52. Thompson, "Why Mass Incarceration Matters," 710; Thompson, *Blood in the Water*, 563.

53. Maclin, "*Terry v. Ohio*'s Fourth Amendment Legacy," 1310 n. 112; McAffee, "Setting Us Up for Disaster," 612–16; Thompson, "Why Mass Incarceration Matters," 712–13.

54. Edsall and Edsall, *Chain Reaction*, 137–53.

55. US Department of Justice, *Attorney General's Task Force on Violent Crime* (1981), v, 1–2, NCJRS. See also, Beckett, *Making Crime Pay*, 47, quoting US Department of Justice, *Final Report* (1981), v.

56. US Department of Justice, *Final Report* (1981), viii–xiv. See also Davis, "Production of Crime Policies," 121.

57. US Department of Justice, *Final Report* (1981), viii.

58. Davis, "Production of Crime Policies," 127.

59. "Reagan, In Radio Talk, Vows Drive against Drugs," *New York Times*, October 3, 1982, 38; "Administration Plans a Wider War on Drugs," *New York Times*, October 17, 1982, E4. See also Alexander, *New Jim Crow*, 49; Beckett, *Making Crime Pay*, 54.

60. Jonny Anderson, "Black Nation behind Bars: Prelude to Genocide," *Final Call* 3, no. 5 (1984): 12.

61. See, for example, Bro. Jalil Muhammad, "Thankful to Minister Farrakhan," *Final Call*, April 1, 1987, 13; Gregory X. Moore, "Death Plot on Muslims in Prison," *Final Call*, April 22, 1987, 13; Darryl P. King, "Black Inmates Forgotten by Their Own Community," *Final Call*, April 22, 1987, 13; Steven Theus, "Imam Remains Steadfast," *Final Call*, May 27, 1988, 15; Gregory Muhammad, "Applauds Muhammad's Program," *Final Call*, August 30, 1988, 15; Timothy X. Jackson, "Brothers in Prison Ready to Soldier for Muhammad," *Final Call*, January 7, 1991, 15; Deer Island Study Group, "Muhammad's Teachings Cure Illness Blacks Suffer in America," *Final Call*, November 18, 1991, 17.

62. Anderson, "Prelude to Genocide," 12.
63. Anderson, "Prelude to Genocide," 12.
64. Anderson, "Prelude to Genocide," 12.
65. "Black Nation behind Bars: A.I.D.S.: A Killer behind Bars," *Final Call* 4, no. 1 (1984): 24.
66. "Black Nation behind Bars," 24.
67. "Black Nation behind Bars," 24.
68. For more on the activism of Nation prisoners in the 1940s–60s, see Felber, *Those Who Know Don't Say*.
69. James E. Smith, "Black Nation behind Bars: Blacks on Death Row Call for Execution Rather Than Torturous Wait," *Final Call*, July 1985, 29.
70. Curtis, *Black Muslim Religion*, 95–174.
71. Smith, "Blacks on Death Row Call for Execution," 29.
72. Smith, "Blacks on Death Row Call for Execution," 29, emphasis added.
73. Jacqui Lopes, Deborah McCants, and Susan Johnson, "Black Nation behind Bars: Black Women Cry Out, *Final Call*, 29.
74. Taylor, *Promise of Patriarchy*, 1–6.
75. Taylor, *Promise of Patriarchy*, 74–124.
76. Alexander, *The New Jim Crow*, 52.
77. Richard M. Smith, "The Plague among Us; the Drug Crisis," *Newsweek*, June 16, 1986, 15.
78. See, Peter Kerr, "Crack Addiction Spreads among Middle Class," *New York Times*, June 8, 1986, 1, 42; John T. McQuiston, "At Rally in Bronx, Hundreds Clamor for Aid in Drug Fight," *New York Times*, June 8, 1986, 42; Shelly Feuer Domash, "Use of the Drug 'Crack' Growing on L.I.," *New York Times*, June 8, 1986, Section 21, 5; Peter Kerr, "Cuomo Says State Is Widening Effort to Combat Crack," *New York Times*, June 18, 1986, 37; Crystal Nix, "'We're Not Going, So They Have To': The Bronx Battle Cry against Crack," *New York Times*, June 19, 1986; Peter Kerr, "Battle against Crack," *New York Times*, June 27, 1986, 39; James Feron, "New Training Program for Police Bolsters Efforts against Cocaine," *New York Times*, June 29, 1986, Section 22, 1; Peter Kerr, "Morgenthau Calls U.S. Bid to Fight Cocaine 'Minimal,'" *New York Times*, July 11, 1986, 33, 36; "Cocaine Draws New Attention," *New York Times*, July 13, 1986, Section 4, 1; "Attack Crack, Not Each Other," *New York Times*, July 15, 1986, 28; "Ex-Drug Addict Warns Panel of Cocaine Peril," *New York Times*, July 16, 1986, 12; John T. McQuiston, "10 in a Family Are Arrested in 5 Drug Raids," *New York Times*, July 18, 1986, 31; Isabel Wilkerson, "Governor Urges Adding Judges for Drug Cases," *New York Times*, July 19, 1986, 31; Gary Gately, "On City Street Corners, Night of Antidrug Vigils," *New York Times*, July 22, 1986, 27, 30; "City Is Doubling Anticrack Force," *New York Times*, July 25, 1986, 34; Russell Baker, "Observer: Same Old Junk," *New York Times*, July 26, 1986, 27; Joyce Furnick, "Officials Join Koch to Press New Attack on Drug Abuse," *New York Times*, July 31, 1986, 25.
79. Murch, "Crack in Los Angeles," 162–63.
80. Lamont X Curry, "A Hard Habit to 'Crack': Cocaine-Based Drug Leaves Bodies Twisted in Streets of the U.S.," *Final Call*, August 30, 1986, 4.
81. Curry, "A Hard Habit to 'Crack,'" 5.
82. Curry, "A Hard Habit to 'Crack,'" 5.

83. Curry, "A Hard Habit to 'Crack,'" 6.
84. Curry, "A Hard Habit to 'Crack,'" 6.
85. Curry, "A Hard Habit to 'Crack,'" 6.
86. Curry, "A Hard Habit to 'Crack,'" 27.
87. Andrew Rosenthal, "National Guard in 12 States Gets Pentagon Money to Battle Drugs," *New York Times*, March 31, 1989, A11.
88. Rosenthal, "National Guard," A11.
89. See, for example, "Forum on Crack Set," *New York Amsterdam News*, April 26, 1986, 36; "N.Y. Police Fight 'Crack' Epidemic," *Afro-American*, May 31, 1986, 1.
90. Murch, "Crack in Los Angeles," 168–73; Forman, *Locking Up Our Own*, 3–14.
91. Abdul Wali Muhammad, "Open War on Black Youth," *Final Call*, July 31, 1989, 11.
92. Abdul Wali Muhammad, "U.S. Gov't Declares War on Youth under Guise of War on Drugs," *Final Call*, September 11, 1989, 10–11.
93. Wali Muhammad, "U.S. Gov't Declares War," 10.
94. Wali Muhammad, "U.S. Gov't Declares War," 10–11.
95. Wali Muhammad, "U.S. Gov't Declares War," 11.
96. Wali Muhammad, "U.S. Gov't Declares War," 11.
97. James Muhammad, "National Guard to 'Fight Drugs' in Brooklyn, NY," *Final Call*, December 31, 1989, 1; Simon Anekwe, "Owens Calls National Guard against E. New York Dealers," *New York Amsterdam News*, October 28, 1989, 4; J. Zangba Browne, "Gov. Approves Use of National Guard," *New York Amsterdam News*, December 9, 1989, 11; Fidel Louis, "Guardsmen to Help Clean Brownsville, E. New York," *New York Amsterdam News*, December 30, 1989, 9.
98. "U.S. Declares War on Blacks," 1; Muhammad, "Thousands Dead," 2.
99. Robert Muhammad, untitled cartoon, *Final Call*, January 29, 1990, 12.
100. "Lessons from Panama," 16.
101. "Lessons from Panama," 16.
102. Schrader, *Badges without Borders*, 27–51.
103. Abdul Wali Muhammad, "Reagan's War on Freedom," *Final Call*, October 15, 1986, 24.
104. James D. Addy, "Drugs Are Tool of Colonizer," *Final Call*, June 17, 1991, 12.
105. Ruth Muhammad, "Report Card," 1990, *Final Call*, May 31, 1990, 3.
106. For more on Siraj Wahhaj's Sunni Muslim drug patrols, see Merle English, "Taking Stand against Drug Dealers," *Newsday* (Brooklyn Edition), March 9, 1986, 34; Peter Noel, "Group Warns of 'Jihad' if Muslims Go to Prison," *New York Amsterdam News*, February 7, 1987, 1.
107. Merle English, "Taking Stand against Drug Dealers," *Newsday* (Brooklyn Edition), March 9, 1986, 34; Peter Noel, "Group Warns of 'Jihad' if Muslims Go to Prison," *New York Amsterdam News*, February 7, 1987, 1; Richard 3X Bryant, "'Dopebusters': Muslim Anti-Drug Patrols Bring Calm in D.C.," *Final Call*, June 16, 1988, 2.
108. Bryant, "Community Welcomes Muslim 'Dopebusters,'" 3, 12; Rupert, "Muslim Dopebusters," B1; "Muslims at the Mayfair," *Time*, May 9, 1988, 30; "Los Angeles Black Community Outraged: Muslim Killed during LA Sheriffs [sic] Attack," *Final Call*, February 5, 1990, 26; Lamont X. Curry, "Muslims Aid Elderly," *Final Call*, April 30, 1992, 7, 11; Rosalind X. Moore, "HUD Puts Muslims on Hold," *Final Call*, April 20, 1992, 7, 19; Richard

Muhammad, "Community, Police, Muslims Form United Front," *Final Call*, June 29, 1992, 5; Rosalind X. Moore, "Tenants, NOI Security Win in L.A.," *Final Call*, October 6, 1992, 3; J. Hugo Warren, III, "N.O.I. Security: The Real Peacekeepers," *Final Call*, October 6, 1992, 23–24; Richard Muhammad, "Police Join Dealers in Clash with Muslims," *Final Call*, June 15, 1992, 3, 10; "Nation of Islam Restores Calm," *Pittsburgh Courier*, January 8, 1992, 1; R. Muhammad, "Community, Police, Muslims," *Final Call*, June 29, 1992, 5.

109. Carl T. Rowan, "We Mustn't Stoop to Vigilantism in Our War against Drugs," *Chicago Sun Times*, April 27, 1988, 35; "Review & Outlook: Frontier Justice," *Wall Street Journal*, June 6, 1988, 1; Carl T. Rowan, "New Lynch Mobs: Drug Vigilantes," *Washington Post*, April 27, 1988, A21; Rowan, "We Mustn't Stoop to Vigilantism," 35.

110. Michael White, "Farrakhan Supporters Wage Street War on Drugs," *The Guardian*, April 22, 1988, 8; "Muslims at the Mayfair," 30; Bryant, "Community Welcomes Muslim 'Dopebusters,'" 12.

111. "Muslims at the Mayfair," 30. See also Bryant, "Community Welcomes Muslim 'Dopebusters,'" 12.

112. Bryant, "Community Welcomes Muslim 'Dopebusters,'" 12.

113. Bryant, "Community Welcomes Muslim 'Dopebusters,'" 12.

114. Bryant, "Community Welcomes Muslim 'Dopebusters,'" 12.

115. Bryant, "Community Welcomes Muslim 'Dopebusters,'" 12; Richard 3X Bryant, "N.O.I. Drug Program Cures: Min. Farrakhan Cites Success of Program," *Final Call*, January 15, 1989, 7.

116. Louis Farrakhan, "'Stop the Killing': Minister Farrakhan Brings Message of Crime-Ravaged New Orleans," *Final Call*, August 3, 1990, 13.

117. Bryant, "N.O.I. Drug Program Cures," *Final Call*, August 22, 1989, 7.

118. "Muslim Program Hailed," *Final Call*, August 22, 1989, 7.

119. Felber, *Those Who Know Don't Say*, 2–3.

120. Bryant, "Community Welcomes Muslim Dopebusters," 3; Lynne Duke, "Big Demand for Drug Patrols Forces Muslims to Face Economics," *Washington Post*, February 12, 1989, B11.

121. Duke, "Big Demand for Drug Patrols," B1.

122. untitled photograph in *Final Call*, October 3, 1988, 3.

123. Rupert, "Muslim Dopebusters," B4.

124. Richard 3X Bryant, "'Dopebusters': Muslim Anti-Drug Patrols Bring Calm in D.C.," *Final Call*, June 16, 1988, 2.

125. "Community Outraged: D.C. Police Assault 'Dopebusters,'" *Final Call*, October 3, 1988, 3; untitled photograph, October 3, 1988, 3.

126. "L.A. Cops Attack Fruit of Islam," *Final Call*, January 29, 1990, 2; "Los Angeles Black Community Outraged: Muslim Killed During L.A. Sheriff Attack," *Final Call*, February 5, 1990, 2, 26; James Muhammad, "'Never Again': Minister Farrakhan Eulogizes FOI Slain by Los Angeles Sheriff," *Final Call*, February 12, 1990, 3.

127. Mary B.W. Tabor, "Muslim Guards: Security Unit Maintaining Pride," *New York Times*, January 6, 1992, B3.

128. Bryant, "Community Welcomes Muslim 'Dopebusters,'" 3, 12; Rupert, "Muslim Dopebusters," B1; "Muslims at the Mayfair," 30; "Los Angeles Black Community Outraged," 26; Curry, "Muslims Aid Elderly," 7, 11; Moore, "HUD Puts Muslims on Hold," 7, 19;

R. Muhammad, "Community, Police, Muslims Form United Front," 5; Moore, "Tenants, NOI Security Win in L.A.," 3; Warren, "N.O.I. Security," 23–24; Muhammad, "Police Join Dealers in Clash with Muslims," 3, 10; "Nation of Islam Restores Calm," 1; Muhammad, "Community, Police, Muslims," 5.

129. Lynne Duke, "Big Demand for Drug Patrols Forces Muslims to Face Economics," *Washington Post*, February 12, 1989, B11.

130. Clarence Page, "Who to Call? Muslim Dopebusters," *Hartford Courant*, April 25, 1989, B9E; Clarence Page, "D.C.'s Black Muslim Dopebusters," *Chicago Tribune*, April 23, 1989, C3.

131. Tabor, "Muslim Guards," B3; Hamil R. Harris and Marcia Davis, "Potomac Gardens Quiet after Fights: Residents Ask City Officials to Keep Nation of Islam Guards on Duty," *Washington Post*, May 13, 1995, C3.

132. Harris and Davis, "Potomac Gardens Quiet after Fights," C3; Joseph P. Fried, "Tenants Seek Black Muslim Guards at Project in Queens," *New York Times*, July 12, 1992, 27.

133. Raymond Hernandez, "Nation of Islam Guards Ordered to Leave Housing Project," *New York Times*, September 13, 1996, B3.

134. Harris and Davis, "Potomac Gardens Quiet after Fights," C3; Fried, "Tenants Seek Black Muslim Guards at Project in Queens," 27.

135. "N.O.I. Security Patrol Service, Inc.," Maryland Department of Assessments and Taxation; "X-Men Security Services, Inc.," Maryland Department of Assessments and Taxation; "N.O.I Security Agency, Inc.," Pennsylvania Department of State; "New Life Self-Development Group, Ltd.," Illinois Department of State; "X-Men Security, Inc.," New York Department of State; "N.O.I. Security Agency, Inc.," NYDS; "N.O.I. Security of New York," NYDS; "NOI Security Agency, Inc.," District of Columbia Office of the Secretary.

136. Harris and Davis, "Potomac Gardens Quiet After Fights," C3; Vernon Loeb, "D.C. Hires Nation of Islam Guards for SE Complex," *Washington Post*, May 4, 1995, C1; Sonya Ross, "Again! Federal Government Probes Nation of Islam," *New Pittsburgh Courier*, May 6, 1995, 3.

137. Ross, "Again!" 3; "Security Firms Found Separate from Farrakhan," *Washington Post*, March 3, 1995, A7.

138. Ross, "Again!," 3; "HUD Cancels Nation of Islam Security Contract," *Chicago Tribune*, November 10, 1995, D10; "Muslim Guards to Stop Work in Baltimore," *New York Times*, November 19, 1995, A23.

139. Hernandez, "Nation of Islam Guards," B3.

140. Hernandez, "Nation of Islam Guards," B3.

141. Vernon Loeb, "Nation of Islam Security Firm Seeks Bankruptcy Protection," *Washington Post*, June 3, 1995, B1, B5.

142. Amy Goldstein, "IRS Freezes Assets of AIDS Clinic Affiliated with Nation of Islam," *Washington Post*, September 13, 1996, B1, B3.

143. "N.O.I. Security Patrol Service, Inc.," Maryland Department of Assessments and Taxation; "X-Men Security Services, Inc.," Maryland Department of Assessments and Taxation; "N.O.I. Security Agency, Inc.," Pennsylvania Department of State; "New Life Self-Development Group, Ltd.," Illinois Secretary of State; "X-Men Security, Inc.," NYDS; "N.O.I. Security Agency, Inc.," NYDS; "N.O.I. Security of New York," NYDS; "NOI Security Agency, Inc.," District of Columbia Office of the Secretary.

Epilogue

1. Rasheed interview.
2. Erakat, "Geographies of Intimacy."
3. "World Report 2015: Israel/Palestine: Events of 2014," *Human Rights Watch*, 2015, https://www.hrw.org/world-report/2015/country-chapters/israel/palestine#:~:text=Israel%20continued%20to%20expand%20unlawful,including%20children%20and%20peaceful%20protesters.
4. Frances Robles and Julie Bosman, "Autopsy Shows Michael Brown Was Struck at Least Six Times," *New York Times Online*, August 17, 2014, https://www.nytimes.com/2014/08/18/us/michael-brown-autopsy-shows-he-was-shot-at-least-6-times.html.
5. Taylor, *From #BlackLivesMatter to Black Liberation*, 171–72, citing John Richardson, "Michael Brown Sr. and the Agony of the Black Father in America," *Esquire*, January 5, 2015, http://www.esquire.com/features/michael-brown-father-interview-0115.
6. Taylor, *From #BlackLivesMatter to Black Liberation*, citing Mark Follman, "Michael Brown's Mom Laid Flowers Where He Was Shot—and the Police Crushed Them," *Mother Jones*, August 27, 2014, http://www.motherjones.com/politics/2014/08/ferguson-st-louis-police-tactics-dogs-michael-brown.
7. "On the Streets of America: Human Rights Abuses in Ferguson," *Amnesty International*, October 23, 2014, https://www.amnestyusa.org/reports/on-the-streets-of-america-human-rights-abuses-in-ferguson/.
8. Al Baker, J. David Goodman, and Benjamin Mueller, "Beyond the Chokehold: The Path to Eric Garner's Death," *New York Times Online*, June 13, 2015, https://www.nytimes.com/2015/06/14/nyregion/eric-garner-police-chokehold-staten-island.html.
9. Lizette Alvarez and Cara Buckley, "Zimmerman Is Acquitted in Trayvon Martin Killing," *New York Times Online*, July 13, 2013, https://www.nytimes.com/2013/07/14/us/george-zimmerman-verdict-trayvon-martin.html.
10. Louis Farrakhan, "The Troubled World: What Should We Be Doing?," *Final Call*, August 19, 2014, http://www.finalcall.com/artman/publish/Minister_Louis_Farrakhan_9/article_101694.shtml.
11. Farrakhan, "The Troubled World."
12. Farrakhan, "The Troubled World."
13. Robert Mackey, "Advice for Ferguson's Protesters from the Middle East," *New York Times Online*, August 14, 2014, https://www.nytimes.com/2014/08/15/world/middleeast/advice-for-fergusons-protesters-from-the-middle-east.html?searchResultPosition=63.
14. "Black Lives Matter Endorses BDS: Israel Is 'Apartheid State,'" *Haaretz*, August 4, 2016, https://www.haaretz.com/israel-news/2016-08-04/ty-article/black-lives-matter-endorses-bds-israel-is-apartheid-state/0000017f-e0f3-d7b2-a77f-e3f730ed0000.
15. Erakat, "Geographies of Intimacy," 479–90.
16. "Protests across the Globe after George Floyd's Death," *CNN*, June 13, 2020, https://www.cnn.com/2020/06/06/world/gallery/intl-george-floyd-protests/index.html; Zamira Rahim and Rob Picheta, "Thousands around the World Protest George Floyd's Death in Global Display of Solidarity," *CNN*, June 1, 2020, http://www.cnn.com/2020/06/01/world/george-floyd-global-protests-intl/index.html; "George Floyd: Protests around the World Show Solidarity with US Demonstrators," *USA Today*, July 18, 2020, http://www.usatoday

.com/picture-gallery/news/world/2020/06/03/george-floyd-protests-around-world-show-solidarity-us-demonstrators/3133960001; "How George Floyd's Death Sparked Protests around the World," *Washington Post*, June 10, 2020, http://www.washingtonpost.com/graphics/world/2020/06/10/how-george-floyds-death-sparked-protests-around-world.

17. "Protests across the Globe after George Floyd's Death"; Rahim and Picheta, "Thousands around the World Protest George Floyd's Death"; "George Floyd: Protests around the World"; "How George Floyd's Death Sparked Protests."

18. Erakat, "Geographies of Intimacy"; Bailey, "Black-Palestinian Solidarity in the Ferguson-Gaza Era," 1017–26; Lubin, *Geographies of Liberation*.

19. Malcolm X, "Zionist Logic," *Egyptian Gazette*, September 17, 1964. See also Baig, "Spirit in Opposition," 47–71.

20. Erakat, "Geographies of Intimacy," 475–76.

21. Lubin, *Geographies of Liberation*.

22. Morgan, "Historical *Sankofa*," 582–91.

23. Divest from Death USC, "News Release," April 24, 2024, https://ugc.production.linktr.ee/63344e8e-21c4-427a-9ae2 7fc3c8c34fcb_ DivestFromDeath.NewsRelease.pdf.

24. S.C.A.L.E. at USC (@uscscale), Instagram.

25. Valeria Macias, Daniel Park, Myriam Alcala, Tess Patton, Lyla Bhalla-Ladd, Estelle Atkinson, Corinne Smith, Jules Feeney, Lindsey Miller, Nolan Ezzet, and Muhammed Zain Shafi Khan, "UPDATES: A USC Pro-Palestinian Group Hosts an Occupation on Campus in Solidarity with Gaza," *USC Annenberg Media*, April 24, 2024, https://www.uscannenbergmedia.com/2024/04/24/live-updates-a-usc-pro-palestinian-group-has-begun-an-occupation-on-campus-in-solidarity-with-gaza/; "LAPD Arrests 93 People at USC Amid Israel-Hamas War Protests," *Los Angeles Times*, April 23, 2024, https://www.latimes.com/california/story/2024-04-24/usc-pro-palestinian-encampment#:~:text=More%20than%2090%20people%20were,Southern%20California%20on%20April%202024.

26. @uscscale, Instagram.

27. Maya Yang, "Police Dismantle Palestinian Solidarity Encampment at USC," *The Guardian*, May 5, 2024, https://www.theguardian.com/us-news/article/2024/may/05/police-palestinian-solidarity-camp-usc.

28. Stefano Ausenda, "Muslim Community to Host Peace Walk in Support of Palestine," *Royal Gazette*, November 3, 2024, https://www.royalgazette.com/general/news/article/20231103/muslim-community-to-host-peace-walk-in-support-of-palestine/.

29. Niraj Warikoo, "Farrakhan Addresses Gaza War in Speech at Nation of Islam Event in Detroit," *Detroit Free Press*, February 25, 2024, https://www.freep.com/story/news/local/michigan/detroit/2024/02/25/farrakhan-calls-for-muslims-to-help-palestinians/72738292007/.

30. Naba'a Muhammad, "A Divine Warning and Why Soft Words Won't Stop Gaza Genocide," *Final Call*, March 4, 2024, https://new.finalcall.com/2024/03/05/a-divine-warning-and-why-soft-words-wont-stop-gaza-genocide/.

Bibliography

Primary Sources

ARCHIVES

Bermuda
Bermuda National Archives (BNA), Hamilton
 Records of the Cabinet, Cabinet Memoranda (RC)
 Records of the Chief Secretary's Office (CSO), Black Power Movement Files (BPM)
Bermuda National Library
 Abdurrahman, Al Hajj Waheed. *Historical Roots of Proper Islamic Governance in Bermuda: Bermuda Islamic History 1977–1999 and Its Analysis*. Hamilton, Bermuda: Independently Published, 1999.

United Kingdom
The British National Archives (TNA), Kew Gardens, Richmond
 Board of Trade: Commercial and Statistical Department and Successors: Inwards Passenger Lists, BT 25
 Colonial Office: West Africa Original Correspondence, CO 554
  Colonial Office and Commonwealth Office: West Indian Department: Registered Files (WIS Series), CO 1031
  Commonwealth Office: West Indian Department 'B' and Foreign and Commonwealth Office, West Indian Department: Registered Files, Smaller Commonwealth West Indian Territories (WB and HW Series), FCO 44
  Foreign and Commonwealth Office: North American and Caribbean Department and Caribbean Department: Registered Files (AN Series), FCO 63

United States
National Archives and Records Administration (NARA), College Park, MD
 Department of State Central Files, Record Group (RG) 59
 General Records of the Department of Justice, RG 60
 Records of the United States Customs Service, RG 36
New York Municipal Archives, New York
 New York Police Department (NYPD) Intelligence Unit Records, Series V: Large Organizations Files, 1934–90
Schomburg Center for Research in Black Culture (SCRBC) (New York)
 Hymns Composed by Arnold J. Ford and others (Hymns)
 Malcolm X Papers
 Moorish Science Temple (MSTA) Collection, 1926–27

Nation of Islam (NOI) Collection
Photographs, Robert Haggins Collection
Western Michigan University, Archives and Regional History Collection
  Brown & Gold. Kalamazoo, MI: Western Michigan College of Education, 1948.
  Brown & Gold. Kalamazoo, MI: Western Michigan College of Education, 1949.
  Brown & Gold. Kalamazoo, MI: Western Michigan College of Education, 1952.

ONLINE DATABASES

California Birth Index, 1905–1995. Provo, UT: Ancestry, 2005.
Federal Bureau of Investigation (FBI) Vault
  FBI Monograph on Elijah Muhammad, https://vault.fbi.gov/elijah-muhammad
  FBI Monograph on Marcus Garvey, https://vault.fbi.gov/marcus-garvey
  FBI Monograph on Malcolm X, https://vault.fbi.gov/malcolm-little-malcolm-x
  FBI Monograph on the Moorish Science Temple of America (MSTA), https://vault.fbi.gov/Moorish%20Science%20Temple%20of%20America
  FBI Monograph on Wallace Fard Muhammed, https://vault.fbi.gov/Wallace%20Fard%20Muhammed/
U.S. Phone and Address Directories, 1993-2000. Lehi, UT: Ancestry, 2005.

PUBLISHED BOOKS AND MANUSCRIPTS

Ahmad, Hazrat Mirza Ghulam. *A Gift for the Queen (Tohfa-e-Qaisariyyah)*. Translated by Syed Sajid Ahmad. Surrey, UK: Islam International Publications, 2018.
———. *Star of the Empress (Sitara-e-Qaisarah)*. Translated by Sharmeen Butt. Surrey, UK: Islam International Publications, 2013.
———. *Tadhikirah*. Translated by Hadrat Chaudry Muhammad Zafrullah Khan. Qadian, India: Islam International Publications, 2019.
Ford, Arnold Josaih. *The Universal Ethiopian Hymnal of the Congregation Beth B'nai*. Edited by Muhammad Abdullah Al-Ahari and Sidney S. Smith. Chicago: Magribine Press, 2019.
Garvey, Marcus. *Philosophy and Opinions of Marcus Garvey or Africa for the Africans*. Edited by Amy Jacques Garvey. New York: Majority Press, 1986.
Hill, Robert A., ed. *Marcus Garvey and the Universal Negro Improvement Association Papers*. Vol. 1. Berkeley: University of California Press, 1983.
———. *Marcus Garvey and the Universal Negro Improvement Association Papers*, Vol. 5. Berkeley: University of California Press, 1983.
———. *Marcus Garvey and the Universal Negro Improvement Association Papers*, Vol. 7. Berkeley: University of California Press, 1983.
Macartney, Earl George. *An Account of Ireland in 1773: By a Late Chief Secretary of That Kingdom*. London: Privately Published, 1773. Gale Eighteenth Century Collections Online.
Muhammad, Elijah. *The Supreme Wisdom: Solution to the So-Called Negroes' Problem*. Newport News, VA: National Newport News and Commentator, 1957.
Wegener, Alfred L. *The Origin of Continents and Oceans*. Translated by J. G. A. Skerl. London: Methuen, 1924.

GOVERNMENT PUBLICATIONS

Bermuda

Bermuda Census Office. *Census of 23rd October 1960*. Hamilton, Bermuda: The Bermuda Government, 1961.

Bermuda Census Office. *The 1991 Census of Population and Housing*. Hamilton, Bermuda: The Bermuda Government, 1991.

Bermuda Census Office. *Report of the Population Census 1970*. Hamilton, Bermuda: The Bermuda Government, 1973.

Department of Statistics. *Facts and Figures 2018*. Hamilton, Bermuda: The Bermuda Government, 2019. https://www.gov.bm/sites/default/files/2018-Facts-Figures_0.pdf.

Wooding, Hugh O. B., Hugh W. Springer, and Lawrence Peter Reginald Browning. *Bermuda Civil Disorders of 1968: Report of Commission and Statement of the Government of Bermuda*. Hamilton, Bermuda: The Bermuda Government, 1968.

United Kingdom

Scarman, Leslie George. *The Scarman Report: The Brixton Disorders 10–12 April, 1981*. London: Her Majesty's Stationery Office, 1981.

United States

Georgia Writers' Project (Savannah Unit). *Drums and Shadows: Survival Studies among the Georgia Coastal Negroes*. Athens: University of Georgia Press, 1940.

Gibson, Campbell, and Kay Jung. "Working Paper No. 81: Historical Census Statistics on the Foreign-Born Population of the United States, 1850–2000." Washington, DC: United States Census Bureau (Population Division), February 2006.

United States Census Bureau. *Fifteenth Census of the United States: 1930*. Provo, UT: Ancestry, 2002.

——— . *1950: United States Census of Population*. Washington, DC: Government Printing Office, 1952.

United States Department of Justice. *Attorney General's Task Force on Violent Crime: Final Report*, August 17, 1981 (Washington, DC, 1981). National Criminal Justice Reference Service Online (NCJRS). https://www.ncjrs.gov/pdffiles1/Digitization/78548NCJRS.pdf.

INTERVIEWS

All interviews were conducted by the author, unless otherwise noted.
Abdul Hadee, Ameenah. Hamilton, Bermuda. February 13, 2016.
Brown, Wayne. Hamilton, Bermuda. April 22, 2015.
Hill, Milton. Hamilton, Bermuda. April 30, 2015.
——— . Hamilton, Bermuda. February 8, 2016.
Khaldun, Michelle. St. George, Bermuda. March 2, 2016.
Madyun, Arifah. Hamilton, Bermuda. February 29, 2016.
Muhammad, Kenneth Castle. Southampton, Bermuda. February 17, 2016.
Rasheed, Mustapha. St. George's, Bermuda. February 13, 2016.
Salaam, Norwood. Hamilton, Bermuda. April 24, 2015.
Salaam, Safiyyah. Hamilton, Bermuda. February 12, 2016.

Seifuddin Stowe, Dyab. Hamilton, Bermuda. April 14, 2015.
Shamsiddeen. Najiyyah. Hamilton, Bermuda. April 15, 2015.
Shakir, Cromwell. Hamilton, Bermuda. April 17, 2015.
Shakir, Zakiyyah. Hamilton, Bermuda. April 2015.
———. Hamilton, Bermuda. February 16, 2016.
———. Hamilton, Bermuda. February 26, 2016.
Sharrieff, Takbir. Hamilton, Bermuda. April 14, 2015.
Wasi, Khalid. Skype. April 23, 2015.

JOURNAL ARTICLES

Beynon, Erdmann Doane. "The Voodoo Cult among Negro Migrants in Detroit." *American Journal of Sociology* 43, no. 6 (1938): 894–907.
Naeem, Abdul Basit. "Current Topics: Pakistan and the U.S.A." *The Muslim World* 41, no. 3 (July 1951): 227.

PERIODICALS

African Times and Orient Review (London)
Afro-American (Baltimore)
Atlanta Daily World
Bermuda Recorder (Hamilton)
Bermuda Sun (Hamilton)
Bilalian News (Chicago)
Chicago Defender
Chicago Herald & Examiner
Chicago Tribune
Des Moines Register
Detroit Free Press
Egyptian Gazette (Cairo)
Esquire (New York)
Final Call (Chicago)
Guardian (London)
Haaretz (Tel Aviv, Israel)
Hartford Courant
Iowa Crest (Cedar Rapids)
Los Angeles Herald-Dispatch
Los Angeles Times
Mid-Ocean News (Hamilton)
Moslem Sunrise (Chicago)
Moslem World & the U.S.A. (Cedar Rapids & Brooklyn)
Mother Jones (San Francisco)
Muhammad Speaks (Chicago)
Muhammad Speaks/Bilalian News (Chicago)
Negro World (New York)
New Pittsburgh Courier
Newsday (Hempstead)
Newsweek (New York)
New York Amsterdam News
New York Times
Philadelphia Tribune
Pittsburgh Courier
Review of Religions (Rabwah-Punjab)
Royal Gazette (Hamilton)
Sheffield Evening Telegraph
USA Today (Tysons, VA)
U.S. News and World Report (Washington)
Voice of Islam (Karachi)
Wall Street Journal (New York)
Washington Post

PRIVATE CORRESPONDENCE

All correspondence is between the listed party and the author, unless otherwise noted. All items are in the possession of the author.
Castle, Sasha. Email. February 18, 2016.
Khaldun, Michelle. Email. April 11, 2016.
Naeem, Shahid. Email. April 24, 2024.
———. Email. August 19, 2024.
Stewart, Ronald X. Facebook message. October 1, 2023.

UNPUBLISHED PERSONAL AND PRIVATE PAPERS

Copies in the author's possession.
Personal Papers of Norwood Salaam (NSP). Hamilton, Bermuda.
Private Papers of the Clara Mohammed Elementary School—Bermuda (CMS). Hamilton, Bermuda.

Secondary Sources

BOOKS

Abu-Lughod, Janet L. *Race, Space, and Riots in Chicago, New York, and Los Angeles.* New York: Oxford University Press, 2007.
Alexander, John. *A History of Organized Labor in the English-Speaking West Indies.* Westport, CT: Praeger, 2004.
Alexander, Michelle. *The New Jim Crow: Mass Incarceration in the Age of Colorblindness.* New York: The New Press, 2010.
Anderson, Benedict. *Imagined Communities: Reflections on the Origins and Spread of Nationalism.* London: Verso, 1983.
Anderson, Jervis. *This Was Harlem: A Cultural Portrait, 1900–1950.* New York: Farrar, Strauss & Giroux, 1981.
Azaransky, Sarah. *This Worldwide Struggle: Religion and the International Roots of the Civil Rights Movement.* New York: Oxford University Press, 2017.
Bald, Vivek. *Bengali Harlem and the Lost Histories of South Asian America.* New York: Cambridge University Press, 2013.
Balto, Simon. *Occupied Territory: Policing Black Chicago from Red Summer to Black Power.* Chapel Hill: The University of North Carolina Press, 2019.
Beckett, Katherine. *Making Crime Pay: Law and Order in Contemporary American Politics.* New York: Oxford University Press, 1999.
Bedasse, Monique. *Jah Kingdom: Rastafarians, Tanzania, and Pan-Africanism in the Age of Decolonization.* Chapel Hill: The University of North Carolina Press, 2017.
Bender, Jill C. *The 1857 Indian Uprising and the British Empire.* Cambridge, UK: Cambridge University Press, 2016.
Benjamin, Jules R. *The United States and the Origins of the Cuban Revolution: An Empire of Liberty in an Age of National Liberation.* Princeton, NJ: Princeton University Press, 2020.
Berger, Dan. *Black Prison Organizing in the Civil Rights Era.* Chapel Hill: The University of North Carolina Press, 2014.
Berlin, Ira. *The Making of African America: The Four Great Migrations.* New York: Penguin, 2010.
Bhatt, Purnima Mehta. *The African Diaspora in India: Assimilation, Change, and Cultural Survivals.* London: Routledge, 2018.
Blain, Keisha N. *Set the World on Fire: Black Nationalism Women and the Global Struggle for Freedom.* Philadelphia: University of Pennsylvania Press, 2018.
Brown, Walton. *Bermuda and the Struggle for Reform: Race, Politics, and Ideology, 1944–1998.* Bermuda: Cahow Press, 2011.
Carey, Elaine, and Alfred J. Andrea, eds. *Protests in the Streets: 1968 across the Globe.* Indianapolis, IN: Hackett Publishing, 2016.

Chan-Malik, Sylvia. *Being Muslim: A Cultural History of Women of Color in American Islam*. New York: New York University Press, 2018. Kindle.

Clegg, Claude. *An Original Man: The Life and Times of Elijah Muhammad*. New York: St. Martin's Press, 1997.

———. *The Price of Liberty: African Americans and the Making of Liberia*. Chapel Hill: The University of North Carolina Press, 2004.

Close, David, Salvador Martí i Puig, and Shelley A. McConnell, eds. *The Sandinistas and Nicaragua Since 1979*. Boulder, CO: Lynne Rienner Publishers, 2012.

Conniff, Michael. *The United States and Panama: The Forced Alliance*. Athens: University of Georgia Press, 2012.

Cronon, David. *Black Moses: The Story of Marcus Garvey and the Universal Negro Improvement Association*. Madison: University of Wisconsin Press, 1955.

Curtis, Edward. *Black Muslim Religion in the Nation of Islam, 1960–1975*. Chapel Hill: The University of North Carolina Press, 2006.

———. *Islam in Black America: Identity, Liberation, Difference*. Albany: State University of New York Press, 2002.

Dannin, Robert. *Black Pilgrimage to Islam*. New York: Oxford University Press, 2005.

Darrell, Neville T. *Acel'dama: The Untold Story of the Murder of the Governor of Bermuda, Sir Richard Sharples*. Surrey, BC: Coastline Mountain Press, 2003.

Dawisha, Adeed. *Arab Nationalism in the Twentieth Century: From Triumph to Despair*. Princeton, NJ: Princeton University Press, 2003.

DeCaro, Louis. *On the Side of My People: A Religious Life of Malcolm X*. New York: New York University Press, 1995.

de la Fuente, Alejandro. *A Nation for All: Race, Inequality, and Politics in Twentieth-Century Cuba*. Chapel Hill: The University of North Carolina Press, 2001.

Dhulipali, Venkat. *Creating a New Medina: State Power, Islam, and the Quest for Pakistan in Late Colonial India*. Delhi: Cambridge University Press, 2017.

Diouf, Sylviane. *Servants of Allah: African Muslims Enslaved in the Americas*. New York: New York University Press, 1998.

Dorman, Jacob. *The Princess and the Prophet: The Secret History of Magic, Race, and Moorish Muslims in America*. New York: Beacon, 2020.

Edsall, Thomas Byrne, and Mary D. Edsall. *Chain Reaction: The Impact of Race, Rights, and Taxes on American Politics*. New York: W. W. Norton & Company, 1992.

Edwards, Brent Hayes. *The Practice of Diaspora: Literature, Translation, and the Rise of Black Internationalism*. Cambridge, MA: Harvard University Press, 2003.

Elfbein, Jessica I., Thomas L. Hallowak, and Elizabeth M. Nix, eds. *Baltimore '68: Riots and Rebirth in an American City*. Philadelphia: Temple University Press, 2011.

Emerson, Rupert. *From Empire to Nation: The Rise to Self-Assertion of Asian and African Peoples*. Cambridge, MA: Harvard University Press, 1960.

Esposito, John L., ed. *The Oxford Dictionary of Islam*. New York: Oxford University Press, 2003.

Evanzz, Karl. *The Messenger: The Rise and Fall of Elijah Muhammad*. New York: Vintage, 2001.

Fanon, Franz. *Wretched of the Earth*. New York: Grove Press, 1963.

Felber, Garrett. *Those Who Know Don't Say: The Nation of Islam, the Black Freedom Movement, and the Carceral State*. Chapel Hill: The University of North Carolina Press, 2020.

Flamm, Michael. *In the Heat of the Summer: The New York Riots of 1964 and the War on Crime*. Philadelphia: University of Pennsylvania Press, 2017.

———. *Law and Order: Street Crime, Civil Unrest, and the Crisis of Liberalism in the 1960s*. New York: Columbia University Press, 2007.

Forman, James. *Locking Up Our Own: Crime and Punishment in Black America*. New York: Farrar, Strauss & Giroux, 2017.

Foucault, Michel. *Discipline and Punish: The Birth of the Prison*. Translated by Alan Sheridan. New York: Vintage, 1995.

Frankel, Henry R. *The Continental Drift Controversy: Volume 1: Wegener and the Early Debate*. Cambridge, UK: Cambridge University Press, 2012.

Fraser-Rahim, Muhammad. *America's Other Muslims: Imam W. D. Mohammed, Islamic Reform, and the Making of American Islam*. Lanham, MD: Lexington Books, 2020.

Friedmann, Yohanan. *Prophecy Continuous: Aspects of Ahmadi Religious Thought and Its Medieval Background*. Berkeley: University of California Press, 1989.

Gardell, Mattias. *In the Name of Elijah Muhammad: Louis Farrakhan and the Nation of Islam*. Durham, NC: Duke University Press, 1996.

Gerard, Emmanuel, and Bruce Kuklick. *Death in the Congo: Murdering Patrice Lumumba*. Cambridge, MA: Harvard University Press, 2015.

GhaneaBassiri, Kambiz. *A History of Islam in America*. New York: Cambridge University Press, 2010.

Gibson, Dawn Marie. *A History of the Nation of Islam: Race, Islam, and the Quest for Freedom*. Santa Barbara, CA: ABC-CLIO, 2012.

Gilmore, Ruth Wilson. *Golden Gulag: Prisons, Surplus, Crisis, and Opposition in Globalizing California*. Berkeley: University of California Press, 2007.

Gilroy, Paul. *The Black Atlantic: Modernity and Double Consciousness*. Cambridge, MA: Harvard University Press, 1993.

Gomez, Michael. *Black Crescent: The Experience and Legacy of African Muslims in the Americas*. New York: Cambridge University Press, 2005.

———. *Exchanging Our Country Marks: The Transformation of Identities in the Colonial and Antebellum South*. Chapel Hill: The University of North Carolina Press, 1997.

Gordon, Edmund T. *Disparate Diasporas: Identity and Politics in an African Nicaraguan Community*. Austin: University of Texas Press, 1998.

Grant, Colin. *Negro with a Hat: The Rise and Fall of Marcus Garvey and His Dream of Mother Africa*. Oxford: Oxford University Press, 2008.

Green, Nile. *Terrains of Exchange: Religious Economies of Modern Islam*. New York: Oxford University Press, 2014.

Greene, Mott T. *Alfred Wegener: Science, Exploration, and the Theory of Continental Drift*. Baltimore: Johns Hopkins University Press, 2015.

Greewal, Zareena. *Islam Is a Foreign Country: American Muslims and the Global Crisis of Authority*. New York: New York University Press, 2013.

Gualtieri, Sarah. *Between Arab and White: Race and Ethnicity in the Early Syrian American Diaspora*. Berkeley: University of California Press, 2009.

Haddad, John Rogers. *Cultures Colliding: American Missionaries, Chinese Resistance, and the Rise of Modern Institutions in China*. Philadelphia: University of Pennsylvania Press, 2023.

Haddad, Yvonne, and Jane Smith. *Mission to America: Five Islamic Sectarian Communities in North America*. Gainesville: University Press of Florida, 1993.

Hall, Simon. *Ten Days in Harlem: Fidel Castro and the Making of the 1960s*. New York: Faber & Faber, 2020. Kindle.

Haney-López, Ian. *White by Law: The Legal Construction of Race*. New York: New York University Press, 1996.

Hardiman, David, ed. *Healing Bodies, Saving Souls: Medical Missions in Asia and Africa*. Amsterdam: Editions Rodopi B.V., 2006.

Hiney, Tom. *On the Missionary Trail: A Journey through Polynesia, Asia, and Africa with the London Missionary Society*. New York: Grove Press, 2000.

Hinton, Elizabeth. *America on Fire: The Untold History of Police Violence and Black Rebellion in the 1960s*. New York: Liveright Publishing, 2021.

———. *From the War on Poverty to the War on Crime: The Making of Mass Incarceration in America*. Cambridge, MA: Harvard University Press, 2017.

Hodgson, Eva. *A Storm in a Teacup: The 1959 Bermuda Theatre Boycott and Its Aftermath*. 3rd ed. Warwick, Bermuda: Atlantic Publishing House, 2009.

Horne, Gerald. *Facing the Rising Sun: African Americans, Japan, and the Rise of Afro-Asia in Solidarity*. New York: New York University Press, 2018.

Hourani, Albert. *Arabic Thought in the Liberal Age, 1738–1939*. Cambridge, UK: Cambridge University Press, 1962.

Hoyland, Robert G. *In God's Path: The Arab Conquests and the Creation of an Islamic Empire*. New York: Oxford University Press, 2015.

Jackson, Sherman. *Islam and the Blackamerican: Looking toward the Third Resurrection*. New York: Oxford University Press, 2005.

Jeffries, Bayinnah. *A Nation Can Rise No Higher Than Its Women: African American Muslim Women in the Movement for Black Self-Determination, 1950–1975*. Lanham, MD: Lexington Books, 2014.

Kelley, Robin D. G. *Freedom Dreams: The Black Radical Imagination*. New York: Beacon, 2002.

Khan, Aisha, ed. *Islam in the Americas*. Gainesville: University Press of Florida, 2015.

Kurzman, Charles, ed. *Modernist Islam, 1840–1940: A Sourcebook*. New York: Oxford University Press, 2002.

Kusmer, Kenneth. *A Ghetto Takes Shape: Black Cleveland, 1870–1930*. Urbana-Champaign: University of Illinois Press, 1978.

Lee, Erika. *At America's Gates: Chinese Immigration during the Exclusion Era, 1882–1943*. Chapel Hill: The University of North Carolina Press, 2003.

Lee, Martha F. *Nation of Islam: An American Millenarian Movement*. Lewiston, NY: E. Mellen Press, 1988.

Levy, Peter B. *The Great Uprising: Race Riots in Urban America during the 1960s*. New York: Cambridge University Press, 2018.

Lubin, Alex. *Geographies of Liberation: The Making of an Afro-Arab Political Imaginary*. Chapel Hill: The University of North Carolina Press, 2014.

Makalani, Minkah. *In the Cause of Freedom: Radical Black Internationalism from Harlem to London, 1917–1939*. Chapel Hill: The University of North Carolina Press, 2011.

Makalani, Minkah, and Davarian L. Baldwin, eds. *Escape from New York: The New Negro Renaissance beyond Harlem*. Minneapolis: University of Minnesota Press, 2013.

Marable, Manning. *Malcolm X: A Life of Reinvention*. New York: Penguin, 2012.
Markarian, Vania. *Uruguay 1968: Student Activism from Global Counterculture to Molotov Cocktails*. Berkeley: University of California Press, 2011.
Marks, Carole. *Farewell—We're Good and Gone: The Great Black Migration*. Bloomington: Indiana University Press, 1989.
Marsh, Clifton. *From Black Islam to Islam: The Transition from Separatism to Islam*. Lanham, MD: Lexington Books, 1984.
Martin, Tony. *Race First: The Ideological and Organization Struggles of Marcus Garvey and the Universal Negro Improvement Association*. Dover, MA: The Majority Press, 1976.
McCloud, Aminah Beverly. *African American Islam*. London: Routledge, 1994.
McKittrick, Katherine. *Demonic Grounds: Black Women and the Cartographies of Struggle*. Minneapolis: University of Minnesota Press, 2006.
Moreno, Paul D. *Black Americans and Organized Labor: A New History*. Baton Rouge: Louisiana State University Press, 2005.
Moses, Wilson Jeremiah. *Afrotopia: The Roots of African American Popular History*. Cambridge, UK: Cambridge University Press, 1998.
———. *The Golden Age of Black Nationalism, 1850–1925*. New York: Oxford University Press, 1978.
Muhammad, Elijah. *The Supreme Wisdom: Solution to the So-Called Negroes Problem*. 1st ed. Newport News, VA: The National Newport News and Commentator, 1957.
Mumford, Kevin. *Newark: A History of Race, Rights, and Riots in America*. New York: New York University Press, 2007.
Nelson, Cary, and Lawrence Grossberg, eds. *Marxism and the Recreation of Culture*. London: Macmillan, 1988.
Ngai, Mae. *Impossible Subjects: Illegal Aliens and the Making of Modern America*. Princeton, NJ: Princeton University Press, 2004.
Osman, Suleiman. *The Making of Brownstone Brooklyn: Gentrification and the Search for Authenticity in Postwar New York*. New York: Oxford University Press, 2011.
Packwood, Cyril Outerbridge. *Chained on the Rock: Slavery in Bermuda*. Hamilton, Bermuda: The Island Press, 1975.
Patterson, Thomas G. *Contesting Castro: The United States and the Triumph of the Cuban Revolution*. New York: Oxford University Press, 1995.
Philip, Ira A. *The History of the Bermuda Industrial Union*. Pembroke: Bermuda Press, 2003.
Pinkney, Alphonso. *Red, Black, and Green: Black Nationalism in the United States*. New York: Cambridge University Press, 1979.
Pirbhai, M. Reza. *Fatima Jinnah: Mother of the Nation*. Cambridge, UK: Cambridge University Press, 2017.
Plummer, Brenda Gayle. *In Search of Power: African Americans in the Era of Decolonization, 1956–1974*. New York: Cambridge University Press, 2013.
Robinson, David. *Muslim Societies in African History*. New York: Cambridge University Press, 2004.
Robinson, Michael F. *The Lost White Tribe: Explorers, Scientists, and the Theory That Changed a Continent*. New York: Oxford University Press, 2016.
Ross, Kristin. *May '68 and Its Afterlives*. Chicago: University of Chicago Press, 2002.

Schoult, Lars. *That Little Infernal Cuban Republic: The United States and the Cuban Revolution*. Chapel Hill: The University of North Carolina Press, 2009.

Schrader, Stuart. *Badges without Borders: How Global Counterinsurgency Transformed American Policing*. Chapel Hill: The University of North Carolina Press, 2019.

Sharkey, Heather, ed. *Cultural Conversions: Unexpected Consequences of Christian Missionary Encounters in the Middle East, Africa, and South Asia*. Syracuse: State University of New York Press, 2013.

Skæerlund Risager, Bjarke, Laurence Cox, and Sala Mohadesi, eds. *Voices of 1968: Documents from the Global North*. London: Pluto Press, 2018.

Springhall, John. *Decolonization Since 1945: The Collapse of European Overseas Empires*. New York: Palgrave, 2001.

Stoler, Ann Laura. *Along the Archival Grain: Epistemic Anxieties and Colonial Common Sense*. Princeton, NJ: Princeton University Press, 2009.

Swan, Quito. *Black Power in Bermuda: The Struggle for Decolonization*. New York: Palgrave Macmillan, 2009.

Tankard, Radell. *The Development of Islam in Bermuda*. Warwick, Bermuda: Educational & Inspirational Publishers, 2012.

Taylor, Keeanga-Yamhatta. *From BlackLivesMatter to Black Liberation*. New York: Haymarket Books, 2016.

Taylor, Ula. *The Promise of Patriarchy: Women and the Nation of Islam*. Chapel Hill: The University of North Carolina Press, 2017.

———. *The Veiled Garvey: The Life and Times of Amy Jacques Garvey*. Chapel Hill: The University of North Carolina Press, 2002.

Thompson, Heather Ann. *Blood in the Water: The Attica Prison Uprising of 1971 and Its Legacy*. New York: Pantheon, 2016.

Trouillot, Michel Rolph. *Silencing the Past: Power and the Production of History*. Boston: Beacon Press, 1995.

Tsant, Rachel, and Eric Taylor Woods, eds. *The Cultural Politics of Nationalism and Nation-Building*. London: Routledge, 2013.

Turner, Joyce Moore. *Caribbean Crusaders and the Harlem Renaissance*. Urbana-Champaign: University of Illinois Press, 2005.

Turner, Richard Brent. *Islam in the African American Experience*. Bloomington: Indiana University Press, 1997.

———. *Soundtrack to a Movement: African American Islam, Jazz, and Black Internationalism*. New York: New York University Press, 2021.

Van DeBurg, William L. *Modern Black Nationalism*. New York: New York University Press, 1997.

von Eschen, Penny. *Race against Empire: Black Americans and Anti-Colonialism*. Ithaca, NY: Cornell University Press, 1997.

Walker, Thomas W., ed. *Reagan Versus the Sandinistas*. Boulder, CO: Westview Press, 1987.

Watkins-Owens, Irma. *Blood Relations: Caribbean Immigrants and the Harlem Community, 1900–1930*. Indianapolis: Indiana University Press, 1995.

Weisenfeld, Judith. *New World A-Coming: Black Religion and Racial Identity during the Great Migration*. New York: New York University Press, 2017.

Wilford, Hugh. *America's Great Game: The CIA's Secret Arabists and the Shaping of the Modern Middle East*. New York: Basic Books, 2013.
Wilson, Peter Lamborn. *Sacred Drift: Essays on the Margins of Islam*. San Francisco: City Lights, 1993.
Zubok, Vladislav M. *A Failed Empire: The Soviet Union in the Cold War from Stalin to Gorbachev*. Chapel Hill: The University of North Carolina Press, 2007.

JOURNAL ARTICLES

Abou-El-Fadl, Reem. "Neutralism Made Positive: Egyptian Anti-Colonialism on the Road to Bandung." *British Journal of Middle Eastern Studies* 42, no. 2 (2015): 219–40.
Baig, Hamzah. "'Spirit in Opposition': Malcolm X and the Question of Palestine." *Social Text* 37, no. 3 (September 2019): 47–71.
Bailey, Kristian Davis. "Black-Palestinian Solidarity in the Ferguson-Gaza Era." *American Quarterly* 67, no. 4 (December 2015): 1017–26.
Bayoumi, Moustafa. "Racing Religion." *CR: The New Centennial Review* 6, no. 2 (Fall 2006): 267–93.
Beynon, Erdmann Doane. "The Voodoo Cult among Negro Migrants in Detroit." *American Journal of Sociology* 43, no. 6 (1938): 894–907.
Chakrabarty, Dipesh. "Postcoloniality and the Artifice of History: Who Speaks for 'Indian' Pasts?" *Representations* 37 (Winter 1992): 1–26.
Crowder, Ralph L. "Fidel Castro and Harlem: Political, Diplomatic, and Social Influences of the 1960 Visit to the Hotel Theresa." *Afro-Americans in New York Life and History* 24, no. 1 (January 31, 2000): 79.
Davis, David S. "The Production of Crime Policies." *Crime and Social Justice* 20 (1983): 121–37.
Diouf, Christophe. "The Cultural Resistance to Missionary Schools in Kenya: A Study of Ngugi Wa Thiong'o's *The River between* and *a Grain of Wheat*." *Journal of Pan-African Studies* 7, no. 7 (2014): 26–35.
Erakat, Noura. "Geographies of Intimacy: Contemporary Renewals of Black-Palestinian Solidarity." *American Quarterly* 72, no. 2 (June 2020): 471–96.
Fitzgerald, Tanya. "Jumping the Fences: Māori Women's Resistance to Missionary Schooling in Northern New Zealand." *Paedagogica Historica* 37, no. 1 (2001): 175–92.
Frazier, Taj Robeson. "Afro-Asia and Cold War Black Radicalism." *Socialism and Democracy* 25, no. 1 (March 2011): 257–65.
Freas, Erik. "Hajj Amin al-Husayni and the Haram al-Sharif: A Pan-Islamic or Palestinian Nationalist Cause?" *British Journal of Middle Eastern Studies* 39, no. 1 (2012): 19–51.
Hoganson, Kristin. "Cosmopolitan Domesticity: Importing the American Dream, 1865–1920." *American Historical Review* 107, no. 1 (February 2002): 55–83.
James, Leslie E. "'Playing the Russian Game': Black Radicalism, the Press, and Colonial Office Attempts to Control Anti-Colonialism in the Early Cold War, 1946–50." *Journal of Imperial and Commonwealth History* 43, no. 3 (2015): 509–34.
Lewis, Earl. "To Turn as on a Pivot: Writing African Americans into a History of Overlapping Diasporas." *American Historical Review* 100, no. 3 (June 1995): 765–87.
Maclin, Tracey. "*Terry v. Ohio*'s Fourth Amendment Legacy: Black Men and Police Discretion." *St. John's Law Review* 72, no. 3–4 (Summer–Fall 1998): 1271–1322.

McAffee, Thomas B. "Setting Us Up for Disaster: The Supreme Court's Decision in *Terry v. Ohio*." *University of Nevada Law Review* 12, no. 3 (2012): 609–25.

McDuffie, Erik S. "Chicago, Garveyism, and the History of the Diasporic Midwest." *African and Black Diaspora: An International Journal* 8, no. 2 (2015): 129–45.

Morgan, Alaina M. "Historical *Sankofa*: On Understanding Violence in the Present through the African Diasporic Past." *Modern Intellectual History* 20 (2023): 582–91.

Murch, Donna. "Crack in Los Angeles: Crisis, Militarization, and Black Response to the Late Twentieth-Century War on Drugs." *Journal of American History* 102, no. 1 (June 2015): 162–73.

Nawaz, Mohammad. "Afro-Asians and the United Nations." *Pakistan Horizon* 15, no. 1 (First Quarter 1962): 42–48.

Roberts, Nicholas E. "Making Jerusalem the Centre of the Muslim World: Pan-Islam and the World Islamic Congress of 1931." *Contemporary Levant* 4, no. 1 (2019): 52–63.

Sultana, Farhat. "Ethnicity and Healing Rituals in Gwadar, Balochistan, Pakistan." *Journal of the Middle East and Africa* 4, no. 2 (2013): 169–85.

Thomas, Deborah. "Rastafari, Communism, and Surveillance in Late Colonial Jamaica." *Small Axe* 21, no. 3 (November 2017): 63–84.

Thompson, Heather Ann. "Why Mass Incarceration Matters: Rethinking Crisis, Decline, and Democracy." *Journal of American History* 97, no. 3 (2010): 703–34.

White, Bob. "Talk about School: Educational and the Colonial Project in French and British Africa (1860–1960)." *Comparative Education* 32, no. 1 (March 1996): 9–25.

Wilson, Jamie J. "'Come Down off the Cross and Get under the Crescent': The Newspaper Columns of Elijah Muhammad and Malcolm X." *Biography* 36, no. 3 (Summer 2013): 494–506.

Index

Italic page numbers refer to illustrations.

Abdul-Hadee, Ameenah, 149, 155
ibn-Abdullah, Muhammad (Prophet Muhammad), 11, 26, 33, 48, 58, 85, 143, 191
Abyssinian Baptist Church, 75, 221n9
Abundant Life Clinic, 185, 186, 187, 189
activism: anticolonial, 15, 64–65, 136, 144–50; anti-drug, 162–63; 183–87, 189; and Bermudian independence, 120, 121–24, 125, 134,154; contemporary, 197–99; educational, 134, 144–50; and labor radicalism, 121–24; of NOI members, 14–15, 134, 136, 144, 161; NOI membership, impact on, 135, 137, 139; and Palestine, 196, 197–200; in prison, 119, 173–77; and students, 199–200; and uprisings, 123–24; use of violence in, 123, 127, 130, 133; and voting rights, 117–18; and women, 132–34, 135, 144–52–155. *See also* labor unions; Nation of Islam (NOI); voting rights
Africa: Noble Drew Ali and, 8; decolonization of, 77, 92; educational systems in, 139; Islam in, 3, 114, 139; Elijah Muhammad in, 70, 72; *Muhammad Speaks*, 90–91, 92, 101, 161–62; proposed recolonization of, 40, 91; Malcolm X in, 79–80
Africa Freedom Day, 86
Africa House, 75
African-Asian World (magazine), 69
African Times and Orient Review (periodical), 25
Afro-Asia: and Bandung, 45, 50, 60, 72; Black solidarity with, 66–67, 78–87, 92; and Cold War and, 56, 61, 74; and decolonization, 66, 74; and Garveyism, 27; and MSTA, 29, 30; and Muslim world, 56; and NOI, 44, 50, 66, 78, 87, 90, 92; and politics, 56, 66, 72–73, 74; and the Third World, 60; United Nations bloc, 73, 74, 89. *See also* Atlantic Crescent; Bandung Conference (1955); Cold War; Garvey, Marcus Mosiah; geography; identity formation; Moorish Science Temple of America (MSTA); Nation of Islam (NOI); Third World; X, Malcolm
Afro-Asian People's Solidarity Conference (1957), 75
Afro-Caribbean immigration, 5, 24, 25, 105, 193. *See also* immigration
Ahmad, A. Mirza (F. L. Andersen), 37
Ahmad, Hazrat Mirza Ghulam, 32–33, 41, 141. *See also* Ahmadiyya Movement in Islam (AMI)
Ahmad, Yusuf, 78
Ahmadiyya Movement in Islam (AMI), 11, 27, 31–43; and anticolonialism, 40, 41; in Bermuda, 116; and Black communities, 27, 39; as Black movement, 43–44; in Britain, 41; on British presence in India, 41; founding of, 32–33; goals of, 33; missionary efforts, 19, 35–36; *Moslem Sunrise* (newspaper), 20, 33–35, 36, 41, 43, 34; as multiracial movement, 43; Abdul Basit Naeem's views on, 58; and proselytization, 19, 27, 32–33, 36–39, 38; and Muhammad Sadiq, 19, 32–34; and UNIA alliance, 40. *See also* Bermuda; missionary work; *The Moslem Sunrise* (AMI newspaper); Sadiq, Muhammad; Universal Negro Improvement Association (UNIA)
Ahmed, Abu (James Harvey Thomas), 126

AIDS epidemic, 174–75
Al-Barahin-al-Ahmadiyya (Ahmad), 33
Alexander, Sandford, 91
Algeria, 60, 69, 92; US policy on, 60
Ali, Ashmead, 144
Ali, Dusé Mohamed, 25, 26, 27, 30
Ali, Noble Drew, 8, 194; Canaanite Temple (Newark, NJ), 22–24; in Chicago, 28; death of, 44; early life, 23; Marcus Mosiah Garvey and, 24, 26, 28; Islamic theology of, 28–31; in Newark, 23; potential aliases, 22–23; relationships with South Asian and Arab immigrants, 23. *See also* Moorish Science Temple of America (MSTA); Universal Negro Improvement Association (UNIA)
"Allah-Hu-Akbar" (song), 26
Alwan, Mahmoud, 76–77. *See also* Islamic and African Institute (Philadelphia)
American Friends of the Middle East (AFME), 57–58
Amexem, 8, 30–31; and alternative geographies and, 8; and Asiatics, 22. *See also* geography; Moorish Science Temple of America (MSTA); Pangaea
Andersen, F. L. (A. Mirza Ahmad), 37
Anderson, Jonny, 174
Armstrong, Louis, 76
'asabiyah (local or tribal community), 9, 10, 89
Asbury Park, NJ, 24
Ashwood, Amy, 6
Asiatic identity: Noble Drew Ali and Asiatic worlds, 22, 30–31; "Asiatics of America," 22, 29; Asiatic Black Man, 50; NOI teachings on, 47. *See also* Afro-Asia; geography; identity formation; Nation of Islam (NOI)
Atlantic Crescent, 3, 9, 43–44, 62, 73, 89, 102, 104, 105, 107, 163; and Afro-Asia, 46; and diaspora, 20–22; and non-Muslims, 56, 89–90, 165
atomic weapons, 97–98
The Autobiography of Malcolm X (X), 133
Al-Azhar University, 79

Bahamas, 93
Bahar, Pauline, 51, 53
Bandung Conference (1955), 45, 50, 59–60, 61, 72; engagement of by Black people, 67, 68
Barbados, 122
Barge, Tomas, 165
Bassett, John Hilton "Bobbie," Jr., 127–28, 132, 136. *See also* Black Beret Cadre (BBC)
Bassett Building, Hamilton, Bermuda, 128–30, 129. *See also* Bermuda; Black Beret Cadre (BBC); Nation of Islam (NOI)
Batista, Fulgencio, 94
Ben Bella, Ahmed, 81
Belgium, 91
Ben Khedda, Ben Youssef, 92
Bengalee, Sufi Mutuir Rahman, 43. *See also* Ahmadiyya Movement in Islam (AMI)
Bennett, William, 184
Bermuda, 101; and AMI, 116; Anglican Church in, 115; Black Beret Cadre (BBC), 127–34; Black Power movement, 124–27; boycotts and strikes in, 116, 130, 231n28; Christianity in, 149; civil rights in, 115; and cruise ships, 111, 112; and decolonization, 112–13; Floral Pageant Uprisings, 123–24; Foreign Commonwealth Office (FCO), 116, 124, 125; history and geography of, 105–6, 111, 114, 136–37; Human Rights Commission, 151, 152, 154; Islam in, 114–19; Islam and revolution in, 135–36; labor movements in, 122–23; Ministry of Education, 150–52; and *Muhammad Speaks*, 111–14, 116, 119, 120–21, 122, 123, 124, 125, 135; Muslim parochial schools in, 138–41, 146–147; 150–52, 153–55, 155–57; and NOI influence, 113–14, 119–24, 131, 138; political parties in, 117–18; Prohibited Publications Act, 112, 120; racial hierarchies in, 130, 133; Schools Act (1926), 146–47; voting rights in, 117; Wooding Commission, 125. *See also* Ahmadiyya Movement

in Islam (AMI); Black Beret Cadre (BBC); labor unions; Masjid Muhammad Sunni community, Bermuda; *Muhammad Speaks* (NOI newspaper); Nation of Islam (NOI)
Bermuda Dock Workers Union (BDWU), 122–23. *See also* labor unions
Bermuda Industrial Union (BIU), 115, 122. *See also* labor unions
Bermuda Recorder (newspaper), 118
Bermuda Sun (newspaper), 152
Bermuda United Workers Party (BUWP), 117–18. *See also* labor unions
Beynon, Erdmann Doane, 48, 215n3
Bight of Benin, 3
Bilalian News (WCIW newspaper), 137, 142; circulation statistics, 143
Black Beret Cadre (BBC), 103, 127–34; persecution of, 136
Black homeland, 90, 91–92, 106
Black Islam: and agency for Black migrants, 4–5; and Black nationalism, 5–6; and Garveyism, 5–6; history and overview of, 3–7; and imperial resistance, 7–9, 163; as radical, 7, 43. *See also* Ahmadiyya Movement in Islam (AMI); Garvey, Marcus; Islam; Great Migration; Moorish Science Temple of America (MSTA); Muhammad, Elijah; Nation of Islam (NOI); Universal Negro Improvement Association (UNIA); X, Malcolm
Black Lives Matter movement, 197, 198
Black nationalism, 5–6, 20, 25–26, 30, 44; in Bermuda, 113; in West Indies, 25
Black Panther Party (BPP): Black Beret Cadre (BBC), 103, 127–34; in United States, 128–30
Black populations, racial origins: Noble Drew Ali's framework, 22, 29–30, 47; Asiatic Tribe theories, 47
Black Power: and anticolonialism, 125–27; 128; and colonial backlash, 126–127; and NOI, 126, 127, 128. *See also* Black Beret Cadre (BBC)
Black Power Conference (1969), 125–27

Black supremacy: Malcolm X on, 80; NOI on, 82
Bourguiba, Habib, 68
Boycott, Divestment, and Sanctions Movement, 197
Briggs, Cyril, 6
Brister, Walter (Noble Drew Ali), 23. *See also* Ali, Noble Drew
British Guiana (Guyana), 122
Bronzeville neighborhood (Chicago), 7, 20. *See also* Chicago, IL
Brown, Michael, 195
Brown, Roosevelt, 117, 125–26, 131. *See also* Committee for Universal Adult Suffrage (CUAS); Progressive Labour Party (PLP)
Browne, Lois, 112
Burchall, Carlton, 122–23, 131
Burrows, Erskine "Buck," 136
Bush, George H. W., 168, 171–72, 182, 196
Butler, Eugene 12X, 179

Cairo Conference (1957), 75
Canaan, 29
Canaanite Temple (Newark, NJ), 22, 24, 26, 194
Caribbean: and Black Islam, 6; independence movements in, 93, 164; NOI and, 163–71, 182. *See also* Bermuda; *Final Call* (NOI newspaper)
Carr, Denzel (Abdullah Omar), 37
Castle Muhammad, Kenneth, 120, 122–23, 131
Castro, Fidel, 93, 94–95; and Malcolm X, 95–97, 96; Marxism in Cuba, 98–99
Cedar Rapids, IA, 45, 54, 56, 57
Chauvin, Derek, 198
Chicago, IL: Black migrant communities in, 20; Bronzeville neighborhood, 7, 20; and MSTA, 28; Muslim migration to, 36; radical movements in, 115–16; Temple No. 2 in, 51; UNIA chapters in, 28
Chicago American (newspaper), 87
Chicago Defender (newspaper), 28, 54
Chicago Herald & Examiner (newspaper), 40
China, 100

264 Index

Christianity: as antidemocratic, 60; in Bermuda, 149; in Caribbean, 93; Christian propaganda, 66; condemnation of, 39; and control of enslaved populations, 3–4; and racism, 77; segregation within, 39; and white supremacy, 4
CIA (Central Intelligence Agency): Office of Policy Coordination, 57–58
The Circle Seven Koran (Ali), 28, 29, 31
civil rights movement, 100, 115, 119, 124, 177, 199
Clara Mohammed Schools, 156
Clara Muhammad-Bermuda Muslim School, 139–41, 148–49, 152–55; curriculum development for, 155–57
Cobb, Ty, 32
Cold War, 1, 53, 56, 58, 59, 74, 95, 105, 161–62. *See also* empire
Colombia, 25
colonialism: AMI as response to, 33; drugs as tool of, 183–84, 185–86; and education, 139–40; and Palestine, 198; resistance to, 192; spiritual colonization of North America, 35
Committee for Universal Adult Suffrage (CUAS), 117. *See also* Brown, Roosevelt
Congo, 90–91, 97
Costa Rica, 25
Cox, William, 148, 151, 152, 154
crack cocaine crisis, 177–79, 180–81. *See also* drug crisis; War on Drugs
Crawford, H. R., 185
crescent (symbol of Islam), 9, 22, 27, 159, 186
criminalization of urban space, 159, 160–61. *See also* War on Drugs
Crummell, Alexander, 30
Cuba, 1, 93, 94, 97–98, 98–100; Cuban Revolution, 98. *See also* Castro, Fidel
Cuomo, Mario, 181–82
Curry, Lamont X., 178–79

Dalil, Mustafa, 76
Dawud, Talib, 76, 85; assault on, 86; international travels (1959), 81; lawsuit against Elijah Muhammad, 84; on Muslim Brotherhood, 78; on NOI, 83–84; use of print media, 76, 81, 83, 193; on racial equality, 77. *See also* Muslim Brotherhood USA
décalage (concept), 9
decolonization, 14, 66, 89–90; and African American sovereignty, 92; in Bermuda, 106, 114; Islam's role in, 45–46, 58, 66, 75, 113
Department of Housing and Urban Development (HUD), 188–89. *See also* Dopebusters
Detroit, MI: Black Bottom neighborhood, 7; Black neighborhoods in, 47, 215–16n16; police surveillance of NOI in, 51. *See also* Great Migration; Nation of Islam (NOI)
Diab, Jamal, 62, 83
diaspora: Afro-Caribbean, 67–68; African, 49; connections, 2, 58; "overlapping diasporas," 5–7, 9, 44, 47, 105, 192; South Asian, 6–7, 49. *See also* Great Migration; immigration
Din, Maulvi Muhammad, 40–43
Divest from Death, 199–200
Dock Strike of 1959 (Bermuda), 116
Dodd, Wallace, 49. *See also* Fard Muhammad, W. D.
Dopebusters, 159, 162–63, 184–88; Department of Housing and Urban Development (HUD) and, 188–89. *See also Final Call* (NOI newspaper); War on Drugs
Dowling, Norwood X (Norwood Salaam), 120
draft (Selective Service Act registration), 51–52
Drew, Timothy, 22. *See also* Ali, Noble Drew
drug crisis, 159–63. *See also* crack cocaine crisis; War on Drugs
DuBois, W. E. B., 6, 30, 67
Duckett, George, 136

Ecuador, 25
education: in British Empire, 139–40; in colonial Bermuda, 139–40; Islamic curricula, 155–57; Islamic education and

"God-consciousness," 148; and missionaries, 32; Muslim parochial schools in Bermuda, 138–41; University of Islam parochial schools, 51, 146–47. *See also* Clara Muhammad-Bermuda Muslim School
Eleta Almarán, Carlos, 171
Ellington, Duke, 76
empire: American, 1–3, 43–44, 145, 160; British, 1, 25, 33 43–44, 139–40; and Cold War, 1, 105; European, 33, 53, 56, 92; Islamic, 35; Garvey on, 25; Muslim resistance to, 43–44, 139–40; visual representations of, 1–2. *See also* activism; Garvey, Marcus Mosiah; *Muhammad Speaks* (NOI newspaper)
Endara, Guillermo, 170–71
enslaved people: Christianity and control of, 3–4; defenders of, 30; Islam and, 3; legacy of in Cuba, 98–99; Middle Passage, 3; and religious practice in Bermuda, 114; slave trade in Bermuda, 114–15. *See also* Islam; Middle Passage
Exchange Club (Grand Haven, MI), 32
Ezekiel's Wheel (NOI teaching), 48, 52. *See also* Mother Plane

Faisal, Sheikh Daoud, 45, 61–62. *See also* Islamic Mission of America
Fanon, Frantz, 133, 139–40. *See also Wretched of the Earth* (Fanon)
Fard, Beatrice, 49
Fard, Wallace Dodd. (W. D. Fard Muhammad), 48, 49
Fard, Zared, 49
Fard Muhammad, W. D., 44, 47; aliases, 48, 215n3; background and origins, 48–50, 216n18; and converts, 44, 48, 50–51; and Pakistan, 49; parentage of, 49; Saudi identity of, 49; teachings of, 47–48, 66; and women, 44, 47, 50
Farr, George (W. D. Fard Muhammad), 48
Farrakhan, Louis, 8, 103–4, 137, 160; and Abundant Life Clinic, 185; and Circum-Caribbean outreach, 163–71; on Gaza (2014), 196–97; on genocide against Black community, 180–81; and NOI reestablishment, 161, 163; political alliances of, 162; Saviour's Day (2024), 200; recording of "A White Man's Heaven is a Black Man's Hell," 117
Fazl-ur-Rahman Ansari, Muhammad, 84
Federal Bureau of Investigation (FBI), 52, 53
Ferguson, MO, 195–97
Final Call (NOI newspaper), 160, 162, 164–65, 166, 168–69; "Black Nation behind Bars," 173–76; on crack crisis, 178–79, 181; on Dopebusters, 187–88; on Gaza, 200–201; on Nicaragua, 179–80; on Panama, 170–71
Floral Pageant Uprisings (Bermuda), 123–24
Floyd, George, 198
Fonseca, Carlos, 165
Ford, Arnold Josiah, 26–27
Fourth Amendment, 172
Framingham, MA correctional facility, 176
French, Glenn, 185
Fruit of Islam (FOI), 1, 88, 132, 159, 162–63, 184, 186–87, 188–89. *See also* Dopebusters

Gambia, 3, 114
Garner, Eric, 196
Garvey, Marcus Mosiah, 5–6, 20, 25, 44, 67, 73; and Afro-Asia, 27; and Dusé Mohamed Ali, 25, 26; and black nationalism, 5, 25; in Harlem, 25; goals of, 26; imprisonment of, 27, 28; on Islam, 26; and labor organizing, 25; in London, 25; and *Negro World*, 25; on Pan-Africanism, 25; publishing, 25; and UNIA, 25–26. *See also* Garveyism; Universal Negro Improvement Association (UNIA)
Garveyism, 6, 20, 24–28. *See also* Garvey, Marcus Mosiah; Universal Negro Improvement Association (UNIA)
Gaza Strip, Palestine, 195, 196–97, 199–200
gender: gender politics, 7; "manhood and womanhood training," 185; and modest clothing, 83, 138, 150; in NOI, 7, 48, 134, 135, 176. *See also* modesty; women

General Civilization Classes (GCC), 135
genocide: in Algeria, 92; mass incarceration and drugs as, 174, 180–81, 189; and Palestine, 197, 199, 200–201
geography: Afro-Asia and, 31, 70, 74; alternative geographies, 3, 7–9, 30–31, 70, 93; and Atlantic Crescent, 43, 70, 89, 167; of imperial resistance, 8, 10, 12, 22, 70, 93, 161, 162, 173; and *Final Call*, 162, 163, 167, 173; and Islam, 8–9, 88, 113; and *Muhammad Speaks*, 88, 89, 92. 113, 161; and the Third World, 88, 162. *See also* Atlantic Crescent; Black Islam; map; Third World; ummah
Ghana, 3, 198
Gibson, Ernest, 185
Gillespie, Dizzy, 76
"God Bless Our President" (song), 26
"God's Angry Men" column *(New York Amsterdam News)*, 74, 78
Gold Coast, 3
Gottschalk, Arthur, 84
Goula, Ibrahim (Sayeed Ramadan), 115
Grand Haven, MI, 31–32
Great Migration, 4, 20, 46, 50, 192; in Chicago, IL, 115; in Detroit, MI, 47; in New York, 24, 68; in Newark, NJ, 23–25
Grenada, 93, 167
Guinea Coast, 114

Hajj (pillar of Islam), 223n34, 224n54; Elijah Muhammad's attempt to make, 79, 86; and Malcolm X, 80
Ham (Old Testament), 29–30
Hamas (Islamic Resistance Movement), 195
Hamitic curse, 30; reframing of, 30; and slavery, 30
Harlem, NY: Abyssinian Baptist Church, 75; crack crisis in, 178–79; as cultural and intellectual center, 67–68; Hotel Theresa, 68, 94–95, 96; Temple No. 7 in, 104, 134; United Nations General Assembly, 94
Harrison, Hubert, 6, 67

The Hate That Hate Produced (television investigation), 80, 83, 87
Highland Park, MI, 33, 36
Hill, Milton, 111–12, 120, 130–31, 133
Hilton G. Hill travel agency, 72
HIV and AIDS, 174–75
Ho, Chi Minh, 56
Hoffman, Edith, 40
Hoffman, John, 32
The Holy Koran of the Moorish Science Temple of America (Ali), 28
Honduras, 25
Horsa (Great Dane), 136
Hotel Theresa (Harlem), 68, 94–95, 96
housing projects, 15; Mayfair Mansions (Washington, DC), 159–60, 184–87; NOI security contracts in, 188; Ocean Towers (New York), 188. *See also* Mayfair Mansions housing project; Ocean Towers housing project
Howard, Charles, 98, 99–100
Hunt, Robert, 135
Hurston, Zora Neale, 67
al-Husseini, Haj Amin, 81

identity formation: American, 142; *'asabiyah* and *ummah*, 10, 52; Asiatic, 22; Atlantic Crescent and, 9, 45; Bermudian, 144, 157; citizenship and, 52, 143; diasporic identities, 9, 45, 46, 62, 77, 133; Muslim, 9, 22, 29, 73, 138–39, 143, 157, 191; of NOI, 48, 88–89, 136; and racial violence, 4; religio-political, 10, 104, 136; religio-racial, 5, 9, 22, 30, 43, 52, 73, 121, 140, 157; renaming and, 22; in South Asian communities, 24; and the Third World, 46, 60
"I Have a Dream" (speech), 132
Ikwan al-Muslimun (Muslim Brotherhood), 77
immigration: from British India, 20; from Caribbean region, 5, 20, 24, 67; from Europe, 5, 6–7; Immigration and Naturalization Service (INS), 19; quota systems, 6–7; restrictions on Asian

immigration, 6–7; South Asian immigrants, 19, 31; US resistance to, 19
imperialism: neo-imperialism, 2, 15, 106, 160, 162, 166–67; resistance to, 43–44, 89
incarceration: "carceral state," 159–60, 178, 240n7; crisis of in Black community, 173–77; in United States, 159–60
India: British rule of, 33; immigration from, 6–7
Indonesia, 53; Indonesian Muslims in Bermuda, 143
Intellectualism: in Black communities, 5, 6, 67–68; at grassroots level, 10; and internationalism, 6, 10, 11; and radicalism, 6; as result of diaspora, 5, 6, 67–68
Iranian Revolution (1979), 164
Islam: adaptability of, 11, 58; in Africa, 3, 64, 114; and alternative geographies, 8–9; among enslaved people, 3; as anticolonial mechanism, 42, 60, 62, 64, 105; and Black liberation, 40, 45; as Black religion, 5, 26, 27, 29, 31, 39, 40, 64, 66; and conservatism, 7, 73; and gender, 48; and Garveyism, 5–6; and Great Migration, 4; Islamic curriculum, 155–57; and masculinity, 48; and modernism, 141; and particularism, 11, 24, 36, 47, 50, 116; pillars of, 3, 64, 223n34; in prisons, 173–77; and religious education, 134, 155–57; Sunni Islam, 11, 62, 141; ummah (universal Muslim community), 8–9, 39, 47, 52, 66, 72, 89; and unification of Black populations, 3, 27, 31, 194–95; and views on race, 41, 77; vis-à-vis Christianity, 3–4, 4–5, 39, 60, 64, 66, 77; and women, 48, 64, 176–77. *See also* 'asabiyah; gender; geography; women; Sunni Islam; ummah
Islamic and African Institute (Philadelphia), 76–77
Islamic Center of Bermuda, 144
Islamic Education Conference (1992), 156
Islamic Mission of America, 45; *Madinat-asslam* (City of Peace), 61; and Abdul Basit Naeem, 45. *See also* Faisal, Sheikh Daoud

Islamic News (NOI magazine), 88
Israel, 195, 199–200; formation of, 198; Israeli Defense Forces, 195

Jack, Hulan, 78
Jacob, John, 181
Jamaica, 25, 93, 122; Marcus Garvey's work in, 25
Jamal, Ahmad, 78
James, C. L. R., 127
jam'iat-ul-falah (Society of Salvation), 55–56. *See also* Naeem, Abdul Basit.
Japan, 51, 52, 66, 74. *See also* Nation of Islam (NOI); Afro-Asia.
jazz music, 76
Jet (magazine), 84, 85
jihad: in Africa, 3; and antidrug activism, 160; of words, 35, 40, 59, 62, 138
Jim Crow era segregation, 5, 50, 92, 171, 176
Johnson, Susan, 176
Johnston, Albert, 122–23, 131
Jones, Claudia, 6
Jordan, 29

Karroub House (Highland Park, MI), 36
Kasa-Vubu, Joseph, 91
Kenya, 97; Kukuyu *Mau Mau* fighters, 56
Kenyatta, Jomo, 81
Khaldun, George, 103–4
Khaldun, Michelle, 103–4, 133–34
King, Martin Luther, Jr., 101, 117, 124, 132
Ku Klux Klan, 83

labor unions, 115; and NOI in Bermuda, 122–23
Ladgham, Bahi, 68
La Nación (newspaper), 25
La Prensa (newspaper), 25
Lateef, Yusuf, 76
"law and order" rhetoric, 168, 171–72. *See also* Bush, George H. W.; crack crisis; drug crisis; Reagan, Ronald; War on Drugs
Lawson, James R., 69, 75, 85, 94. *See also* United African Nationalist Movement (UANM)

Lebanon, 29
"Letter from Birmingham Jail" (King), 133
Liberia, 91
Locke, Alain, 67
Logan, James, 86
Lopes, Jacqui, 176
Los Angeles Evening Herald-Examiner (newspaper), 49
Los Angeles Herald-Dispatch (newspaper), 74, 87, 91
Los Angeles Police Department (LAPD), 200
Lowery, Jacob, 181
Lumumba, Patrice, 91, 227n99

Madinat-asslam (City of Peace), 61
Madyun, Arifah, 149
mahdi, 33, 35
Mahmud Ahmad, Mirza Bashirud-Din, 35
Majied, Eugene, 1, 101
Malcolm X Liberation School (Bermuda), 128
Mali, 92
Manley, Michael, 165
maps: alternative mapping, 1–3, 8–9; Mercator projection, 1
Mao, Zedong, 100
Martin, Trayvon, 196
Masjid al-Quba, 144
Masjid Muhammad Sunni community (Bermuda), 138–41, 144–47, 145, 147–48; and education, 149, 150–52; and NOI, 143
Matthews, Dilton, 115. *See also* Ramadan, Sayeed
Martonmere, Baron Lord (John Roland Robinson), 127
Mau Mau fighters (Kenya), 56. *See also* Kenya
Mayfair Mansions housing project (Washington, DC), 159–60, 184–87
McCants, Deborah, 176
McKay, Claude, 67
media: Black urban newspapers, 73–74; social, 197. *See also* names of individual publications

memory, 138, 141, 152, 154
Mercator projection, 1. *See also* maps
Message to the Blackman (Muhammad), 132
Messenger (NOI magazine), 88
Middle Passage, 3. *See also* enslaved people
Mid-Ocean News (newspaper), 152
migration: Caribbean, 5–6, 20, 24, 25; labor, 25; South Asian, 6–7, 23. *See also* Great Migration; immigration
"minority" (term), 8, 163
Miranda warnings, 172
missionary work: of AMI, 32; and Christianity, 32; and colonialism, 32; Islamic, 19, 32, 33, 55, 84
modesty, 83, 138, 150
Mohamet, Bilali, 23
Moorish Science Temple of America (MSTA), 6, 11, 21, 192; and Afro-Asia, 28; and Afro-Caribbean diaspora, 24–25; beliefs of, 22, 28–31; decline of, 44, 48; and Garveyism, 5–6, 25–26, 27; and NOI, 48; recruitment to, 27; and South Asian diaspora; and UNIA, 26, 48
Moslem Sunrise (AMI newspaper), 20, 33–35, 34, 36, 38, 41; resumption of (1930), 43; suspension of (1924), 42
Moslem World & the U.S.A. (periodical), 45, 46, 57–59, 60; circulation of, 58; and decolonization, 61; Islam in Africa, 65; Elijah Muhammad's columns in, 73–74; on NOI, 62–64; termination of, 69. *See also* Naeem, Abdul Basit
Mother Plane (NOI teaching), 48, 52. See also, Ezekiel's Wheel (NOI teaching)
Movement for Black Lives, 198
Mr. Muhammad (NOI magazine), 88
"Mr. Muhammad Speaks" column (*Pittsburgh Courier*), 74, 78
Muhammad, A. Alim, 159, 184, 186
Muhammad, 'Abd al-Haqq, 156
Muhammad, Abdul, 50
Muhammad, Akbar, 72, 79, 81–82
Muhammad, Clara, 50–51, 53, 72, 79, 81, 217n48; and leadership of the NOI, 53;

marriage to Elijah Muhammad, 50; transforming views on race, 50. *See also* gender; women

Muhammad, Elijah, 8, 45, 46, 81–82; arrest of (1942), 51; attacks on the Muslim Brotherhood USA, 85–86; and Black homeland movement, 90; and Cairo Conference, 75; on China, 100; death of, 103, 136–37; on Fard Muhammad's origins, 49; and Great Migration, 50; international travel (1959), 72, 81–83, 86–87, 223n36; lawsuit against using "Islam," 84; legacy and impact of, 197; and Mecca pilgrimage, 86–87, 89; media exposure in Black press, 73–78; *Moslem World* editorials, 63; NOI, leadership of, 50–53; on superiority of Black people, 77. *See also* Nation of Islam (NOI)

Muhammad, Herbert, 72, 79, 81–82; as *Muhammad Speaks*, editor, 91–92, 97–98

Muhammad, Naba'a, 201

Muhammad, Robert, *169*, *182*, 182

Muhammad, Umm Salamah, 135

Muhammad, Wali, 169–70, 181

Muhammad, Wallace, 15, 103, 104, 105, 137, 142, 143, 144. *See also* Warith Deen Muhammad, World Community of al-Islam in the West (WCIW)

Muhammad, Warith Deen, 8, 138–39, 141, 191. *See also* Wallace Muhammad; World Community of al-Islam in the West (WCIW)

Muhammad Speaks (NOI newspaper), 1, 88–90, 101; ban on in Bermuda, 120–21, *121*, 123, 124, 135; as *Bilalian News*, 137, 142; on Black separatism, 91–92; and cruise industry, 116, 120; on Cuba, 93, 97–98; on decolonization, 89, 90–91, 106, 161; distribution of in Bermuda, 116, 119–20; expansion of circulation, 101–2, 106; international outreach of, 101–2, 106; "The Muslim Program" section, 92–93; Abdul Basit Naeem's work with, 45, 70, 93

Muhammad Speaks to the Black Man (NOI magazine), 88

Muslim Brotherhood *(Ikwan al-Muslimun)*, 77

Muslim Brotherhood USA, 11, 76; in Bermuda, 116–17; and NOI, 84–86

Muslim Girls Training (MGT), 134, 135

Muslim Mosque, Inc., 100

Muslim Teachers College (VA), 156

Naeem, Abdul Basit, 45–47, *46*, 50, 54–56, *55*, 193; as ambassador and translator, 83, 89; and Bandung, 59–60; in Brooklyn (1956), 61; on Cold War, 59, 60; on colonialism, 58; and correspondence with Elijah Muhammad, 101; and Daoud alliance, 61–62; in Iowa, 56, 57, 58; and *Moslem World* (periodical), 56–59; and *Muhammad Speaks*, 70; and NOI, 63–64; as travel agent, 70, 72, 79; and UANM (United African Nationalist Movement), 69; on uplift, 64–66. *See also* Shalimar International Travel Agency

Naeem, Selma, 56

Naeem, Shahid, 55, 70

Naeem, Shereen, 55

Naeem, Zuleikha, 45–46, *46*, 55

Namibia, 92

Nasir, Dawud, 148, 149, 150–51, 152

Nasser, Gamal Abdel, 70, 75–76, 79

Nation of Islam (NOI), 11, 45–47; alternative geographies and, 1–3; in Afro-Asian world, 56–59, 66–67, 74; and anti-imperialism, 93–100, 162–63; Bandung-type conferences, 78–79; in Bermuda, 14, 126–27, 134, 135; and Black homeland movement, 90; Black nationalism and, 73; Black supremacy and, 88, 141–42; Black and white racial hierarchies, 47–48; on citizenship, 52; and communism in Bermuda, 117–18; criticism of, 80, 82–83, 87; early history of, 47–50; Louis Farrakhan and Wallace Muhammad conflict, 103–4; Louis Farrakhan, reestablishment by, 161; FBI raid and arrests, 51, 53–56,

Nation of Islam (NOI) (cont.)
217n49; identity formation and, 88–89; on internationalism, 89–90; as model for Bermudan revolutionary movement, 131; and *Moslem World* as publicity tool, 63; after Elijah Muhammad's death, 143; Elijah Muhammad's travels, 81–82, 87–88; and *Muhammad Speaks* (newspaper), 88–90; and Muslim Brotherhood USA, 84–86; and Abdul Basit Naeem, 62–67, 70–71; on police brutality, 160; and prayer instruction, 86–87; on racial solidarity, 52, 53–54; and Saudi Arabia, 48–49; Saviour's Day, 63, 64, 101, 136, 200; and Selective Service Act registration, 51–52; surveillance of by Detroit police, 51; teachings of, 73; texts of, 48; Temple No. 2 (Chicago), 51; Temple No. 7 (Harlem), 74, 104, 134; and UANM, 69; on War on Drugs, 183–87; "The World Serpent" map, 1–3, 2; Malcolm X's travels on behalf of, 79;

National Guard (US), 181–82. *See also* War on Drugs

nationalist and independence movements, 90, 92, 121–22, 161–62, 164; post–World War II, 53–54; and UANM (United African Nationalist Movement), 68–69. *See also* Afro-Asia

Nation of Islam Security Agency, 189

The Negro: Man or Myth? (pamphlet), 116–17

Negro World (UNIA newspaper), 25, 26, 40

Nehru, Jawaharlal, 69

neo-imperialism, 2, 15, 106, 160, 162, 166–67

Newark, NJ, 22, 23. *See also* Great Migration; Ali, Noble Drew

New Crusader (newspaper), 87; on NOI, 83–84

New York Amsterdam News (newspaper), 54, 74, 87, 90; "God's Angry Men" column, 74, 78; on Malcolm X's travels, 80

New York City: New York Police Department (NYPD), 74; United Nations Secretariat, 68. *See also* Harlem, New York

Ngileruma, Alhaji Muhammad, 70

Nicaragua, 25, 165–67; US embargo on, 166–67

Nigeria, 3, 92

Nkrumah, Kwame, 78

Noah (Old Testament), 29

Noriega, Manuel, 168–71, 181, 183. *See also* Panama

OAU League (Organisation of African Unity), 166

Ocean Monarch (cruise ship), 111, 112, 120

Ocean Towers housing project, 188

Omar, Abdullah (Denzel Carr), 37

O'Meally, J. A., 27, 40, 41

Operation Just Cause, 169, 171

Operation Protective Edge, 195, 200

Organization for American States (OAS), 171

Organization of Afro American Unity, 100, 101

Organization of American States, 97

Origins of the Continents and Oceans (Wegener), 31

Ortega, Daniel, 166, 167

Orthodox Brotherhood of Islam, 144

Owens, Major, 181–82

Pakistan, 54, 222n18; African-descended Muslims in, 49; W,D. Fard Muhammad's engagement with, 49

Palestine, 29, 195

Pan-Islamism, 25

Pan-Africanism, 6, 25, 30, 101, 113. *See also* Garveyism

Panama, 25, 26, 168–71, 181. *See also* internationalism; *Muhammad Speaks* (NOI newspaper), Noriega, Manuel

Pangaea, 30–31. See also Amexem

Pantaleo, Daniel, 196

Perinchief, Edna, 134

Perinchief, Gary, 111–12, 120–21, 134, 234–35n108

Perinchief, Wanda, 104, 134

Philadelphia, PA: Islamic and African Institute, 76–77; Mosque No. 12, 63

Philadelphia Detention Center (Gloucester, NJ), 19
Philip, Byron, 131, 135, 137, 146, 147
Pittsburgh Courier (newspaper), 54, 74, 76, 87, 90; "Mr. Muhammad Speaks" column, 74, 78; on NOI, 84; on Malcolm X's travels, 80
Point Pleasant, NJ, 24
policing, 159–60; militarized forces, 195–96. *See also* crack crisis; drug crisis; "law and order" rhetoric; War on Drugs
Pomares, German, 165
Powell, Adam Clayton, 74–75
Progressive Labour Party (PLP), 118, 123, 125, 131; Youth Wing of, 125, 126, 127, 131, 132, 133. *See also* Brown, Roosevelt; voting rights
Prophet Muhammad. See ibn-Abdullah, Muhammad

Qalandar, Lal Shahbaz, 49. *See also* Pakistan; Shabazz, Tribe of; Sufism
Queen of Bermuda (cruise ship), 119, 120
quiblah (wall niche), 26
Qur'an: in classroom, 139, 156; education on, 63–64

ibn-Rabhah, Bilal, 137
racial hierarchies: in Bermuda, 130, 133; and historical oppression, 191; in US South, 30
racism: and Christianity, 77; labor and exploitation of Black workers, 25; in segregated Christian churches, 39
Rainey, Alfonso Nelson (Talib Dawud), 76
Ramadan, Sayeed (Dilton Matthews), 115–16, 119, 131
Ramírez, Sergio, 166
Randolph, A. Philip, 6
Rasheed, Hajj, 76
Rasheed, Mustapha, 191, 194
Rastafarianism, 113
Reagan, Ronald, 159, 166, 168, 169, 169–70, 171–72, 182. *See also* War on Drugs

Rockefeller, Nelson, 172
Rogers, J. A., 76, 77, 78. *See also* Islamic and African Institute (Philadelphia)
Royal Gazette (newspaper), 119, 151, 152

El-Sadat, Anwar, 79
Sadiq, Muhammad, 19–22, 21, 27, 31–32, 35–36; and anticolonialism, 35; and Black communities, 20–21, 39; and Black political and religious activity, 39–40; in Chicago, IL, 20; on Christianity, 39; and experience of racism, 30–40; incarceration of, 19; and *Moslem Sunrise*, 20, 33–35; multiracial approach to *da'wah*, 19, 35, 36, 37; proselytization and *da'wah*, 19; on race, 20; and Universal Negro Improvement Association (UNIA), 20, 40. *See also* Ahmadiyya Movement in Islam (AMI); United Negro Improvement Association (UNIA)
Salaam (NOI magazine), 88
Salaam, Abdus, 20
Salaam, Liaquat Ali, 76
Salaam, Norwood (Norwood X Dowling), 120–21
Salaam, Safiyyah, 149, 154
Salaam International, 143
Sandinista National Liberation Front (FSLN), 165–67. *See also* Nicaragua
sankofa, 198–99
Santería religion, 99
Sapelo Island, Georgia, 4, 22–23
saraka, 4
Saud (king), 78
Seaga, Edward, 165
Sea Islands (GA and SC), 4, 22–23
Selassie, Haile, 81
Selective Service Act registration, 51–52. *See also* draft (Selective Service Act registration); World War II
Senegal, 3
Senegambia, 3
Serag, Issa, 70
el-Shabazz, Malik (Malcolm X), 79

Shabazz, Tribe of, 47, 49. *See also* Muhammad, W. D. Fard; Nation of Islam (NOI); Qalandar, Lal Shahbaz
Shakir, Amir, 152
Shakir, Cromwell, 148, 149, 152
Shakir, Zaheera, 150, 152, 153, 154–55
Shakir, Zakiyyah, 148, 154
Shalimar International travel agency, 70, 93
Shamsiddeen, Najiyyah, 132–33, 135
Sharples, John, 136
Sharrieff, Edna, 154
Sharrieff, Takbir, 151, 152
Sharwarbi, Youssef, 84, 225n69
Shawkat 'Ali, Maulana, 81
Sierra Leone, 3
Simmons, Ottiwell, Jr., 136
slavery. *See* enslaved people
Smith, James E., 175
Smith, Leonard, 27–28
Smith, William French, 173
social media, 197
Society of Salvation, 55–56. *See also jam'iat-ul-faluh*
Somoza Garcia, Anastasio, 165
Sotanki, Armmah (Noble Drew Ali), 23
South Asia: American fixation on, 23; culture of, 23; immigration from, 6–7; and racial identity in United States, 10, 23, 62; religion in, 23. *See also* immigration; Great Migration
Southern Christian Leadership Conference (SCLC), 181
Soviet Union, 161–62; Cuba's alignment with, 97–98; Muslims in, 57, 59; Abdul Basit Naeem on, 60–61; Third World resistance to, 56. *See also* Cold War
Staton, Dakota, 76, 77, 78, 83; *Jet* magazine feature on, 84, 85; on NOI, 84
Stoner, J. B., 83
Student Coalition Against Labor Exploitation (SCALE), 200
Student Nonviolent Coordinating Committee (SNCC), 198
Suez Canal, 69, 76, 80
Suleiman, Dr., 24

suffrage, 117. *See also* voting rights
Sufism, 49; representations of in American culture, 23
Sukarno (president of Indonesia), 53, 221n9
Sunni Islam, 84, 87, 137; Abdul Basit Naeem on, 58; in NOI, 104; and political participation, 144–50; and Sunnah observance, 191; transition to by NOI members, 138, 141–42, 143
The Supreme Wisdom: Solution to the So-Called Negroes' Problem (Muhammad), 63, 64, 87
Swan, John, 152, 154, 155

Tacklyn, Larry, 136
Taylor, Breonna, 198
Third World, 59–60, 66, 74, 160. *See also* Afro-Asia
Thomas, James Harvey (Abu Ahmed), 126
Thompson, Dorothy, 57–58
Touré, Sekou, 77, 86
Trenton State Prison (NJ), 174
Trinidad and Tobago, 93, 122
Tunisia, 68

ummah (universal Muslim community), 8–9, 10, 39, 47, 52, 66, 72, 89. *See also* 'asabiyah; georaphy; identity formation
umrah (lesser pilgrimage), 82, 86, 89, 224n54
United African-Asian Friendship, 75
United African Nationalist Movement (UANM), 68–69, 75, 85–86
United Bermuda Party (UBP), 118, 123
United Fruit Company, 25
United Nations, 62, 68; Afro-Asian bloc, 89, 93–94, 97–98; and Afro-Asian nations, 74; power dynamics in, 91
United Negro Improvement Association (UNIA), 5–6; and Ahmadiyya Movement in Islam (AMI), 21, 40; and anticolonialism, 40; decline of, 44, 48;

international reach of, 21; and Islam, 26–27; mission of, 27; and Moorish Science Temple of America (MSTA), 25–26, 48; music of, 26–27; shared membership with NOI, 48. *See also* Garvey, Marcus; Garveyism

United States: American identity, 142–43; anticommunism and, 57; Central Intelligence Agency (CIA), 57, 166; Christianity in, 3–4; civil rights movement in, 119; and Cuba, 97–98; imperial expansion of, 179–80; interventionism of, 162–63; and Latin America, 164–66; and militarization of urban areas, 180–81; racial hierarchies in, 20; welfare system, attacks on, 172

Universal Ethiopian Hymnal, 26. *See also* Ford, Arnold; Universal Negro Improvement Association (UNIA)

Universal Negro Improvement Association (UNIA), 20, 25. *See also* Garvey, Marcus; Garveyism

University of Islam schools, 51, 146–47. *See also* Nation of Islam (NOI)

uplift: Black nationalism and Islam's role in, 28, 64, 133

Urban League, 181

Venezuela, 25
Vietnam, 97
Voice of Islam (AMI journal), 56
voting rights, 117. *See also* Brown, Roosevelt; Committee for Universal Adult Suffrage (CUAS); suffrage

Wachuku, Jaja, 98
Wahhaj, Siraj, 184
Walker, David, 30
War on Drugs, 160, 163, 171–73; and American neo-imperialism, 180–83; and genocide against Black community, 180–81; ineffectiveness of, 183–87; Islam's role in, 177–79; and prisoners, 173–77. *See also* Bush, George H. W.; crack crisis; Dopebusters; drug crisis; "law and order" rhetoric; Nation of Islam (NOI); Reagan, Ronald

Washington Post (newspaper), 187
Wayside Casino Conference (1958), 75
Wegener, Alfred, 30–31
Welcoming Committee for Harlem's 28th Precinct, 94, 95
West Indies, 25, 165
Western Michigan College of Education, 54
"A White Man's Heaven is a Black Man's Hell" (sound recording), 117
white supremacy: and Christianity, 4; and Islam, 11, 77; resistance to, 4, 66, 89
Williams, Robert, 100
Wilson, Darren, 195
Wilson, Woodrow, 133
WNTA (television station), 80
women: and archival silence, 139, 140, 141, 153; benefits for in Islam, in carceral system, 176; and curriculum development, 155; and intellectual production, 10; 64; labor of, 50; Masjid Muhammad community and school formation and, 153–54; misogyny toward, 84; modesty in dress, 83, 138, 150; and NOI, 44, 64, 134, 135; in prison, 176–77; programs for, 135; roles of in Islam, 176–77; and shortage of men in Black community, 176. *See also* gender

Wooding, Hugh, 125
Wooding Commission, 125
Woodward, Bob, 165
World Community of al-Islam in the West (WCIW), 136, 142–43, 151, 155. *See also* Muhammad, Wallace; Muhammad, Warith Deen
World Federation of Islamic Missions, 84
World Islamic Congress, 81
"The World Serpent" (illustration), 1–3
World War I, 4, 5, 7, 20, 39, 68
World War II, 50, 52, 53, 56, 66, 68, 74, 89, 115, 160; and decolonization, 52–53
The Wretched of the Earth (Fanon), 133, 139–40

X, Catherine, 126
X, Malcolm, 8, 46, 56; on Afro-Asian political situation, 74; assassination of, 100–101; and Fidel Castro, 95–97, 96; and hajj (1964), 79–80; and international travels, 78–80; in *Moslem World*, 63; and *Muhammad Speaks*, 91, 97; on Palestine, 198; Pan-Africanism, 79–80; and Adam Clayton Powell, 74–75

Yakub (NOI teaching), 47

Zimmerman, George, 196
Zionism, 198

www.ingramcontent.com/pod-product-compliance
Lightning Source LLC
Chambersburg PA
CBHW032031230426
43671CB00005B/282